Cultural Heritage in the Realm of the Commons: Conversations on the Case of Greece

Edited by
Stelios Lekakis

]u[

Ubiquity press
London

Published by
Ubiquity Press Ltd.
Unit 322-323
Whitechapel Technology Centre
75 Whitechapel Road
London E1 1DU
www.ubiquitypress.com

First published 2020

Cover design and image by Ioannis Oikonomakis

Print and digital versions typeset by Siliconchips Services Ltd.

ISBN (Paperback): 978-1-911529-60-6
ISBN (PDF): 978-1-911529-61-3
ISBN (EPUB): 978-1-911529-62-0
ISBN (Mobi): 978-1-911529-63-7

DOI: https://doi.org/10.5334/bcj

The full text of this book has been peer-reviewed to ensure high academic standards. For full review policies, see http://www.ubiquitypress.com/

Suggested citation:
Lekakis, S. (ed.) 2020. *Cultural Heritage in the Realm of the Commons: Conversations on the Case of Greece*. London: Ubiquity Press. DOI: https://doi .org/10.5334/10.5334/bcj. License: CC-BY

To read the free, open access version of this book online, visit https://doi.org/10.5334/bcj or scan this QR code with your mobile device:

Contents

Foreword: The Wisdom of the Commons: 'Together' is
Always Better (Graham Fairclough) v

Introduction: Cultural Heritage in the Realm of the Commons:
Reading a Letter from the Future (Stelios Lekakis) 1

Part 1 15

Chapter 1. A Political Economy of Heritage and the Commons:
A First Sketch Focusing on Greece (Stelios Lekakis) 17

Chapter 2. An Economic Analysis of Heritage as Commons:
Reflections on Theory, Methodology and Social Imagery
(Mina Dragouni) 45

Chapter 3. Heritage, Openness and the Commons in Urban
Environments: Some Thoughts on the Archaeological Parks of
Philopappos Hill and Plato's Academy in Athens (Despina
Catapoti, Ioulia Skounaki and Georgia Gkoumopoulou) 67

Part 2 95

Chapter 4. Cultural Life Reconfigured: From the Ancestral to the
Digital Commons and Beyond (Nicholas Anastasopoulos) 97

Chapter 5. State, Netocrats and the Commons: Developing a
Cultural Policy in the Era of Platforms (Prodromos Tsiavos) 109

Chapter 6. "Capture and Release of the Chthonic Beasts":
Archaeological Heritage as Digital Commons in Contemporary
Art Practice. Various Thoughts on the Occasion of the Artwork
'Future Bestiary' (Marina Markellou and Petros Moris) 127

Chapter 7. Seeds as Common Cultural Heritage
(Vasso Kanellopoulou)   141

Chapter 8. From Cooking to Commoning: The Making of
Intangible Cultural Heritage in OneLoveKitchen, Athens
(Penny Travlou)   159

Chapter 9. Urban Experiments in Times of Crisis:
From Cultural Production to Neighbourhood Commoning
(Giorgos Chatzinakos)   183

Chapter 10. Commoning Over a Cup of Coffee: The Case
of Kafeneio, a Co-op Cafe at Plato's Academy
(Chrysostomos Galanos)   213

Part 3   227

Chapter 11. The Alternative of the Commons, New Politics
and Cities (Alexandros Kioupkiolis)   229

Chapter 12. Making Politics Meaningful: The Pitfalls of the
'Commons' and the Importance of Anthropological Analysis
(Dimitris Markopoulos)   253

Afterword: This is not a Manifesto: Precipitating a Paradigm
Shift in Cultural Management (Stelios Lekakis)   259

Biographical Notes   263

Index   269

The Wisdom of the Commons: 'Together' is Always Better

Graham Fairclough

The idea of commons, quite rightly, has gained an increased currency in recent years. This has happened in many fields, several of which contribute to this collection, but – unsurprisingly given the millennia-long history of land-based commons – it has become increasingly visible in the field of heritage-and-landscape discourse as much as in any field. Unfortunately, however, the word 'commons' is far too often prefaced by the words 'tragedy of'. The blame for this rests on a short, misunderstood paper published half a century ago by the American neo-Malthusian ecologist Garret Hardin, to which far too much attention has been paid (Hardin 1968).

So-called 'seminal' works, recurrently cited as the theoretical basis of research, are not uncommon in the literature of landscape and heritage. In some cases, however, their significance is undeserved, and they are not necessarily celebrated for valid reasons. Some – Carl Sauer's (1925) *'The Morphology of Landscape'*, Marwyn Samuel's (1979) *'Biography of Landscape'*, perhaps even (at a very different level) Simon Schama's (1995) *'Landscape and Memory'* and certainly Garrett Hardin's (1968) *'Tragedy of the Commons'* – have been used in ways neither intended nor anticipated by their authors. They are often the work of people from outside the landscape and heritage field, but this is in itself not problematic; all disciplinary visitors are welcome to fields that are

How to cite this book chapter:
Fairclough, G. 2020. The Wisdom of the Commons: 'Together' is Always Better. In Lekakis, S. (ed.) *Cultural Heritage in the Realm of the Commons: Conversations on the Case of Greece.* Pp. v–xi. London: Ubiquity Press. DOI: https://doi.org/10.5334/bcj.a. License: CC-BY

quintessentially inter-disciplinary. What is problematic however is when these scholars' appropriation of the idea of landscape as a metaphor to explore their own topics and to pursue particular agendas are later adopted uncritically by landscape and heritage researchers, and in isolation from their original aims. Written for one precise purpose but thereafter enlisted by others to achieve other goals, these papers can take research in less than helpful directions. Hardin's use of the commons is a sharp point in case; it has proved a major obstacle to the understanding and promotion of commons in a modern context and has distorted how commons are seen.

'The Tragedy of the Commons', Hardin's paper, approaches commons from a negatively ideological perspective. It does not display an accurate understanding of their historical operation because Hardin was not interested in the history or character of commons, and indeed had little useful to say about them. Whatever his influence may have been on environmental science or (post) human ecology, his was a distorted view of commons and their management, used solely to argue for a Malthusian, neo-liberal approach to what he called the 'population problem'.[1] Hardin invented the 'tragedy of the commons' in order to advocate the destruction of commons by modern-day versions of enclosure. For him, commons will (and should) always self-destruct through individual selfishness in order to give way to private enterprise, a natural and inevitable progression because freedom should always be limited. Applying this to population growth, Hardin's mantra was: 'Freedom to breed will bring ruin to all' (Hardin 1968: 1248).

Hardin blamed the breakdown of commons on over-exploitation caused by the selfish behaviour of commoners. As many have since pointed out (Ostrom 1990; Rodgers 2010), however, the failure of commons came almost invariably not from such internal causes but through being engineered by the imposition (during a relatively short period of history) of the external forces of property ownership and incipient capitalism. He chose not to blame the early capitalist landowners who enclosed the commons, nor to recognise that properly managed commons were complex fit-for-purpose systems. For success and sustainability, commons required only careful consensual co-regulation of an area of land and its resources, in other words collaboration, compromise and cooperation.

It is time to stop citing Hardin. The triumph – far from their tragedy – of the commons was their successful maintenance over a very *longue durée*; there is plenty of evidence in the historical and archaeological record that long-term sustainability can be assured, as in Europe over many centuries if not millennia, when commons are self-regulated by their own community of users for a common good (as evidenced in several chapters in this book, for example Dragouni, Catapoti and Chatzinakos). This applies whether the commons are a tract of rough land for grazing, fuel and other forms of extraction, easily

---

[1] His other example in the paper was the game of 'noughts and crosses' (tic-tac-toe, Hardin 1968: 1243), which should have put readers on their guard.

exhausted shared arable land, water resources, or fish-filled oceans regulated by a 'Common Fisheries Policy'. These of course are all types of resources currently threatened by significant anthropocentric global challenges, and it is interesting that the commons have come back to public awareness precisely at a time of global political and social uncertainty and anxiety. It seems natural that this collection of papers has arisen from Greece in the long aftermath of its post-2008 crisis (see notably the chapter by Markopoulos, but additionally those from Kioupkiolis, Chatzinakos or Lekakis), and it also seems appropriate (in a time of the rising urbanisation of human populations) that its main focus is on modern urban contexts, and specifically multi-functional public spaces (see for example, Catapoti et al. and Kioupkiolis).

Commons seem to offer lessons for the 21st century, perhaps even for addressing Hardin's concerns for the impact of overpopulation but in a gentler, more humanistic way. In the 21st century, however, commons come in many forms, from surviving or reconstituted agricultural rural commons to urban commons as the shared spaces of the cities, in the rise of creative ventures in all fields (as well-exemplified by the present collection by Galanos, Travlou or Chatzinakos) and in the deeply political sphere, where (see Kioupkiolis) commons can offer new alternatives of non-hegemonic or heterarchical democracy. As Markopoulos shows, working with the theoretical frame of 'commons' might even enable 'a more radical criticism in politics', challenging the neo-liberal focus on the individual in favour of recognition of the values of collectivity and communalism.

Several chapters in this collection also show commons emerging in the new territories of virtual space, and in digital and cyber realms, indeed also in relation to the growth in acceptance of the ideas of the intangibility of heritage. One of the most intriguing sections in the book is that (Tsiavos) in which Hardin's so-called 'tragedy' silently rears its head again in the digital sphere: the successful digital realms of wiki (-pedia / - media) are closely self-regulated, guided and managed by wiki-communities whereas the problematic platforms (Facebook, Twitter, Instagram) reside firmly in the top-down, neo-liberal market sphere. Digital and virtual commons also open up what is meant by neighbourhood: neighbourliness, being a part of a community, no longer necessarily needs physical proximity. Members of a community (of place or of interest, of landscape or of heritage) are not necessarily always known to each other: the community building OneLoveKitchen was, we are told by Travlou, composed of strangers. This does not exclude physically based neighbourhoods, of course, but complements them.

Commons are increasingly becoming a focus for practical application as well as academic study and increasingly seen as part of a possible way out of current discontent with political systems and their effects. They are becoming highly visible in European Commission funding programmes because, like landscape itself, they inevitably have an interdisciplinary allure. The commons sit at the heart of most humanistic and cultural definitions of landscape, notably of the pre-Renaissance, customary definitions, and specifically that of the Landscape Convention (Council of Europe 2000). Landscape *is* a commons. Equally, conceptualisations and practices of heritage, and not only through critical heritage discourse, are moving towards the idea and value of the commons, in opposition to globalising and neo-liberal currents within World Heritage (and all other spheres, see Kanellopoulou).

Is it possible to turn to any of the existing heritage treaties and conventions to help us frame commons within the heritage field? The UNESCO World Heritage Convention is in this respect of limited help, and understandably perhaps it is almost invisible in this collection of papers (see Lekakis). Arguably it even undermines the idea of commons altogether. UNESCO rhetoric about cultural heritage refers to 'a commitment to preserving our legacy for future generations', rather than to a shared access to heritage for use and enjoyment. While in theory the Convention asks signatory states to inventorise all their heritage, the Convention and its operationalisation) focuses in practice (and in the eyes of a wider public) on selected 'World Heritage' sites – 'outstanding examples' or 'universally significant properties'. This fosters exclusivity on several fronts, notably social and political, but it also privileges a mainly or wholly 'global' scale of value which can be far removed from any concept of commons.

The UNESCO WH Convention does speak of collective assistance and collective protection, but its collectivity arises from an imagined 'international community' rather than from any form of community operating at a more familiarly human level, for example at local or national scale, or through communities of place, interest or heritage. Commons primarily grow from grass-root activity (see for literally grassroots activity Kanellopoulou, or at macro scale Galanos), production and participation (e.g. Chatzinakos), and from use rights (as Kioupkiolis reminds us), and such issues or vectors are not at the forefront of UNESCO thinking (despite UNESCO in 2007 adding 'community' to its strategic objectives – the 'four Cs', previously only Credibility, Conservation, Capacity-building and Communication). This is not to deny the achievements of the UNESCO WH Convention since 1972, putting to one side the World Heritage List, in encouraging and supporting non-World Heritage conservation activities and awareness at national or local level. Equally, UNESCO's championship of alternative, more wide-ranging and more globally-sensitive approaches to heritage, notably through its 2003 Convention for the Safeguarding of the Intangible Cultural Heritage and its 2005 Convention for the Protection and Promotion of the Diversity of Cultural Expressions, has enabled heritage to be seen as an important aspect of culture, and culture, and to be treated as a significant type of heritage (UNESCO 2003; 2005). But the 1972 starting point of UNESCO World Heritage Convention is too difficult to reconcile with current ideas of shared heritage, localism and democratic participation to connect to the commons agenda.

Such ideas however are now familiar within the European context in two Council of Europe (not European Union) Conventions concerning Landscape (the Florence Convention, the European Landscape Convention (ELC), drafted over many years in the 1990s and finally published in 2000) and Heritage (the Faro Convention). These moved imaginatively towards placing people, citizens and communities at the forefront of their philosophy. The Landscape Convention in 2000 stated in its foundational Preamble that "landscape constitute(s) a common resource", and "contributes to the formation of local cultures ', as 'an important part of the quality of life for people" and "a key element of individual and social well-being". Furthermore, landscape's 'protection, management and planning entail rights and responsibilities for everyone', an important statement of principle in the context of commons (Council of Europe 2000).

Five years later, the Faro Convention went further. Its title – the Value of Cultural Heritage for Society – clearly stated its broad social, or political, aim. Its Preamble recognised "the need to put people and human values at the centre of an enlarged and cross-disciplinary concept of cultural heritage" as "a resource for sustainable development and quality of life in a constantly evolving society" (Council of Europe 2005). This is in marked contrast to the UNESCO World Heritage Convention which comes close to placing people outside of heritage: in its very first sentence ("heritage ... is increasingly threatened with destruction not only by the traditional causes of decay, but also by changing social and economic conditions") it portrays societal processes – which after all, represent people's aspirations and actions, their everyday lives in effect – as a threat to heritage rather than as a valid use of heritage or as the creative force behind heritage (UNESCO 1972). In contrast, the Faro Convention reflects 'the need to involve everyone in society in the ongoing process of defining and managing cultural heritage'. 'Involvement' (and elsewhere in the Faro Convention 'public or democratic participation', 'shared or public responsibility', and the balancing of rights with responsibilities towards other people) is a deep red thread running through the Convention's text.

Faro (in its Article 3) uses the term 'common heritage', as many such documents do, thus risking homogenisation and the heritage marginalisation of less influential, less voiced social groups. But its definition (in Article 2) of heritage as 'a cultural heritage is a group of resources inherited from the past which people identify, independently of ownership' helps to outweigh such risks (Council of Europe 2005). Within the terms of the commons discourse, those words – 'independently of ownership' are all-important. They cover the three dimensions of commons to which Kioupkiolis and Lekakis refer in the present collection: the shared-by-all common asset / resource that heritage can be; the use-rights owned by commoners who are not landowners but have long-term intergenerational responsibilities; the processes of commoning, establishing rights and access above and beyond (or at least alongside) legal property ownership.

At the centre of the commons debate, and frequently visible in this collection (for example Dragouni or Lekakis) is the public / private dichotomy, but not straightforwardly. In western Europe, the 'market' (or whatever term is used) is commonly seen as part of the private realm and held distinct from and sometimes in opposition to the public sector, yet in the voices heard and reported in these papers the market is seen as an element *of* the state apparatus and of the public realm, and is held in contradistinction to the private realm of citizens and commons. Perhaps this is a consequence of the special post-crisis situation in Greece. Yet historical commons rarely belonged to everyone in a community but rather to members of a prescribed (often even hereditary) and exclusive group within a community. Where do the commons reside? Commons have traditionally been places of resistance and of opposition, outlaw places and 'no man's land', but at the same time they functioned as part of public resources. Do commons in fact bridge the public / private realms, having feet in both? The '*commune*' in republican France is a fusion of public and private, but also a form of the type of decentralised governance which is key to the ideal of commons (and frequently exemplified in this collection). Perhaps the relevant dichotomy is not after all public / private but local / national, in which case the challenge is to prevent modern commons discourse from falling into crude localist or nativist, even nationalistic, views? Can a whole nation act as a commons, in the sense that citizens (or only some of them, to follow historical analogies) possess use rights within the imagined community of a nation state? The papers in this collection that contemplate commons in the virtual, cyber world (Anastasopoulos, Tsiavos) are amongst those most interested in showing what future commons should or might look like, and their imagined communities are not even territorially-based, let alone national.

There are two main sources for optimism within heritage thinking, however, and rather surprisingly one arises from UNESCO. Its recommendations on Historic Urban Landscapes (HUL) (UNESCO 2011), offers a set of ideas that follow in the footsteps of the ELC, with a focus on the 'urban everywhere', on heritage and landscape layering and pluralism, and on democratic participation. The other optimistic path is the Faro Convention on the value of heritage for society, with its refocusing of heritage away from the fabric and materiality of objects towards the people who create and enjoy heritage though ascribing values and associations and through shared use; for this convention heritage is not only objects (the *resource* of the commons) but also a verb as well as a noun (and thus the *process* of commoning); while 'societal value' is a simile for *use-right*. Both HUL and Faro seem to stand in support of several of the initiatives and aims described in this rich collection of Greek experience, perhaps most obviously in Chatzinakos' Thessaloniki but in truth in all the papers.

Those two internationally derived but locally-focussed documents are people-centred in ways that many contributors to this book would recognise. They promote forms of ownership of heritage that do not depend on use rights rather than property rights. Strangely, Greece has not signed the Faro Convention (although 24 member states of the Council of Europe have since 2010) – or perhaps it is not strange, given that the Faro is the sort of convention whose influence can be felt and profited from even without the mediation of signatory nation states. It is in short, a form of intellectual commons whose ideas are open for all to follow, as this collection does from the perspective of Greek communities looking for new modes of politics. Whilst the papers in this collection, mainly speak of heritage and politics, community and cooperation, it is, finally, important to recall that the historical origins and evolution of commons lie in landscape and its use and that in the 21st century the growing focus on 'landscape approaches' (even if sometimes erroneously called 'nature-based' solutions) is a vehicle through which commons can be reinvigorated. This collection of papers offers inspirational examples and helpful signposts towards new political, social and environmental landscapes.

Bibliography

Council of Europe. (2000). *Council of Europe European landscape convention.* Retrieved November 20, 2019, from https://www.coe.int/en/web/landscape.

Council of Europe. (2005). *Convention on the value of cultural heritage for society (Faro Convention, 2005).* Retrieved November 20, 2019, from https://www.coe.int/en/web/culture-and-heritage/faro-convention.

Hardin, G. (1968). The tragedy of the commons. *Science, 162*(3859), 1243–1248.

Ostrom, E. (1990). *Governing the commons: The evolution of institutions for collective action.* Cambridge, United Kingdom: Cambridge University Press.

Rodgers, C. (2010). Reversing the 'tragedy' of the commons?: Sustainable management and the Commons Act 2006. *The Modern Law Review, 73*(3), 461–486.

Sauer, C. O. (1925). The morphology of landscape. *University of California Publications in Geography, 2*(2), 19–53.

Samuels, M. S. (1979). The biography of landscape: Cause and culpability. In D. W. Meinig (Ed.), *The interpretation of ordinary landscapes: Geographical essays* (pp. 51–88). London, United Kingdom: Oxford University Press.

Schama, S. (1995). *Landscape and memory.* London, United Kingdom: HarperCollins.

UNESCO. (1972). *Convention concerning the protection of the world cultural and natural heritage.* Retrieved 20 November, 2019, from https://whc.unesco.org/en/conventiontext/.

UNESCO. (2003). *Convention for the Safeguarding of the Intangible Cultural Heritage.* Retrieved 12 May 2020, from https://ich.unesco.org/doc/src/01852-EN.pdf.

UNESCO. (2005). *Convention for the Protection and Promotion of the Diversity of Cultural Expressions.* Retrieved 12 May 2020, from https://en.unesco.org/creativity/convention.

UNESCO. (2011). *Recommendation on the historic urban landscape.* Retrieved 20 November, 2019, from https://whc.unesco.org/uploads/activities/documents/activity-638–98.pdf.

Cultural Heritage in the Realm of the Commons: Reading a Letter from the Future

Stelios Lekakis

> He filled the glasses and raised his own glass by the stem.
> 'What shall it be this time?' he said,
> still with the same faint suggestion of irony.
> 'To the confusion of the Thought Police?
> To the death of Big Brother?
> To humanity? To the future?'
> 'To the past,' said Winston.
> 'The past is more important,' agreed O'Brien gravely.
> G. Orwell, 1984

There is a lingering idea that the reader of the commons often stumbles upon in the bibliography; it suggests that in recent years we have been pondering over the definitions and the nature of the commons because their status is increasingly challenged and their existence compromised by emergent threats prescribing enclosures for goods and services up until now enjoyed freely.

This idea could imply two things: that we might take some goods for granted, becoming uneasy only when they fall out of reach or, conversely, that we might – just recently – be becoming aware of the increasing rate of privatisation

---

How to cite this book chapter:
Lekakis, S. 2020. Cultural Heritage in the Realm of the Commons: Reading a Letter from the Future. In Lekakis, S. (ed.) *Cultural Heritage in the Realm of the Commons: Conversations on the Case of Greece.* Pp. 1–14. London: Ubiquity Press. DOI: https://doi.org/10.5334/bcj.b. License: CC-BY

processes spread by neoliberal politics, enclosing and capitalising on goods such as public space, seeds, software and information but also politics, democracy, personal or communal relationships and other aspects of our culture.

Cultural heritage might be a paradigmatic category for both arguments. Invented in the realm of nation-states, from an early point it was considered a public asset, stewarded to narrate the historic deeds of the ancestors, on behalf of their descendants; As the neoliberal narrative would have it, it is for the benefit of these tax-paying citizens that privatisation logic on heritage sector have been increasing over recent decades, to cover their needs in the name of social responsibility and other truncated views of the welfare state.

This volume examines whether we can place cultural heritage at the other end of the spectrum, as a common good and potentially as a commons. It does so by looking at Greece as a case study, lately a battlefield of harsh and experimental austerity measures but also of inspiring grass-roots mobilisation and scholarship, currently blossoming to defend the right of communities to enjoy, collaboratively manage and co-create goods by the people, for the people. Since cultural heritage – and culture in general – is hastily bundled up with other goods and services in various arguments for and against their public character, this volume invites several experts to discuss their views on their field of expertise and reflect on the overarching theme: Can cultural heritage be considered a commons? If so, what are the advantages and pitfalls concerning theory, practice and management of heritage? What can we learn from other public resources with a longer history in commons-based or market-oriented interpretation and governance? Can a commons approach allow us to imagine and start working towards a better, more inclusive and meaningful future for heritage?

Genealogies of the commons

When using the term *commons*, we are normally referring to the historic common land enclosures in Britain from the 16th and 17[th]c. onwards and how these processes contributed to a number of revolutionary changes in the European agricultural and social landscape, mainly facilitating the 'primitive capital accumulation' in favour of the emerging bourgeoise. Land enclosures and capital accumulation were constitutive elements in the transformation from feudalism to capitalism and a catalyst for the deterioration of the living conditions and labour potential of small farmers, who had until that point based their survival on customary use rights of the land and the relevant arrangements (Rodgers et al. 2011; Zuckert 2012).

However, apart from the Marxist exegesis as the prerequisite for the (re)production of the capitalistic frame, the commons actually has a longer history (De Angelis 2017). Perhaps the earliest definition of the common good (*koinón*) can be traced back to Aristotle, where in the context of the city-state (*pólis*), participatory citizen action was needed to deliberate a shared and just communal life. Again, as a civic duty for the common benefit (*koinó symphéron / utilitas communis*), we find it in the Roman law, to explicitly demarcate the inherently inalienable goods (*res communes*), such as the air, running water, the sea and the seashore (Menatti 2017: 650). This Latin definition, where the word derives from (*munus*: obligation & gift) precisely documents the reciprocal core of the term *community* (*cum-munus*) and reflects the collective attempt to sustain a group of people on shared grounds (Dardot & Laval 2019: 9–15). These three elements can be considered as the main constituents of the commons: i.e. the resources at hand, the communities in charge and the regulatory frames to sustain this management system.

Contemporary approaches on commons' theories

In this volume the same tripartite schema comes up quite often; Interested communities collaborate on the protection and (re)production of a resource or a service, following agreed regulations for the shared interest; people collaborate, they *common* in bottom-up, inclusive, just and synergetic ways to produce use value for them and the rest of the people (Dellenbaugh et al. 2015; Linebaugh 2008: 279). The goods produced are left as a patrimony in material or immaterial forms; for example, seed stock, food, cultural systems, management circuits or open-source software. This open-ended interpretation makes classification of the commons both complex and versatile, depending on the resource (material, immaterial, (non)renewable, natural, manmade), the scale (local, regional, national, global), the context (social, cultural, academic) and the enclosure risks (public / private) (Bollier 2014).

Whatever the taxonomic arrangement, commons are better known in the bibliography from Hardin's (1968) paper on the ascertained tragedy in their management, a neoclassical argument that has since been systematically challenged and overthrown as referring to an exploitative, individualistic, antagonistic management steeped in the contemporary market ethos of unregulated, uncontextualized, freely accessible resources,[2] approached by people of the *Homo Economicus* subspecies, i.e. solely interested in their own profit (Olsen 1965; Caffentzis & Federici 2014).

Hardin's approach was particularly criticised by the – only woman – Nobel Prize laureate in Economics, Elinor Ostrom, in her book: *Governing the Commons: The Evolution of Institutions for Collective Action*. Ostrom's lifelong project focuses on the collective management of Common Pool Resources (CPR), natural or man-made resource systems that are subtractable and pose difficulties in excluding potential beneficiaries from obtaining benefits from their use (Ostrom 1990: 30). Although regularly criticised for the (new

---

[2] Hardin's work has contributed to the popularisation of a usual mistake in the discussion of the commons, sometimes solely associated with *common goods*, i.e. open access resources, indeed susceptible to overuse if no other conditions apply.

institutional) economistic approach (De Angelis 2017), Ostrom's contribution[3] attracted a great deal of attention to the field and opened up new horizons in the study of the commons, particularly in relation to the abundant and diverse cultural systems and social interactions of traditional communities that formulate sustainable strategies for land use, crop collection, cultivation differentiation and natural resources management (Ostrom 1990: 88–101). Her work supported several systematic and transdisciplinary approaches to the socio-economic and ecological system of commons, developed in different areas from the 1980s onwards, mostly related to natural resources (animal husbandry, fisheries, forestries, water management, irrigation systems), political studies and economics (van Laerhoven & Ostrom 2007: 3–7).

Ostrom's work resonates in the contemporary discussion of the commons, however in this volume authors are inspired from manifold theories and practices developed since, deriving among others from political theory, law, organisational studies, traditional knowledge, political economy and the proliferation of social movements worldwide.

Re-inventing the commons: The political and the digital

From the 1990s onwards, a diverse group of thinkers and researchers broadened our understanding of the commons, linking in with the rich tradition of political approaches such as Proudhon's mutualism, Bakunin's collectivism, Ricardian and Utopian socialism or drawing on the works of Arendt, Castoriadis and Chomsky, in political economy arguments cutting across production, dissemination and consumption of resources, community organisation, urban and rural life et al.

In later years, a reformist and a radical approach could be discerned, although definite categorization should be avoided (Papadimitropoulos 2017: 566). Thus, we could discuss a 'pragmatic' school of thought (for example, Bauwens, Bollier, Kostakis, Arvidsson & Peitersen, Papanikolaou) that negotiates with the traditional statecraft, proposing and building an alternative paradigm in the shell of the old world (see for example, the concepts of the 'partner state' and the 'chamber of the commons'). This extends to the upcoming Social Economy practice; a diverse bundle of services, products and actors, prioritising social objectives over profit maximisation. On the other hand, a more 'radical', neo/autonomist Marxist approach can be observed, suggesting the assemblage of counter-power for constitutive change (for example, De Angelis, Stavrides, Caffentzis, Federici, Rigi, Kioupkiolis). This approach can be related to calls for egalitarian, action-focused shareholder formations, promoting Solidarity Economies outside and against the capitalistic frame.

---

[3] See 'The International Association for the Study of the Commons' (https://iasc-commons.org).

With the dawn of the new millennium, the spread of the Internet and new digital technologies enacted pioneering patterns of association and self-governance, reinventing and expanding the commons as a mode of co-creation and social sharing in the digital field, outside the traditional limits of forests and grazing grounds. As a response and a probe, a large body of theoretical knowledge has been developed 'on digital commons', coupled with practical applications, spanning software development (Linux, Apache HTTP Server), online encyclopaedias (Wikipedia) and social media platforms (Benkler 2006: 117–120; Bollier 2008: 2–4; Bauwens & Niaros 2017). This form of commons-based peer-governance and production in the digital realm holds a prefigurative promise, and enables the proliferation of decentralized communities, with their own (im)material output, against platform capitalism and the omnipresent aspect of the extractive digital economy (Kostakis et al. 2019; Benkler 2006; Anastasopoulos this volume; Tsiavos this volume).

However, commons have also been physically present in more radical ways. They feature in various protesting platforms around the world against neoliberal appropriation of resources, state violence and democracy enclosures: from the 1970s ecological movements to the Chipko Andolan in India, the Landless Workers' Movement in Brazil, the Zapatistas movement in Chiapas, the Water wars in Cochabamba, the Occupy movement and its spill over effects on the Square movements at the beginning of the 2010s (Gezi Park Istanbul, Syntagma Square Athens, Puerta del Sol Madrid, Tahrir Square Cairo, Bouazizi Square Tunisia) and the recent 'municipalist' politics in Spain and Italy. Following different trajectories, these movements make commoning incremental to the emergence of a new historical paradigm, a democratic and caring culture that helps us prefigure politics beyond the normalised capitalist hegemony and statist socialism (Caffentzis & Federici 2014; Kioupkiolis this volume; Markopoulos this volume).

Even if it is difficult – if not impossible – to compile a solid or linear genealogy, commons emerge as an all-encompassing theoretical and practical process in communities across the physical and the digital realm, charged politically but not necessarily ideologically, holding the promise of a more egalitarian and sustainable future. To understand this multifaceted phenomenon, university courses and modules on commons are growing across the world, related to law, environment, governance and Social & Solidarity Economy. Lately arguments are spilling over to thematics as intellectual property, digital information, traditional knowledge, biodiversity and genetic material, urban life, gender and alternative economies (Bollier 2003; Scharper & Cunningham 2006; Kanellopoulou this volume; Harvey 2016; Federici 2012; Gibson et al 2013).

Cultural heritage as a commons: The research field

In this emerging scientific arena of debate and practice, culture and heritage appear in notably few discussions while the current available bibliography can be considered rather fragmented in terms of theoretical enquiries and applications (Lekakis et al. 2018).

Cultural commons are broadly interpreted as cognitive/intellectual commons, involving concepts as social structures, regulatory frames and processes of commoning, along with their immaterial outputs (Hess 2012: 25; Bertacchini et al. 2012). In this pluralistic but opaque approach, cultural commons reflect a number of values and include such diverse goods as ethics, languages, codes, symbols, rites, customs, information, traditional knowledge, but also the creative aura of a cultural district or the collaboration patterns between online peers over the production of open-source software (Benesch et al. 2015). On the other hand, treating them as "new commons", may pinpoint their vulnerability (enclosures, overuse, social dilemmas) and the need for a governance system (Hess 2008). It does not however ameliorate their under-theorisation or encourage further exploration in terms of meanings, boundaries and affordances. On the contrary, it may act as a pretext to the distortion of the goods and practices involved, i.e. their economistic appreciation or even marketisation through impact assessment models.

Heritage commons appear in the bibliography even less frequently, mainly inferred through discussions in heritage theory (values, tangible-intangible resources, indigenous heritage), community inclusion, institutions & management (public / private, ownership, rights), criticism to economic development & sustainability practices (tourism, management) (Gould 2017). When explored, heritage commons are regularly presented as similar to environmental commons or considered as cultural commons, a treasury of the community's imagined identity, part of the aspired and yet utopian democracy of the commons (Bollier 2016; Lieros 2016: 232). In some instances, they are idiosyncratically conceptualised or examined in very specific hypotheses and case studies (Erickson 1992; Benesch 2016; Gonzalez 2014), inadequately theorised or approached through economistic viewpoints (Bertacchini et al. 2012) but rarely treated as a container of values, worthy of meticulous research to better understand local, regional and global identities but also inform potential arrangements for their viable management (Catapoti et al. this volume; Dragouni this volume).

Case study and scope of the volume

As mentioned earlier, this volume invites a number of experts to converse on heritage commons, from their own standpoint and field of expertise (environmental, digital, urban, political, cultural resources and processes of governance and production) that in many cases has a longer history on the commons' front; an interdisciplinary research question that developed out of a session in the 2015 Dialogues in Archaeology Conference. Their approaches depart either from the 'reformist', the 'radical' school of thought or somewhere in the middle, shifting between academic and/or on-the-ground perspectives, tangible and intangible resources, broader and theoretical to narrower and practical contexts (for example, national politics vs neighborhood dynamics) but also ontological, political, economic and managerial considerations in an attempt to raise key issues and map this newly constituted field without though prescribing a canonical model of heritage (commons). Providing the latter is beyond the scope of this exploratory volume.

Geographically, the volume focuses on Greece, reflecting on the lingering narratives of economic crisis (2010–2017). Nowadays, it is largely admitted that the austerity measures, a result of the Greek government-debt crisis, brought about an incipient disintegration of the welfare state, a desert of unmet social needs and relentless neoliberal restructuring of provisions, job precarity and increased unemployment rates but also the rise of new forms of nationalist and neo-fascist movements that settled into the political scene (Bekridaki & Broumas 2016: 233; Bloemen & De Groot 2019). Alongside summer tourism, the sun, Zorba the Greek, souvlaki and the Parthenon, 'the crisis' became and currently remains the new, dominant folkloric image of the country, a popular icon reproduced on the news around the world, a totem and an axiom in the sociopolitical domain but also in humanities' research (see e.g. contributions in Tziovas 2017).

In this context, public institutions responsible for the management of the natural/cultural resources faced insurmountable difficulties. Budget cuts, lack of adequate infrastructure, political instability and the umbrella argument of the lazy Greeks, living beyond their means, supported a peer pressure to 'mobilise untapped resources' (Plantzos 2018; Voudouri 2014). This gave rise to recurring arguments of privatisation on different levels, in different fields and in different processes. However, the narratives of 'how to gain from cultural heritage' are not really systematic, even though empty axioms on synergy, sustainability and lately participatory processes recur in the omnipresent deliberation of culture for tourism.

This deregulatory process instigated by the economic recession, urging for the privatization of the public and common wealth, and the humanitarian crisis that had befallen the citizenship, was met with the emergence of a number of grassroots movements and solidarity collectives that sprang up to ameliorate the hardship the people were going through, organising and delivering social goods (Chatzinakos this volume; Galanos this volume). Among others, one can list food initiatives ('without middlemen' networks, solidarity kitchens, cooperative social groceries; Travlou this volume), education initiatives, solidarity clinics and social pharmacies, (precarious) workers' mutual aid funds and campaigns, housing, legal support, initiatives against water privatization or for immigrants/refugees. This, however, is still a minority of the wide range of goods and processes that were once taken care of by state provisions (De Angelis 2017; Lieros 2016: 350).

This colourful range of initiatives has contributed to the theorization of the commons, their governance and production, through research projects,

Figure 1: The Academy of Athens (T. Hansen 1859) during debt-crisis demonstrations (Source: author, 2017).

academic publications, workshops and festivals (Papanikolaou 2019). What is more, in recent years a number of government initiatives have emerged, aimed at systematizing the Social and Solidarity Economy framework in Greece (L.4430/2016; L.4605/2019; L.4608/2019), the energy and education commons (L.4513/2018; L.4485/2017) and attempting to establish a developmental framework involving the concept of the commons; it remains to be seen if these will have an impact on society and the economy in the long run.

Thus, the first part of this volume delves into the core of the issue, discussing current considerations of heritage commons; Stelios Lekakis comments on the concept of heritage commons as inferred from his work in Greece and the relevant management context, bringing forward a new theoretical framework for the conceptualisation of cultural heritage, grounded in the tripartite structure of the commons, i.e. resources managed by communities through commoning. Mina Dragouni discusses whether heritage goods can be related to the economic conceptualisation of Common Pool Resources (CPR), proposing novel research tools (economic experiments) to explore collective management alternatives in the field. Despina Catapoti, Ioulia Skounaki and Georgia Gkoumopoulou examine the concept of *openness* in urban archaeological sites in relation to public / private (*open-closed*) parameters. They seek answers in the Archaeological Park of Plato's Academy (see also Galanos in this volume) and the Philopappos Hill case studies.

Part two takes us to a number of different fields, and a mix of academic and opinion papers, addressing current debates from the common's front in Greece. Styles differ significantly, however they all can be considered as 'notes from the field', providing examples of 'commoning' patterns, processes of collaboration and conflicts around property rights and/or institution-creating from unusual but useful perspectives. Nicholas Anastasopoulos discusses the continuum between traditional commons and their digital configurations, along with the social process of coming together to produce, curate and inherit use-valuable resources. Prodromos Tsiavos looks at the limitations and prohibitions imposed by the Greek Archaeological Law in managing representations of heritage material and how that plays out in the digital sphere, where 'regulators' and mainly 'netocrats' (sharing mega-platforms run by private bodies) operate on different rules. On the same note, Marina Markellou & Petros Moris discuss a contemporary art project and how it attempted to incorporate heritage material in the final product, raising questions about traditional notions of originality and authenticity along with issues concerning the legal framework for the use of heritage elements in digital creations.

Vasso Kanellopoulou looks at the case of seeds, discussing how the current legal provisions hinder the circulation of traditional varieties of seeds – as a CPR – and are intended to protect industrial seeds in the name of commerce regulations. Also, on the matter of food, Penny Travlou discusses the activities of the OneLoveKitchen collective in Athens, considering the transnational context of cultural production and the shifting concept of intangible heritage, that coalesce in acts of commoning. Giorgos Chatzinakos explores the long-standing neighbourhood initiative in Thessaloniki, attempting to provide the physical and immaterial space for communicating, sharing, and eventually commoning. In parallel, Chrysostomos Galanos describes the story of Plato's Academy co-op Café, as a hands-on endeavour in urban commons, along with relevant tools needed in the process; a prototype that was then followed in other cases in Athens and beyond.

Finally, in Part 3, on a more political note, Alexandros Kioupkiolis sets the focus on the horizon, commenting on the lack of strategic thinking in terms of potential political transformation, bringing forward interesting practices from Italy while Dimitris Markopoulos questions the set-up of the discussion on commons in relation to the private and the public when it comes to politics.

Aspirations

At the end of the rather long session held at the 2015 Dialogues in Archaeology Conference, a colleague raised their hand and posed a somewhat general comment that went along the lines of: 'I don't agree with all of this. Products have always been circulated, people have always paid a price for a service and middlemen got what they were entitled to'. Although panel members had pinpointed the character of the CPRs historically and the processes of sharing and commoning as embedded in the history of humanity, I think that the nub of the question remains unanswered; indeed in the framework of normalized capitalism, the market can seem the only legitimate venue to interact with others over resources, in a surveilled, monetized system set to handle all types of transactions, related to material or immaterial goods. It feels somehow natural to be expected to pay for everything.

Social and cultural goods are processed through the same framework, shaped by the same tools and diligently prepared for audit accounting reports. In fact, aggressive neoliberal agendas now claim deeper subordination of vital elements, unexplored niches of people's everyday lives, cultural aspects included.

Attempting to re-consider given 'truths', we need to focus on solid theoretical but also relatable and feasible schemata. It is interesting that the commons have come back to public awareness precisely at a time of global political and social uncertainty and anxiety. The main argument of the commons, reflecting processes of collaboration and sharing, should be considered a political principle, fashioning a new political subjectivity, making it possible to theorise the conditions of collective action, formulate new principles and link dispersed activities towards a new model of governance (Dardot & Laval 2019: 4). This provides the social and political framework to examine a case study from a holistic approach, uniting economic, ideological, cultural and political points of reference on an alternative basis, rather than the dominant public/private hiatus paradigm.

In the field of heritage, commons theory and practice allow for critical exploration on ontological features of the entities involved, the role of the surrounding stakeholders and the exigent frames for the protection and management, but most importantly open the discussion for further argumentation, frameworks and potential implementation models (institutions) for heritage commons. Discussing heritage within the framework of the contemporary socio-political system of Europe and especially within the dispossessed framework of Greece, allows us to delve further into the strengths, opportunities and potential pitfalls of such an endeavour.

Enveloped in the emerging scene of critical heritage studies, this volume should be considered as an initial step forward, a primary sketch aimed at precipitating a paradigm shift, while at the same time furthering the element of amazement and disbelief that we encounter when we present the possibility of cultural heritage in the realm of the commons.

Acknowledgements

This volume, which aspires to describe and discuss the boundaries of the emerging field of 'heritage commons', through a focused case study on Greece and from an interdisciplinary perspective, would not have been possible without the generous contributions of the authors, two insightful reviews by Dr. Georgios Alexopoulos (UCL) and Dr. Peter G Gould (University of

Pennsylvania), the concise proof-editing by Dr. Emmet Marron, the reference list editing by Konstantina Nikolopoulou and the timely arrangements by Ubiquity Press (Imogen Clarke and colleagues). The artwork on the cover was crafted by Ioannis Oikonomakis. Support received from the Faculty of Humanities and Social Sciences, Newcastle University. To support the dissemination of ideas and contribute further to the wider discussions in the field, the volume is published under the Creative Commons BY-NC licence.

Bibliography

Bauwens, M., Kostakis, V. & Pazaitis, A. (2019). *Peer to peer: The commons manifesto*. London, United Kingdom: University of Westminster Press.

Bauwens, M. & Niaros, V. (2017). *Value in the commons economy: Developments in open and contributory value accounting*. Chiang Mai, Thailand: Heinrich-Böll-Foundation & P2P Foundation.

Bekridaki, G. & Broumas, A. (2016). The Greek society in crisis and in motion: Building the material bases for an alternative society from the bottom up. Retrieved November 20, 2019, from https://papers.ssrn.com/sol3/papers.cfm?abstract_id=2853050.

Benesch, H., Hammami, F., Holmberg, I. & Uzer, E. (Eds.). (2015). *Heritage as common(s) – Commons as heritage*. Gothenburg, Sweden: Makadam.

Benkler, Y. & Nissenbaum, H. (2006). Commons-based peer production and virtue. *The Journal of Political Philosophy, 14*(4), 394–419.

Bertacchini, E. Saccone D. & Santagata, W. (2011). Embracing diversity, correcting inequalities: towards a new global governance for the UNESCO World Heritage. *International Journal of Cultural Policy, 17* (3), 278–288.

Bloemen, S. & De Groot, T. (Eds.). (2019). *Our commons: Political ideas for a new Europe*. Retrieved November 20, 2019, from https://www.commonsnetwork.org/ourcommons/.

Bollier, D. (2008). *Viral spiral: How the commoners built a digital republic of their own*. New York, NY: New Press.

Caffentzis, G. & Federici. S. (2014). Commons against and beyond capitalism. *Community Development Journal, 49*(suppl. 1), i92–i105. DOI: https://doi.org/10.1093/cdj/bsu006.

Dardot, P. & Laval, C. (2019). *Common: On revolution in the 21st century*. London, United Kingdom: Bloomsbury Academic.

De Angelis, M. (2017). *Omnia sunt communia. On the commons and the transformation to postcapitalism*. London, United Kingdom: ZED books.

Dellenbaugh, M., Kip, M., Bieniok, M., Müller, A. K. & Schwegmann, M. (Eds.). (2015). *Urban commons: Moving beyond state and market*. Berlin, Germany: Birkhäuser.

Erickson, C. (1992). Applied Archaeology and Rural Development: Archaeology's Potential Contribution to the Future. *Journal of the Steward Anthropological Society, 20* (1–2): 1–16.

Federici, S. (2012). Feminism and the politics of the commons. In D. Bollier & S. Helfrich (Eds.), *The wealth of the commons: A world beyond the market & state* (pp. 45–54). Amherst, MA: Levellers Press.

Gibson-Graham, J. K., Cameron, J. & Healy, S. (2013). *Take back the economy: An ethical guide for transforming our communities.* Minnesota, MN: University of Minnesota Press.

Gonzalez, P. A. (2014). From a given to a construct: Heritage as a commons. *Cultural Studies, 28*(3), 359–390. DOI: doi.org/10.1080/09502386.2013 .789067.

Gould, P. G. (2014). A tale of two villages: Institutional structure and sustainable community organizations. *Public Archaeology, 13*(1–3), 164–177.

Gould, P. G. (2017). Considerations on governing heritage as a commons resource. In P. G. Gould & K. A. Pyburn (Eds.), *Collision or Collaboration. Archaeology Encounters Economic Development* (pp. 171–187). Cham, Switzerland: Springer.

Hardin, G. (1968). The tragedy of the commons. *Science, 162*(3859), 1243–1248.

Hardt, M. & Negri, A. (2012). *Declaration.* Argo-Navis Author Services.

Harvey, D. (2012). *Rebel cities: From the right to the city to the urban revolution.* London, United Kingdom: Verso.

Harvey, D. (2016). *The ways of the world.* London, United Kingdom: Profile books.

Hess, C. (2012). The unfolding of the knowledge commons. *St. Anthony's International Review, 8*(1), 13–24.

Law 3028/2002. *On the protection of antiquities and cultural heritage in general.* Retrieved November 20, 2019, from https://www.bsa.ac.uk/wp-content /uploads/2018/11/Archaeological-Law-3028-2002.pdf.

Law 4430/2016. Κοινωνική και αλληλέγγυα οικονομία και ανάπτυξη των φορέων της και άλλες διατάξεις. Retrieved November 20, 2019, from https://www.taxheaven.gr/laws/law/index/law/781.

Law 4485/2017. *Οργάνωση και λειτουργία της ανώτατης εκπαίδευσης, ρυθμίσεις για την έρευνα και άλλες διατάξεις.* Retrieved November 20, 2019, from https://www.taxheaven.gr/laws/law/index/law/829.

Law 4513/2018. *Ενεργειακές κοινότητες και άλλες διατάξεις.* Retrieved November 20, 2019, from https://www.taxheaven.gr/laws/law/index/law/859.

Law 4605/2019. *Εναρμόνιση της ελληνικής νομοθεσίας με την Οδηγία (ΕΕ) 2016/943 του Ευρωπαϊκού Κοινοβουλίου και του Συμβουλίου ...... - Μέτρα για την επιτάχυνση του έργου του Υπουργείου Οικονομίας και Ανάπτυξης και άλλες διατάξεις [Προστασία πρώτης κατοικίας].* Retrieved November 20, 2019, from https://www.taxheaven.gr/laws/law/index/law/923.

Law 4608/2019. *Ελληνική Αναπτυξιακή Τράπεζα και προσέλκυση στρατηγικών επενδύσεων και άλλες διατάξεις.* Retrieved November 20, 2019, from https://www.taxheaven.gr/laws/law/index/law/926.

Lekakis, S., Shakya, S. & Kostakis, V. (2018). Bringing the community back: A case study of the post-earthquake heritage restoration in Kathmandu valley. *Sustainability, 10*(8), 2978. DOI: https://doi.org/10.3390/su10082798.

Lieros, G. (2016). Κοινά, κοινότητες, κοινοκτημοσύνη, κομμουνισμός: Από τον κόσμο των κοινών στον κοινό κόσμο. Athens, Greece: Ekdoseis ton synadelfon.

Linebaugh, P. (2008). *The Magna Carta Manifesto: Liberties and commons for all*. Berkeley, CA: California University Press.

Olsen, M. (1965). *The logic of collective action: Public goods and the theory of groups*. Cambridge, MA: Harvard University Press.

Ostrom, E. (1990). *Governing the commons: The evolution of institutions for collective action*. Cambridge, United Kingdom: Cambridge University Press.

Papadimitropoulos, V. (2017). The politics of the commons: Reform or revolt? *Triple C, 15*(2), 563–581. DOI: https://doi.org/10.31269/triplec.v15i2.852.

Papanikolaou, G. (2018, July 9). Η ανάδυση του ιδεολογικοπολιτικού ρεύματος των κοινών. *Avgi*. Retrieved November 20, 2019, from http://www.avgi.gr /article/10811/9023370/e-anadyse-tou-ideologikopolitikou-reumatos-ton -koinon.

Plantzos, D. (2018). Crisis, austerity measures and beyond: Archaeology in Greece since the global financial crisis. *Archaeological Reports, 64(November)*, 171–180. DOI: https://doi.org/10.1017/S0570608418000261.

Rodgers, C. P., Straughton, E. A., Winchester, A. J. L. & Pieraccini, M. (2011). *Contested common land: Environmental governance past and present*. Abingdon, United Kingdom: Earthscan.

Scharper, S. & Cunningham, H. (2006). The genetic commons: Resisting the neo-liberal enclosure of life. *Social Analysis, 50*(3), 195–202. DOI: https:// doi.org/10.3167/015597706780459403.

Tziovas, D. (Ed.). (2017). *Greece in crisis: The cultural politics of austerity*. London, United Kingdom: I. B. Tauris.

Van Laerhoven, F. & Ostrom, E. (2007). Traditions and trends in the study of the commons. *International Journal of the Commons, 1*(1), 3–28. DOI: https://doi.org/10.18352/ijc.76.

Voudouri, D. (Ed.). (2014). *Διαχείριση πολιτιστικών οργανισμών σε περίοδο κρίσης. Πρακτικά διημερίδας, 31 Μαΐου-01 Ιουνίου 2013*. Athens, Greece: Panteion University.

Zückert, H. (2012). The commons: A historical concept of property rights. In D. Bollier and S. Helfrich (Eds.), *The wealth of the commons: A world beyond market and state* (pp. 125–131). Amherst, MA: Levellers Press.

PART I

A Political Economy of Heritage and the Commons: A First Sketch Focusing on Greece

Stelios Lekakis

The commons today constitute a hotly debated topic with wide research range spanning from the natural resources to social and digital goods. However, discussions on heritage as commons are limited, considered mostly as part of the state politics and economics agenda. This chapter attempts to provide an initial sketch of the emerging field of heritage commons, based on empirical work carried out by the author in Greece; a country at the forefront of the development of the 'cultural property' notion for heritage, currently negotiating the public texture of its monuments and cultural economy. Commenting on the state enclosure of the past and subsequent practices by other agencies within this appropriation, this chapter attempts to redefine heritage and its components, drawing on their social and economic values and the tripartite schema of the commons (resources, involved communities, regulatory frame) towards a more democratic governance perspective.

How to cite this book chapter:
Lekakis, S. 2020. A Political Economy of Heritage and the Commons: A First Sketch
    Focusing on Greece. In Lekakis, S. (ed.) *Cultural Heritage in the Realm of the
    Commons: Conversations on the Case of Greece*. Pp. 17–44. London: Ubiquity Press.
    DOI: https://doi.org/10.5334/bcj.c. License: CC-BY

A political economy of heritage

The national appropriation of the past

The concept of heritage goes hand in hand with the emergence of nation-states in the 18th and 19th c. Modernity and the complementary processes developing in Europe (urbanization, industrialization and their effects in social differentiation) changed long-standing views of the 'familiar ruins' – the remains of the past encountered in everyday life – as antiquity was distanced from the present and recast as 'cultural heritage'; socially significant tangible and intangible remains that should be protected and studied to document the glory of the nation (Anderson 1991). Artifacts, buildings, landscapes and figures of the past were thus acknowledged as landmarks in an eclectic narrative, the national history, to be managed by public servants (i.e. archaeologists, historians, conservators, archivists), who were responsible to project national identity to the past and narrate the deeds of the newly-established collective political subject, the nation-state, through the centuries (Lekakis et al 2018).

In this way, nation-states enclosed areas of the past and appropriated them as cultural heritage; a body of tangible and intangible material, imbued with symbolic meaning of belonging, pride and exceptionalism of the nation; a public good, stewarded in a top-down way by the state services, for the benefit of all.

Cultural Property & Cultural Economy

After the end of WWII, a number of intergovernmental organisations emerged in an attempt to bridge the gap left by the hostilities (UNESCO: 1945; ICOM: 1946; ICCROM: 1956; ICCROM 1959; ICOMOS: 1965). Their vision had a cultural horizon, implemented through the shared platform of 'cultural policy', an element of soft diplomacy aiming to establish good practice in heritage management across Europe and progressively organise the niche economic sector of 'cultural economy' with touristic and educational outputs. Main goal in this international network was the protection of and raising awareness for cultural heritage through 'shared ownership', attempting to introduce a common platform in heritage management and project inspirational feelings of unity and belonging onto a venerated, pre-war past, 'for the benefit of humanity'. This narrative, mainly expressed and utilised through normative documents, featured for the first time in the preamble of the Hague Convention for the Protection of Cultural Property in the Event of Armed Conflict in 1954, where (national) heritage is considered as common "heritage of all mankind" (UNESCO 1954).[4] Again, in the Hague Convention, the concept of "cultural property" was introduced as a generic term to assert the national appropriation of heritage "irrespective

---

[4] The concept was since reiterated to represent other entities, among others, the open sea, outer space and the human genome.

of origin or ownership" (UNESCO 1954: par.1). This concept of 'cultural property of mankind, reiterated in the UNESCO World Heritage Convention, still remains a pivotal theme in European cultural policy and a recurring subject in intergovernmental documents that followed (UNESCO 1972; Council of Europe 2015; Council of the European Union 2014); As we have examined elsewhere (Lekakis 2012: 686–8), there is no antagonism between the national and the international heritage ownership schemes; heritage still remains under the jurisdiction of the individual state, while sharing with the 'rest of the humanity' is implied as a moral obligation, a field for scientific collaboration but also a touristic potential, an encouragement to visit each other's monuments, promoted as finished and singular products for visitors' consumption.

Thus, cohesively organized and managed in-house to document and propagate the national self but also a point of reference for the reconciliation and collaboration of the nations, heritage as 'cultural property' became an element for the tourism industry, establishing progressively the 'cultural economy' sector, already traceable after World War II (Hobsbawm & Ranger 1983; Urry 1990; Goodwin 2006; Bertacchini et al 2012; Lekakis 2013a: 108–118).

The economistic horizon of heritage management

The last three decades, however, have seen a new series of discussions on the economistic horizon of heritage. The surfacing of neoliberal politics and the establishment of the New Public Management dogma in Europe, requiring adequate investment return in parallel to the shrinkage of state provisions, have highlighted the need to include cultural/heritage elements in the developmental plans in more productive ways than mere 'outputs' for tourism. Heritage is explored in these approaches, as a dynamic resource that can be measured, invested in and protected from exhaustion, an 'input' rather than an 'output', that can inform growth potentials, in the spectrum of sustainability; i.e. development that does not compromise natural resources or the social capital. In current narratives, culture is incremental in these schemata as a coordinating aspect that allows contextualization of tools and processes to promote productiveness, competitiveness and effectiveness (Sørensen 2007: 75). In fact, UNESCO and the United Nations support the introduction of culture as the fourth circle in the sustainability Venn diagram (Nurse 2006).

To cater for this set up, support the translation of culture/heritage in the economistic parole, and better the distribution and dynamics of the goods, a number of formalistic models and accounting practices have been transferred from the business sector to cultural/heritage management (Power 1997; Shore & Wright 2000: 60; Clark 2006: 60). Heritage management, in general, involves tools and practices from business administration and the management of the natural environment, processed into a resource in the 1960s (Mason 1999; Throsby 2002). It is already a theoretically laden and politically, culturally and technically organised set of activities that can contribute in the further reification of cultural heritage and its deliberation into a private good; for example, as an added value in a capital-driven gentrification scheme (Herzfeld 2010).

The 'cultural capital' modification is characteristic in this assortment. Through this, culture/heritage is considered as an input; a cumulatively homogeneous aggregation of tangible and intangible remains of the past and the relative cultural services, collectively taking into account its cultural and social values and the economic potential (Throsby 2001: 46). A homogeneous total that can work in parallel with the social and natural capital (Mason 1999: 12), managed through processes of valuation and valorization, that is fit for audit and accrual accounting and also has the potential to be consumed in terms of stock and flow (Throsby 2002: 102; Rizzo & Throsby 2006: 986). Heritage still remains a public good shared across the humanity ('cultural property'), it is however manipulated to fit the framework of the market, inventing or highlighting properties that we normally encounter in private goods, such as rivalry, excludability and substitutability.

Challenging the trend, researchers have swiftly identified that heritage commonly resists accounting standards prescribed for other assets to satisfy conventional market metrics, as assessing the economic outcome of an investment (Hooper et al 2005). The public character of heritage holds values that cannot be easily measured or exchanged for fiscal and commercial gains. In the bibliography of cultural economics, these are described from a negative perspective, as 'non-use values': relational, nonmaterial benefits or positive externalities that people obtain from ecosystems and cultural systems through spiritual enrichment, cognitive development, reflection, recreation, aesthetic experience and other qualities and attributes that cannot be easily quantified in financial terms (MA 2005: 40; Hølleland et al. 2017: 212; Gerber & Hess 2017: 715). These are now the centre of the attention, manipulated to fit the "holistic impact" of heritage resources on the social and economic landscape (Bakhsi et al. 2015).

Following the 'social turn'

The last four decades have also witnessed a marked turn in the heritage management debate towards the social values of cultural heritage. This could be considered a result of several processes ongoing, for example political decolonisation, economic refocusing of development, and reflexive, post-modern criticism in social science research. Respective criticism on Europe-centred cultural concepts (for example, the 'humanity' ownership) formed cracks in the national appropriation of monuments and raised the 1980s question of 'who owns heritage' (Lekakis 2012). Despite the abundant bibliography, the enquiry led to a dead-end. Arguments developed, however, allowed us to consider the public in a plural and inclusive form and track the emergence of hybrid disciplines around heritage, such as 'public archaeology' and 'cultural communication' that acknowledged the stake of the non-expert communities and sought methods to understand their views and collaborate towards a more inclusive present in heritage management (Schadla-Hall et al. 2010; Lekakis et al 2018: 3).

This 'social turn', acknowledged widely (Council of Europe 2000; European Commission 2008; Council of Europe 2005), is nowadays considered to have limited success and pay lip-service to effective inclusion and participatory processes. A frequent argument relates this trend again to the repercussions of New Public Management; Managerialism requires public sector entities to be as effective and efficient as their private sector counterparts, covering the social responsibility and respecting tax-payers' money to revert the liability character of heritage assets. Public choice is thus seen as an overarching strategy, guiding the attempts to generate economic benefit by materializing values and services embodied in the 'asset' (Hooper et al. 2005: 420). The public is thus taken into account, however shallowly considered either as tax-payers or customers/tourists for whom heritage should be managed. A mindset that further reinforces the economistic appraisal of heritage but also leaves social needs unaddressed; Results, currently observable around Europe, can be considered a far cry from democratic governance attempts (Council of Europe 2000), or the deliberation of culture as a human right (UNESCO 2007), to mention just a few of the 'social turn' aspirations in normative documents.

Organised as a state property with international scope, the national enclosure of the past has thus been progressively stripped from social meanings and cultural content into a micropolitical and economic niche to generate national identity and revenues through its connection to tourism and other supporting sectors, compromising its public character and potential.

Heritage commons: The research field today

As we are examining in this volume, commons theory and practice have been emerging globally as a hybrid academic discipline but also as a sensitive process of managing resources collectively and on the ground (Dardot & Laval 2019); Goods and processes used and produced in the commons realm are governed in democratic ways by the managing communities, making them accessible on regulated terms.

Nevertheless, heritage as a commons appears infrequently in the bibliography and remains largely unrelated to the critique of the dominant model described above. Sometimes, heritage commons are encountered in descriptive arguments, inspired by the 'common heritage of mankind' narrative and in relevant shallow interpretations of the term; the most prominent of them derives from UNESCO 1972 Convention and the World Heritage List holding assets of 'Outstanding Universal Value', asserting the vague 'common ownership' for heritage as discussed above (Zhang 2012; Council of the European Union 2014).

On a similar note and extending somehow the width of the economistic horizon of heritage management, relevant scholarship focuses on the economic reading of the resources, attempting to discern the affordances of cultural capital as a Common Pool Resource and fend off potential 'tragedies'. In these studies, there are a number of attempts to: incorporate cultural assets as input in other systems (Briassoulis 2002), frame, measure and commodify non-use values or capture non-market preference (Serageldin 2000; Throsby 2016) and based on that treat heritage services and cultural expression as 'flow', protecting them from depreciation and overconsumption in a quasi-sustainable horizon (Bertacchini et al 2012: 244; Gonzalez 2014).

However, in the last decade, parallel to the cultural commons broad and inclusive narratives examined in the Introduction of the volume, there has been a number of theoretical attempts, based on but also lagging behind well-established commons theories from economic, social or political perspectives (e.g. Ostrom 1990; Harvey 2012; Hardt & Negri 2009; Dardot & Laval 2019). The enquiries focus on management patterns, institutions, design principles but also social dilemmas in their governance (Gould 2014; Benesch et al 2015; Bertacchini 2015; Uzer 2015; Hammami 2015; Baillie 2015). In this spectrum, even though some studies engage in the exploration of specific cases, discussing applied heritage management aspects in detail (processes of inclusion, production and governance, see for example contributions in Gould & Pyburn 2017), they regularly fail to address ontological enquiries related to the resources, critically explore their (ethnographic) context in its historicity and/or consider the future of the heritage commons arrangements, giving rise to a number of queries: Can we actually consider the heritage commons potential in the contemporary (public) management settings? And what would it mean for heritage and the communities involved? How is it different from the 'sustainable heritage management' models and aspirations currently trending in the bibliography? But for a limited amount of scholarship (Gould 2014), lack of holistic arguments keeps the field relatively untapped, offering sparse and narrow narratives on specific case-studies (for example, Menatti 2017; Gonzalez 2014), limiting horizons to the deliberation of heritage services (Kolembas & Billas 2019: 104). Although a reality for other public resources, commons as an organisational principle for heritage has not been explored systematically and largely remain unrelated to the current problematic management of cultural heritage.

The case of Greece

Greece has been at the forefront of 'cultural property' concept development, focusing on the nationalisation of cultural heritage along with other open-access resources (e.g. mines, forestries) by the nascent nation-state, pioneering what later became a mainstream activity for antiquities' source-countries (Lekakis 2012; Carman 2018: 167).

In Greece, attempts to prevent the haemorrhage of antiquities abroad date to even before the emergence of the nation-state, preparing the ground for the establishment of the Archaeological Service in 1834, one of the oldest public services in the country. In the first Archaeological Law, antiquities were declared as "national property" (ἐθνικόν κτῆμα) (A. 61) (Petrakos 1987: 55–56). However, this was a nominal regulation due to the widespread looting and the traditional ownership practices that encouraged the illegal trade of antiquities for many decades before the establishment of the modern state. Sixty-five years later, the new law "On Antiquities" (Law 2646/1899) smoothed out any chances of co-ownership left behind (A.1) and prescribed heavy penalties for looters (A.15) (Lekakis 2016). Following closely, by the end of the 19thc. most European countries had acquired a legal framework for heritage as 'state property', including Spain (1860), Italy (1872), Hungary (1881), Egypt (1881) and the United Kingdom (1882).

In Greece, the tradition of heritage as public property (domaine publique) owned by the state, was reiterated in the following Archaeological Law (Law 5351/1932) that established antiquities as inalienable goods, in the realm of *res sanctae*, exempting them from trade or transactions, for the benefit of the public (Voudouri 2003). State ownership and its obligation to preserve heritage for the public benefit (i.e. over private ownership, A.17:1) was reinstated in the Constitution of Greece (Hellenic Parliament 2008, A.24), introducing also the right of the people to preserve cultural goods and enjoy the right of cultural freedom (A.5:1, A.16:1) (Pantos 2001: 265). Finally, in the most recent Archaeological Law 3028/2002, the 'public' features as the final the recipient of heritage protection and enhancement, both important public goods that should be "incorporated in contemporary social life" (A. 3:1.6).

Enclosures within the enclosure

These early developments and later appraisals had set a solid framework for public heritage management in Greece, nurturing however further enclosures within the national one.

The tourism industry in Greece

Following the heritage as an 'output' pattern for the tourist industry described above, the Greek National Tourism Organization was established in 1929 to promote cultural heritage and littoral summer destinations as a homogenized touristic product (Tziovas 2011). This was shaped accordingly and included various stereotypes, such as traditional and monumental architecture, ancient art, the natural environment, but also the 'naïve and benign inhabitants of the islands', formulating an aesthetically inviting cultural identity for Greece, ready

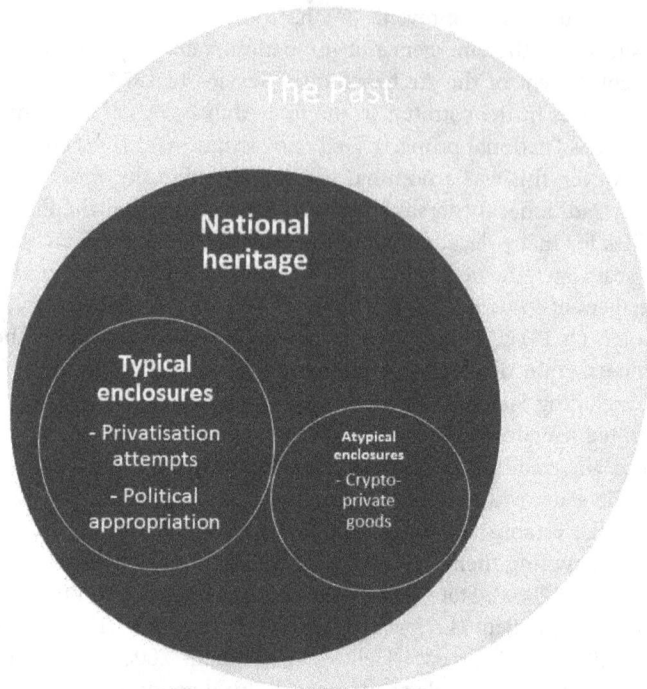

Figure 1: A political economy of the past: New enclosures within the national appropriation of the past, also known as: Cultural Heritage.

to be experienced through the lenses of neo-classicism and philhellenism by subjects imbued in European modernity (Lekakis 2013b). This touristic product became the basis of a mass tourism pattern that, while lacking a cohesive promotion strategy, still operates today. However, apart from inviting the consumption of this truncated view of the Greek identity, this schema created a space that allowed locals to "rapproach" cultural heritage (Lekakis 2013b). Thus locals, organising an idiosyncratic enclosure within the national one, have been operating as cultural mediators, promoting expected and easy to digest heritage elements and services with high-exchange value, such as souvenir shops, rooms-to-let and restaurants. Heritage in the form of 'cultural property' is further appropriated, this time at a local level, to satisfy the omnipresent national narrative but also fulfil the neoliberal aspiration of short-term profit-making from it.

Crisis narratives & new enclosures: Typical and Atypical

In the last decade, however, this homogeneous tourist product and its appropriation was somehow lost in the crisis narratives that dominated media reports about the European South and specifically Greece with the potential economic default and debt restructuring (Tziovas 2017). This context paved the way for urgent austerity measures including repeated cutbacks in wages, the abrogation of numerous social rights (especially related to labour), an effective disregard for political liberties and systematic privatizations. All of these were considered cataclysmic changes that would have been unthinkable without the rhetoric and biopolitics of terror deployed in an undeclared state of exception and led to new enclosures of social and cultural goods (De Angelis 2017: 155–8).

The cultural heritage management field in Greece was accordingly affected, since further cuts were introduced in terms of budget and staff, while fast track processes for large developmental projects were introduced to reduce the costs and delays incurred by archaeological works (L.4072/2012; L.4146/2013). The private sector, in the form of large philanthropic foundations, rose to dominate heritage preservation and the new cultural production (Plantzos 2018). Critique soared: the receding state proved unable to adapt to the patron/facilitator patterns of management policy (Craik 2007), while chronic, palpable pathogenies in Greek cultural management (low state budget on culture, problematic prioritisation of spending, lack of infrastructure and tools, understaffing, clientelism) were further aggravated (Kouki & Liakos 2015). The 'state deficit model' steadily became a commonplace argument in academic narratives, while 'self-explanatory' flexible models emerged as one of the dominant modalities in the relevant bibliography, focusing on profit generation, entrepreneurship and cross-sectoral competitiveness; currently, proposals float between the synchronisation of public and private sectors, synergies and the preparation of the ground for investment on culture and heritage (Gazi 2017; Antoniadou et al 2018; Čopič & Srakar 2012). In the same frame, relevant (empty of meaning) terminology like 'cultural capital mobilization', 'rebranding', 'returns on investment', 'sustainable management for heritage', was put forward and currently plagues narratives in cultural/heritage management in Greece (Lekakis & Dragouni forthcoming; Lekakis 2016; Hadjimichael 2014).

Typical enclosures

This climate provided fertile ground for narrow and mainly shallow economic interpretations of cultural heritage, in various attempts to promote 'heritage-led development' in cultural management. Sometimes promoted as a disenclosure/liberation from the state's grip, the case studies that follow are just a small number that surfaced in the years of economic recession, suggesting new enclosures inside the national one and the dismemberment of cultural heritage to fit an unhinged neoliberal logic for public resources management.

Privatisation attempts

In the majority of the case studies, antiquities are presented as an obstruction to development, a factor that will result in the loss of invested money for the sake of a 'few old stones' and the state archaeologists' inflexible modi operandi. At the time of writing (July 2019), this is still the case with Elliniko airport, the disused Athens airport, where Lamda Development, backed by Chinese and Gulf funds claimed the tender – part of a post-bailout agreement between Greece and its lenders – and plans to turn the area into a complex of luxury residences, hotels, a yachting marina and casino at the expense of listed (moveable and immovable) heritage. The heritage preservation claims of archaeologists and activists are considered the final barrier to the alleged $8.97 billion investment that will transform the 'derelict' area and 'provide numerous work-places' (The hellinikon project 2017). The same mishmash of arguments have been repeated verbatim in the case of Agrotera Artemis temple, an important landmark of classical Athens, claimed for a hotel development project (https://www.artemisagrotera.org/?history=1). In cases such as these, heritage assigned for preservation, is to be delimited within the framework of a glass-box for touristic purposes, to provide space for the building activities, while the protesters should be silenced not to scare away the investors.

In less publicised cases, cultural heritage is aggressively undermined, as in the case of Cavo Sidero in Crete and the proposals for the development of a golf course (Bellos 2019) or the earlier case of Aiglitis Apollo temple on Anafi Island, where the development company started utilising their religious tourism facilities, without any permit from the Ministry of Culture (Kazalotti 2009). Less known is the case of many historic and/or listed buildings in Athens that have been demolished or left to decay, due to lack of resources or aggressive urban investment strategies (Smith 2017) (Figure 2).

Cases of direct privatisation of heritage are infrequent; an example is the attempt (allegedly due to an administrative error) to include a number of monuments and listed buidings on the list of the Hellenic Corporation of Assets and Participations S.A., alongside the other properties to be expropriated again according to the country's international bail-out obligations and the Medium-Term Fiscal Strategy (GTP editing team 2019).

Crisis' heritage enclosures also include accessibility limitations, in favour of more profitable activities by private firms, as in the Platos' Academy & Philopappou Hill cases discussed in this volume or in the case of Apollo Zoster temple, where the real estate company managing the promontory, encompassing the adjacent beach and hotels, limits the accessibility to their customers, sometimes charging potential visitors to access the ruins (Figure 3). Relevant to the latter, i.e. from a 'heritage services' enclosure viewpoint, is the case of Messini archaeological site, where a project of archaeological tourism was organised (but not utilised) in collaboration with a nearby resort, inviting visitors to participate, as part of their all-inclusive cultural experience (Myrilla 2014).

Finally, a frequent scenario of enclosure relates directly to the operative management framework of cultural heritage, for the benefit of a private entity. Thus, in a well-known case in 2013, the excavator of the Nemea archaeological site, in light of the lack of staff and the potential closure of the visitor facilities, proposed a new scheme for the archaeological site and the museum:

Figure 2: Ktima Drakopoulou. Drakopoulou estate contains a complex of buildings from the 19th c. bequeathed to the Greek Red Cross in 1977. Delisted in 2003 and partially demolished in 2009, buildings and green space are now in grave danger of complete destruction to make space for new development (Source: author, 2020).

Figure 3: Observing Apollo Zoster's temple outside the fence (Source: author, 2019).

following an international call, a private firm would rent out the site and adjacent facilities, a model that held the potential to be adopted by many small and overlooked archaeological sites in Greece (Pournara 2013). Elements of this operative framework hijacking can be observed in the touristic study by Ralph Applebaum and Associates for the cultural resources in Athens and Attica (Bellos 2012). Indeed, it has even been suggested that this concept is already up and running, fully-fledged, in the form of the Legal Entity of Public Law scheme, under which a number of museums in Greece currently operate (Krimnioti 2019). A different branch of the same scenario, reflects resources mobilisation for the protection and promotion of ancient sites, including excavation and extensive restoration projects, such as those envisaged by the association 'Diazoma', who in recent years have been promoting various agendas for the management of culture in Greece, and going as far as to suggest that state heritage management is "post-ottoman" in terms of agility, bureaucracy and effectiveness (Pantazopoulos 2019).[5]

Political appropriation

On another note, one can frequently observe the appropriation of heritage in favour of political parties and politicians' agendas in the frame of the state management or at the borders of it, mainly using the imagery and connotations of classical antiquities. Following the decline of the foundational stories of Europe and the rise of the far-right throughout the continent (Bloemen & de Groot 2019), the most prominent manifestation of this phenomenon is the symbolic adaptation of classical antiquities by far-right political elements in Greece; a typical process observed historically in totalitarian states that call upon ancient heritage to promote an exclusionary sense of belonging and persecution of the *other*, paradigmatic in Nazi Germany but also during the military junta in Greece (1967–1974) (Chapoutot 2012; Kokkinidou & Nikolaidou 2004). In contemporary Greece, such scenarios still exist, constructing racist and sexist narratives in favour of an imagined, pure, national, mostly white, able-bodied, male agent; more often than not, narratives like these formulate biopolitical discourses against the other, as immigrants, refugees or the LGBTQI+ community (Plantzos 2012).

---

[5] It is interesting to observe that 'Diazoma' also complements every post on social media with the hashtag *culture, common good* (#πολιτισμός #κοινό_ αγαθό). This is influenced from the 'heritage of the mankind' arguments discussed above, however it can also be considered as a feat of 'commons washing', a neoliberal attempt to hijack commons' semantics and retract value for private benefit.

Atypical enclosures

Apart from the typical enclosures, i.e. attempts to enclose part of the resources, the relevant services or the operative framework by undermining the public management body in charge, in favour of a private agent, other types of enclosures can also be discerned. These are collectively examined here as 'atypical'.

A large category of these can be considered the enclosures within the management body, producing idiosyncratic crypto-private goods. These relate to the pathogeny of state management practices and current framework, pinpointed in catchword rhetoric of leftish pedigree and bureaucratic ankylosis coupled with chronic reservation against any private contribution for heritage protection and management, even if they come from well-intended, nongovernmental bodies (Lekakis 2016).

The 2012 conference of the professional association of archaeologists working in the Ministry of Culture affirmed that 'monuments belong to all' (Syllogos Ellinon Archaiologon 2002). However, in many cases priorities are set by monopoly interests of persons or groups. Thus, even though a detailed description of the structures and power struggles within the Greek Archaeological Service is yet to be composed, a number of templates producing crypto-private heritage resources are familiar to individuals either working or liaising with the Ministry of Culture services, relating to heritage resources, framework

Figure 4: Demonstrating outside the Acropolis of Athens (Source: author, 2008).

or knowledge. Excavators, for example, have unlimited *de facto* rights to the material sometimes even transferable to people of their liking, contrary to the current Law (Bournia et al. 2014). What is more, they commonly retain documentation paperwork at their houses, jeopardising its safety and limiting the study of the material or rejecting the contribution to the national or European data repositories, claiming them as (scientifically) unpublished. In addition to this, on the operative framework side, it is observed that short term hires – a process sometimes hijacked in favour of local politicians and other extra-institutional factors – regularly work on other projects or cover administrative and immediate needs of the Ministry's branches throughout Greece. The refusal to collaborate can lead to a compromise in the trust relationship between the precarious archaeologist and the state frame. Finally, various allegations have highlighted the need to liaise personally with people in vital positions that can promote or withhold cases that need approval at a local level (Tsaravopoulos & Fragkou 2013: 95).

Re-reading heritage as commons in Greece

Although these case studies could be interpreted as markers of a current state of emergency for heritage, our discussion suggests that it could all be related to the framework organised by the modern state, enclosing the past and assembling a malleable product to exploit for micropolitics and profit. In view of the present challenges, the need for effective heritage protection and the defense of its public character, a question arises as to whether we can move the slider away from the privatisation spectrum towards the opposite end, i.e. democratic and socially relevant patterns for its viable governance as a commons.

As noted, the commons are goods and processes used and produced collectively, administered in egalitarian and participatory ways by the communities that manage them. Communities' involvement in the process of commons production and reproduction is 'commoning'. This is also a rule of thumb to discern whether the activity we are examining or designing is actually a commons; i.e. (i) if it involves tangible or intangible resources, public or common, (ii) if it is managed by one or more communities of 'commoners' and (iii) if it is protected by a framework or rules organised and actively defended by the commoners, in the participatory act of 'commoning'. This tripartite schema is regularly characterised as a 'commons-based governance' and/or a 'production system' that sustains itself, protects the resources at hand and empowers the communities involved in social, political and economic ways, caring at the same time for the common benefit (Dellenbaugh et al. 2015: 13). There are many different categories of commons, from natural Common Pool Resources, such as pastures and irrigation canals to digital goods, such as open-source software or common productive assets, such as co-operatives (Ostrom 1990: 30; Benkler & Nissenbaum 2006). Even though a complete taxonomy is difficult to sketch

Figure 5: Re-reading heritage as commons: Resources, Communities, Commoning.

out, as commons are dynamic and porous processes, they always involve shared resources which are managed, produced and distributed collectively – in common stewardship – in ways that contest both private and state property logic (Hardt & Negri 2012: 69–80).

Can heritage fit this schema? Can a conceptual and practical shift from a resource-based to a commons-based approach be supported? Following the intertwined social and economic discussion of heritage affordances in the private and public realm and our observations on the case of Greece, we will attempt to discuss whether heritage can be read and managed as a commons. Getting back to the core of the commons conceptualization (the resources, the communities that manage them and the regulatory framework for the management process), we can discern: (i) the tangible and intangible material (for example, a historic building, an archaeological site and the social/traditional knowledge/beliefs or local practices and visions surrounding them), (ii) the communities and their values (local and distant stakeholders surrounding the resources, the public in a plural and diverse form, e.g. archaeologists, administrative bodies, locals, tourists etc.) and (iii) commoning (namely, the present and aspired governance arrangements along with the products in the process, either in the form of (scientific) knowledge and information or as relevant tourism and education activities).[6]

---

[6] A prior version of this schema has been presented in Lekakis et al. 2018.

Resources

Examining further this tripartite schema, it seems that cultural heritage resources, or better cultural heritage goods, should be examined in a broad sense, including tangible and intangible, moveable and immovable assets of cultural and social significance, varying from monumental antiquities and museum collections to modern and contemporary heritage and oral history. Produced by communities and re-interpreted in each historic moment on cultural grounds, cultural heritage goods bear a composite biography, being essentially alive and potentially relevant to different communities.

Nowadays the past is commonly materialised through its national appropriation, segmented in an abstract, unchanging, cartographic space to be meaningful in the national narrative and as private goods in the form of reified exchangeable objects or assets for tourism. However, heritage is not easily scalable. Cultural heritage is compiled collectively over the course of time and ionised according to the social, political and economic circumstances of the era. As in the discussion of the 'archaeological site', concepts are invented to circumscribe these cultural phenomena, leaving behind tangible and intangible fabric that hold significant and/or alternative meaning to the delimitated area (Olwig 2015: 93). The synthesis of cultural heritage should be contextual and considered as a negotiation of historic identities, contemporary views and future visions in the present, overcoming the sterile economic approach. Preservation and research are resource-intensive activities, meaningful when utilizing heritage's widespread ownership and public textures, bringing out the concrete possibility of collective enjoyment.

Communities

As the 'social turn' narrative has attested, cultural heritage goods should also be considered as social goods, forged in the iterations between historical memory and its contemporary interpretation by various communities that participate in the process, investing values in a dominant or more marginal way. Thus heritage, apart from the fabric and the intangible characteristics – related but not always depending on it – includes particles of identity of a society in its historicity, and the vision for the future in the present. This is a deeply sociocultural process that is always conditional and "in the making" (Lekakis & Dragouni 2020), negotiating the affordances of cultural goods, depending on the needs, the challenges, the local, national and global conditions and the vision for the future. It is common knowledge that societies choose monuments to reflect themselves and co-create their significance in the present, in an unfolding relationship between the past, present and future.

In this context, heritage stakeholder communities should be acknowledged plurally, taking into account alternative values and significance ascribed or brought out from heritage, in parallel with or against the national overarching agenda. This collective storehouse of cultural values (Carman 2005: 74) should be examined in context and at a local level contrary to the nebulous 'humanity ownership' argument, examined above.

Communities can be unbound geographically, as the new digital environment enables the participation of decentralized communities, already with critical contribution in the proliferation of digital commons (Benkler 2006: 2; Bollier 2008: 1–20, 117). Thus, contrary to the economistic approach that considers stakeholders as customers and tax-payers, the concept of participant communities needs to be re-assessed, in a more open, inclusive and political way, acknowledging the power imbalances and their relevant contribution in the formation of heritage. Also, contrary to the essentialist understanding of meanings ascribed, we need to listen tentatively and allow the re-enchantment of cultural heritage goods.

Commoning: Commons-based governance & production

The socially mediated, collective and distributed activity for management and production is inherent in the commons and can be summarised as a verb; "to common" (Linebaugh 2008; Dardot & Laval 2019). Commoning is a central set of functions and the social network in which the resource is situated, but also a prevailing ethic among the participant communities, utilizing and providing normative valence to the resources while also allowing self-reflection and progressive maturity in the establishment of management mechanisms and institutions (Roe 2018: 409).

Governance: Institutions & frame

Thus, governance implies new forms of social gatherings and networks that decide on the common resources in participatory and democratic ways, forging the sense of collective ownership (Gerber & Hess 2017: 725). Apart from these basic characteristics, implying co-operative, free associational networks and mutual decision-making processes, it is difficult to suggest a formalistic pattern for commons governance as it will be related to the relevant social and cultural context and should retain its versatility and adaptability, while protecting the resource, generating values and bringing people together (Bauwens & Niaros 2017). Ostrom suggested governance patterns following eight design principles (Ostrom 1990), however there is an imperative need to focus on a case by case basis, dealing with the resources and the communities in question, deliberating among others: access rights, extraction rights, management rights and exclusion rights (Hess & Ostrom 2003: 127).

There are no pre-modern utopias to go back to. However, we can learn from the past; studying the values emerging from the management of the CPR prior to being purged by modern life and incorporating them into contemporary designs. Neighbouring commons fields can also provide interesting case studies and tools for examination. For example, over the last decade social movements for the cultural and natural resources in Greece have made their presence felt by implementing important projects; however, they have failed to consolidate this into wider networks of power circulation, let alone accumulate it into such a constituent power or commons-based production (Bekridaki & Broumas 2016: 232; Nikolopoulou 2019). These case studies suggest that examples of synergetic behaviour in heritage management do exist, however commons-based governance is a new and largely undefined field, based on 'proposals' (Tsaravopoulos & Frangou 2013; Gonzalez 2014) or participatory based approaches with references to the commons theory (L-D Lu 2007). Most of these, fall under the 'aspirational' bibliography of heritage management, without significant practice-based evidence. This is undeniably an area that heritage commons research should turn to.

Production: knowledge & services

Hybrid systems of governance based on communal validation and negotiated coordination are focused on commons production, in the form of knowledge, information or service. In this locally based but globally oriented production process, use value is generated through the collaboration of people with access to the distributed capital and means of production (Bauwens et al. 2019). Economic efficiency, profit, and competitiveness are not cast away however they cease to be the guiding principles of the process. In this context of peer-production, the boundaries between producers and consumers become blurred, enabling the so-called "prosumers" or "produsers" (Bruns 2008) hybrid model and other novel forms of social formulations. Relevant licences can protect the products in an emerging post-capitalist landscape focusing on commons accumulation in a co-op mentality, as documented in 'public licences': 'contributors can use, enterprises need to pay'.

Commenting on the products, social and scientific knowledge is one of the main spin-offs from the commons-based governance patterns for heritage, non-rival and sharable, that we can focus on as a straightforward way in the heritage commons scheme. Knowledge can be considered part of the resources, but also a result of commoning, a product of social interaction and production by the various communities mobilized around the cultural resources, providing new meanings in their biography, as described in the 'Resources' section of this chapter. Social knowledge produced can also feed back to the governance process and in a wider sense to the cultural context of the heritage commons, re-invigorating cultural commons that is essentially part of all commons. Scientific knowledge produced must be open and accessible to the communities related to the heritage commons. Digital ways of sharing came to revolutionise knowledge commons and various possibilities can be discerned, ranging from digital repositories (Europeana) to open licences in Galleries, Libraries, Archives or Museums (Sanderhoff 2014). Finally, knowledge can be transliterated to information, the basis for heritage interpretation opening up to current and future participants, who are thus invited to co-create.

On the other hand, services' development requires more careful planning, again being informed by practices in relevant fields, away from capital-centric modalities (Gibson-Graham 2006). Community based museums or locally run touristic enterprises can be organised in the form of co-operatives that have been making their presence felt over the last decade in the European South. The Social Economy sector is currently a small niche, although it holds significant potential, comprising of co-operatives, associations, foundations, non-profit and voluntary organisations (Gibson-Graham et al 2016). What is more, Solidarity Economy initiatives have contributed to the alleviation of numerous issues instigated by the economy recess and the default of the welfare state in many European countries; among others these include work collectives (cafes, restaurants), social grocery stores, networks for distribution of goods without middlemen, social kitchens and movements for the collection and distribution of food, social clinics, pharmacies for the uninsured and time-sharing banks.[7] Heritage services organised in Social or Solidarity Economy patterns can be the main line of defence against the expansionist modality of cultural economics and co-optation attempts by market and state forces but also hold prefigurative potential to an alternative commons-based cultural economy (Lekakis & Dragouni forthcoming).

Cultural heritage in the realm of the commons

In this chapter, we attempted to discuss and describe an alternative understanding of cultural heritage, as a commons, looking at problems in the crisis-laden Greek heritage context. Cultural heritage goods include material and immaterial resources but also the communities deciding on their significance and participating on their governance and production. The past can be considered as part of the things that were there before we came to life, as a 'passed down' common resource. However, it is materialised through its national appropriation – where the concept of heritage derives from – having only superficial relation to the surrounding communities. Focusing on social values is part of the contemporary heritage management agenda, however it is still a limited field of endeavour, rigged in favour of the managing authorities and the overarching economistic appropriation of heritage. By focusing on the commons agenda, we attempt to hack the concept of heritage and regain accessibility to the past.

---

[7] For Greece: https://www.solidarity4all.gr/. Last accessed 15.08.2019.

Commons-based heritage governance can provide a solid ground to perform our social endeavours in the field but also a socio-political horizon to move to.

In this frame, cultural heritage goods are to be protected but also considered in the making, reshaping organically through participation and praxis, providing the possibility to connect and self-reflect for the interested communities that derive and assign values to it. This is a vital function for the people participating in heritage governance, the heritage commoners. Heritage can be a hub of social activity, facilitating values and holding imaginary and symbolic meanings. Community-based rules can define patterns of production and reproduction of further cultural goods and services, without negating use values and profit, closing in with neighbour commons-based products. Even though there is still a long way to go, especially when designing and implementing the specific governance patterns and institutions, commons can be the basis for a new political economy for heritage, one that can be truly considered as a human right.

Bibliography

Anderson, B. (1991). *Imagined communities. Reflections on the origin and spread of nationalism*. London, United Kingdom: Verso.

Antoniadou, S. (Ed.), Vavouranakis, G. (Ed.), Poulios, I. (Author) & Raouzaiou, P. (Ed.). (2018). *Culture and perspective at times of crisis: State structures, private initiative and the public character of heritage*. Oxford, United Kingdom: Oxbow books.

Baillie, B. (2015). Heritage and the right/the right to heritage. In H. Benesch, F. Hammami, I. Holmberg & E. Uzer (Eds.). (2015). *Heritage as Common(s) – Common(s) as Heritage* (pp. 255–264), Gothenburg, Sweden: Makadam.

Bakhshi, H., Fujiwara, D., Lawton, R., Mourato, S. & Dolan, P. (2015). *Measuring economic value in cultural institutions*. Swindon: Arts and Humanities Research Council.

Bauwens, M., Kostakis, V. & Pazaitis, A. (2019). *Peer to peer: The commons manifesto*. London, United Kingdom: University of Westminster Press.

Bauwens, M. & Niaros, V. (2017). *Value in the commons economy: Developments in open and contributory value accounting*. Chiang Mai, Thailand: Heinrich-Böll-Stiftung & P2P Foundation.

Bekridaki, G. & Broumas, A. G. (2016). The Greek society in crisis and in motion: Building the material bases for an alternative society from the bottom Up. Retrieved November 20, 2019, from https://ssrn.com/abstract=2853050.

Bellos, I. (2012, October 29). Plan to revamp Athens tourism to boost visitor numbers. *ekathimerini*. Retrieved November 20, 2019, from http://www.ekathimerini.com/145775/article/ekathimerini/business/plan-to-revamp-athens-tourism-to-boost-visitor-numbers.

Bellos, I. (2019, February 24). State officials strive to block major investment projects. *ekathimerini*. Retrieved November 20, 2019, from http://www

.ekathimerini.com/238034/article/ekathimerini/business/state-officials
-strive-to-block-major-investment-projects.

Benesch, H., Hammami, F., Holmberg, I. & Uzer, E. (Eds.). (2015). *Heritage as Common(s) – Common(s) as Heritage*. Gothenburg, Sweden: Makadam.

Benkler, Y. (2006). *The wealth of networks: How social production transforms markets and freedom*. New Haven, CT: Yale University Press.

Benkler, Y. & Nissenbaum, H. (2006). Commons-based peer production and virtue. *The Journal of Political Philosophy, 14*(4), 394–419.

Bertacchini, E., Bravo, G., Marrelli, M. & Santagata, W. (Eds.). (2012). *Cultural Commons: A new perspective on the production and evolution of cultures.* Cheltenham, United Kingdom: Edward Elgar Publishing.

Bertacchini, E., Saccone, D. & Santagata, W. (2011). Embracing diversity, correcting inequalities: Towards a new global governance for the UNESCO World Heritage. *International Journal of Cultural Policy, 17*(3), 278–288.

Bloemen, S. & De Groot, T. (Eds.). (2019). *Our commons: Political ideas for a new Europe* [e-Book]. Retrieved November 20, 2019, from https://www.commonsnetwork.org/ourcommons/.

Bollier, D. (2008). *Viral spiral: How the commoners built a digital republic of their own*. New York, NY: New Press.

Bollier, D. & Helfrich, S. (2015). *Patterns of commoning*. Amherst, MA: The Commons Strategies Group & Off the commons Books.

Bournia, E., Gerousi E. & Kakavogianni, O. (Eds.). (2014). *Αρχαιολογική έρευνα και διαχείριση του αρχαιολογικού υλικού. Πρακτικά Επιστημονικής Ημερίδας. Παρασκευή, 9 Μαρτίου 2012. Πολιτιστικό Κέντρο του Δήμου Αθηναίων*. Athens, Greece: Enosi Archaiologon Ellados "Ios".

Briassoulis, H. (2002). Sustainable tourism and the question of the commons. *Annals of Tourism Research, 29*(4), 1065–1085.

Bruns, A. (2008). The future is user-led: The path towards widespread produsage. Retrieved November 20, 2019, from https://www.researchgate.net/publication/27472557_The_Future_Is_User-Led_The_Path_towards _Widespread_Produsage.

Carman, J. (2005). Good citizens and sound economics: the trajectory of archaeology in Britain from 'heritage' to 'resource'. In C. Mathers, T. Darvill & B. J. Little (Eds.), *Heritage of value, archaeology of renown: Reshaping archaeological assessment and significance* (pp. 43–57). Florida, FL: University Press of Florida.

Carman, J. (2018). Links: Going beyond cultural property. *Archaeologies, 14*, 164–183. DOI: https://doi.org/10.1007/s11759-018-9337-y.

Chapoutot, J. (2012). *Le nazisme et l'antiquité*. Paris: Presses Universitaires de France-PUF.

Clark, K. (2006). From significance to sustainability. In K. Clark (Ed.), *Capturing the public value of heritage: The proceedings of the London conference, 25–26 January 2006* (pp. 59–60). London, United Kingdom: Historic England.

Čopič, V. & Srakar, A. (2012). Cultural governance: A literature review. *EENC Paper, January 2012 [updated February 2012]*. Retrieved November 20, from www.interarts.net/descargas/interarts2549.pdf.

Council of Europe. (2000). *Council of Europe Landscape Convention*. Retrieved November 20, 2019 from https://www.coe.int/en/web/landscape.

Council of Europe. (2015). *The wider benefits of investment in cultural heritage: Case studies in Bosnia and Herzegovina and Serbia*. Strasbourg Cedex, France: Council of Europe Publishing.

Council of the European Union. (2014). *Conclusions on cultural heritage as a strategic resource for a sustainable Europe*. Retrieved November 20, 2019, from https://www.consilium.europa.eu/uedocs/cms_data/docs/pressdata /en/educ/142705.pdf.

Craik, J. (2007). *Re-visioning arts and cultural policy: Current impasses and future directions* [e-book]. Canberra ACT, Australia: ANU Press. DOI: http://doi.org/10.22459/RACP.07.2007.

De Angelis, M. (2013). *Κοινά, περιφράξεις και κρίσεις*. Thessalonica, Greece: Ekdoseis ton Xenon.

De Angelis, M. (2017). *Το ξεκίνημα της ιστορίας, αξιακοί αγώνες και παγκόσμιο κεφάλαιο*. Athens, Greece: autopoiesis.squat.gr.

Dellenbaugh, M., Kip, M., Bieniok, M., Müller, A. K. & Schwegmann, M. (Eds.). (2015). *Urban commons: Moving beyond state and market*. Berlin, Germany: Birkhäuser.

European Commission. (2001). *The Aarhus Convention*. Retrieved November 20, 2019, from https://ec.europa.eu/environment/aarhus/.

Gazi, A. (2017). Greek museums in times of crisis. In D. Tziovas (Ed.). *Greece in Crisis: The Cultural Politics of Austerity* (pp. 158–179). London, United Kingdom: I.B. Tauris.

Gerber, J.-D. & Hess, G. (2017). From landscape resources to landscape commons: focussing on the non-utility values of landscape. *International Journal of the Commons, 11*(2), 708–732.

Gibson-Graham, J. K. (2006). *A postcapitalist politics*. Minneapolis, MN: University of Minnesota Press.

Gibson-Graham, J. K., Cameron J. & Healy, S. (2016). Commoning as a postcapitalist politics. In A. Amin & P. Howell (Eds.). *Releasing the commons: rethinking the futures of the commons* (pp. 192–212). London, United Kingdom: Routledge.

Gonzalez, P. A. (2014). From a Given to a Construct: Heritage as a commons. *Cultural Studies, 28*(3), 359–390.

Goodwin, C. (2006). Art and culture in the history of economic thought. In V. A. Ginsburg & D. Throsby, *Handbook of the economics of art and culture*, Vol. 1 (pp. 25–68). Retrieved November 20, 2019, from https://www .sciencedirect.com/science/article/pii/S1574067606010027.

Gould, P. (2014). A tale of two villages: Institutional structure and sustainable community organizations. *Public Archaeology*, *13*(1–3), 164–177. DOI: https://doi.org/10.1179/1465518714Z.00000000066.

Gould, P. G. (2017). Considerations on governing heritage as a commons resource. In P. G. Gould & K. A. Pyburn (Eds.), *Collision or Collaboration. Archaeology Encounters Economic Development* (pp. 171–187). Cham, Switzerland: Springer.

Gould, P. G., Pyburn, K. A.(Eds.). (2017). *Collision or Collaboration. Archaeology Encounters Economic Development*. Cham, Switzerland: Springer.

GTP editing team. (2019, January 22). Decision allowing transfer of Greece's archaeological sites for private use upheld. *Gtp-Greek Travel Pages Headlines*. Retrieved November 20, 2019, from https://news.gtp.gr/2019/01/22/decision-transfer-greeces-archaeological-sites-private-use-upheld/.

Hadjimichael, M. (2014, June 4). In Greece, a battle to reclaim the seashore as commons. *ROAR*. Retrieved November 20, 2019, from https://roarmag.org/essays/greece-seashore-privatization-bill/.

Hammami, F. (2015). New commons and new heritage: negotiating presence and security. In H. Benesch, F. Hammami, I. Holmberg & E. Uzer (Eds), *Heritage as common(s) – Commons as heritage* (pp. 287–307). Gothenburg, Sweden: Makadam.

Hardt, M. & Negri, A. (2012). *Declaration*. Argo-Navis Author Services.

Hellenic Parliament. (2008). *The Constitution of Greece: As revised by the parliamentary resolution of May 27th 2008 of the VIIIth Revisionary Parliament*. Retrieved November 20, 2019, from https://www.hellenicparliament.gr/UserFiles/f3c70a23-7696-49db-9148-f24dce6a27c8/001-156%20aggliko.pdf.

Herzfeld, M. (2010). Engagement, gentrification, and the neoliberal hijacking of history. *Current Anthropology*, *51*(S2), S259–S267. DOI: https://doi.org/10.1086/653420.

Hess, C. (2012). The Unfolding of the Knowledge Commons. *St. Anthony's International Review*, *8*(1), 13–24.

Hess, C. & Ostrom, E. (2003). Ideas, artifacts, and facilities: Information as a common-pool resource. *Law and Contemporary Problems*, *66*(1–2), 111–146.

Hobsbawm, E. & Ranger, T. (Eds.). (1983). *The invention of tradition*. Cambridge, United Kingdom: Cambridge University Press.

Hølleland, H., Skrede, J. & Holmgaard, S. B. (2017). Cultural Heritage and Ecosystem Services: A Literature Review. *Conservation and Management of Archaeological Sites*, *19*(3), 210–237. DOI: https://doi.org/10.1080/13505033.2017.1342069.

Hopper, K., Kearins, K. & Green, R. (2005). Knowing "the price of everything and the value of nothing": Accounting for heritage assets. *Accounting Auditing & Accountability Journal*, *18*(3), 410–433. DOI: https://doi.org/10.1108/09513570510600765.

Mitsopoulou, C., Nikolopoulos, E. & Filimonos, M. (Eds.). (2016). *Η αρχαιολογία στην Ελλάδα του σήμερα: Μνημεία και άνθρωποι σε κρίση. Πρακτικά Διεπιστημονικού Συνεδρίου, 19–20 Μαρτίου 2015*. Athens, Greece: Enosi Archaiologon Ellados "Ios".

Kazalotti, E. (2009, September 11). Προφήτης Ηλίας κατά... Απόλλωνα: Μοναστήρι της Καλαμιώτισσας. Οι μοναχοί χτίζουν πάνω σε αρχαία. *Enet.gr*. Retrieved November 20, 2019, from http://www.enet.gr/?i=news .el.ellada&id=81173.

Kioupkiolis, A. (2019). *The common and counter-hegemonic politics. Re-thinking social change*. Edinburgh, United Kingdom: Edinburgh University Press.

Kokkinidou, D. & Nikolaidou, M. (2004). *On the stage and behind the scenes*: Greek archaeology in times of dictatorship. In M. M. L. Galaty & C. Watkinson (Eds.), *Archaeology Under Dictatorship* (pp. 155–190). New York, NY: Springer. DOI: https://doi.org/10.1007/0-387-36214-2_8.

Kolembas, G. & Billas, G. (2019). *Για την κοινότητα των κοινοτήτων: Με το πρόταγμα της αυτονομίας, της αποανάπτυξης, του κοινοτισμού και της άμεσης δημοκρατίας*. Athens, Greece: Ekdoseis ton synadelfon.

Kostakis, V., Niaros, V. & Giotitsas, C. (2015). Production and governance in hackerspaces: A manifestation of commons-based peer production in the physical realm? *International Journal of Cultural Studies, 18*(5), 555–573.

Krimnioti, P. (2019, August 2). Επιστροφή στις παλιές πρακτικές... *Avgi*. Retrieved November 20, 2019, from http://www.avgi.gr/article/10964/ 10093456/1-epistrophe-stis-palies-praktikes-.

Kouki, H. & Liakos, A. (2015). Narrating the story of a failed national transition: discourses on the Greek crisis, 2010–2014. *Historein, 15*(1), 49–61. DOI: http://dx.doi.org/10.12681/historein.318.

Law 3028/2002. *On the protection of antiquities and cultural heritage in general*. Retrieved November 20, 2019, from https://www.bsa.ac.uk/wp-content /uploads/2018/11/Archaeological-Law-3028-2002.pdf.

Law 4072/2012. *Βελτίωση επιχειρηματικού περιβάλλοντος – Νέα εταιρική μορφή – Σήματα – Μεσίτες Ακινήτων – Ρύθμιση θεμάτων ναυτιλίας, λιμένων και αλιείας και άλλες διατάξεις*. Retrieved November 20, 2019, from https:// www.taxheaven.gr/laws/law/index/law/430.

Law 4146/2013. *Διαμόρφωση φιλικού αναπτυξιακού περιβάλλοντος για τις στρατηγικές και ιδιωτικές επενδύσεις και άλλες διατάξεις*. Retrieved November 20, 2019, from https://www.kodiko.gr/nomologia/document _navigation/72227/nomos-4146-2013.

Lekakis, S. (2006). Αρχαιοκαπηλία και τοπικές κοινωνίες. Η περίπτωση των Κυκλάδων το 18° και 19° αιώνα. *Ναξιακά* 20 (58): 7–19.

Lekakis, S. (2012). The cultural property debate. In T. J. Smith & D. Plantzos (Eds.), *A Companion to Greek Art*, vol. I (pp. 683–697). Oxford, United Kingdom: Wiley-Blackwell.

Lekakis, S. (2013a). *Κοινωνικές και οικονομικές οπτικές της πολιτισμικής κληρονομιάς: Η διαχείριση σε τοπικό επίπεδο: Η περίπτωση της νήσου Νάξου*

(Unpublished PhD thesis). National & Kapodistrian University of Athens, Athens. Retrieved November 20, 2019, from https://www.didaktorika.gr /eadd/handle/10442/33304.

Lekakis, S. (2013b). Distancing and rapproching: Local communities & monuments in the Aegean Sea: A case study from the island of Naxos. *Conservation and Management of Archaeological Sites*, 15(1), 76–93. DOI: https://doi .org/10.1179/1350503313Z.00000000048.

Lekakis, S. (2016). Η διαχείριση της πολιτιστικής κληρονομιάς στην Ευρώπη και την Ελλάδα: Μια επισκόπηση. In C. Mitsopoulou, E. Nikolopoulos & M. Filimonos (Eds.), *Η αρχαιολογία στην Ελλάδα του σήμερα: Μνημεία και άνθρωποι σε κρίση. Πρακτικά Διεπιστημονικού Συνεδρίου, 19–20 Μαρτίου 2015* (pp. 115–132). Athens, Greece: Enosi Archaiologon Ellados "Ios".

Lekakis, S. & Dragouni, M. (2020). Heritage in the making: Rural heritage and its mnemeiosis on Naxos island, Greece. *Journal of Rural Studies, 77*, 84–92. DOI: https://doi.org/10.1016/j.jrurstud.2020.04.021.

Lekakis, S. & Dragouni, M. (forthcoming). Can cultural economy be social? Discussing about the rural heritage of Greece. *The Greek Review of Social Research.*

Lekakis, S., Shakya, S. & Kostakis, V. (2018). Bringing the community back: A case study of the post-earthquake heritage restoration in Kathmandu valley. *Sustainability, 10*(8), 2798. DOI: https://doi.org/10.3390/su10082798.

Lieros, G. (2016). *Υπαρκτός καινούργιος κόσμος: Κοινωνική/αλληλέγγυα και συνεργατική οικονομία.* Athens, Greece: Ekdoseis ton synadelfon.

Linebaugh, P. (2008). *The Magna Carta Manifesto: Liberties and commons for all.* Berkeley, CA: California University Press.

Lowenthal, D. (1998). *The heritage crusade and the spoils of history.* Cambridge, United Kingdom: Cambridge University Press.

Lu, L.-D. T. (2007). The management of two world heritage sites: Xidi and Hongcun in Anhui, China. In R. White & J. Carman (Eds.), *World heritage: Global challenges, local solutions. Proceedings of a conference at Coalbrookdale, 4–7 May 2006, hosted by the Ironbridge Institute* (pp. 87–94). Oxford, United Kingdom: Archaeopress.

MA. (2005). *Millennium Ecosystem Assessment.* Washington DC: World Resources Institute.

Mason, R. (Ed.). (1999). *Economics and heritage conservation: A meeting organized by the Getty Conservation Institute, December 1998,* Getty Center, Los Angeles. *Los Angeles, CA: Getty Conservation Institute.*

Menatti, L. (2017). Landscape: From common good to human right. *International Journal of the Commons, 11*(2), 641–683.

Mercouri, M. (2012). *Cultural heritage.* Retrieved November 20, 2019, from http:// melinamercourifoundation.com/en/cultural-heritage/cultural-heritage-2/.

Myrilla, D. (2014, July 16). «Ανασκαφικός τουρισμός» με το… αζημίωτο. *Imerodromos.gr.* Retrieved November 20, 2019, from https://www.imerodromos .gr/anaskafes-tourismos/.

Nikolopoulou, K. (2019). Grass-roots Initiatives and bottom-up musealisation mechanisms in urban space: The case of Heraklion Crete. *Heritage*, 2, 1912–1926. DOI: https://doi.org/10.3390/heritage2030116.

Nurse, K. (2006). Culture as the fourth pillar of sustainable development. In *Small states: Economic review and basic statistics*, vol. 11 (pp. 28–40). Retrieved November 20, 2019, from https://read.thecommonwealth -ilibrary.org/commonwealth/economics/small-states/culture-as-the -fourth-pillar-of-sustainable-development_smalst-2007-3-en#page1.

Olwig, K. R. (2015). Heritage as common(s) – Commons as heritage: Things we have in commons in the political landscape of heritage. In H. Benesch, F. Hammami, I. Holmberg & E. Uzer (Eds.), *Heritage as common(s) – Commons as heritage* (pp. 89–115). Gothenburg, Sweden: Makadam.

Pantazopoulos, G. (2019, July 14). Ο Σταύρος Μπένος μιλά για το «Διάζωμα», την κόντρα του με το υπουργείο πολιτισμού και την «μετα-οθωμανική» δημόσια διοίκηση. *Lifo.gr*. Retrieved November 20, 2019, from https:// www.lifo.gr/articles/greece_articles/244496/o-stayros-mpenos-mila-gia-to -diazoma-tin-kontra-toy-me-to-ypoyrgeio-politismoy-kai-tin-meta -othomaniki-dimosia-dioikisi.

Pantos, P. A. (2001). *Κωδικοποίηση νομοθεσίας για την πολιτισμική κληρονομιά κατά θέματα. Τόμος Ά. Ελληνική νομοθεσία*. Athens, Greece: Ministry of Culture-National Archive of Monuments.

Petrakos, V. Ch. (1987). Τα πρώτα χρόνια της ελληνικής αρχαιολογίας. *Αρχαιολογία & Τέχνες, 25*, 54–63.

Plantzos, D. (2012). The kouros of Keratea: Constructing subaltern pasts in contemporary Greece. *Journal of Social Archaeology, 12*(2), 220–244. DOI: https://doi.org/10.1177/1469605311433368.

Plantzos, D. (2018). Crisis, austerity measures and beyond: Archaeology in Greece since the global financial crisis. *Archaeological Reports, 64*, 171–180.

Pournara, M. (2013, October 23). Crisis comes calling at Ancient Nemea. *E-Kathimerini.com*. Retrieved November 20, 2019, from http://www .ekathimerini.com/154866/article/ekathimerini/life/crisis-comes-calling -at-ancient-nemea.

Power, M. (1997). *The audit society: Rituals of verification*. Oxford, United Kingdom: Oxford University Press.

Rizzo, I. & Throsby, D. (2006). Cultural heritage: Economic analysis and public policy. In V. A. Ginsburgh & D. Throsby (Eds.), *Handbook of the economics of art and culture, Vol. 1* (1st Ed.) (pp. 984–1016). Amsterdam, The Netherlands: North Holland.

Roe, M. (2018). Landscape and participation. In P. Howard, I. Thompson, E. Waterton, & M. Atha (Eds.), *The Routledge companion to landscape studies* (2nd ed.) (pp. 412–417). London, United Kingdom: Routledge.

Sanderhoff, M. (Ed.). (2014). *Sharing is caring: Openness and sharing in the cultural heritage sector*. Copenhagen, Sweden: Statens Museum for Kunst.

Schadla-Hall, T., Moshenska, G. & Thornton, A. (2010). Editorial. *Public Archaeology, 9*(3), 1.

Serageldin, I. (2000). Florence 1999: Culture counts in so many ways… (A recapitulative summation of the events). In World Bank, *Culture counts: Financing, resources, and the economics of culture in sustainable development. Proceedings of the Conference, Florence Italy, 4–7 October 1999* (pp. 162–171). Washington, DC: World Bank.

Shore, C. & Wright, S. (2000). Coercive accountability: The rise in audit culture in higher education. In M. Strathern (Ed.), *Audit cultures: Anthropological studies in accountability, ethics and the academy* (pp. 57–89). London, United Kingdom: Routledge.

Smith, H. (2017, September 12). Forget the Parthenon: how austerity is laying waste to Athens' modern heritage. *The Guardian*. Retrieved November 20, 2019, from https://www.theguardian.com/cities/2017/sep/12/athens-modern-heritage-austerity-neoclassical-architecture-acropolis-greece.

Sørensen, M. L. S. (2007). What does sustainability have to do with it?: Reflections upon heritage language and the heritage of slavery and missionaries. In R. White & J. Carman (Eds.), *World heritage: Global challenges, local solutions: Proceedings of a conference at Coalbrookdale, 4–7 May 2006 hosted by the Ironbridge Institute* (pp. 75–79). Oxford, United Kingdom: Archaeopress.

Syllogos Ellinon Archaiologon (2002). *Το μέλλον του παρελθόντος μας: Ανιχνεύοντας τις προοπτικές της Αρχαιολογικής Υπηρεσίας και της ελληνικής αρχαιολογίας, 4ο Συνέδριο, Αθήνα, 24–26 Νοεμβρίου 2000*. Athens, Greece: Syllogos Ellinon Archaiologon.

The Hellinikon Project (2017, November 10). Protection of Antiquities. Retrieved November 20, 2019, from https://thehellinikon.com/protection-of-antiquities/.

Throsby, D. (2002). Cultural capital and sustainability concepts in the economics of cultural heritage. In M. de la Torre (Ed.), *Assessing the values of cultural heritage* (pp. 101–117). Los Angeles, CA: Getty Conservation Institute.

Throsby, D. (2012). *Investment in urban heritage. Economic impacts of cultural heritage projects in FYR Macedonia and Georgia*. Retrieved July 6, 2018, from http://siteresources.worldbank.org/INTURBANDEVELOPMENT/Resources/336387-1169585750379/UDS16_Investment+in+Urban+Heritage.pdf.

Throsby, D. (2016). Investment in urban heritage conservation in developing countries: Concepts, methods and data. *City, Culture and Society, 7*(2), 81–86.

Tsaravopoulos, A. & Fragou, G. (2013). Archaeological sites as self-sustained resources for economic regeneration: Towards the creation of living archaeological parks on the islands of Kythera and Antikythera. *Conservation & Management of Archaeological Sites, 15*(1), 94–108.

Tziovas, D. (2011). *Ο μύθος της γενιάς του τριάντα. Νεοτερικότητα, ελληνικότητα και πολιτισμική ιδεολογία.* Athens, Greece: Polis Publications.

Tziovas, D. (Ed.). (2017). *Greece in crisis: The cultural politics of austerity.* New York, NY: I.B. Tauris.

UNESCO. (1954). *1954 Hague Convention for the protection of cultural property in the event of armed conflict.* Retrieved November 20, 2019, from http://www.unesco.org/new/en/culture/themes/armed-conflict-and-heritage/convention-and-protocols/1954-hague-convention/.

UNESCO. (1972). *Convention concerning the protection of the world cultural and natural heritage.* Retrieved November 20, 2019, from https://whc.unesco.org/en/conventiontext/.

UNESCO. (2007, August 15). *Fribourg declaration on cultural rights.* Retrieved November 20, 2019, from https://www.humanrights.ch/en/standards/international/un-bodies/launch-fribourg-declaration-cultural-rights.

Urry, J. (1990). *The tourist gaze: Leisure and travel in contemporary societies.* London, United Kingdom: SAGE Publications.

Uzer, E. (2015). Commoning in resistance: Gezi Park protests and "Yeryüzü Sofraları". In H. Benesch, F. Hammami, I. Holmberg & E. Uzer (Eds), *Heritage as common(s) – Commons as heritage* (pp. 309–327). Gothenburg, Sweden: Makadam.

Voudouri, D. (2003). *Κράτος και μουσεία: Το θεσμικό πλαίσιο των αρχαιολογικών μουσείων.* Athens, Greece: Sakkoulas.

Voudouri, D. (2010). Law and the politics of the past: Legal protection of cultural heritage in Greece. *International Journal of Cultural Property, 17*(3), 547–568. DOI: https://doi.org/10.1017/S094073911000024X.

Voudouri, D. (Ed.). (2014). *Διαχείριση πολιτιστικών οργανισμών σε περίοδο κρίσης. Πρακτικά διημερίδας, 31 Μαΐου-1 Ιουνίου 2013.* Athens, Greece: Panteion University.

World Bank. (2000). *Culture counts: Financing, resources and the economics of culture in sustainable development. Proceedings of the Conference, Florence, Italy, 4–7 October 1999.* Washington, DC: World Bank.

Zhang, C. Z. (2012). Three emerging variables influencing tourism development and study of world heritage protection. *Tourism Tribune, 27*(5), 5–6.

CHAPTER 2

An Economic Analysis of Heritage as Commons: Reflections on Theory, Methodology and Social Imagery

Mina Dragouni

The term 'commons' is used to describe a particular type of institutional arrangement for governing the availability and use of a good. As Hardt and Negri (2009) observe, we tend to see the world as divided between the public/ state and private/market spheres. This perceptual dichotomy creates implications not only in conceptualising heritage commons but also in addressing issues related to their political economy. To deal with these complexities, this chapter embraces economics and seeks to position heritage commons within the relevant theoretical and methodological approaches – in particular, the branch of behavioural experimental economics that provides tools for exploring the mechanics of collective decision-making and individuals' responses to social dilemmas. Moreover, the chapter engages in a discussion on macro-economic issues and the interplay between a potential (local) self-governing arrangement and the external economic and political influences that threaten to undermine its effectiveness to resolve commons problems.

According to economic theory, the concept of the common or Common Pool Resource is imbued with the attributes of non-excludability and rivalry (Ostrom et al., 1994). Indeed, there is a plethora of heritage resources that

How to cite this book chapter:
Dragouni, M. 2020. An Economic Analysis of Heritage as Commons: Reflections on Theory, Methodology and Social Imagery. In Lekakis, S. (ed.) *Cultural Heritage in the Realm of the Commons: Conversations on the Case of Greece.* Pp. 45–66. London: Ubiquity Press. DOI: https://doi.org/10.5334/bcj.d. License: CC-BY

bear these traits and are in principle (and often in practice) communal goods, implying that it is particularly difficult to exclude their potential beneficiaries from enjoying them. While the imposition of certain restrictions can set some limits on our encounters with heritage physically, it remains impossible to defend, both legally and economically, the enclosure of intangible values that we derive from the remains and practices of the past. Parallel to this, heritage goods can be viewed as rival in the sense that the (over)extraction of value by certain users can reduce availability for others. This is manifested, for example, in places where there is limited capacity and excessive development, or in cases where the uses of heritage antagonise disparate value systems.

Investment in common and non-market heritage goods is supposed to generate positive externalities that benefit society as a whole (Frischemann 2005). However, it is argued here that current regimes, such as centralized management, often fail to serve the communal interests of heritage sufficiently, whereas recently emerging market-led policies further jeopardise the communal character of heritage goods. As will be discussed, when the state follows management practices (e.g. selection, interpretation, public representation) that are expert-driven and exclusionary, it essentially de-socialises heritage resources and causes the alienation of non-expert communities. At the same time, when central administration adopts neoliberal strategies that prescribe funds for allocation that disproportionately favour private interests (e.g. the real estate and tourism sectors), it again fails to summon up the heritage communal principle. Given these shortcomings, the commons, which increasingly generate debate over public access to environmental and cultural resources, are viewed as an alternative to government control and an antidote to privatisation (Frischemann, 2005; Hardt & Negri 2009).

Admittedly, a central complexity imbued within the commons relates to provision arrangements and the behavioural responses of appropriators when it comes to contributing resources for maintaining them (Ostrom et al. 1994). In principle, commons are managed and sustained by communities themselves, through social networks that rely on solidarity and exchange (De Angelis 2003). Based on economic thinking, complexity stems from the fact that provision to and appropriation of heritage goods are disconnected, meaning that the former is not a precondition for the latter due to non-excludability. This leads to dilemmas between individual and collective interests, as personal gains compete with the provision of an optimal mix of communal benefits. To address these complications, this chapter analyses some key ideas of mainstream economics related to the subject, drawing mainly on the seminal work of Elinor Ostrom. Ostrom (1990) challenged the prevailing notions surrounding common goods, primarily those conceptualised in Olson's *Logic of Collective Action* (1965) and Hardin's *Tragedy of the Commons* (1968). The prediction of these theories was that in situations where resources are jointly shared, potential collective benefits will not be achieved due to excessive appropriation and the temptation to free ride. Contrary to these gloomy prognoses, in her book, *Governing the Commons* (1990), Ostrom compiled a series of micro-level cases in which users had in fact avoided tragic outcomes. Rather, these small communities had managed to sustain their commons by establishing their own rules, or in the author's terms, 'institutional arrangements' to regulate contribution and appropriation.

Economic studies on Common Pool Resources have been systematic in exploring mainly natural resources, focusing on individuals and the circumstances that drive their decisions. However, as is shown here, the common-pool metaphor is particularly relevant to heritage, the collective management of which entails control assignment to local actors and a horizontal collaboration between experts and citizens. In some respects, the heritage commons call for a socio-political arrangement located at Arnstein's (1969) highest rungs of 'citizen participation' ladder. Although there is high interest in the concept of managing heritage goods such as commons, there is considerably less evidence on how to do so in an effective and viable way. For those engaging in scientific research on the subject, the idea of commons inevitably leads to some serious methodological considerations. As it is outlined, there is a serious limitation to the empirical study of heritage commons due to the scarcity of naturally occurring data that are vital for gaining a better understanding of how models of heritage self-governance can work in practice.

Considering these limitations and bearing in mind that understanding human behaviour towards the commons is itself a great challenge (Ostrom et al. 1994), this chapter proposes the use of economic experiments as complementary methodological tools to address the implications of empirically investigating heritage commons and increase our current knowledge of the communal drivers and arrangements that can make collective management a viable alternative. As will be shown, there are two features of economic experiments that render this possible. Firstly, the mechanics of economic experiments that mimic real-world incentives and secondly, their capacity to elicit participants' social preferences (e.g. altruism, fairness, reciprocity) when making decisions. As such, experiments can be combined with historical, ethnographic and survey research, enabling us to study social behaviour in the field and to gain *ex-ante* some insight into the dynamics of community collective action. To illustrate this point, an example of a field experiment is presented here, along with some interesting findings that have been drawn empirically.

Finally, the chapter raises some additional political economy issues that deserve our attention. In particular, our discussion extends to the ramifications that emerge as we move from the microcosm of decision-making mechanics to broader concerns regarding the users and uses of heritage commons. This provides us with the space to reflect on and set certain critical parameters with which future scholarly work and public debates need to engage methodically. In turn, these reflections illustrate that the commons project is not simply a management model but a radical proposal that touches on and challenges deeply rooted principles and norms of our social, political and economic organisation. As is highlighted, at a time when options for socio-economic organisation seem so closely narrowed, approaching cultural heritage from a commons perspective requires us to set in motion our social imagination.

State vs markets: The (pseudo)dilemma of fulfilling communal interests

Since the 19th century, Western European conservation and preservation practices shaped the perception of 'heritage' as monumental, aesthetic, largely material and universally significant (Kuutma 2013). The ideological roots of heritage-making and its management practices grew between Bourdieu's (1984) symbolic distinctions of elitist spaces and Anderson's (1983) fabricated communities of national imagination. Heritage policy and control of the past and its remains was granted predominantly to the state and its officials (Smith 2006; Harrison 2012). State management prescribed for the material protection of heritage resources at the expense of public engagement and socialisation, creating inequality and distancing the broader public (Smith 2009). Participatory practice, introduced to museums and heritage spaces in recent decades to tackle the latter, is still largely flawed, in many cases creating the deception of collaboration while critical power continues to rest with experts (Waterton & Smith 2010; Lynch 2017).

Across the wider macro-economic policy landscape, recent years have seen the weakening of Keynesian politics and the destabilisation of state control over cultural heritage. However, the new policy 'shift' seems to also pay lip-service to the communal dimension of the remnants of the past. What is particularly disturbing in this case is that emerging policy trends are presented as reinstating commons qualities although in reality they serve predominantly business interests. In the current neoliberal climate, the concept of heritage commons is heavily challenged by market pressures, individualisation and the crisis of the welfare state (Callon 2007). The state is increasingly attacked for lacking the efficiency to satisfy *individual* needs as compared to the market. As in other sectors, recommended remedies to cure inefficiency are public sector reduction, increased marketisation and commodity consumption (e.g. by introducing user-fee services, privatisation and outsourcing schemes; Chhotray & Stoker 2009).

Cultural heritage does not remain impervious to these changing trends. Neoliberal politics advance the idea that, similar to other types of non-marketed goods, expenditure on heritage protection and enhancement must contribute somehow to economic development (Harvey 2012). Consequently, public policy for heritage is gradually adopting a market-approach, evaluating the conservation of the past against economic impacts and measurable indicators.

Countries such as the UK showcase this new apparatus of cultural politics by popularising the notion that the assignment of public funding to heritage must be justified in terms of its contribution to the economy (see for example, Heritage Lottery Fund 2016; Historic England 2017) and perceptual life satisfaction (see indicatively Fujiwara et al. 2014; Wheatley & Bickerton 2017). Undeniably, reducing a collective political economy issue to a matter of individual subjective well-being is perfectly aligned with new market instrumentalism.

Parallel to this, in less affluent states, heritage-led development is presented as a solution to diversify declining or emerging economies. Related strategies position heritage as compensation for the loss of agricultural and manufacturing activities, advancing the growth of service sector industries in tourism and leisure. European policy guidelines and reports by multilateral organisations increasingly promote the conservation of the past as an 'investment' option, a source of destination 'branding' and an 'asset' that needs to be capitalised in order to contribute to material wealth (see, for example, Throsby 2012; Council of Europe 2015). This new heritage vocabulary that has taken over policy narratives illustrates quite disturbingly the intrusion of market reasoning into the sphere of heritage commons. According to this rhetoric, heritage-led development projects hold the potential to generate multiple socio-economic benefits for local communities, although these come mainly indirectly (e.g. through employment 'opportunities'). However, what the narrative conceals is that these projects establish new 'synergies' between the state and the markets. While we are left to wonder how trading 'tax-payers' money with low-paid insecure employment can contribute substantially to the public benefit and socio-economic equality, private capital directly reaps the profits of increased tourism numbers and real-estate values. Economic analyses measuring the impact of heritage sites upon real estate through hedonic pricing illustrate this point eloquently (e.g. Lazrak et al. 2014).

State practices and norms determining the relationship between cultural heritage and Greek society do not deviate much from their European counterparts. Here, heritage management has long been viewed as state responsibility and a public service (Alexopoulos & Fouseki 2013). State authority over heritage was expressed as privileged control to official experts, exclusionary interpretation practices and political manipulation; long-standing 'traditions' that contributed to the alienation of communities from the 'official' past (Hamilakis 2007; Damaskos & Plantzos 2008; Lekakis 2013; Fouseki & Dragouni 2017). Furthermore, commitment to materiality was combined with a strict regulatory framework, to which compliance was hardly monitored or hindered by lengthy bureaucratic procedures and constraints on human and financial resources. In response to these shortcomings, non-expert communities developed confused, apathetic and occasionally hostile behaviour towards the ostensibly common heritage goods that had largely been isolated from their social surroundings (Stroulia & Sutton 2009). In more recent years, Greece's sovereign debt crisis led to the imposition of draconian austerity measures that lessened its welfare state considerably and shrunk its public goods provisions dramatically, also compromising the heritage sector (Georganas 2013; Howery 2013). Perhaps not surprisingly, the predicament of the national economy served as a fertile ground in public dialogue for entertaining ideas favourable to the private appropriation of heritage commons (see for instance, Chasapopoulos 2012, January 09; Pournara 2013, October 14; see also Lekakis, 2017), whereas post-crisis governments showed clear intentions to promote heritage tourism more intensively (Kouri 2012).

Overall, the problem with heritage resources, in Greece and elsewhere, is that state management often fails to fulfil their common interests and effectively address their public role, operating instead as a mechanism that controls, limits and excludes (Graham 2017). Heritage resources under state authority regimes have lost their societal relevance, whereas the state-market alliances legislating for enclosures and rents threaten to further strip their communal features. As the current economic and political landscape suggests, seeing the state and markets as opposing forces is misleading (Hann & Hart 2011). Rather, both models are imbued with failures to materialise common qualities and generate value and positive externalities that benefit society as a whole (Frischemann 2005). To our mind, any state-market synergy is condemned to fail in bringing about communal heritage benefits because private interests inherently favour specific (profit-seeking) uses of heritage, thus creating negative externalities such as the overuse and further detachment of heritage goods from their social context (Young 2011). This does not imply that heritage-related tourism and economic activities are intrinsically flawed, but rather that the economic system within which they function normally transforms them into unsustainable and destructive forces.

In this context, the management of heritage would need to move beyond the public / private logic and the choice of either the Keynesian or neoliberal canon (Hardt & Negri 2009). The failures of public management and market-oriented development projects suggest that it is worth exploring alternative models for heritage resources management, such as those that rely on political social action on behalf of citizens in order to (re)appropriate them. Economic analysis of Common Pool Resources and Ostrom's work on self-governance provide a conceptual framework to explore the subject and most importantly, to start thinking of a socio-economic formation of collectives that would operate outside current state and market rules.

The tragedy and triumph of the commons in rational economic thought

In mainstream economic theory, the terms 'commons' or 'common-pool resources' are used to describe a particular type of institutional arrangement for governing the availability and use of a good. This arrangement suggests that despite their rival character (i.e. use by one agent may affect use by another), no single agent can have exclusive control over their appropriation (Ostrom et al. 1994; Benkler 2003). Rather, the commons can be used and disposed by anyone under certain formal or informal rules. Cultural heritage can be formally defined as a Common Pool Resource based on these traits. Its non-excludability lies in the fact that it is in principle a shared good, given that exclusion from enjoying heritage is not socially and ethically acceptable. Moreover, heritage bears tangible and intangible elements of which the boundaries are often, by nature, hard to delineate. Consequently, even when access to heritage is restricted (e.g. to privately-owned historic houses) or conditional (e.g. when admission charges apply), it maintains qualities that are impossible to control, such as aesthetic pleasure or pride. In terms of rivalry, heritage is conflicting and attached to diverse use and non-use values that are often competing (Tunbridge & Ashworth 1996; Porter & Salazar 2005). For example, mass tourism or extreme commercialisation may generate economic benefits but lead to physical deterioration, decay and distortion of the heritage 'essence' (thus, affecting social and cultural values negatively).

Management-wise, the conceptual framework of the commons applied to the heritage realm calls for the substitution of paternalistic (state) regulation and market restrictions with recognition of commoners' rights to maintain the heritage resources of their locality (Benkler 2003). Here, economic analysis underlines the complexity of such an arrangement, suggesting that due to their non-excludable character, investment in the commons and returns of investment are disconnected. Said isolation creates externalities, as those not contributing to heritage commons cannot be excluded from enjoying the benefits of its protection and enhancement. Therefore, according to the rationality theorem, heritage resources are caught in social dilemmas, defined as situations where it is individually preferable to pursue one's personal interests instead of contributing to the commons' collective provision. This might hold especially true when social agents do not directly use heritage (as in the case of alienated communities) or when they can reap heritage-induced profits by free-riding (as in the case of tourism entrepreneurs; see Gonzalez 2014). Apart from limited incentives to invest in the maintenance and enhancement of heritage commons, the feature of rivalry, entailing the existence of certain interests pushing for heritage appropriations that clash with the uses and values of other interest groups, bears the inherent risk of excessive exploitation, overdevelopment and over-extraction of value (Briassoulis 2002).

Considering the complexities in the management of common goods, in 1968, Hardin put forward his famous proposition of the 'tragedy of the commons', advancing the idea that the collective management of a shared resource under these circumstances (i.e. no enclosures or external control) was doomed to fail. The foundation of his argument was the selfishness axiom, namely the assumption that social actors have a 'natural' tendency for profit-maximisation (Hann & Hart 2011). Based on this line of economic thought, dilemma situations are critical because the temptation to refuse cooperation can lead to less optimal provisions of communal benefits and eventually impair heritage goods, leaving everyone worse-off. To resolve such dilemmas, Hardin (1968) recommended either a top-down management or the privatisation of heritage goods (the failures of which we discussed earlier in this chapter).

Contrary to Hardin, Elinor Ostrom (1990) took the opposite stance towards the subject. In her seminal work, *Governing the commons*, she moved beyond both centralised government and private sector management to propose collective choice arrangements as a means of avoiding 'tragedy' situations. She suggested that communities can solve social dilemmas through a process of self-governance, which was subject to institutional arrangements (i.e. locally set rules). Based on Ostrom's (1990) metaphor, heritage resources can be positioned as the 'common-pools' of a locality, community members as 'providers' of these pools and the broader public as their 'appropriators' (e.g. through joint use and visitation). In a decentralised governance arrangement, invested provisions will benefit all appropriators but community agents will be granted the authority to collaboratively maintain heritage common resources.

The latter generates interest in the processes and dynamics of participation in decision-making, with regards to how heritage goods will be managed by commoners. Admittedly, a core problem of collective action relates to the interplay between individual action and outcomes dependent on others (Berge & van Laerhoven 2011). Nonetheless, presuming that individuals will *de facto* engage in the anti-social pursuit of profit is an oversimplification of human reasoning. In fact, both economic history and social anthropology suggest otherwise, rejecting the idea that humans strive to maximise utility and instead emphasising the existence of psychological drivers as complex structures shaped by the interplay between personal gain, consideration for others and social acceptance (Eriksen 2004). Thus, research into heritage commons needs to explore the internal mechanics of a collective process, as these would ultimately determine the viability of the resources in question.

While Ostrom's work exhibited cases where a commons regime could be successful at a micro level (mainly on natural resources management), we have little evidence at hand regarding its feasibility in a heritage context. Undeniably, one of our main challenges as scholars with an interest in the subject is the fact that both self-governance and the autonomy to make decisions are extremely uncommon phenomena. In some respects, the heritage commons call for a socio-political system that resembles Arnstein's (1969) citizen power levels, at a time when the prevailing paradigm for heritage management is top-down state control (Cleere, 2012). Thus, inevitably, we face the problem of limited, naturally occurring data on collective behaviour for heritage commons in order to study the cooperative capacity of social actors. This not only weakens the convincing power of theoretical arguments in favour of the commons but also hinders empirical enquiry on the subject as a means to inform the implementation of self-governance models in the real world. Since traditional observational approaches are not easily applicable to heritage commons studies, we propose here the use of economic experiments as alternative methodological tools that open up a novel avenue of research into the topic. Considering the growing experimental work on critical issues related to people's preferences, behaviour and decision-making, it is plausible to argue that experimental protocols can be adapted to respond to questions related to heritage self-governance and community cooperation in places where top-down management culture still prevails.

More specifically, economic experiments can capture participants' behaviour in a real setting by implementing actual pay-off structures associated with their choices (Exadaktylos et al. 2013). As such, they have been used to explore policy issues through the study of social preferences, where human subjects are asked to make economic decisions with real stakes. Experimental economics have consistently exposed the flaws of normative assumptions rooted in the selfishness axiom by demonstrating that human subjects do not innately engage in an anti-social pursuit of individual gain. Rather, systematic experimentation through economically incentivised protocols have shown that pro-social behaviour is associated with some form of conditional cooperation (Brandts & Fatas 2012). Exploring such conditions, therefore, deserves our scientific attention. In addition, experimental evidence has linked subjects' choices with the economic, social and cultural environments in which they operate.[8] These observations are highly relevant to a commons-based socio-economic organisation and can inform research in communities that currently have limited experience of collective action.

Similar to other policy contexts, experimental tools could be employed to elicit community commitment to heritage commons at the cost of personal rewards and generate observational data on their revealed preferences. In essence, this means that there is potential for studying community-based management of heritage *ex-ante* by devising experimental procedures that imitate circumstances of self-governance with the view to testing relevant hypotheses empirically and by design. Such hypotheses may relate to social interaction and cooperation, where heritage protection depends upon the collective decisions of participants. A model of self-governance for heritage commons presupposes direct responsibility on behalf of community members for both policy formulation and outcomes (Ansell & Gash 2008). This would suggest that, similar to Ostrom's (1990) framework, where self-governance is based upon the voluntary cooperation of community members, the maintenance and enhancement of heritage commons will be dependent on collective decisions to contribute.

Therefore, we argue that experimental research in the field of heritage can complement qualitative (e.g. ethnographic) and quantitative approaches (e.g. surveys) by increasing our understanding of cooperation dynamics in action.

---

[8] In this regard, the cross-cultural field experiments of Henrich et al. (2004) were particularly revealing in demonstrating the influence of socio-economic organisation systems upon people's responses to social dilemmas.

Given the similar arrangements needed for Common Pool Resources and public goods (Ostrom et al. 1994), researchers can create variations of public-good experiments in order to investigate behaviour when individual interests clash with social returns (Van Winden et al. 2008). In order to illustrate how experimental protocols can be employed to explore heritage commons questions, the next section will describe a hands-on application and briefly discuss its empirical results.

Studying the dynamics of collectives: A field experiment

During the Autumn of 2015, we ran a series of field experimental sessions with the community of Kastoria in Greece with the view to testing collaborative decision-making for heritage in a locality with no recent experience of self-governance. Kastoria was an interesting case study that exemplified a remote community and heritage at risk. This was highlighted by the 2014 Europa Nostra '7 most endangered' list,[9] which included the city's historic districts and by the dramatic socio-economic circumstances that heavily affected the area at the time (i.e. national debt crisis, decline in local manufacturing, extreme unemployment, increasing migrant population).

The experiment drew all of its subjects from the local community, encompassing residents, heritage professionals and government representatives. The key aim was to explore the collective processes of decision-making for heritage and the effect of different local group compositions upon cooperation. With this in mind, we organised participants into small groups and assigned them three different treatments. These imitated (a) conventional top-down management by state experts and officials, (b) bottom-up citizen leadership and (c) mixed arrangements of both officials and citizens that reflected a more pluralist form of heritage governance (Figure 1).

Inspired by public good protocols, the experiment featured two realistic management scenarios for heritage development projects, specifically designed

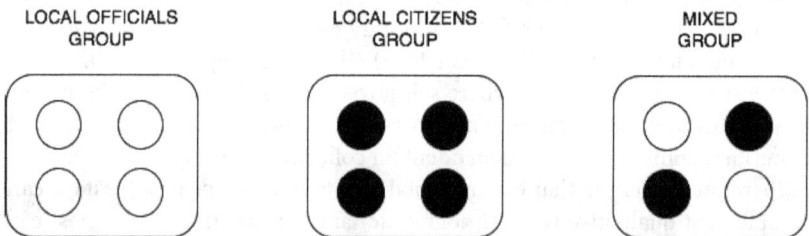

Figure 1: Experimental treatments (Source: author, 2019).

---

[9] Available at: http://7mostendangered.eu/sites/neighbourhoods-of-dolcho-and-apozari-kastoria-greece/. Last accessed 20 November 2019.

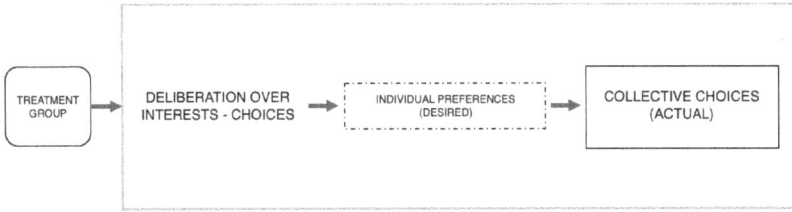

Figure 2: Process followed by each group and observed during experimental sessions (Source: author, 2019).

to fit with the local context. The actual implementation of these scenarios relied upon participants' choices and the resources they would be willing to contribute to the proposed projects. At each round, a voluntary contributions mechanism assigned the groups with an endowment and a simple task to allocate resources between a heritage account and a private account. Contributions to the heritage account would be used to fund the heritage project in question whereas contributions to the private account would be shared amongst group members for any other use. Each group was requested to reach a joint decision on how to use their endowment and note their decisions in privacy (to avoid any inter-group influences). Intra-group deliberation was recorded to extract data on individuals' (desired) choices and conflict (Figure 2). Responses to a personal questionnaire were also collected at the beginning of the sessions in order to observe how participants' background and beliefs shaped individual and group preferences during decision-making. Overall, the generated data allowed us to compare behaviour across different collective settings, the causes and impact of conflict upon collaboration and negotiations between an individual's own preferences and communal choices.

Based on the widely accepted assumptions about the tragedy of the commons, we would expect that in this collective-action situation, community members would act as rational egoists, generating a deficient equilibrium of zero or very low contributions to heritage (Ostrom 2005). However, as revealed by the experimental results, the local community of Kastoria presented significantly high social preferences and generosity towards heritage, despite its serious socio-economic problems, its lack of previous political traditions of collective action and its relative alienation from what was considered 'official' heritage.[10] Composition-wise, groups aligning with top-down management and pluralist groups that included officials and citizens as equal partners made equally pro-social choices. Interestingly, autonomous citizen groups were less co-operative in the first round, but equally co-operative in the second round.

---

[10] Based on survey-based empirical research that preceded the experiment (see Dragouni & Fouseki 2018).

This heterogeneity was possibly related to the different uses of heritage proposed by each scenario.[11]

In terms of deliberation dynamics, citizen and mixed groups were more susceptible to conflict situations, but interestingly their disagreement was positively related with their contributions to the heritage account (the opposite held true for the groups of officials). Furthermore, their collective decisions were consistently higher than the average individual preferences of group members. These suggest that conflict played a positive role during deliberation as it increased cooperation for heritage, showing higher resistance to egotistical interests compared to counterfactuals. In fact, the content of the group discussions revealed that negotiation dynamics (e.g. accommodating vs. contending behaviour) were instrumental in determining whether conflict would act favourably or against heritage commons. This has important implications for heritage self-management, highlighting that dealing with internal conflict can be a constructive democratic process rather than a destructive force. Conflict resolution reflects participants' freedom to challenge the direction of a common project (Kallis & March 2015) and in our case, it mobilised contributions to heritage commons. This mobilisation was dependent on certain negotiation merits and in particular, tolerance to participants' right to hold a different opinion and continuous deliberation on the available options.

In terms of drivers to cooperation, we found that trust (either in citizens or experts, depending on the sub-sample) played a significant role in determining social preferences at an individual level. Likewise, doubts within groups over the credibility of central authorities and external private players to manage heritage impacted positively on cooperation. In contrast, groups exhibiting high discrepancies with regards to the credibility of local actors, such as local heritage experts and community associations, tended to invest less in heritage commons. These findings are important because they underline the decisive role of trust at local level as a condition of cooperation and successful management of heritage by communities themselves. Qualitative data extracted from deliberation lent support to this argument, as distrust was one of the most frequent causes of dispute during decision-making. The role of trust in our experimental setting contradicts conventional theories of collective action problems, which emphasise the importance of material incentives (Kahan 2005). Rather, our results subscribe to a shift away from pure incentives towards the cultivation of trust as a key driver to cooperation.[12]

Although it is acknowledged that this empirical study would benefit greatly from future replication and comparison, it is maintained that it can introduce

---

[11] According to deliberation content analysis, the first scenario was seen as benefitting mostly tourism stakeholders whereas the second was mainly educational in nature.

[12] For a full description of the experimental design and results please refer to Dragouni et al. 2018.

a new and exciting line of research into the subject. Based on our experience of using an experimental method to observe community behaviour at the field, it is argued that diversifying our research tools and being scientifically 'creative' can be particularly rewarding not only in terms of research outputs but also as a process in itself. As discussed by Cardenas and Carpenter (2005), field experiments create benefits for both experimenters and participants, as a process of reflection on communal issues and problems. Indeed, as researchers we felt that the experimental sessions provided a platform for local stakeholders to meet and share their thoughts on heritage, while the whole process eventually led to the implementation of one of the project scenarios by the local heritage office, producing additional benefits to the community under study. It is hoped that our experience and results will provide an eloquent example of the methodological directions available at hand from other disciplines – in this case, experimental economics – and their capacity to meaningfully inform scientific research and public debate regarding heritage commons.

Moving from micro to macro: reflections on broader issues of political economy

Exploring the mechanics of decision-making processes and management arrangements at a micro level would be valuable for informing questions regarding heritage commons. Nonetheless, we maintain that the discussion on heritage commons also needs to engage in broader issues of political economy, as these are critical for understanding our current position, defending the concept, and visualising future steps towards self-governance. In particular, we argue that there are important parameters that deserve further consideration and these relate primarily to (i) the *users* and (ii) the *uses* of heritage commons. In turn, these reflections raise broader questions of political economy that touch upon the self-governance of heritage shared resources. By raising these questions, our intention is not to respond but rather to start painting the wider picture of the subject as an economic and political problem.

As previously implied, the ideal of the heritage commons is to form the groundwork for non-exclusive politics of collectivism. By encouraging processes of collective working, the commons arrangements are expected to tackle community alienation and promote equality (i.e. rectify the failures of current management approaches). Heritage studies have long been advocating for the 'opening up' of heritage management systems from top-down to more community-inclusive processes. However, this proposition, rooted in ideas of post-colonial justice, cannot be easily applied to the fragmented and shifting communities located in Western European territories. Therefore, a critical question arises regarding which community or communities are entitled to manage heritage commons. As Waterton and Smith (2010) stress, the concept of community seeks to draw arbitrary divisions across society to construct supposedly homogeneous sub-collectives.

Considering the multiplicity of interest groups with stakes in heritage resources it becomes clear that a key parameter that deserves consideration is whether heritage commons and their management will be open to anyone or only to specific groups. Ostrom's examples describe limited-access commons collectively 'owned' by a village or an association. Having clearly defined communities can become particularly problematic in the heritage field because heritage communities are not static or spatially defined entities. In addition, even if communities are somehow defined (e.g. based on physical proximity to the shared resource), they may still have hidden hierarchical divisions. Internal hierarchies are of particular concern as they can end up changing power relations amongst stakeholders without disposing their repressive character locally (Herzfeld 2010). Yet, truly democratic systems, such as those envisaged through commons ideology, need to provide space for the expression of minorities and appease socio-economic inequalities amongst its members. A decentralised heritage governance arrangement that maintains its inner antagonisms can merely shift but cannot eliminate power imbalances. Failure to do so will hamper the capacity of communities to address commons problems successfully (Bowles & Gintis 2005).

Thus, a true and meaningful change would call for a horizontal management model in order to effectively promote equality. This marks a break from the 'top-down' and 'bottom-up' heritage management schemata that exist in current theory and practice. Furthermore, it suggests that behind questions on the commons lie acute social and political interests. While our vision is that the democratic advantages of decentralised horizontal processes will lead to heritage and citizenship enhancement to multiply societal benefits, our present reality is imbued with top-down rules and political norms, essentially leaving us with minimum experience of said social organisation structure. Again, Ostrom's work provides limited solutions to these concerns as it proposes the function of the commons as nested enterprises, working within wider systems, requiring again some sort of hierarchical organisational forms (Harvey 2012). For other researchers, such as Frischmann (2005), the degree of openness depends ultimately on economic considerations, the ways in which the resource is used to generate value, the community setting and its demands.

This leads us to our second key consideration of whether heritage commons management should discriminate certain uses of the heritage resource. If the heritage commons are constructed to address the failures of current management regimes (e.g. alienation, over-extraction of value and unfair distribution of benefits), the question that follows is what objectives and goals would their 'rules-in-use' serve in order to do so (Maddison et al. 2010). According to Harvey (2012), commons should be treated as non-commodified resources, lying outside of the market exchange logic. Yet heritage goods, even if they are not commodities themselves, can be traded to extract economic rents (e.g. through tourism and leisure activities). Still, their viability would require commitments that are antithetical to market competition and bear costs to the local economy since, despite the rhetoric, growth and sustainability are contradictory in nature. At the same time, given that heritage resources exert and receive pressures from competing economic interests, they may be seen as 'liabilities' in the eyes of alienated communities (Chirikure et al. 2010). It is therefore important to consider and explore the broader contextual economic factors that frame the present reality, should we wish to engage meaningfully in a discussion of heritage self-governance.

Small-scale economies functioning along the commons lines provide some valuable insight into effective solutions based on solidarity. However, jumping from clearly defined social and economic boundaries to larger-scale problems of socio-economic organisation increases complications dramatically (Harvey 2012). It is on this point that a major question needs to be posed; if heritage commons operate locally but still in dependency to broader politico-economic forces, can they really manage to refrain from serving markets and industries? Contradictions between the ideals of commons self-governance and the broader economic fixes could easily threaten their long-term survival. At a macro level, market capitalism has been crystallised as the global economic paradigm. This paradigm promotes the delusion of unlimited choice at the same time that practically favours scarcity through enclosures, inequalities and the 'fetishisation' of economic growth (Harvey 2007; Kallis & March 2015). The quest for growth should not be underemphasised as it is an imperative that is maintained by the relevant institutions that make up the 'rules of the game' macro-economically, as seen in 'grow-or-die' competition (Kallis 2011). Since the ideal of the commons marks a sharp contrast to such mechanics and rules, the question that inevitably plagues us is whether heritage commons can be implemented effectively within the context of market economies and their property rights, their financial and political institutions and their lack of effective income redistribution mechanisms.

Heritage commons is therefore not merely a management concept – it is a radical political project. Our argument is that public debate and scholarly work in the heritage commons apart from negotiating with internal issues and complexities needs to move a step further and challenge directly the current economic system. This is not an option but rather a necessity as the economic system is a central function of our social organisation (Polanyi 1957). Therefore, it is possible that the theoretical and practical development of heritage commons as a political project needs to be linked to the vision of a shift from the prevalent economic paradigm. Needless to say, advocating for and planning such a shift would be anything but an easy task. This is because the foundations of our present economic and social organization, such as ownership, inheritance rights and central state administration, are persistent long-lived concepts that have determined not only our institutional structures and political constitutions but also our intuitive understanding of social reality (Badiou 2017). Thus, we hold that the first step would be for our imagination to escape the diachronic dictates of growth and material accumulation, sustained diachronically by hierarchical ideologies that defined the social evolution of Western societies (Latouche 2009). In essence, the idea of the commons is a quest for an alternative polity. Thinking about such alternative is not merely a methodological problem but an ontological one (Curtis 2013). It is time to dare to think of a different world, if we wish to provide the heritage commons project with the opportunity to be realised or at least, pursued.

Conclusion

This chapter attempted to pose and reflect on some theoretical, methodological and broader macro-economic questions related to heritage commons. It provided an analysis of the economic thinking that dictates the present reality and policy along with the theoretical economic concepts that lie behind it. As analysed, neoclassical economics predicts that communities using heritage collectively will face a tragic situation in which individual rationality will lead to destructive outcomes. The neoclassical paradigm and its obsession with the utility calculations of *Homo Economicus* epistemologically undermined the sociological and psychological dimensions of economic exchanges. In contrast, Ostrom's theory, although remaining consistent to the rational choice hypothesis, departed from the mainstream economic thinking of her time. In her work, self-governance was set as a central characteristic of commons' success, granting community the power to devise its own rules of participation and use. Her research demonstrated the impact of formal and informal institutions on human behaviour and showed that collective forms of ownership can be successful at a micro level.

Inspired by Ostrom's principles, this chapter proposed the use of experimental approaches as a means to address the implications that arise from the scarcity of naturally-occurring data in modern-state polities. Experimental economics, although rooted in rational economic thinking, allow us to observe not merely rational elements but also behavioural aspects that often contradict the utility axiom. As such, they can serve to empirically study critical features of collective decision-making for heritage resources management under a commons arrangement and thus inform the transferring of the concept to the real world. Our field experiment in Kastoria provided an actual example of how experimental protocols can be adapted to elicit community attitudes, processes and responses to communal heritage problems.

Undeniably, a mere understanding of institutions and rules at micro-environments is not sufficient in itself. As we move from controlled environments to the macro levels of our social ecosystem, critical questions of political economy emerge. Who would be involved in the commons management, how power relations would work, what aims and uses of the heritage resources would be acceptable and favourable are amongst the many critical considerations that we need to explore further. The commons project marks a sharp contrast to the rules and workings of central-state administration and market economy and it is antithetical to political norms and power relations that diachronically shaped our social evolution. Since the commons cannot operate autonomously from these forces, it is imperative that relevant research and future debate does not remain confined to internal mechanics but also looks at the broader politico-economic picture to identify the conditions that call for change in order to make the concept feasible.

Overall, this chapter attempted to provide a first touch rather than an in-depth analysis of some fundamental theoretical, methodological and macro-economic issues that permeate the realm of heritage commons. Our position is that the concept of self-governance is largely an unknown territory to Western political traditions and current socio-economic forms of organisation. Nevertheless, considering the management failures of state and market agents, the concept and questions around heritage commons are particularly worthy of negotiation. Addressing them effectively will be anything but easy. In our capacity as scientists, we need to remain open-minded and embark on mixed methodological approaches that along with traditional tools, such as ethnography and historical research, will also draw on 'unorthodox' research methods inspired by other disciplines. In our capacity as social actors and citizens, we need to employ our social imagination and think of a radically different world. Confronted with the limitation of space, this chapter attempted to stimulate its readers to set their imagination in motion.

Bibliography

Alexopoulos, G. & Fouseki, K. (2013). Introduction: Managing archaeological sites in Greece. *Conservation and Management of Ar chaeological Sites, 15*(1), 1–12.

Anderson, B. (1991). *Imagined communities: Reflections on the origin and spread of nationalism*. London, United Kingdom: Verso.

Ansell, C. & Gash, A. (2008). Collaborative governance in theory and practice. *Journal of public administration research and theory, 18*(4), 543–571. DOI: https://doi.org/10.1093/jopart/mum032.

Arnstein, S. R. (1969). A ladder of citizen participation. *Journal of the American Institute of Planners, 35*(4), 216–224. DOI: https://doi.org /10.1080/01944366908977225.

Badiou, A. (2017). On the Russian October revolution of 1917. *Crisis and Critique, 4*(2), 13–23.

Benkler, Y. (2003). The political economy of commons: Upgrade. *The European Journal of the Informatics Professional, 4*(3), 6–9.

Berge, E. & van Laerhoven, F. (2011). Governing the commons for two decades: A complex story. *International Journal of the Commons*, 5(2), 160–187. DOI: http://doi.org/10.18352/ijc.325.

Bourdieu, P. (1984). *Distinction: A social critique of the judgement of taste.* London, United Kingdom: Routledge.

Bowles, S. & Gintis, H. (2005). Social capital, moral sentiments, and community governance. In H. Gintis, S. Bowles, R. Boyd & E. Fehr (Eds.), *Moral sentiments and material interests: The foundations of cooperation in economic life* (pp. 379–398). Cambridge, MA: The MIT Press.

Brandts, J. & Fatas, E. (2012). The puzzle of social preferences. *Revista Internacional de Sociologia*, 70(Extra_1), 113–126. DOI: https://doi.org/10.3989/ris.2011.09.03.

Briassoulis, H. (2002). Sustainable tourism and the question of the commons. *Annals of tourism research*, 29(4), 1065–1085. DOI: https://doi.org/10.1016/S0160-7383(02)00021-X.

Callon, M. (2007). An essay on the growing contribution of economic markets to the proliferation of the social. *Theory, Culture & Society*, 24(7–8), 139–163. DOI: https://doi.org/10.1177/0263276407084701.

Cardenas, J. C. & Carpenter J. P. (2005). Three themes on field experiments and economic development. In J. P. Carpenter, G. W. Harrison, & J. A. List (Eds.), *Field experiments in economics. Research in Experimental Economics*, Vol. 10 (pp. 71–123). Oxford, United Kingdom: Elservier.

Chasapopoulos, N. (2012, January 9). Γιακουμάτος: Νοικιάστε τώρα την Ακρόπολη. *To Vima*. Retrieved 6 July, 2018, from http://www.tovima.gr/politics/article/?aid=437898.

Chhotray, V. & Stoker, G. (2009). *Governance theory and practice: A cross-disciplinary approach.* Basingstoke, United Kingdom: Palgrave Macmillan.

Chirikure, S., Manyanga, M., Ndoro, W. & Pwiti, G. (2010). Unfulfilled promises?: Heritage management and community participation at some of Africa's cultural heritage sites. *International Journal of Heritage Studies*, 16(1–2), 30–44.

Cleere, H. (2012). Introduction: the rationale of archaeological heritage management. In H. Cleere (Ed.), *Archaeological heritage management in the modern world* (pp. 1–22). London, United Kingdom: Routledge.

Council of Europe. (2015). *The wider benefits of investment in cultural heritage.* Retrieved July 6, 2018, from https://book.coe.int/usd/en/cultural-heritage/6454-the-wider-benefits-of-investment-in-cultural-heritage.html.

Curtis, N. (2013). *Idiotism: Capitalism and the privatisation of life.* London, United Kingdom: Pluto Press.

De Angelis, M. (2003). Reflections on alternatives, commons and communities. *The Commoner*, 6, 1–14.

Dragouni, M. & Fouseki, K. (2018). Drivers of community participation in heritage tourism planning: an empirical investigation. *Journal of Heritage Tourism*, 13(3), 237–256. DOI: https://doi.org/10.1080/1743873X.2017.1310214.

Dragouni, M., Fouseki, K. & Georgantzis, N. (2018). Community participation in heritage tourism planning: is it too much to ask? *Journal of Sustainable Tourism,* 26(5), 759–781. DOI: https://doi.org/10.1080/09669582.2017 .1404606.

Eriksen, T. H. (2004). *What is anthropology?* London, United Kingdom: Pluto Press.

Exadaktylos, F., Espín, A. M. & Brañas-Garza, P. (2013). Experimental subjects are not different. *Scientific Reports,* 3(1213), 1–6.

Fouseki, K. & Dragouni, M. (2017). Heritage spectacles: the case of Amphipolis excavations during the Greek economic crisis. *International Journal of Heritage Studies,* 23(8), 742–758. DOI: https://doi.org/10.1080/13527258 .2017.1321573.

Frischmann, B. M. (2005). An economic theory of infrastructure and commons management. *Minnesota Law Review, 89,* 917–1030.

Fujiwara, D., Cornwall, T. & Dolan, P. (2014). *Heritage and wellbeing.* London, United Kingdom: English Heritage.

Georganas, I. (2013). The effects of the economic crisis on Greek heritage: A view from the private cultural sector. *Journal of Eastern Mediterranean Archaeology & Heritage Studies,* 1(3), 242–245. DOI: https://doi.org /10.5325/jeasmedarcherstu.1.3.0242.

Gonzalez, P. A. (2014). From a given to a construct: Heritage as a commons. *Cultural Studies,* 28(3), 359–390. DOI: https://doi.org/10.1080/09502386 .2013.789067.

Graham, H. (2017), Horizontality: Tactical politics for participation and museums. In B. Onciul, M. L. Stefano & S. Hawke (Eds.), *Engaging heritage: Engaging communities* (pp. 73–87). Woodbridge, United Kingdom: The Boydell Press.

Hamilakis, Y. (2007). *The nation and its ruins: Antiquity, archaeology, and national imagination in Greece.* Oxford, United Kingdom: Oxford University Press.

Hann, C. & Hart K. (2011). *Economic anthropology.* Cambridge, United Kingdom: Polity Press.

Hardin, G. (1968). The Tragedy of the commons. *Science, 162*(3859), 1243–1248.

Hardt, M. & Negri, A. (2009). *Commonwealth.* Cambridge, MA: Belknap Press.

Harrison, R. (2012). *Heritage: Critical Approaches.* London, United Kingdom: Routledge.

Harvey, D. (2007). *The limits to capital.* London, United Kingdom: Verso.

Harvey, D. (2012). *Rebel cities: From the right to the city to the urban revolution.* London, United Kingdom: Verso.

Henrich, J., Boyd, R., Bowels, S., Camerer, C., Fehr, E. & Gintis, H. (Eds.). (2004). *Foundations of human sociality: Economic experiments and ethno-graphic evidence from fifteen small-scale societies.* Oxford, United Kingdom: Oxford University Press.

Heritage Lottery Fund. (2016). *Values and benefits of heritage: A research review.* Retrieved July 6, 2018, from https://visionforsidmouth.org/wp-content /uploads/2019/05/values_and_benefits_of_heritage_2015.pdf.

Herzfeld, M. (2010). Engagement, gentrification, and the neoliberal hijacking of history. *Current Anthropology, 51*(S2), S259–S267. DOI: https://doi .org/10.1086/653420.

Historic England. (2017). *Heritage counts 2017: Heritage and the economy.* Retrieved July 6, 2018, from https://historicengland.org.uk/content/heritage -counts/pub/2017/heritage-and-the-economy-2017-pdf/.

Howery, C. (2013). The effects of the economic crisis on archaeology in Greece. *Journal of Eastern Mediterranean Archaeology & Heritage Studies, 1*(3), 249–250. DOI: https://doi.org/10.5325/jeasmedarcherstu.1.3.0249.

Kahan, D. M. (2005). The logic of reciprocity: Trust, collective action and law. In H. Gintis, S. Bowles, R. Boyd & E. Fehr (Eds.), *Moral sentiments and material interests: The foundations of cooperation in economic life* (pp. 339–378). Cambridge, MA: The MIT Press.

Kallis, G. (2011). In defence of degrowth. *Ecological Economics, 70*(5), 873–880. DOI: https://doi.org/10.1016/j.ecolecon.2010.12.007.

Kallis, G. & March, H. (2015). Imaginaries of hope: The utopianism of degrowth. *Annals of the Association of American Geographers, 105*(2), 360–368. DOI: https://doi.org/10.1080/00045608.2014.973803.

Kouri, M. (2012). Merging culture and tourism in Greece: An unholy alliance or an opportunity to update the country's cultural policy? *The Journal of Arts Management, Law, and Society, 42*(2), 63–78. DOI: https://doi.org/10 .1080/10632921.2012.685688.

Kuutma, K. (2013). Between arbitration and engineering: Concepts and contingencies in the shaping of heritage regimes. In R. F., Bendix, A. Eggert & A. Peselmann (Eds.), *Heritage regimes and the state* (pp. 21–36). Göttingen, Germany: Universitätsverlag Göttingen.

Latouche, S. (2009). *Farewell to growth.* Cambridge, United Kingdom: Polity Press.

Lazrak, F., Nijkamp, P., Rietveld, P. & Rouwendal, J. (2014). The market value of cultural heritage in urban areas: An application of spatial hedonic pricing. *Journal of Geographical Systems, 16*, 89–114.

Lekakis, S. (2013). Distancing and rapproching: Local communities and monuments in the Aegean Sea: A case study from the island of Naxos. *Conservation and Management of Archaeological Sites, 15* (1), 76–93. DOI: https://doi.org /10.1179/1350503313Z.00000000048.

Lekakis, S. (2017, May 4–7). *Cultural heritage in the realm of the commons.* Paper presented at the 1st National Conference on Commons and Social & Solidarity Economy in Greece, Thessaloniki. Retrieved July 6, 2018, from https://www.academia.edu/32902575/Cultural_heritage_in_the_realm _of_the_commons.

Lynch, B. (2017). The gate in the wall: Beyond happiness-making museums. In B. Onciul, M. L. Stefano & S. Hawke (Eds.), *Engaging heritage, engaging communities* (pp. 11–29). Woodbridge, United Kingdom: The Boydell Press.

Ostrom, E. (1990). *Governing the commons.* Cambridge, United Kingdom: Cambridge University Press.

Ostrom, E. (2005). Policies that crowd out reciprocity and collective action. In H. Gintis, S. Bowles, R. Boyd & E. Fehr (Eds.), *Moral sentiments and material interests: The foundations of cooperation in economic life* (pp. 253–275). Cambridge, MA: The MIT Press.

Ostrom, E., Gardner, R. & Walker, J. (1994). *Rules, games, and common-pool resources.* Ann Arbor, MI: University of Michigan Press.

Polanyi, K. (1957). *The great transformation: The political and economic origins of our time.* Boston, MA: Beacon Press.

Porter, B. W. & Salazar, N. B. (2005). Heritage tourism, conflict, and the public interest: An introduction. *International Journal of Heritage Studies, 11*(5), 361–370. DOI: https://doi.org/ 10.1080/13527250500337397.

Pournara, M. (2013, October 14). Στέφανος Μίλερ, μια ζωή αφιερωμένη στη Νεμέα. Kathimerini. Retrieved July 6, 2018, from http://www.kathimerini .gr/71445/article/proswpa/synentey3eis/stefanos-miler-mia-zwh-afierw menh-sth-nemea.

Smith, L. (2006). *Uses of heritage.* London, United Kingdom: Routledge.

Stroulia, A. & Sutton, S. B. (2009). Archaeological sites and local places: connecting the dots. *Public Archaeology, 8*(2–3), 124–140. DOI: https://doi .org/10.1179/175355309X457187.

Throsby, D. (2012). *Investment in urban heritage. Economic impacts of cultural heritage projects in FYR Macedonia and Georgia.* Retrieved July 6, 2018, from http://siteresources.worldbank.org/INTURBANDEVE LOPMENT/Resources/336387-1169585750379/UDS16_Investment+in +Urban+Heritage.pdf.

Van Winden, F., Van Dijk, F. & Sonnemans, J. (2008). Intrinsic Motivation in a Public Good Environment. In C. R. Plott & V. L. Smith (Eds.), *Handbook of Experimental Economics: Results, vol.1* (pp. 836–845). Amsterdam, The Netherlands: Elsevier.

Waterton, E. & Smith, L. (2010). The recognition and misrecognition of community heritage. *International Journal of Heritage Studies, 16*(1–2), 4–15. DOI: https://doi.org/10.1080/13527250903441671.

Wheatley, D. & Bickerton, C. (2017). Subjective well-being and engagement in arts, culture and sport. *Journal of Cultural Economics, 41*, 23–45.

Young, O. (2011). Land use, environmental change, and sustainable development: the role of institutional diagnostics. *International Journal of the Commons, 5*(1), 66–85.

CHAPTER 3

Heritage, Openness and the Commons in Urban Environments: Some Thoughts on the Archaeological Parks of Philopappos Hill and Plato's Academy in Athens

Despina Catapoti, Ioulia Skounaki and
Georgia Gkoumopoulou

Until recently, the dominant management model of archaeological sites in Greece largely drew upon a logic of *enframing* (Thomas 2004: 79; *see also* Díaz-Andreu & Champion 1996; Dietler 1994; Olsen 2012), which understood the past as "gone" and "completed", a temporal entity in other words, whose closure and finitude needed to be guaranteed through physical demarcation (Olsen, 2012: 215). We shall call this "the enclosure model", for in essence, it sought to isolate monuments from the sphere of the everyday. The tendency to spatially distinguish the past from the present has its roots in modernity, particularly the 19th century: at the time, prominent archaeological sites across the Mediterranean were marked out (and henceforth rendered "visible") as *loci* of exclusive membership (i.e. products of archaeological activity, arenas of intellectual/scientific discourse) but above all, as representational spaces of collective appeal, accommodating both nationalist and colonialist narratives (*cf.* Catapoti 2013; Catapoti & Relaki 2013; Hamilakis 2007; Plantzos 2014: 104, 260–272;

How to cite this book chapter:
Catapoti, D. Skounaki, I. and Gkoumopoulou, G. 2020. Heritage, Openness and the Commons in Urban Environments: Some Thoughts on the Archaeological Parks of Philopappos Hill and Plato's Academy in Athens. In Lekakis, S. (ed.) *Cultural Heritage in the Realm of the Commons: Conversations on the Case of Greece.* Pp. 67–94. London: Ubiquity Press. DOI: https://doi.org/10.5334/bcj.e. License: CC-BY

Sack 1986; Smith 2008; Thomas 2004; Vavouranakis 2018: 23–25; White 1973; Wylie 2005; Yalouri 2001). On the one hand, the archaeological site was perceived as a bounded and protected area, in which the public could only enter under certain conditions stipulated by the relevant authorities (Carman 2005; Hamilakis 2007: 17; Smith 2008; Buck Sutton & Stroulia 2010: 3). The boundaries set between the public and past material remains, on the other hand, moved beyond the spatial to also encapsulate the ideological and the conceptual, with both the state and the scientific community assuming a higher-order role, that of the custodian of the past, its meanings, value and symbolisms (Appadurai 2008; Catapoti 2013: 263–266; Hall 2008: 220; Nicholas & Hollowell 2007: 60; Pels 1997; Smith 2004: 68–74, 2008: 62–3).

The Greek legal framework stipulates that all monuments dating up to 1453 are the property of the State, not subject to exchange and long-term private use (Law 3028/2002).[13] In practice, this should not be taken to imply that the Greek Archaeological Service fences off every archaeological excavation or monument in the country, thereby cancelling out any other potential private or public use. It does, however, set out that state authorities have the final say in every potential use of such monuments. What stands out as a paradox here is that although experts (i.e. archaeologists, conservators etc.) and the public in Greece share a broad consensus with regard to the value of archaeological heritage – defending a standard "protocol" for its protection, study and promotion – the long-established state monopoly on archaeological monuments and the "overcentralisation of the administrative system" (Tziotas 2015: 49) is systematically accused of clientelism, opportunism and favouritism (Alexopoulos & Fouseki 2013; Hamilakis 2007: 37; Tziotas 2015: 49), while leaving little or no room for the cultivation of bottom-up processes of participation, dialogue and negotiation (Stroulia & Buck Sutton 2010). As a result, archaeology is commonly referred to as "the State's bureaucratic face" (Fotiadis 2010: 454) and often results in feelings of social distrust as well as a proliferation of conspiracy theories against the Archaeological Service.

---

[13] "[A]ll antiquities belong to the state and their administration is the duty of the Ministry of Culture and its dedicated Archaeological Resource Management (ARM) service, the so-called General Directorate of Antiquities and Cultural Heritage, and informally dubbed as the "Archaeological Service", namely the body of state archaeologists in Greece" (Vavouranakis 2018: 23). Vavouranakis has argued that a "strong" Archaeological Resource Management has always been necessary for the Greek State largely due to the fact that the latter needs "to reclaim illicitly circulating antiquities" (ibid: 24). It is for this reason perhaps that "the ownership of monuments is a standard feature of the Greek archaeological legislation. Law 2646, which came into effect in 1899, its codification Law 5351, which substituted it in 1932, and the current Law 3028, which replaced the previous laws in 2002, all state that all antiquities are owned by the state" (ibid); See also Lekakis this volume.

As a result of this, archaeologists in Greece display a schizoid socio-political profile, acting as both enemies and guardians of the past (*cf.* Plantzos 2018: 106). Thus, for instance, in certain cases the Service is heavily scrutinized (as biased, nationalist, bureaucratic, outdated) for its insistence on the spatial demarcation and sacralisation of antiquities, whereas in others, it is the Service that is called upon to protect these vulnerable and exhaustible resources from looting, abuse or overuse. Equally interesting is the fact that although the "enclosure model" has received much criticism for supporting the activation and harvesting of the economic value of heritage resources (in other words, their transformation into a tourist product) (Catapoti 2013: 270; Hamilakis & Duke 2007; Holtorf 2005; Kehoe 2007; Lowenthal 2002; Silberman 2007: 179–182; Walsh 1992), this is a strategy also frequently supported by local communities, who recognise the opportunity for economic profit that the existence of an organised archaeological site in their area affords (*cf.* Bianchi 2003; Boissevain 1996; Galani-Moutafi 2002; Urry 1990; Zarkia 1996).

Over the last two decades, however, the situation described above regarding heritage management in Greece has undergone significant transformations. Currently, a plethora of initiatives are promoting the idea of *opening up* sites and monuments to a wider audience. Catapoti (2013) has argued that "openness" refers to a wide variety of practices and strands such as the use of monuments and archaeological sites outside of opening hours for the organization of cultural events and performances; calls for the reuse of ancient and historical monuments (i.e. ancient theatres); increased participation of non-specialist groups and volunteers in excavation projects; the promotion of archaeological experience and tourism packages; the growing number of archaeological parks and ecomuseums; programmes and funding devoted to the visual and functional unification of archaeological sites and monuments in urban centres; the increasing emphasis on urban walks and heritage walking tours; the advancement and development of digital applications in archaeology and cultural heritage (i.e. open access digital resources, VR and AR reconstructions and tours, digital apps for museum visits, increasing museum presence in social media platforms and digital marketing). Interestingly, in certain cases, these initiatives are spearheaded by the Archaeological Service itself in an obvious attempt to move beyond its customary *modus operandi* concerning heritage management. Equally significant is the fact that, quite often, the call for openness is also supported by urban social movements or specific stakeholder groups (e.g. parent groups) – with the aim of widening the availability of leisure spaces and educational facilities within the city (green areas and parks, spaces for children, physical exercise etc.). In other cases, these efforts mask implicit or explicit claims for further touristic development, as is also the situation in most rural parts of Greece.

In recent years, what has been emphasized by several scholars[14] is the fact that the emergent pluralism and cornucopia of approaches in the heritage

---

[14] See Catapoti 2013 for a review of the literature.

sector does not merely form part of a wider theoretical regime that favours openness; what is equally noteworthy is that this regime has developed the ability to fully embrace seemingly opposing ideological agendas, ranging from neoliberal marketing strategies to small-scale, non-institutionalized political action (Antoniadou et al 2018). Jameson (1984) eloquently demonstrated how this pluralistic logic constitutes the backbone of late capitalism, supporting social fragmentation, subjectivity, fluidity of all boundaries (spatial, temporal, social, political, and even corporeal), individuality and the self, the constant reinvention of all aforementioned categories, and with them, a constant rein-vention of consumer goods as markers of identity and the self (Harvey 1989; *see also* Anderson 1998; Catapoti 2013: 269–70). In view of the above, it becomes readily apparent how the continuous renewal of the past and by extension, the creation of a steadily growing heritage surplus, become totally attuned with the idea of openness and contribute to its very sustenance. What also becomes increasingly crystallised, however, as Frank rightly stresses (2015: 25), is that this process of "breaking down" boundaries *simultaneously* leads to the democ-ratisation as well as the commercialisation of the past.

An immediate consequence of these developments has been on the one hand, that the dearth of quantitative and qualitative data described above is accom-panied by an obvious paucity of criteria for evaluating the ways in which the steadily increasing body of cultural spaces is managed, leading to an absence of critical, coherent, and substantiated suggestions for the preservation or re-assessment of cemented practices. Despite this lack of systematization on the other hand, what is particularly noteworthy is that in recent years, a new con-cept appears to be gaining ground (and popularity) as an alternative against the polarized distinction between "closure" and "openness" and this is the concept of the "commons":

"We live in the midst of a social and economic crisis, one of the worst in capitalism's history; at the same time the environmental crisis, accord-ing to the predictions of the vast majority of scientists, is approaching catastrophe. Neither states nor markets seem able to offer solutions. On the contrary, many believe that they are the main sources of these crises. It is in this context that talks of – and social movements for – commons have become not only increasingly commonplace, but also increasingly relevant" (De Angelis & Harvie 2014: 280).

In thinking about what commons are, an obvious point of departure is that they refer to shared resources that are neither public nor private. Sharing is a parameter of crucial importance here, for it implies a form of ownership (or responsibility) that is constituted through collective use and negotiation rather than as a predetermined condition (e.g. a property relation). Although initially, the commons were mainly linked with the study and improvement of the man-agement of natural, eco-social systems and common pool resources, currently they embrace other sociopolitical fields, including urban contexts (for an over-view of urban commons literature *cf.* Parker and Johansson 2011). From as far back as the early stages of the 20th century, important thinkers like Georg Sim-mel (1903/1971) and Louis Wirth (1938) pointed out that in urban contexts, public space exhibits an unparalleled degree of heterogeneity and density and that as such it constitutes "a place where modern society as a market-medi-ated and state-protected association of strangers could first be experienced as *a new social form*" (Frank 2015: 22, *our emphasis*). In light of the above and for the purposes of this paper, we wish to examine whether (and under what conditions) the notion of the urban commons could also bear relevance on an important sub-category: urban heritage. Do the principles that apply to the study of urban commons apply equally to the study of heritage? Should com-mons and openness in urban cultural spaces and/or heritage *loci* of the city be treated as synonymous, compatible, or complementary terms? Is it possible to move beyond centralised and strictly hierarchical forms of social organization (i.e. state governance) in urban heritage management, without equating open access to *laisser-faire* and other neoliberalist managerial formats? Last but not least, what happens in an urban context like Athens, a city whose identity is to a very large extent fuelled by its past and the materialities of that past (Hamilakis 2007; Leontis 1995; Loukaki 2008; McNeal 1991; Planztos 2011; Yalouri 2001)?

A brief note on the concept of the commons

Although we could describe the commons as an umbrella term, encompass-ing a wide variety of definitions, at the most basic level it refers to resources (natural and/or cultural) that are accessible to all members of a given social unit and are managed through governance mechanisms aiming at collective benefit (Caffentzis 2010; An Architektur 2010; Hardt and Negri 2009; Ostrom 1990). At the moment, the consensus is that anything may fall into the category of common resource as long as a certain social entity decides to share and man-age it collectively, setting the rules through which it is accessed, used, sustained and/or reproduced (Bollier 2014: 15; An Architektur 2010; Stavrides 2016):

> "The word 'commons' refers to resources for which people do not have to pay for to exercise their user and access rights within a confine of a set of institutions or rules to protect the resources from overuse by people who do not respect the resources' fragility or limits" (Jumbe 2006: 5).

According to a number of scholars, however (*see* Caffentzis 2005; De Angelis & Harvie 2014), this mode of understanding is not so straightforward, but rather a definition that encapsulates a wider (and highly complex) nexus of opinions, involving even opposing political ideologies and strategies. In certain cases, for instance, we find approaches that set themselves strongly against privatization and yet maintain a line of thought that sees capitalism and the commons as relatively compatible:

"Many of the capabilities of a parallel adaptive system can be retained in a polycentric governance system. By polycentric, I mean a system where citizens are able to organize not just one but multiple governing authorities at differing scales... Each unit may exercise considerable independence to make and enforce rules within a circumscribed scope of authority for a specified geographical area. In a polycentric system, some units are general-purpose governments while others may be highly specialized. Self-organized resource governance systems, in such a system, may be special districts, private associations, or parts of a local government. These are nested in several levels of general-purpose governments that also provide civil, equity, as well as criminal courts" (Ostrom 1998: 27).

Another major trend that may be identified in the literature is largely based upon social dynamics (Caffentzis 2010; An Architektur 2010; De Angelis 2007; Federici 2010; Hardt and Negri 2009). At the centre of this enquiry is the idea of *commoning,* namely the process whereby something becomes a common resource, but at the same time the process through which a resource creates forms of social being that are collective yet not emancipatory in nature. Under this scheme, the commons is something that "is continuously being produced" (Harvey 2011: 105).

Particularly within the context of urban theory, practices of commoning become even more emphatic. What is of cardinal analytical importance in a city with reference to the triptych "resources, commoners and rules" is its fluid nature (Kornberger & Borch 2015). Analytical focus is thus primarily laid upon substantiating the theory that the relations established between people and resources, or more specifically the conditions and social processes that create, reproduce (and even challenge) the commons, are in a constant state of flux (Harvey 2011; 2012):

"The human qualities of the city emerge from our practices in the diverse spaces of the city, even as those spaces are subject to enclosure both by private and public state ownership, as well as by social control, appropriation, and countermoves to assert what Henri Lefebvre called "the right to the city" on the part of the inhabitants. Through their daily activities and struggles, individuals and social groups create the social world of the city and, in doing so, create something common as a framework within which we all can dwell" (Harvey 2011: 103–4).

Thus, the question addressed here focuses more on architecture, namely it is a question of spatiotemporal *responsivity* (Kärrholm 2015: 54). This concerns the need for any (emerging) group or issue to go through *a trial by space* (ibid). As Lefebvre notes in *The Production of Space* (1991):

> "[G]roups, classes or fractions cannot constitute themselves, or recognize one another as "subjects", unless they generate (or produce) a space. Ideas, representations or values which do not succeed in making their mark on space, and thus generating (or producing) an appropriate morphology, will lose all pith and become mere signs, resolve themselves into abstract descriptions, or mutate into fantasies (*ibid*: 416–17).

This shift of emphasis towards commoning and social dynamics opens up the way for a better understanding of how urban heritage, among other resources, is introduced in the discussion of the urban commons. Heritage itself, very much like the concept of the commons, cannot be perceived as a predetermined, neutral category but must be seen instead as a concept with heavy ideological, economic, social and political connotations (*cf.* Gero n.d.; Layton 1989; Lowenthal 1985; Miller et al. 1989; Shennan 1989; Silverman 2011). Heritage is a mnemonic resource that never ceases to be under scrutiny and reconfiguration. What also goes without saying is that this condition is further complicated within the highly heterogeneous context that is the urban landscape of cities like Athens, a landscape exhibiting an even higher density of past spatiotemporal materialities, thus rendering their interpretation and use even more difficult.

But what if, on the other hand, those conflicting, asymmetrical, discontinuous forms of engagement with heritage were not considered an obstacle but a boon? What if we decided to approach the conflicting social demands and aspirations revolving around heritage as an expression of commoning, as a process of actively negotiating urban being and identity through the past, a dynamic form of exploring the mnemonic within the urban sphere? In what follows, therefore, we argue for a more rigorous and nuanced consideration of the use and management of archaeological sites in urban contexts. This will consider the relationship between openness, the commons and the transformation of urban space engendered by historically specific dynamics of heritage management strategies. To exemplify this final point, in the following sections of this chapter we will focus our attention on two case studies: Philopappos Hill and Plato's Academy Archaeological Park, both located at the centre of Athens.[15] Both case studies involve spaces officially classified as archaeological sites but also as public green spaces. The dual role served by these two sites makes them

---

[15] The fieldwork and data collection for each case study were conducted as part of a research project funded by the Research Centre for the Humanities under the topic: "The 'open' archaeological site as an alternative management model in an urban environment: Plato's Academy and Philopappos Hill". https://www.rchumanities.gr/en/catapoti-skounaki-gkoumopoulou/. Last accessed 20 November 2019.

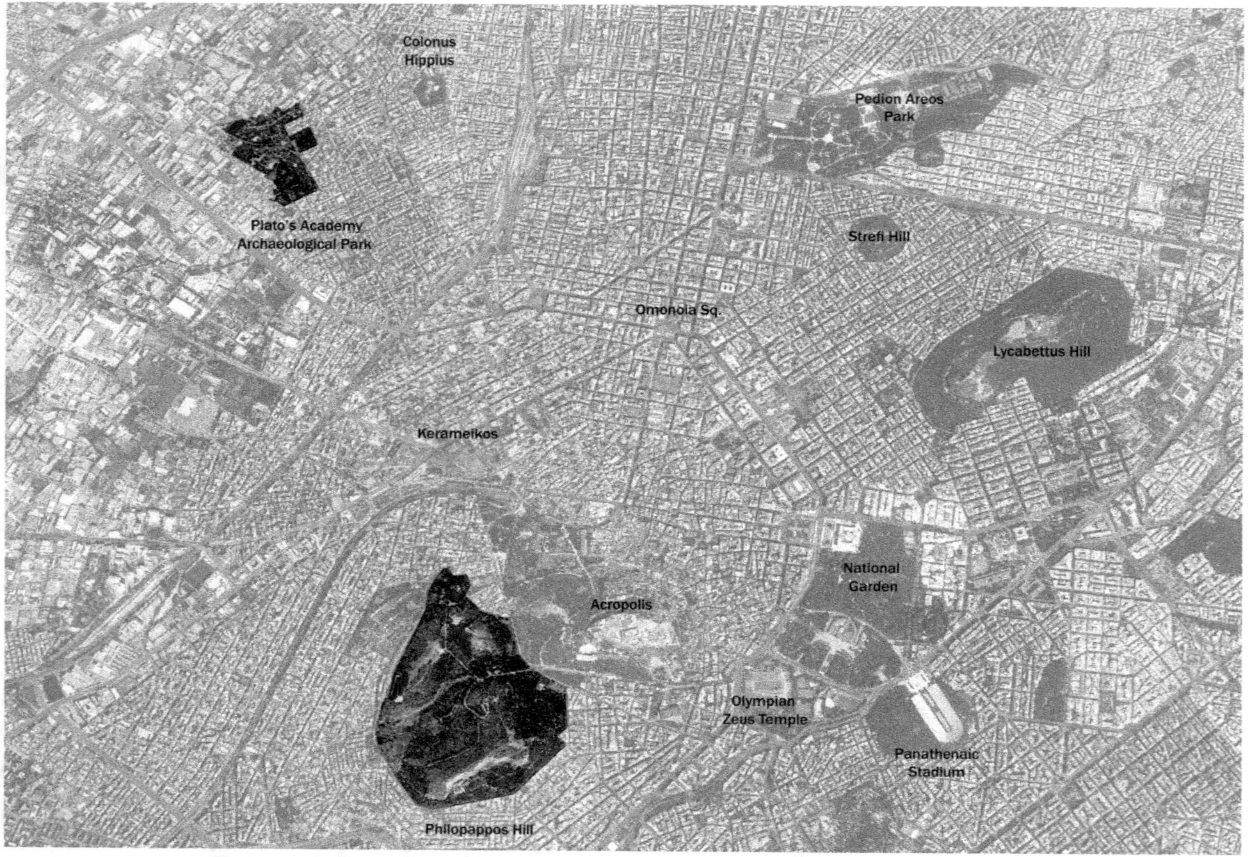

Figure 1: Location of the two case studies in the boundaries of the city of Athens. (Source: Map background: Google Maps; Map editing: authors).

notable exceptions to the Greek rule, i.e. the 'enclosure model'. Both case studies are the 'products' of institutional management choices and top-down planning methods. At the same time, however, they play a crucial role as open green spaces, serving not only the daily needs of adjacent neighbourhoods but also operating as a broader urban imaginary, an ideal conjunction point of archaeological and environmental features/values. In fact, over the past decade, these two areas have been transformed into regions of pronounced territorial claim, not only of the state and the Archaeological Service, but also of urban movements and political groups of the surrounding neighbourhoods as well as the wider city of Athens. To date there has been no systematic investigation of (a) how either the Hill or the Park perform their twofold role (archaeological site/urban park); (b) whether (and when) these two functions are compatible or at variance; (c) how the dynamic *in situ* presence of different social groups and collectivities on the Hill and the Park affects institutional decision-making and ultimately; or (d) how such forms of bottom-up political engagement contribute to the establishment of alternative models of heritage management and use within an urban setting. The final part of the paper identifies the connections established between the commons and openness at Philopappos Hill and Plato's Academy and discusses both promising elements and weak points in the conceptualization and/or pragmatism of these interconnections. How is this phenomenon to be associated with the wider forum on the commons and which approach to the commons in particular? Is this a phenomenon of only limited relevance to broader issues of cultural heritage management, or does it act as a preface for more radical developments in the future?

The Archaeological Park of Plato's Academy

The Archaeological Park of Plato's Academy is located at the centre of Athens, near the neighbourhood of Colonus, approximately 1.5 km north of Dipylon Gates at Kerameikos. If we were to describe the broader area of the Akademia, then this would have to include the Industrial Park (*Viomihaniko Parko*), comprising, in turn, notable examples of industrial architecture, flanked by historic buildings and neighbourhoods, all agents of urban memory. Along the length of the axes of Lenorman Street and Athinon Avenue (Kavalas), lies the residential area. Between the industrial and the residential sectors an intermediate zone is found, where functions would seem to overlap; meanwhile, there are also many "voids" serving the purposes of heterogeneous activities (parking lots, orchards and gardens, playgrounds etc.). Within this area we also find the Park and within it, the few archaeological remains related to Plato's famous Academy.

In ancient times, the Academia (Ακαδήμεια) was an Athenian suburb, named, perhaps, after the mythical local hero Academos (or Ecademos). Although the area bears archaeological traces from as early as prehistoric times, it is best known for hosting (from the 4th century BC onwards) the most famous of all philosophical schools of the ancient city. The Academy was set up in or beside a sacred precinct (Garden of Academos) and one of the three Gymnasia of classical Athens. It operated in the same place for several centuries and even today the location maintains its name as a tribute to the famed philosopher Plato. Around 86 BC, the Roman General Lucius Cornelius Sulla destroyed the tree-covered area to build siege engines. It appears, however, that the Academy remained a memorial and place of worship until the period of Neoplatonism (5th century AD) that reactivated philosophical activity in the area. The school was permanently closed down under the rule of the Byzantine emperor Justinian, during the 6th century AD (Panagiotopoulos & Chatziefthimiou 2017; Carouso 2013).

In the early part of the 20th century (and mainly during the 1950s), the area experienced increased housing development while an industrial zone was also built on the outskirts of the Park. Between 1929 and 1939, the architect Panagiotis Aristophron funded excavations in the area,[16] which were conducted under the supervision and the collaboration of archaeologists and archaeophiles such as K. Kourouniotes, A. Philadelpheus and J. Travlos. Among the buildings that were unearthed during fieldwork were the Gymnasium's Palaestra and the square Peristyle. Work recommenced after World War II and the Civil War, between 1956 and 1961, under the direction of Phoivos Stavropoulos and with the financial support of the Greek Archaeological Society.[17] Stavropoulos' excavations brought to light the so-called House of Academos and the Sacred House. Since then, fieldwork in the area has been conducted by the Ephorate of Antiquities of West Attica (Panagiotopoulos & Chatziefthimiou 2017).

Since its first official designation as an archaeological site in 1937, the site has continuously shrunk in size. In 1979, it was designated as an urban park (*alsos*) and only relatively recently, in 2000, the term Archaeological Park was introduced (see c.f. Chazapis 2015; Perpinia 2014). In the 1990s, the Archaeological Service directed an ambitious demolition programme of expropriated buildings. The areas cleared through this process underwent planting and garden landscaping by the Technical Service of the Municipality of Athens, to fulfil the vision of a fully green Plato's Academy. It is worth mentioning that, despite the extensive fencing, the Park has remained open to access with numerous entry/exit gates.

---

[16] It is worth mentioning here that Aristophron, who envisioned the revival of Plato's Academy and a 'Commons of Academies', excavated the area using his own funds and acquired (through paying compensations) a large expanse of land, much larger than hitherto known.

[17] The Greek Archaeological Society is an independent society founded in 1837 with the aim of encouraging the archaeological excavation, protection and exhibition of antiquities in Greece. https://www.archetai.gr. Last access 20 November 2019.

Figure 2: Archaeological finds from various excavations in the city of Athens have been placed freely inside the park to empower the site's monumental identity (Plato's Academy Park). (Source: authors).

The archaeological site constitutes an important landmark of the Athenian landscape endowed with supra-local symbolic value as noted in the first Regulatory Master Plan of Athens (RPA) (Law 1515/1985) as well as by the intention of the official authorities to include the site in the Unification Project of Archaeological Sites at the centre of Athens (UPASA) (see below). The current vision for the archaeological site and the wider area of Plato's Academy involves the creation of a "Supra-Local Centre of Cultural Activities", the Academy of Nations and the Archaeological Museum of the City of Athens, all to be achieved within the framework of integrated metropolitan interventions (cf. Regulatory Plan of Athens 2014; Municipality of Athens 2009). It is worth noting that the role of the area as a "green space" has been further underlined by the location of defined playground areas, sport facilities, and other kinds of open-air recreation. However, the archaeological and monumental identity of the site is simultaneously strengthened by the positioning of freestanding archaeological objects from various excavations from the broader catchment area of Athens throughout the Academy park.

Despite its history, the Archaeological Park is not visited by large numbers of tourists and/or locals; it seems to function mainly as a public green space for the adjacent residential areas. Although the lack of good public transport provision and the poor connectivity with the city centre of Athens compound this situation, a more important factor is the exclusion of Plato's Academy from

Figure 3: A way of appropriating the Gymnasium's archaeological remains in Plato's Academy Park (Source: authors).

the UPASA programme, as well as the more general delay in the realisation of the overall developmental plan discussed above. However, what makes this case study particularly noteworthy is the 'social workshop' that has been taking place in the area with direct (spatial and symbolic) reference to the archaeological site: the workshop comprises collectivities that organise discussions, activities and interventions within the boundaries of the site, relevant to a range of social, economic, political and cultural themes. At the same time, the highly engaged 'Residents Committee', as well as other local groups, stage dynamic interventions in the public dialogue about the site's use, negotiating (a) the expansion of the archaeological site's boundaries (already crowned with some success through their 2008 campaign);[18] (b) the protection of the unique character of the park; (c) its upgrade and connection with the archaeological site of Kerameikos; (d) the broader regeneration of the area through an appropriate institutional framework (e.g. low building elevations, co-operative structures

---

[18]   A substantial tract of private land had been acquired through public funds and subsequently incorporated into the official boundaries of the archaeological site. However, although institutional approval of this transaction has been secured, its financial fulfilment remains unresolved, endangering the overall completion of the initiative.

for local business activities, etc.) and (e) the further enhancement of its public character through a wide array of actions and workshops (e.g. common
co-operative economy, organic agriculture, permaculture etc.) (see Chazapis
2015). In general, residents and other groups are guided by a desire to protect
the archaeological space because they consider it to be a 'public good'.

In summary, even though there is no official model of collaborative
management of the Park, it is notable that the personnel of the local Archaeological Ephorate and the local groups enjoy a relatively smooth working
relationship, exemplified by the constant presence of the resident groups
within the archaeological site, where they perform a range of their initiatives
and activities (See Galanos in this volume), often without the need for a 'special
permit' from the authorities.

Philopappos Hill

The archaeological site of Philopappos Hill comprises three distinct hills; the
Hill of the Muses, the Pnyx and the Hill of the Nymphs, forming a rocky out-
crop to the west of the Acropolis. The three sites are collectively known as
Philopappos Hill, with the site deriving its name from a Roman mausoleum
and monument dedicated to a prince from the Kingdom of Commagene, Gaius
Julius Antiochus Epiphanes Philopappos, and situated at the SW side of the
Acropolis, on the Hill of the Muses.

Today, Philopappos Hill represents a collective of archaeological sites of great
symbolic and environmental significance for the local population, but also a
major tourist attraction (particularly on the eastern part where there are views
of the Acropolis). In contrast to the archaeological park in Plato's Academy,
archaeological remains in this area have been taken into account as far as the
design of green spaces on the Hill is concerned. More specifically, we refer to
those archaeological remnants that have been designated significant by the
Ministry of Culture and the Archaeological Ephorate (e.g. the Pnyx), but also
to Pikionis' work[19] which is classified as a monument of modern cultural heritage. The archaeological landscape is therefore in a dialogue with the natural
landscape, yet it must be emphasised that this does not apply equally to all three
hills comprising Philopappos (Figure 4).

---

[19] The work of the architect Dimitris Pikionis represents a ground-breaking
intervention on the eastern side of the Philopappos Hill. Through personal
effort and persistence, he created a unique landscape, which, in contrast
to the norms of his time, materialises an idea of "Greekness" whereby the
ancient is in dialogue with folk, modern and contemporary cultural elements as well as the natural landscape of Attica, using a broad spectrum of
collages that bring together ancient *spolia* and neo-classical, Byzantine and
traditional elements.

Figure 4: At Pnyx (eastern side of the archaeological site), at dusk: once the meeting place of the ancient Athenian democratic assembly, today a gathering point for tourists, as well as youth residents in search of a (non-commercialized) evening out in the city centre (Source: authors).

Figure 5: Experiencing the loveliness, as well as loneliness of the western part of Philopappos' Hill, while walking on the ancient commercial road traversing the deme Koile (η δια Κοίλης οδός) and the Long Walls, from the city of Athens to the port of Piraeus (Source: authors).

Looking briefly at the history of area, what ought be stressed is its diachronic use as an open space, its distinctiveness as a natural feature of the Athenian landscape, its multifunctional character, as well the diversity of its forms of management. During antiquity, it accommodated the demes of Melite, Kolyttos and Koile, while in early modern times, it was used as a refugee residential area extending to the outskirts of the ancient site (Figure 5). During medieval times and subsequently under Turkish rule, the hill was transformed into agricultural and pastoral land, while in the 17th century it attracted the interest of the first European travellers to Greece. In the 19th century it survived the damages caused to the broader area during the Greek War of Independence. 1833 was a crucial date in the recent history of the city of Athens and Philopappos Hill was no exception; this was the year when the town was officially named the capital of the newly formed Greek State. According to the prevalent historical narrative of the period, Athens was expected to express and represent a Western ideal of classical antiquity, in which the Acropolis Hill and the Parthenon constituted an absolute ideological construct that provided an official incentive for the establishment of the modern capital. Already in the first urban planning proposal for the new city a suggestion was made to keep the Philopappos area free of buildings, incorporating it into the broader archaeological space around the Acropolis. However, until the mid 20th century, the Hill was encroached

Figure 6: The daily walk of pet dogs on Philopappos' Hill (Source: authors).

upon and subjected to dangerous over-mining, the marks of which are still visible today. Also, even though large building projects have taken place in the area, a large part of the Hill was spared and protected largely due to extensive projects of reforestation since 1900. Lately (1997–2004), the area formed part of the Unification Programme of the Archaeological Sites of Athens (UPASA) (Dakoura-Voyatzoglou 2013; Noukakis et al. 1998).

Today, the residents of neighbourhoods situated close to the Hill (such as Koukaki, Petralona), as well as other sociopolitical groups, strive to defend the public character of the area – against the demands and acts of trespassing by private actors – and to safeguard the cultural landscape and its function as an open green space.[20] Despite a firm official proposal to introduce controlled, albeit free, access to the site, currently the Hill remains accessible on a 24-hour basis (Figure 6). In fact, this was the explicit aim of a legal campaign mounted by the residents' committee which had a ground-breaking positive result in a decision by the Supreme Court in 2015:[21]

"…in the case of the movement against the enclosure of the Philo-pappos Hill in Athens, we could assume that the incentives for taking action were linked with practices developed in relation to the hill, such

---

[20] https://filopappou.wordpress.com/. Last access 20 November 2019.

[21] The Supreme Court decided in favour of the Residents' request to keep the space accessible 24 hours (including during the night) based on the argument that the citizens have a constitutional right to access and enjoy public cultural spaces and that the counter-arguments for the enclosure of the hill were not adequately supported by evidence.

as spatiotemporal patterns of roaming, but also related to memories, experiences and general representations of the Philopappos Hill as an open space. The practice of taking action thus can be considered as an important aspect in the daily routine of the neighbourhood, even if expressed differently for each person" (Chaidopoulou-Vrychea 2016: 95).

Up until today, local residents' demands do not seem to be directed towards models of exclusive participatory management and/or cooperative governance; or to be more precise, these have not been made known as such in any official way. Instead the main concern of the residents appears to be the protection and improvement of the existing green area.[22] It is for precisely this reason that they frequently instigate planting initiatives as well as other gardening upkeep activities (e.g. watering, pruning of the existing vegetation etc.). However, quite often the lack of dialogue and collaboration between the various local collectivities and the central authorities leads to unilateral actions on both sides which result in and keep feeding tensions and confrontation.

Discussion

What becomes readily apparent from the discussion so far is that both Philopappos Hill and Plato's Academy Park have managed to unmask deeper structural shortcomings of the hegemonic model of archaeological site management, particularly in urban contexts such as Athens. What has been the main issue at stake is the involvement of organised collectivities in decision making as far as both planning and daily experience of these spaces are concerned. The Hill and the Archaeological Park represent clear manifestations of sharing and participation, setting themselves apart from the ownership and enclosure models of the past that the Archaeological Service has long envisaged and advocated. Equally interesting, however, is the fact that the situation as it currently stands does not seem to call for a radical reconfiguration of their governance, since on several occasions operational aspects have existed that continue to be resolved with recourse to existing administrative structures, often with the support of local communities. This implies that perhaps the shift from enclosure to openness in archaeological sites such as Philopappos hill and the Academy Park necessitates a shift towards a more evolved framework of collective, multi-level, multi-stakeholder governance.

---

[22] In December 2008, following an official request by the hill's Residents Committee, a group of scientists conducted a specialised inquiry on the condition of the vegetation on the Philopappos Hill. Their scientific report outlined the poor state of the plant material on the hill and urged for its immediate regeneration. For details see: https://filopappou.wordpress .com/2008/12/12/1–3/. Last access 20 November 2019.

But what exactly would collective governance of urban heritage entail? The first issue to take into account is the very concept of the 'collective'. Who is involved in governance, what is the degree of official/formal involvement? As Sani has recently pointed out (2015: 4), this issue is very difficult to tackle:

> "If the Framework Convention on the Value of Cultural Heritage for Society opened for signature by Council of Europe Member States in 2005 at Faro, Portugal, defines a "heritage community" as consisting of "people who value specific aspects of cultural heritage which they wish within the framework of public action, to sustain and transmit to future generations", the current literature refers to a variety of other communities all of which are to be taken into account when developing participatory processes: *"source communities"* or *"communities of origin"* which are the ones from which, in the case of museums for example, collections originate; *"user communities"*, e.g. visitors to a site or a museum, *"interpretive communities"* referring to the active contribution in the interpretive and meaning making process of heritage according to constructionist theories, *"contemporary communities"*, *"communities of practice"* or *"communities of interest"* defined as "informal, self-organized network of peers with diverse skills and experience in an area of practice or profession, held together by the members' desire to help others (by sharing information) and the need to advance their own knowledge (by learning from others)"; *"virtual communities"* or *"online communities"*, emerging as a result of the use of Web 2.0 where the increasing production of user generated content can in principle lead to the merging of all the above mentioned communities" (Sani 2015: 4).

The significance of the above passage lies in its demonstration, first of all of how our field of enquiry widens up enormously when referring to openness and participation. Although we could indeed associate these dynamic fluctuations with the concept of commoning discussed above, it is important to remember that heritage is not merely a value under constant negotiation, but, above all, constantly contestable. By extension, heritage not only solidifies communities, but also results in the formation of transient socio-political groupings. What we need to bear in mind from the onset, therefore, is that heritage results from, reproduces (and even) re-establishes asymmetrical and confrontational relations.

Let us consider an archaeological site in Athens: can we really take this heritage to constitute the material and symbolic resource of some local community? Cultural heritage may have a local, supra-local, national or international value. Classical antiquity may be understood as a common resource for (and by) many that do not belong to the citizen body of the Greek state. Philopappos Hill is an indicative example of multi-layered archaeological value. At the same time, the state remains the official entity that maintains the right to manage the archaeological heritage resources legally located within its physical borders, since heritage, apart from representing a cultural phenomenon and ultimately a universal value, remains a modernist institutional category still at work (Lekakis 2012). And of course, the modernist legacy of the current state is not the only reason why this form of management is maintained. Since participation recognizes a role for both public and private actors, the state could be seen as a regulatory mechanism operating more against the 'private' and less so against bottom-up social formations.

Following this line of argument, the regulatory role of the state may even be strengthened by bottom-up participation, in contributory or collaborative types of projects (through the creation of focus groups, the setting up of advisory groups representing different segments of the local population, the hosting of specific actions in the heritage site and/or *Grassroots* projects etc.). If such initiatives are context specific and adapted to particular conditions and/ or circumstances (Sani 2015: 6), *overall responsibility* for the area is not necessarily challenged or contested: even in the two case studies examined here, it is obvious (at least so far) that local communities mainly express demands relating to the role of the areas as open green parks and less to their role as archaeological sites. According to Tsavdaroglou's classification (2015), the situation at Philoppappos Hill and the Archaeological Park at Plato's Academy are closer to Ostrom's vision of commoning and the so-called "polycentric" system of governance (1998: 27).

A polycentric system of governance raises issues not only about the level of involvement of different communities and/or groups, but also about the very nature and character of scientific practice. To begin with, antiquities are not inexhaustible or self-regenerating resources like, for example, some types of immaterial cultural heritage. The performance of mnemonic practices is what keeps them alive and sustains them by renewing their nature and character. However, in the case of the archaeological sites protection, conservation and longevity depend on scientific know-how and interdisciplinary work (by archaeologists, conservators, architects, engineers etc.). It is reasonable therefore, to question which urban groups or organisations could adopt such a rigorous social constitution so as to allow them to also acquire the institutional mandate for the management of such complex public archaeological parks like Philopappos Hill and Plato's Academy Park, hence guaranteeing their sustainability. From this perspective, and since no local community strives for a thoroughly collective governance regime for the Hill or the Park, the interaction that takes place between local authorities and official institutions moves towards distributing roles and actions to each entity depending on its particular character and reach. These are context-specific distributions and this makes it clear once more that commoning is what mainly emerges in the urban context of heritage use, not so much as a process leading to a standardized managerial practice, but more as a negotiation between groups over a 'common issue', the distribution and redistribution of roles but within a dialectic spirit and commitment. This is a process that leaves issues pending and unresolved, without, however, surrendering its political stance neither to the state/closed model nor to the neoliberalist model of social fragmentation.

An equally important point to address is whether openness may operate effectively at the level of interpretation. On the one hand, the obsessive insistence of the Greek state to monumentalise all classical period ruins adds a further weight that the Philopappos Hill, for example, finds difficult to bear, with its residents paying less attention to classical antiquity monuments and more on material traces linked with lived experiences and more recent chronological periods (Plantzos 2018: 106). This is certainly important as, although the Archaeological Service prioritises certain periods (and associated materialities) in its heritage management strategy and promotion, local communities are calling for more room in our interpretations for the so-called contemporary period (or in any case the more recent past). Of course, this is not only a demand of the non-specialists; in fact, the academic world has long stressed the need to direct analytical attention to other periods and in this respect, it finds itself largely attuned with the demands and/or objections expressed by the public. What needs to be stressed, however, is that the opening up of interpretation to a wider audience (and why not the private sector itself?) entails a fundamental risk: are we really ready for any kind of interpretation? Is there really room at a site such as the Pnyx for an anti-classicist narrative of how the ancient Athenians took advantage of the Delian League treasury to finance the ambitious building programme of the Acropolis? After all, nationalist and extreme right-wing narratives revolving around classical antiquity have already proven to be very popular, especially in the years following the Greek financial crisis. How many difficult or contested narratives can such an open space sustain or even bring to the fore? And what is the role of archaeologists in this newly emerging picture?

Along with openness at the level of narrative and interpretation, there also exists openness at the level of experience. The affordances of an 'open' and 'shared' space for transformation and flexibility also need to be considered when dealing with openness: how and to what extent does a particular place enable the incorporation of different uses, functions and practices (hence groups of people) under its auspices? In this respect, sites like Philopappos Hill and the Archaeological Park at Plato's Academy, which involve several and diverse social uses, can fulfil this specific criterion. By contrast, other archaeological sites which have a more restricted operational identity lack this potential. However, it would be naïve to suggest that the communal use of a large archaeological site in a capital city like Athens, results only in positive forms of appropriation. As in many other public spaces, similarly urban monuments and archaeo-logical sites can easily be transformed into dystopias of the dense, fast shifting and impossible to contain urban reality. For instance, the overuse and abuse of antiquities are also all part of the contemporary landscape of Philopappos Hill and although everyone, from the official authorities to the local communities seek solutions to such problems, they do not do so in common.[23] Perhaps this dichotomy in reaction stems from the fact that 'openness', 'open use' (and even 'abuse') are not that straightforward and uncontested terms. To state a simple example, openness at the level of experience, according to environmental psychology (Canter 1977; Stokols & Altman 1987) depends on factors that determine how 'hospitable' and/or attractive a site is for different groups of people. Sound, noise, light or darkness, the ability to enjoy a view of the part or the city, to contact or set one's self apart from other people, the clear signposting of the space or the room to manoeuvre in, or intervene upon that space, changing variables like the complexity or the coherence of the space, emotional reactions or expectations (such as feelings of fear or safety) can create multiple sensory and psychological responses that alter the experience of different subjects and/ or groups and provoke highly heterogeneous social (re)actions.

Of course, all the above are also radically influenced by a new parameter concerning openness, stemming from the newly emerging condition of dwelling which combines real space with digital space. In particular, what would be analytically worthwhile to investigate in future research is, for instance, how intensely controlled and closely supervised archaeological sites and/or monuments (like the Acropolis), often inaccessible for certain groups of people (e.g. people with reduced mobility) can be transformed into a wholly open space in social media platforms, mobile apps and VR or AR virtual environments (Catapoti & Vavouranakis 2016). Would digital presence and/or visibility be considered to fall into the category of the 'open'? And how would this affect interpretations as well as experiences of an archaeological site such as Philopappos or Plato's Academy Park?

Concluding remarks

This article has attempted to move beyond the polarized distinction between 'open' and 'closed' management models for archaeological sites and monuments, by suggesting that strategies of *openness* may be present in a host of different approaches ranging from resistance politics and attacks on the conventional centralised managerial systems to implicit and explicit assimilation and expansion attempts of the commercialised logic of neoliberal capitalism. The two case studies examined – Philopappos Hill and Plato's Academy Archaeological Park – empirically demonstrated that strategies and actions, deriving both from institutions and non-institutional entities, have rendered these archaeological sites relatively open, a condition that marks a clear shift

---

[23] For the lack of communication, see for example: https://www.news247 .gr/koinonia/to-pepromeno-enos-fonoy-me-archaiofylakes-se-rolo -parkadoroy; https://insidestory.gr/article/filopappou-apofaseis-skia-enos -thanatou. Last access 20 November 2019.

from the dominant model of archaeological site management in Greece. Within this framework, the concept of the 'commons' opens up an alternative pathway between a state-based and market-oriented system of resource management. Largely drawing upon the concept of *commoning*, it is argued that the processes that bring different actors, collectivities and institutions into constant negotiation over a common resource is a more advantageous way of grasping the reality that takes shape in hybrid spaces (heritage sites – public parks). It was also discussed whether the two case studies revealed practices that could lead towards a regime of closer resemblance to radical definitions of the commons. The conclusion reached was that this is not as yet the case, or perhaps even the expectation. The chapter concluded by describing the idiosyncrasies of urban archaeological heritage, which appear to play a significant role in the maintenance of a more symmetrical ('polycentric') condition in its governance.

Both the conditions of openness and of commoning, as well as the complexity of the sites examined here certainly point to the need to redefine current management models and to explore more collaborative and participatory schemes for the future. One must be careful, however, to not cancel out, but rather to amplify the dynamics and inventiveness of commoning as a constant process of becoming and reinventing the past (the sites, the materialities, memories, identities, and groups involved), as opposed to any static labelling ('state', 'private', 'top-down', 'bottom-up', including even the very concept of the 'commons').

Bibliography

Alexopoulos, G. & Fouseki, K. (2013). Introduction: Managing archaeological sites in Greece. *Conservation and Management of Archaeological Sites, 15*(1), 1–12. DOI: https://doi.org/10.1179/1350503313Z.00000000043.

An Architektur (2010). Beyond markets or states: Commoning as collective practice. Public interview with Massimo de Angelis and Stavros Stavrides. *An Architektur, 23*, 4–27.

Anderson, P. (1998). *The origins of postmodernity*. London, United Kingdom: Verso.

Antoniadou, S., Vavouranakis, G., Poulios, I. & Raouzaiou, P. (Eds.). (2018). *Culture and perspective at times of crisis: State structures, private initiative, and the public character of heritage*. Oxford, United Kingdom: Oxbow.

Appadurai, A. (with Chadha, A., Hodder, I., Jachman, T. & Witmore, C.). (2008). The globalization of archaeology and heritage: A discussion with Arjun Appadurai. In G. Fairclough, R. Harrison Jnr., J. H. Jameson & J. Schofield (Eds.), *The Heritage Reader* (pp. 209–218). London, United Kingdom: Routledge.

Bianchi, R. V. (2003). Place and power in tourism development: Tracing the complex articulations of community and locality. *Pasos, 1*(1), 13–32.

Retrieved October 10, 2018, from http://www.pasosonline.org/Publicados /1103/PS020103.pdf.

Boissevain, J. (Ed.). (1996). *Coping with tourists: European reactions to mass tourism.* Oxford, United Kingdom: Berghahn.

Bollier, D. (2014). *Think like a commoner: A short introduction to the life of the commons.* Gabriola Island, BC.: New Society Publishers.

Buck Sutton, S. & Stroulia, A. (2010). Archaeological sites and the chasm between past and present. In A. Stroulia & S. Buck Sutton (Eds.), *Archaeology in situ: Sites, archaeology, and communities in Greece* (pp. 3–50). Plymouth, United Kingdom: Lexington Books.

Caffentzis, G. (2005). Dr Sachs, Live8 and neoliberalism's 'Plan B'. In D. Harvie, K. Milburn, B. Trott & D. Watts (Eds.), *Shut them down!: The G8, Gleneagles 2005 and the Movement of Movements* (pp. 51–60). Leeds: Dissent! & Brooklyn, NY: Autonomedia.

Caffentzis, G. (2010). The future of 'The Commons': Neoliberalism's 'Plan B' or the original disaccumulation of capital? *New Formations, 69* (Summer), 23–41. DOI: https://doi.org/10.3898/NEWF.69.01.2010.

Canter, D. (1977). *The psychology of place.* London, United Kingdom: Architectural Press.

Carman, J. (2005). *Against cultural property: Archaeology, heritage and ownership.* London, United Kingdom: Duckworth.

Caruso, A. (2013). *Akademia: Archeologia di una scuola filosofica ad Atene da Platone a Proclo (387 a.C.–485 d.C.). SATAA: Studi di Archeologia e di Topografia di Atene e dell'Attica, 6.* Paestum, Italy: Pandemos.

Catapoti, D. (2013). To own or to share?: The crisis of the past at the onset of the 21st century. In M. Relaki & D. Catapoti (Eds.), *An archaeology of land ownership* (pp. 260–290). London, United Kingdom: Routledge.

Catapoti, D. & Relaki, M. (2013). An archaeology of land ownership: Introducing the debate. In M. Relaki & D. Catapoti (Eds.), *An archaeology of land ownership* (pp. 1–20). London, United Kingdom: Routledge.

Catapoti, D. & Vavouranakis, G. (2016). Parthenon 2.0. Από το μνημείο στο μεταδεδομένο. In C. Petropoulou & T. Ramadier (Eds.), Αστικές γεωγραφίες: Τοπία και καθημερινές διαδρομές (pp. 196–207). Athens, Greece: Kappon Publications.

Chaidopoulou-Vrychea, M. (2016). Η υπεράσπιση του βιωμένου χώρου: Καθ ημερινότητα και κοινωνικά κινήματα πόλης/περιφέρειας. In C. Petropoulou, A. Vitopoulou & C. Tsavdaroglou (Eds.), *Urban and regional social movements* (pp. 94–104). Thessaloniki, Greece: Research Group 'Invisible Cities'.

Chazapis, A. (2015, September 24–27). Οράματα και σχεδιασμοί για την πόλη: Το παράδειγμα της Ακαδημίας Πλάτωνος. Paper presented at the 4th National Conference of Urban Planning and Regional Development, Department of Planning and Regional Development, School of Engineering, University of Thessaly, Volos.

Coase, R. (1960). The problem of social cost. *The Journal of Law and Economics, 3,* 1–44.

Dakoura-Vogiatzoglou, O. (2013). Αναδιφώντας την ιστορία των Δυτικών Λόφων. In S. Oikonomou & M. Dogka-Tolis (Eds.), *Αρχαιολογικές συμβολές. Τόμος Β΄: Αττική. Α΄ και Γ΄ Εφορείες Προϊστορικών και Κλασικών Αρχαιοτήτων* (pp. 193–212). Athens, Greece: Museum of Cycladic Art.

De Angelis, M. (2007). *The beginning of history: Value struggles and global capital.* London, United Kingdom: Pluto Press.

De Angelis, M. (2013). *Κοινά, περιφράξεις και κρίσεις.* Thessaloniki, Greece: Ekdoseis ton xenon.

De Angelis, M. & Harvie, D. (2014). The commons. In M. Parker, G. Cheney, V. Fournier & C. Land (Eds.), *The Routledge companion to alternative organizations* (pp. 280–294). Abingdon, United Kingdom: Routledge.

Dellenbaugh, M. & Schwegmann, M. (2017). Actors of urban change from an urban commons perspective. *Actors of urban change: Urban Commons, Urban Change Talk Newspaper, 3,* 15–17. Retrieved August 30, 2018, from https://marydellenbaugh.files.wordpress.com/2017/06/actors-of-urban -change-from-an-urban-commons-perspective.pdf.

Díaz-Andreu, M. & Champion, T. (Eds.). (1996). *Nationalism and archaeology in Europe.* London, United Kingdom: University College London Press.

Dietler, M. (1994). 'Our ancestors the Gauls': Archaeology, ethnic nationalism and the manipulation of Celtic identity in modern Europe. *American Anthropologist, 96*(3), 584–605.

Federici, S. (2010). Feminism and the politics of the commons in an era of primitive accumulation. In C. Hughes, S. Peace & K. Van Meter – for the Team Colors Collective (Eds.), *Uses of a whirlwind: Movement, movements, and contemporary radical currents in the United States* (pp. 283–293). Edinburgh, United Kingdom: AK Press.

Fotiadis, M. (2010). There is a blue elephant in the room: From state institutions to citizen indifference. In A. Stroulia & S.Buck Sutton (Eds.), *Archaeology in situ: Sites, archaeology, and communities in Greece* (pp. 447–456). Plymouth, United Kingdom: Lexington Books.

Frank, S. (2015). Urban commons and urban heritage: Input for the urban heritage seminar series, University of Gothenburg, 23rd August 2013. In H. Benesch, F. Hammami, I. Holmberg & E. Uzer (Eds.), *Heritage as common(s) – Common(s) as heritage* (pp. 19–29). Gothenburg, Sweden: Makadam.

Galani-Moutafi, V. (2002). *Έρευνες για τον τουρισμό στην Ελλάδα και την Κύπρο: Μια ανθρωπολογική προσέγγιση.* Athens, Greece: Propobos.

Gero, J. (n.d.). *The history of World Archaeological Congress.* Retrieved October 10, 2018, from http://www.worldarchaeologicalcongress.org/about -wac/history/146-history-wac.

Hall, S. (2008). Whose heritage?: Un-settling 'the heritage', re-imagining the post-nation. In G. Fairclough, R. Harrison Jnr., J. H. Jameson & J. Schofield (Eds.), *The Heritage Reader* (pp. 219–228). London, United Kingdom: Routledge.

Hamilakis, Y. (2007). *The nation and its ruins: Antiquity, archaeology, and national imagination in Greece.* Oxford, United Kingdom: Oxford University Press.

Hamilakis, Y. & Duke, P. (Eds.). (2007). *Archaeology and capitalism: From ethics to politics.* Walnut Creek, CA: Left Coast Press.

Hardt, M. & Negri, A. (2009). *Commonwealth.* Cambridge, MA: Belknap Press.

Harvey, D. (1989). *The condition of postmodernity: An enquiry into the origins of cultural change.* Cambridge, MA: Blackwell.

Harvey, D. (2011). The future of the commons. *Radical History Review, 109,* 101–107. DOI: https://doi.org/10.1215/01636545-2010-017.

Harvey, D. (2012). *Rebel cities: From the right to the city to the urban revolution.* London, United Kingdom: Verso.

Holtorf, C. (2005). *From Stonehenge to Las Vegas: Archaeology as popular culture.* Walnut Creek, CA: AltaMira Press.

Jameson, F. (1984). Postmodernism, or the cultural logic of late capitalism. *New Left Review, I*(146), 53–92.

Jumbe, C. B. L. (2006). Short commentary on "The name change; or what happened to the P?", authored by Charlotte Hess and Ruth Meinzen-Dick. *Commons Digest, 2,* 5–6.

Kärrholm, M. (2015). On 'crowd space' as urban commons-some notes on responsivity and the transformation of an urban square. In H. Benesch, F. Hammami, I. Holmberg & E. Uzer, *Heritage as common(s) – Common(s) as heritage* (pp. 53–62). Gothenburg, Sweden: Makadam.

Kehoe, A. B. (2007). Archaeology within marketing capitalism. In Y. Hamilakis & P.Duke (Eds.), *Archaeology and Capitalism: From ethics to politics* (pp. 169–178). Walnut Creek, CA: Left Coast Press.

Kornberger, M. & Borch, C. (2015). Introduction: Urban commons. In C. Borch & M. Kornberger (Eds.), *Urban commons: Rethinking the city* (pp. 1–21). London, United Kingdom: Routledge.

Layton, R. (Ed.). (1989). *Conflict in the archaeology of living traditions.* One World Archaeology. London, United Kingdom: Routledge.

Law 3028/2002. *On the protection of antiquities and cultural heritage in general.* Retrieved November 20, 2019, from https://www.bsa.ac.uk/wp-content/uploads/2018/11/Archaeological-Law-3028-2002.pdf.

Law 1515/1985. *Ρυθμιστικό σχέδιο και πρόγραμμα προστασίας περιβάλλοντος της ευρύτερης περιοχής της αθήνας.* Retrieved November 20, 2019, from https://www.e-nomothesia.gr/kat-periballon/skhedia-poleon/n-1515-1985.html.

Lefebvre, H. (1991). *The Production of Space.* Oxford, United Kingdom: Blackwell.

Lekakis, St. (2012). The cultural property debate. In T. J. Smith & D. Plantzos (Eds.), *A Companion to Greek Art, Vol. I* (pp. 683–697). Malden, MA: Wiley-Blackwell.

Leontis, A. (1995). *Topographies of Hellenism: Mapping the homeland.* Ithaca, NY: Cornell University Press.

Loukaki, A. (2008). *Living ruins, value conflicts*. Aldershot, United Kingdom: Ashgate.

Lowenthal, D. (1985). *The past is a foreign country*. Cambridge, United Kingdom: Cambridge University Press.

Lowenthal, D. (2002). The past as a theme park. In T. Young, & R. Riley (Eds.), *Theme park landscapes: Antecedents and variants* (pp. 11–23). Washington, DC: Dumbarton Oaks Press.

Lynch, K. (1960). *The image of the city*. Cambridge, MA: The MIT Press.

McNeal, R. A. (1991). Archaeology and the destruction of the later Athenian acropolis. *Antiquity, 65*(246), 49–63. DOI: https://doi.org/10.1017/S000 3598X00079291.

Miller, D., Rowlands, M. & Tilley, C. (Eds.). (1989). *Domination and resistance*. London, United Kingdom: Unwin Hyman.

Municipality of Athens. (2009). *Ακαδημία Πλάτωνος: Έγκριση μελέτης πολεοδομικού ανασχεδιασμού & διαδικασιών διαβούλευσης από το Δ.Σ.* Retrieved October 10, 2018, from http://www.cityofathens.gr/node/9806.

Nicholas, G. & Hollowell, J. (2007). Ethical challenges to a postcolonial archaeology: The legacy of scientific colonialism. In Y. Hamilakis & P. Duke (Eds.), *Archaeology and capitalism: From ethics to politics* (pp. 59–82). Walnut Creek, CA: Left Coast Press.

Noukakis, A. (1998). Μελέτη συνολικής ανάδειξης αρχαιολογικού χώρου Φιλοπάππου. *Architektones. Magazine of the Association of Greek Architects /Syllogos Architektonon Diplomatouchon Anotaton Scholon-Panellinia Enosi Architektonon (SADAS-PEA), 12*/B(November-December), 41–43.

Olsen, B. (2012). Symmetrical archaeology. In I. Hodder (Ed.), *Archaeological theory today* (2nd ed.) (pp. 208–228). Cambridge, United Kingdom: Polity Press.

Ostrom, E. (1990). *Governing the commons: The evolution of institutions for collective action*. Cambridge, United Kingdom: Cambridge University Press.

Ostrom, E. (1998). *Coping with tragedies of the commons*. Retrieved October 10, 2018, from https://pdfs.semanticscholar.org/7c6e/92906bcf0e590e6541 eaa41ad0cd92e13671.pdf.

Panagiotopoulos, M. & Chatziefthimiou, T. (2017). Επιστροφή στην Ακαδημία. *Archaiologia kai Technes, 123*, 58–77.

Parker, P. & Johansson, M. (2011, June 23–25). *The uses and abuses of Elinor Ostrom's concept of commons in urban theorizing*. Paper presented at International Conference of the European Urban Research Association (EURA) 2011, Cities without Limits, Copenhagen. Retrieved October 10, 2018, http://muep.mau.se/handle/2043/12212.

Pels, P. (1997). The anthropology of colonialism: Culture, history and the emergence of Western governmentality. *Annual Review of Anthropology, 26*, 163–183. DOI: https://doi.org/10.1146/annurev.anthro.26.1.163.

Perpinia, S. (2014). *Ακαδημία Πλάτωνος: διερεύνηση των αστικών μετασχηματισμών των αναπτυσσόμενων νέων κεντρικοτήτων* (Unpublished

Master's Thesis). National Technical University of Athens. Athens. Retrieved October 10, 2018, from http://www.arch.ntua.gr/project/10998.

Plantzos, D. (2011). Behold the raking geison: The new Acropolis Museum and its context-free archaeologies. *Antiquity, 85*(328), 613–625. DOI: https://doi.org/10.1017/S0003598X00068009.

Plantzos, D. (2014). *Οι αρχαιολογίες του κλασικού: Αναθεωρώντας τον εμπειρικό κανόνα*. Athens, Greece: Ekdoseis tou Eikostou Protou.

Plantzos, D. (2018). Διεκδικώντας το τοπίο: Αντικρουόμενες προσεγγίσεις στη χρήση του Φιλοπάππου. In A. Loukaki & D. Plantzos (Eds.), Τέχνη – Χώρος – Όψεις ανάπτυξης στην Ελλάδα της κρίσης (pp. 95–115). Athens, Greece: Leimon.

Sack, R. D. (1986). *Human territoriality: Its theory and history*. Cambridge, United Kingdom: Cambridge University Press.

Sani, M. (2015). *Participatory governance of cultural heritage*. Retrieved October 10, 2018, from http://www.interarts.net/descargas/interarts2538.pdf.

Shennan, S. J. (Ed.). (1989). *Archaeological approaches to cultural identity*. London, United Kingdom: Unwin Hyman.

Silberman, N. A. (2007). 'Sustainable' heritage?: Public archaeological interpretationand the marketed past. In Y. Hamilakis & P. Duke (Eds.), *Archaeology and capitalism: From ethics to politics* (pp. 179–194). Walnut Creek, CA: Left Coast Press.

Silverman, H. (Ed.). (2011). *Contested cultural heritage: Religion, nationalism, erasure, and exclusion in a global world*. New York, NY: Springer Publications.

Simmel, G. (1971). The metropolis of modern life. In G. Simmel (Author) & D.N. Levine (Ed. & Writer of introduction), *Georg Simmel on individuality and social forms: Selected writings* (pp. 324–339). Chicago, IL: University of Chicago Press.

Smith, L. (2004). *Archaeological theory and the politics of cultural heritage*. London, United Kingdom: Routledge.

Smith, L. (2008). Towards a theoretical framework for archaeological heritage management. In G. Fairclough, R. Harrison Jnr, J. H. Jameson. & J. Schofield (Eds.), *The Heritage Reader* (pp. 62–74). London, United Kingdom: Routledge.

Stavrides, S. (2016). *Common space: The city as commons*. London, United Kingdom: Zed Books.

Stokols, D. & Altman, I. (Eds.) (1987). *Handbook of environmental psychology*. New York, NY: John Wiley & Sons.

Thomas, J. (2004). *Archaeology and modernity*. London, United Kingdom: Routledge.

Tsavdaroglou, C. (2015, August 27–29). *The contentious common space in Greece: From the neoliberal austerity to the SYRIZA left government*. Paper presented at the RC21 International Conference on "The Ideal City: between myth and reality. Representations, policies, contradictions and challenges for tomorrow's urban life" Urbino (Italy). Retrieved October 10, 2018, from https://www.rc21.org/en/wp-content/uploads/2014/12/E10.2-Tsavdaroglou.pdf.

Tziotas, C. E. M. (2015). *The effects of the economic crisis on the cultural heritage of Greece: An Analysis of the EU funding (National Strategic Reference Framework) provided for the Region of Central Macedonia*. Unpublished Master's Thesis. The University of Oslo, Oslo.

Urry, J. (1990). *The tourist gaze: Leisure and travel in contemporary societies*. London, United Kingdom: Sage Publications.

Vavouranakis, G. (2018). Archaeological resource management in Greece: State, private, public and common. In S. Antoniadou, G. Vavouranakis, I. Poulios & P. Raouzaiou (Eds.), *Culture and perspective at times of crisis: State structures, private initiative and the public character of heritage* (pp. 21–39). Oxford, United Kingdom: Oxbow.

Walsh, K. (1992). *The representation of the past: Museums and heritage in the postmodern world*. London, United Kingdom: Routledge.

White, H. (1973). *Metahistory: The historical imagination of nineteenth-century Europe*. Baltimore, MA: Johns Hopkins University Press.

Wirth, L. (1938). Urbanism as a way of life. *American Journal of Sociology*, 44(1), 1–24.

Wylie, A. (2005). The promise and perils of an ethic of stewardship. In L. Meskell & P. Pels(Eds.), *Embedding ethics: Shifting boundaries of the anthropological profession*. (pp. 47–68). Oxford, United Kingdom: Berg.

Yalouri, E. (2001). *The Acropolis: Global fame, local claim*. Oxford, United Kingdom: Berg.

Zarkia, C. (1996). Philoxenia receiving tourists –but not guests– on a Greek island. In J. Boissevain (Ed.), *Coping with tourists: European reactions to mass tourism* (pp. 143–173). Providence, RI: Berghahn Books.

PART 2

CHAPTER 4

Cultural Life Reconfigured: From the Ancestral to the Digital Commons and Beyond

Nicholas Anastasopoulos

Transitioning to the digital universe

The advent of the internet was undoubtedly the milestone of the information era, triggering a chain reaction and setting the stage for a series of revolutions in communication, production and the creative fields of culture, which characterise the period we live in. By its very nature and its operational structure of a loose, highly complex non-hierarchical network, as well as its decentralized management, the internet possesses attributes which justify its classification as a man-made common resource on a planetary scale. Virtually unlimited access to knowledge, information, opportunities for collaboration, communication, sharing, and distributed production, have all heralded the era of a digital commonwealth and of a networked public sphere (Benkler 2007).

The fact that whatever can be produced can just as easily be multiplied, distributed and shared, generated a climate of accessibility and openness. Consequently, this has led to an unprecedented social production, to a transformation of processes of collaboration and exchange, and to a movement of theorists and practitioners advocating the management of information as a digital

How to cite this book chapter:
Anastasopoulos, N. 2020. Cultural Life Reconfigured: From the Ancestral to the Digital Commons and Beyond. In Lekakis, S. (ed.) *Cultural Heritage in the Realm of the Commons: Conversations on the Case of Greece*. Pp. 97–108. London: Ubiquity Press. DOI: https://doi.org/10.5334/bcj.f. License: CC-BY

commons freely accessible to everyone. In this context, open-source software, creative commons, crowdfunding and Wikipedia were born, all of which are concepts that have been shaping a new environment that emerges from a rethink of issues such as copyright, licensing, and consumer and creator relationships.

From the ancestral to the digital commons: Cooperate or Corporate?[24]

According to Yochai Benkler, "culture, shared meaning, and symbols are how we construct our views of life across a wide range of domains – personal, political, and social" (Benkler 2007: 274). Culture encompasses the behaviour, norms and expression of societies and should be understood in its widest possible definition, as forming part of a dynamic and ongoing body of creation in many fields of human activity. Cultural heritage and natural heritage domains are often indistinguishable and historically were bound together.[25] Every aspect of the human condition may therefore be viewed through the cultural lens. For a community, or a nation their natural and cultural heritage remain their most vital common resources, and therefore cultural heritage should be understood as a right, as well as a common resource. Communication, expression and creativity are the components par excellence of both culture and cultural heritage, and the digital sphere currently addresses these aspects of human activity to unprecedented degrees of quantity, efficiency, speed and universality.

The commons in various forms and commoning as a practice, form a significant, uninterrupted and inextricable element of traditional and historical or indigenous populations and cultural heritage in several countries. A considerable body of knowledge concerning cultural heritage, the commons and the implication of the digital age, forms part of an entirely different cosmovision, outside of the sphere of influence of the West and the Global North (not excluding European traditions), which is worth both citing and learning from.[26] This body of knowledge has an archetypical identity and may be found in small communities everywhere. In most such communities the commons remain

---

[24] The title, implying a fundamental dilemma for the present and the future of civilization, was borrowed from the "Jamm'Art" session that Culture Action Europe (CAE) launched on July 4, 2017 addressing a European audience in the form of an online live debate. See http://jammart.eu/discussions/cooperate -or-corporate/. Last access 20 November 2019

[25] In that respect, institutions or entities such as UNESCO, or the Environmental Justice Atlas represent either official or activist digital portals, relating to one of the two, or both. See https://whc.unesco.org & https://ejatlas .org/. Last access 20 November 2019

[26] Also often referred to as Traditional Ecological Knowledge (TEK).

alive as a way of life in the traditions, practices, and the built environment. The rural traditions of festivals, carnivals and *panigyria*[27] in southern Europe, and the shamanic ceremonies in the Andean communities for example, can be thought of as ancestral commons. They all provide a space and a context for people to congregate and to partake in a communal experience which they help co-create and in which they also become participants.

As we experience new enclosures, and various categories and examples of commons are being threatened with extinction, we may observe how simultaneously processes of creating new commons unfold. To a certain extent, the process of sharing today has migrated to the digital sphere, onto social networking sites and for most people the reproduction of digital content has already been a daily routine for many years. The peer-to-peer culture (P2P) is a phenomenon of commoning in the digital realm. Many citizens may produce, distribute and consume at the same time, motivated by the passion and the need for creation, communication, learning, self-realization and self-integrity, i.e. superior positive motives free from the neoliberal doctrine of the market economy that measures each resource solely through the logic of profit (Kostakis & Bauwens 2014). However, the vast majority of users arguably perform mundane, socially or personally driven acts with such incentives as acquiring immaterial goods that previously constituted market products of high commercial value. In this sense, it can be argued that both peer to peer culture and community movements have become second nature and that as a result they are apolitical, perhaps even amoral, since they derive from all parts of the political spectrum, from the far left to the far right. A majority with no political identity, such as those internet and social media users who have developed daily routines of sharing selfies, news and other innocuous content, may be doing so without considering the ethics, morality or the ecological footprint of their actions, or perhaps in their absence altogether.

Meanwhile, the immaterial production that the internet implicitly or explicitly favours forms a new landscape of conflicts and negotiations, because it has been used as the arena for generating both surplus market value, as well as for the production of new commons. Under protocols such as open-source and creative commons, individuals and initiatives offer the fruits of their labour to a common effort, a common pool of resources or a joint project. The terms 'open-source' and 'creative commons' describe practices that promote access to the components of a digital product for its reuse, as well as for the production and development of new products. The basic operational principles and widespread

---

[27] Term used in Greece to describe popular traditional festivities taking place in villages all over the country, usually on the occasion of a saint's name day, in which people congregate to socialize, share, and enjoy food, music and dance. These events are usually produced by the people themselves on a rotating basis.

practices are those of a horizontal relationship arising from the exchange of information and cooperation so that the final product, the code and layout of the structure itself, as well as their documentation, remain open. Some believe it is a philosophy, while others see it as the natural evolution of the concurrent and distributed access to production, use and modification, as opposed to the centrally controlled industrial production models commonly used in commercial software companies.

In this state of affairs, much appears to be offered in the digital sphere for free, while value is created in a variety of alternative ways, such as entering a moneyless agreement with Facebook in which the central, yet unseen part of the deal involves selling the users' personal profiles to commercial, for-profit entities. In this case, should giant enterprises such as Airbnb, Amazon or Facebook be understood as corrupting, co-opting, or facilitating the principles of a sharing economy and peer to peer culture? In a recent mutation of capitalism, referred to as 'platform capitalism', the new practices of flexible forms of work producing value over digital services have profound and largely unintended side effects, both positive and negative. Consequently, in the digital era of globalized capital, overcoming the obstacles enforced by national borders can serve primarily a neo-liberal agenda and secondarily socially radical practices (Delfanti 2018; Langley & Leyshon 2017). Nonetheless, the dog-eat-dog approach of doing anything it takes to be successful, to the detriment of others, seems to contradict some of the innate characteristics of the digital sphere and a habit, if not a culture, of sharing is undeniably on the rise.[28]

Wikipedia, which represents a collectively produced and managed repository of accumulated human knowledge, across languages and territories, may be thought of as the quintessential, universal digital commons. Similarly the Human Genome Project, the world's largest collaborative biological project (1990–2003) could be viewed as both a scientific, as well as a cultural achievement and therefore, cultural heritage of humanity thereafter (Bryant et al. 2007). These considerations, as well as other complicated legal issues of licensing, reproduction and use have been brought to the forefront of the debate over digital commons and to a great extent may be credited with the revival of the current widespread interest by the general public in the digital commons.

All over the world initiatives at various scales and societal levels attempting to highlight, research, expand and redefine our understanding of the commons abound, several of which involve cultural practices bridging the digital and the

---

[28] Some noteworthy examples have been developing in several countries over the last two decades under different circumstances. Since 2009, in Greece and in Spain, among many other countries, a wave of initiatives and processes have sprung as a way of mitigating the effects of the crisis, by experimenting with alternative currencies, time banks, and other forms of exchange, cooperation, commoning practices and cooperative economy.

physical sphere. It is a challenge to delineate digital commons and the cultural heritage field as clearly defined areas, nevertheless some examples serve as references to develop a sense of the inquiry and practices pointing in this direction.

Reviewing European and Latin American case studies

Some noteworthy or emblematic European and Latin American examples that I have experienced or worked with follow, serving to map aspects of interaction and cross-over between the areas of digital commons and cultural heritage.

Several European initiatives form part of a commons-oriented shift in the collective imagination, many functioning with both strong physical and digital presence, while also belonging to wider networks forming extensive rhizomatic evolution, support and empowerment systems. These include the 'Transition Movement' and the 'Transition Towns', which originated in Kinsale, Ireland (2005), then migrated to Totnes, UK, and subsequently to several other cities in Europe and worldwide.[29]

The French/Romanian *Atelier d'Architecture Autogérée* (AAA) and the Ecuadorian *Al Borde* collective of architects employ parallel tactics. They both attempt to address the traditional limitations of the architect's role in responding to the true needs of communities by bypassing the restrictions of the monetary economy, 'hacking' the chain of production, and actively seeking to engage with the communities that they see as the rightful recipients of their skills.[30] This is made possible through a combination of frugal living, pooled resources and the collective's reliance on the support of their digital networks and involvement in international events, which allow sustenance and transfer of monetary resources to their projects. Both of these emblematic case studies point to an updated interpretation of culture, community, the economy and the commons in a digital context.

A number of notable Italian case studies, on a municipal level, address aspects of cultural heritage as commons and experiment with cultural heritage management in a cooperative economy context. Bologna is a pioneering city with a strong tradition in the urban commons among other things, which has taken active steps towards the safeguarding of its cultural heritage, as well as of its public spaces as urban commons.[31] Similarly, the city of Ghent in Belgium has

---

[29] See https://transitionnetwork.org and https://en.wikipedia.org/wiki /Transition_town. Last access 20 November 2019.

[30] See www.albordearq.com and http://www.urbantactics.org/. Last access 20 November 2019.

[31] See http://labgov.city/thecommonspost/bologna-as-a-laboratory-for-urban -commons-urban-change-talk-berlin/. Last access 20 November 2019.

recently taken steps at an institutional level to highlight and reinforce already existing community, heritage and commons characteristics.[32]

In the area of a cooperative economy, CoopCulture is the largest cooperative enterprise in the sector of cultural heritage and activities in Italy, managing the consortium of the largest museums in the country and offering a sophisticated bundle of digital services.[33]

Greek case studies

During the crisis years (2009 to the present) resistance and activism in Greece have often been rooted in both cultural affairs and cultural heritage. A plethora of websites, blogs end portals representing commoning activities was documented in 2014, but many have withered, disappeared, or become inactive since then. Some noteworthy cases that are still active include the Navarinou Park case, and the Embros Theater (Anastasopoulos 2012; 2014). The Victoria Square project on the other hand represents a much younger contender, coming from an entirely different perspective, i.e. the cross-over of an arts institution such as Documenta 14 and the artistic practice of the artist Rick Lowe. It is defined by its initiator as a "social sculpture", resembling a grassroots community empowerment movement based on creativity and cultural production.[34]

The Unmonastery is an experimental collective of young, highly skilled, and well educated people from various parts of the world, disillusioned by their efforts to make a meaningful and satisfying living by offering the fruits of their expertise to society.[35] In their own words, *"When it comes to work, it is increasingly difficult to reconcile making money with making sense. People work to make a living. Others work to make meaning. But the two 'works are not the same work".* The initiative's principles and goals have been attempting to dissect the operating

---

[32] At an institutional level it appears that several forward-thinking European organizations have been recently shifting their attention to the commons, cooperative forms of economy and production, etc. See for example, Culture Action Europe, and the European Commons Assembly.

[33] The company was founded in January 2010 by the merger of two highly specialized companies with over 15 years of experience alongside public and private bodies, with the aim of improving the quality and variety of user services and enhancement at prestigious museums, monuments and libraries of many Italian regions. See Coopculture/Societá Cooperativa Culture: https://www.coopculture.it/. Last access 20 November 2019.

[34] See victoriasquareproject.gr/ and https://www.documenta14.de/en/artists /13512/rick-lowe. Last access 20 November 2019.

[35] The Unmonastery initiative came into being as an initiative on the occasion of Matera awarded the Cultural Capital of Europe (CCoE) title for 2019. https://www.matera-basilicata2019.it/it/. Last access 20 November 2019.

principles, signs and contradictions of our times, seeking to match highly skilled and intelligent individuals possessing a strong sense of ethics, with communities, thus addressing the harsh circumstances imposed on both communities and individuals by the neoliberal economy. Digital culture and open source forms a significant part in their principles and practices, both in the members' expertise, communication, and interface with other communities.[36]

The Ecuadorian experiment

Ecuador is a South American country whose territory encompasses a substantial percentage of the Amazon, the forest with the richest biodiversity on Earth, and it represents an outstanding example. Its natural wealth has been managed by the indigenous communities that have been living there for millennia through accumulated wisdom, the result of producing empirical knowledge through the trial and error of its peoples. The concept of *Sumak Kawsay*, best described as *Life in Harmony,* embodies the very essence of this cultural heritage and the commons, and it encapsulates the belief that humans form part of the ecosystem and do not stand apart from it. [37]

The FLOK Society (Free, Libre, Open Knowledge Society) Project was greatly publicized and appeared as the flagship research project with the task of laying the foundations of a new approach to knowledge and its role in a knowledge-based orientation for the future of the economy of the country.[38] The FLOK

---

[36] The Unmonastery group has had an "Athenian phase", and engagement with the city between 2015 and 2016, as well as an ongoing Greek phase and a remote community of Kokkinopylos on Mount Olympus. See http://unmonastery.org. Last access 20 November 2019.

[37] In 2008 Ecuador was the first nation to vote and put in effect a constitution which acknowledges Rights to Nature. Despite the somewhat poor results, the significance of the precedence of the Ecuadorian Constitution remains, and it has been inspiring ever since in nations such as Bolivia, activists and individuals, setting new standards. These ideas were first adopted at state level and appropriated in the better-known 'Buen Vivir principles', but the relationship between the original holders of this heritage and knowledge, its indigenous populations and the state remains tense and unresolved. Nina Pacari, a representative of the indigenous movement, claims that there is a new academic, state and financial hegemony being established in the name of its peoples' cultural heritage, in their absence, or often in their detriment.

[38] The FLOK society project was a research project aiming to formulate proposals to the Ecuadorian government for policy making in various sectors of the economy and human activity, with the goal of achieving economic, as well as social and ecological emancipation through distributed, knowledge production in the context of a digital environment and economy. The work

Society Project drew inspiration and reference from the indigenous communities of Ecuador and the practice of 'minga', in an attempt to instil it in the sphere of the digital world and technology. The proposals that have emerged concern education, science and culture as well as open source manufacturing and distributed energy production, based on examples from the international sphere (Vila-Viñas et al., 2015). It is not yet known how and in what circumstances the suggestions will apply, and there is much to be debated about this venture that has caused a great deal of agitation among the commoners and scholars worldwide, acting thereafter as a reference and a catalyst for the future, in terms of developments in the digital community.

Challenges around the commons and P2P Ethics

The digital sphere tends to breed illusions of universality generated by a global culture, ease and speed of dissemination of information. Naturally, all of these come into sharp contrast with the diverse lifestyles, production and consumption patterns that form part of the cultural heritage of different regions and the cultural origins of individualities and collectivities that are associated with local characteristics, as well as with specific moments of history. Several gaps and contradictions arise, given that precarity and the inequalities and difficulties in the material world seem to persist and expand rather than diminish. Despite the fact that we interact, coexist, share content and develop common areas beyond national and other boundaries more than ever, we are far from overcoming the barriers stemming from cultural disparities, economic inequalities and geopolitical interests. In the context of a neoliberal global economy, a common cultural heritage is more vulnerable than ever and runs the risk of being eroded, appropriated, privatized or eradicated altogether. Profound transformations in production which gradually coincide with the loss of control and sovereignty over resources, force and coerce people to sacrifice their cultural heritage to the market, in exchange for survival.[39]

Each era is characterized by a set of beliefs, rules, and codes of conduct that are referred to as ethics, but as was explained above, the current period is a transitional one. Therefore, as our time possesses transitional characteristics,

---

of the research group was coordinated by Michel Bauwens and took place between September 2013 and June 2014.

[39] In China, state and neoliberal predatory tactics have massively been destroying, in a matter of years, century-old traditions of *siheyuan* and *hutong* (traditional residences and alleys) replacing them with monstrous megacities. In Athens a state alliance with corporate multinational interests has had no qualms over selling out a cultural heritage site of global proportions such as Plato's Academy to real estate development for a Shopping Mall, which would coopt the site's name to that of Academy Gardens (See Galanos, this volume).

until a new modus operandi is established and becomes universally accepted, we will continue living in a precarious, conflictual and experimental state of affairs of ambiguous ethics. At the beginning of the twentieth century, German philosopher Max Weber wrote an essay titled *Protestant Ethics and the Spirit of Capitalism*. Protestant ethics stemmed from northern Europe, where work was considered an end in itself (the means to avoid inertia, which can lead to sin) and a goal in which the entrusted task must be completed regardless of its value (Furnham 1984). Weber argued that modern bureaucratic capitalism was born out of the confirmation of this Protestant morality of work. In an attempt to map developments in immaterial peer production, Finnish philosopher Pekka Himanen more recently introduced the ethics for the work of hackers (2010). According to Himanen, work must be interesting, entertaining and, above all, it must create value for the worker, the organization and society as a whole. Workers must also have the freedom to organize their work in a more functional way and reach their goals in the way that best suits their needs and ideas (Himanen 2010; Weber et al. 2002).

While ethics in general have been significantly challenged or undermined, one key characteristic of the new era is the emergence of social relations based on a 'commons ethics'. New practices attempt to return to the physical and material environment focusing on resource management and their use at various levels, such as nutritional, spatial, cultural and urban, and most significantly ethical. In these developments we find new attitudes towards ideology and morality, which help shape new political theories and ideas beyond capitalism, even a new meaning for existence. The ethics of the commons permeating mostly unwritten cultural structures and defining rules of conduct, stem from fundamental aspects of the human condition, which have traditionally been characterized by qualities of cooperation and sharing (Costanza-Chock et al. 2018). These ethics embody the concept of commoning, a term that describes the practices of collective creation and active management of the commons. Both traditional and modern communities are the expression of commoning activity and some forms of cooperative economies may be seen as the expression of this common ethics and commoning in practice (Bollier 2014: 147).

Conclusions or, what is at stake?

As with many other technological advances, digital culture remains a double-edged sword. In this respect we observe digital activities that may be classified as commoning activities surviving in the midst of an ocean of predatory actors in the digital sphere. The appropriate national as well as international legal context required in order to support such enterprises and to safeguard it from the risks of perishing or being privatised, is missing. Societies are experiencing recurring cases of enclosure and subsumption of their cultural heritage by neoliberal processes in which the nation-state serves primarily as the agent for this transaction. Despite differences, the same challenges and similar victories and defeats seem to be the case for both European and Latin American case studies.

On the antipode of the commons, citizen initiatives, grassroots culture, Keller Easterling researches and analyses the mechanisms of capital in the digital era (Easterling 2014) and speaks of the complex infrastructure of a global scale that has been put into place in order to facilitate the flaw of capital beyond national laws, local conditions and regional restrictions. She likens the present condition to a David vs Goliath case, which despite the apparently insurmountable difficulties leaves us with the hope that, as the fable goes, and as several of the case studies discussed allow us to hope, size and might do not always determine the outcome.

Where shall we start? Fostering a genuine commons and peer-to-peer ethics climate, through education and the social, political, and legal infrastructure seems to be a safe and sustainable way forward.

Bibliography

Anastasopoulos, N. (2012). Share! In P. Dragonas & A. Skiada (Eds.), *Made in Athens. 13th international architecture exhibition. La Biennale di Venezia* (pp. 91–99). Athens, Greece: Ministry of Environment, Energy and Climate Change & Authors.

Anastasopoulos, N. (2014). The rise of communitarianism and other alternative movements from the Athenian crises. In E. Russell & P. Gallardo (Eds.), *Yesterday's tomorrows on utopia and dystopia* (p. 217–226). Newcastle upon Tyne, United Kingdom: Cambridge Scholars Publishing.

Barandiaran, X. E., Vila-Viñas, D. & Vázquez, D. (2015). Buen Conocer/FLOK Society como proceso de investigación colaborativa y diseño participativo. In Vila-Viñas, D. & Barandiaran, X. E. (Eds.), *Buen Conocer/FLOK Society: Modelos sostenibles y políticas públicas para una economía social del conocimiento común y abierto en el Ecuador* (pp. 7–58). Quito, Ecuador: IAEN-CIESPAL. Retrieved August 21, 2018, from http://book.floksociety .org/ec/0/0-2-metodologia-arquitectura-de-la-participacion-durante-el -proceso-flok/.

Benkler, Y. (2006). *The wealth of networks: How social production transforms markets and freedom.* New Haven, CT: Yale University Press.

Bollier, D. (2014). *Think like a commoner: A short introduction to the life of the commons.* Gabriola Island, BC: New Society.

Bryant, J. A., Collins, M. W. & Atherton, M. A. (2007). *Design and information in biology: From molecules to systems.* Southampton, United Kingdom: WIT Press.

Costanza-Chock, S., Wagoner, M., Taye, B., Rivas, C., Schweidler, C., Bullen, G. & the T4SJ Project. (2018). *#MoreThanCode: Practitioners reimagine the* *landscape of technology for justice and equity*. Research Action Design & Open Technology Institute. Retrieved August 21, 2018, from https://morethancode.cc/T4SJ_fullreport_082018_AY_web.pdf.

Delfanti, A. (2018, August 16). Amazon is the new FIAT. *The worker and the union*, 3. Retrieved August 21, 2018, from http://notesfrombelow.org/article/amazon-is-the-new-fiat.

Easterling, K. (2014). *Extrastatecraft: The power of infrastructure space*. Brooklyn, NY: Verso.

Furnham, A. (1984). The protestant work ethic: A review of the psychological literature. *European Journal of Social Psychology, 14* (1), 87–104. DOI: https://doi.org/10.1002/ejsp.2420140108.

Hardt, M. & Negri, A. (2011). *Commonwealth*. Cambridge, MA: Belknap Press.

Himanen, P. (2010). *The hacker ethic: A radical approach to the philosophy of business*. New York, NY: Random House.

Kostakis, V. & Bauwens, M. (2014). *Network society and future scenarios for a collaborative economy*. London, United Kingdom: Palgrave Pivot.

Langley, P. & Leyshon, A. (2017). Platform Capitalism: The intermediation and capitalization of digital economic circulation. *Finance and Society, 3*(1), 11–31. DOI: https://doi.org/10.2218/finsoc.v3i1.1936.

Virno, P. (2008, June 22). *A grammar of the multitude: For an analysis of contemporary forms of life*. Retrieved August 28, 2018, from https://web.archive.org/web/20080622073210/http://www.generation-online.org/c/fcmultitude3.htm.

Weber, M., Baehr, P. & Wells, G. C. (2002). *The protestant ethic and the spirit of capitalism: And other writings*. New York, NY: Penguin Classics.

CHAPTER 5

State, Netocrats and the Commons: Developing a Cultural Policy in the Era of Platforms

Prodromos Tsiavos

Setting the scene

The question of how we see antiquities is not merely a sensory or factual question;[40] it is equally an existential, political as well as socially constructed and technologically mediated question. It is also a question that cannot be answered at the individual but rather at the collective level.[41] More than anything else, it is a question that while it may not define, it at least influences the way in which we handle, reproduce, and exist in relation to (cultural heritage) objects (Harman 2018).

An Athenian of the Ottoman period would incorporate an antiquity into his house; an Englishman doing the Grand Tour at the same time would bring some antiquities back home; a Greek political exile in Makronisos in the 1950s

---

[40] For a detailed discussion of the issue see Hamilakis 2013.

[41] Hamilakis (2007: 15–17) explores in detail the Anderson's (Anderson 2006) argument in relation to the role of imagined communities in the process of nation formation.

How to cite this book chapter:
Tsiavos, P. 2020. State, Netocrats and the Commons: Developing a Cultural Policy in the Era of Platforms. In Lekakis, S. (ed.) *Cultural Heritage in the Realm of the Commons: Conversations on the Case of Greece*. Pp. 109–126. London: Ubiquity Press. DOI: https://doi.org/10.5334/bcj.g. License: CC-BY

would be forced to build replicas of the Parthenon while confined in a concentration camp; an archaeologist in the 1970s would meticulously document and publish his excavation findings;[42] a film director or a researcher in the 2000s would request permission from the Central Archaeological Council in order to film or publish pictures from ancient Greek monuments; a Chinese tourist or a Greek pupil in the 2010s would search for the Acropolis in Google and Wikipedia before visiting them and share their pictures over Facebook and Instagram during their visit.

Antiquities live a rich, long and multifaceted life. Their sociomateriality[43] is subject to a continuous and rhizomatic transformation process that renders them continuously negotiable and contested, but also central to the collective imagination of the communities they relate to. There is a growing body of research exploring how antiquities constitute sociomaterial agents that form and are formed by the nation state. In this intellectual context, the way in which antiquities are seen, reproduced, surrogated, transformed and disseminated, becomes a question not merely relevant for the antiquities themselves but also for the modern nation and the multitude of its evolutionary trajectories.

The centrality of the antiquities and their core role as a device supporting the collective imagination of the nation state is astutely reflected in the provisions of the Greek Archaeological Law (Law 3028/2002),[44] particularly the sections regulating access, reproduction and the dissemination of such reproductions (Law 3028/2002: A. 46). It is in these provisions that we may identify in the clearest fashion the *effort* of the nation state to control not just the materiality of the antiquities, but also their symbolic dimension by setting conditions for their reproduction and imposing terms on how such reproductions are to be disseminated and published. Especially with regards to the latter, the law

---

[42] For an analysis of these examples see Hamilakis 2007.

[43] "Going forward, we suggest that further work is needed to theorize the fusion of technology and work in organizations, and that additional perspectives are needed to add to the palette of concepts in use. To this end, we identify a promising emerging genre of research that we refer to under the umbrella term: sociomateriality. Research framed according to the tenets of a sociomaterial approach challenges the deeply taken-for-granted assumption that technology, work, and organizations should be conceptualized separately, and advances the view that there is an inherent inseparability between the technical and the social" (Orlikowski & Scott 2008: 434). For an extensive overview of the concept of sociomateriality see (Scott & Orlikowski 2013; Orlikowski & Scott 2008).

[44] In this essay we focus solely on the Greek Archaeological Law 3028/2002. However, since the main elements of the Greek Archaeological law may be found in other jurisdictions (Morando & Tsiavos 2011), the main argument presented in this paper may be applicable in different contexts as well.

makes a series of assumptions in relation to the media landscape that is formed by the devices used to capture and reproduce the antiquities into surrogates. These assumptions extend to the mechanisms, infrastructures and institutions used to edit, reproduce and disseminate the outcome of the capturing process.

This process of translation of the technological landscape, the media technoscape of reproduction and dissemination, is not one that can be taken at face value. As Latour outlines, "there is no transportation without transformation" (Latour 1996: 119)[45] and in the case of the Greek Archaeological Law, only a fragment of technological methods have been legislated for in the Greek legal system. However, when one attempts to apply these provisions in a world that is technologically substantially different, a series of failures emerge. These are not merely failures of enforcing the law, but rather failures of enforcing the broader programme of a state-controlled building of the collective image of the nation-state.

It is important to highlight the two aspects of our main argument:

First, we maintain that the failures in the enforcement of the Archaeological Law are not merely instantiations of the classic problem of legal regulation trying to keep up with technological developments. Instead, we argue that these failures are rather the expression of a much deeper phenomenon: that of the clash between two distinct but very powerful forms of regulation, law and technology. These have different institutional pedigrees but compete with increasing force for dominance over the regulatory space of the nation-state. Thus, the regulation of antiquities, as a form of cultural heritage, becomes a symbolic arena within which the drama of regulatory competition between law and technology unravels.

Second, by "opening the black box of technology" (Winner 1993) and looking into the families of technologies that dominate the collective production of meaning, we are faced with the difficult question of cultural heritage policy making in a world of polycentric regulation. While this is normally posed as a question of how to tighten forms of hierarchical control of content dissemination, we argue that there is a need to devise strategies that take into account the dominance of new forms of digital and symbolic production. These are paradigmatically expressed in the netocratic[46] model of digital platforms and the

---

[45] "In the translation model, there is no transportation without transformation-except in those miraculous cases where everybody is in total agreement about a project" (Latour 1996: 119). See also Schmidgen on Latour: "At the same time, Latour's insistence on transmission as change can be read as a paraphrasing of an insight of the literary scholar and media theorist Marshall McLuhan: "Each form of transport not only carries, but translates and transforms, the sender, the receiver, and the message (McLuhan 1994: 90)" (Schmidgen 2014: 4).

[46] While the term "netocracy" and "netocrats" has been used by Alexander Bard and Jan Söderqvist (2002) in juxtaposition to "consumariat" in order to express the global upper class that is based on high-tech to draw global

sharing economy vis-à-vis the model of commons and peer based production (Benkler 2002; 2006).

Hence, the question of devising a national cultural heritage policy inevitably needs to take into account the fact that that the law is not the only, nor even the most powerful form of regulation. Moreover, classic hierarchy or control and command models of regulatory intervention (Baldwin et al. 2012) are not necessarily the optimum models for serving the objectives of a national narrative on cultural heritage, since sharing economy platforms and the commons dominate both material and immaterial modes of production. At the end of the day, the failures of classic regulatory intervention raise deeper questions over ownership of the nation state and the need to translate a plural, open and commons-based form of national identity into regulatory forms able to resist the ultranationalist, sectarianist and monocultural models of nationalism that digital platforms more often than not invite.

This paper is structured in the form of 'episodes', that is, snapshots of different artefacts, instances or technologies that highlight various facets of the phenomenon of the interaction or clash between the state, the commons and the netocratic platforms that allow us a better understanding of the framing within which contemporary cultural policy is formed and enacted.

Ways of seeing

How can we see the Parthenon today? The process of seeing a monument in our highly mediated society is one that starts before we even approach an antiquity. If we want to know what it is that we are going to visit, then we will search for it on Wikipedia. More precisely, we would carry out a Google search, which in all likelihood will provide us with Wikipedia as the primary source for a particular monument. Even if the relevant Wikipedia entry is not the first search result we get, it is from Wikipedia that the Google search results obtain the data necessary to provide us with an abstract of (a) what the Parthenon is; (b) where it is; (c) how to get there and the times during which we can visit it; (d) other related places and information that other individuals have searched, including images and critiques. The search will most likely be carried out on a mobile phone rather than a desktop or laptop and sometimes it might be during or after the actual visit.

The use of technologies to create representations or reproductions of antiquity is not new. There is a considerable body of literature on the subject of the use of photography as a means of constructing the image of antiquities in

---

power and domination. Our use of the term is to denote a wide range of platform (Gawer 2009) technologies that are based on crowdsourcing (Surowiecki 2005) or community type of activities in an extractive and exclusive manner.

tandem with the objectives and collective imaginary of the artist or society that produced such images (Derrida 2010; Szegedy-Maszak 2001). Similarly, representations of antiquities in paintings operate again as a device to represent the collective imaginary related to antiquities. In addition, once the fixation of the images is completed, the image itself demonstrates an agency, contributing to the collective imagination it chooses to serve. We need only look at the paintings of the Acropolis by the pre-Raphaelites, Nelly's images of Mona Paeva at the Acropolis, the representation of the Acropolis in images of the early 20th century or at the images on contemporary postcards and in textbooks. We could also look at the images of the Acropolis found on Facebook, Instagram, Flickr and Wikimedia Commons.

It is important at this stage to note that an approach to the images as something that stands alone as an artefact is extremely misleading. In order to unravel the Ariadne's thread that leads to an understanding of the framing that an image creates, it is necessary to appreciate it within the broader institutional ecology and dissemination system in which it exists. Nelly's images, for example, were shot to be published in the French magazine *Illustration de Paris* and then disseminated through a market system and a supply chain that involved the publisher, the printer, a dissemination network and shops where people could buy the magazines. We also need to appreciate that the consumption pattern of the magazine was such that it encouraged individual reading or sharing of the physical artefact of the magazine. Finally, those pictures had an afterlife as artworks, parts of the Benaki archive and private collections as well as through exhibitions and events, but also by being re-photographed digitally and placed in circulation anew over the internet.

The patterns of production and consumption of an early 20th century photograph differ substantially from the bulk of photography as it takes place today. The main difference is not merely the ease with which high quality photographs may be taken or the post-production that is possible today. These are important parameters that, as Manovic (Scott & Orlikowski 2013; Orlikowski & Scott 2008) has extensively explained, are framing – if not defining – our aesthetics and understanding of the represented subject. However, what makes the pictures we see on the internet substantially different from everything we have seen in the past is the whole life-cycle of their production and dissemination as well as the mass of the collections of which they are destined to become part of. The introduction of photographs on social media, initially with Facebook, Flickr and Pinterest, but particularly with Instagram has marked an entirely different form of representation: one that is both massive and relies to a large extent on the self-image or 'selfie culture', one that introduces a particular type of frame and filtering of the image through predefined options and one that is followed by – again – a predefined set of reactions or 'impressions' by other participants to those social networks that constantly assess and evaluate the image, the photographer and the humans and non-humans represented on those pictures. In addition, once the photograph is taken it is then placed in a rhizomatic (albeit well defined by algorithms) flow of information on multiple social media platforms and of course the almost unique access point for World Wide Web, i.e. the Google search engine. As such, the photograph becomes part of a massive and algorithmically mediated collection that begs for interpretation not as an isolated item but as part of a much greater, dynamic and controlled whole.

This framing of the image is quite different from what happens in the case of images contained in Wikipedia and Wikimedia Commons. The inclusion of an image in this context once again follows specific rules with regards to the technical specifications of the picture. However, the objective here is quite different: it is not the sharing of a personal moment but rather the search for objective or collectively accepted facts. As such, Wikipedia seeks to both present encyclopaedic entries following a very rigorous set of rules as to what is acceptable or not and to respect the rules regarding the provenance of the images uploaded, so that they conform to copyright and cultural heritage protection rules. In addition, the content found on Wikipedia and Wikimedia Commons is constantly and collectively edited and checked, through a set of common and transparent rules. Finally, this is content that, again, is part of a massive collection constituting the most commonly accessed form of factual resource on the Internet.

This digital ecosystem produced through different forms of mega-platforms, whether Google, Facebook and Instagram or Wikipedia, invites a form of image production and consumption that differs substantially from forms of picture taking we have seen in the past. It departs from picture taking of the past on at least four points. First, the technological framing of the picture in terms of specifications, filters or framings that the technological interface itself imposes. Second, it is an activity that happens through mobile devices throughout the life-cycle of a visit to an antiquity or its representation. Third, it is highly connected, interactive and collective irrespective of whether it is a personal story or the effort to construct a collectively acceptable fact. Fourth, the picture is experienced as part of a massive collection that is algorithmically mediated and thus made accessible to the recipient of the picture in ways that are not always transparent to the end user.

The State of the Law

No matter how appealing it may be, there is no such thing as a technology neutral law. The idea of drafting laws that focus on 'naked' human activity, stripped of any technological context has always been the Holy Grail for legislators and policy makers. However, it has also been an almost impossible task. Laws embody representations of technology precisely because they rely on technology's regulatory capacity to achieve their normative programme. Lessig, in his classics 'New Chicago School' (1998) and 'Code and other laws of cyberspace'

(1999), demonstrated with great clarity that laws, technologies, markets and norms not only interact but that such interactions are the essence of the contemporary regulatory landscape. In societies heavily mediated by technology, understanding the way in which such interactions between different modalities of regulation take place is an essential precondition for assessing the effectiveness and efficiency of both regulation and its underlying policies.

Law 3028/2002 is a classic case of a law that contains technological assumptions. This is particularly clear in the case of the Ministerial Decrees, based on the Archaeological law. These decrees[47] provide the detailed conditions for granting permission to access, reproduce and disseminate the reproductions of antiquities, found both in archaeological sites and museums. The representation of technology is most clearly illustrated in the different categories of acts of reproduction and dissemination that focus on specific types of media. What is even more interesting, is that the law also reflects different conceptualisations of how the market operates in relation to the circulation of reproductions of antiquities. More specifically, we may identify the following elements:

- Access to archaeological sites is divided into access solely for viewing and access for the reproduction of the archaeological artefact.
- Reproductions of the archaeological artefact are again divided into reproductions that are conducted with the use of 'professional equipment', for which a fee is required and other reproductions, for which no fee is required.
- Similarly, there are further categorisations of reproductions with reference to paper and electronic publications, dissemination through broadcast and internet technologies, reproduction for postcards, records, CDs and DVDs, labels, rubber stamps, leaflets, packaging, electronic cards, logos etc.
- Another element that also appears is that of profit, direct or indirect, particularly in relation to the dissemination of the reproductions. Similarly, the fee for the production of an audiovisual work is calculated on the basis of the costs of its production.
- There is a fee waiver in any case where the photography or video recording is used for the documentation of excavations and is conducted by the excavators or the researchers and where the funders have received the necessary licenses for the publication of the results. The fee is also waived when it takes place for purely academic and scientific purposes, such as teaching and documenting archaeological work. Finally, the fee is waived when it relates to a production of the Ministry of Culture and Sports.
- Accordingly, there is a waiver in the case of the use of reproductions, photographic and audiovisual, whose uses fall within the scope of the

---

[47] See Government Gazette (FEK) B' 1138/10.04.2012; Government Gazette (FEK) B' 648/7.3.2012; Government Gazette (FEK) B' 3046/30.12.2011; Government Gazette (FEK) B' 1491/27.10.2005.

Copyright limitations and exceptions, for publications of EU educational establishments, for limited editions by researchers and research institutions that serve and are addressed to the academic community, for PhD and postgraduate publications, for solely academic publications of the Greek Research Performing Organisations and The Archaeological Society at Athens, and for all the Ministry of Culture publications.

There are some clear technological and market assumptions in the Greek Archaeological Law:

- The distinction between amateur and professional photography is mostly based on the equipment and its technological capacities. However, as technology advances, technological features that previously could only be found in professional equipment are now present in almost every mobile phone. Similarly, certain types of digital capturing, such as aerial photographs and videos, while requiring permission, are increasingly taken by non-professionals, using portable devices or mini drones.
- Another criterion to assess whether a fee is required for the taking of photographs or video and their respective distribution is the direct or indirect flows of monetary value. Again, this is a classic market model, where the producer of the content or a distributor/disseminator that the photo producer contracts, gains revenue from the process of distributing the picture.
- The main technological/market assumption is that the dissemination of the content occurs through publishing, broadcasting or film dissemination. This means that the controlling mechanisms put in place by the law mostly focus on the dissemination intermediaries that are required to obtain the necessary permissions every time an act of publishing or distribution takes place.

While these three assumptions make sense in an environment of centralized and formalized collection and distribution of physical or digital surrogates of the antiquities, it makes little sense in a sharing economy or commons-based environment:

- The model of professional vs. amateur photo shooting is one that is difficult to assess since both the quality of equipment and monetary criteria are hard to establish.
- The model of revenue making as a criterion for providing a fee becomes one that is either not easy to enforce or requires specific sets of agreements. In the case of social media platforms, the person taking the picture is not the one that profits from it. While there is a heated legal debate as to the status of such providers, it is still accepted that they are Information Society Providers (ISPs) and as such they are not liable for the content trafficking

over their networks. Increasingly, however, they are required to put in place mechanisms to both ensure that the content uploaded is clear of any third-party Intellectual Property Rights (IPR) and General Data Protection Regulation (GDPR) compliant. This means that there is potential opportunity to impose similar conditions regarding the regulation of antiquities. However, this means that there must be special agreements between the social media companies and the state as how to deal with the dissemination of such content.

– The current system is built on the assumption of a single act of redistribution per licence from the Ministry of Culture. However, this is not how commons-based transaction operate. In the case of Wikipedia, for instance, there is a serious problem in relation to the operation of the licensing regime. The Creative Commons Attribution ShareAlike licence used by Wikipedia and Wikimedia Commons, where most photographs will be uploaded, allows for the downloading, creation of derivative works and redistribution of the work. As a result, while there may be a licence from the Ministry of Culture regarding the original uploading of the material on Wikipedia and its distribution from that point, additional licensing would in principle be required for the subsequent re-publishing and re-distribution of the same picture, as it would constitute a new act of dissemination. This would entail an endless chain of requests for licences from the Ministry or would render all Creative Commons Licences illegal.

– The reference to the Copyright notice as well as the limitations and exceptions as a means for not requiring a fee is rather problematic. The statement "copyright Ministry of Culture", which is a requirement for all images captured and disseminated by an applicant, would seem to imply the acquisition of copyright by the Ministry of Culture as a condition to provide a licence for accessing the content. While the use of real property as a mechanism for obtaining rights over the digitised surrogate is not a new phenomenon, it creates substantial enforcement issues. Moreover, the provision stipulating that the fee is waived in the case of uses falling under the limitations and exceptions of Greek Copyright law[48] is equally problematic. On the one hand it makes reference to a very limited set of uses that in most cases would not satisfy the needs of the person capturing the images. On the other hand, it would still require permission from the state in order to engage in such uses, something that would run contrary to the spirit and function of the limitations and exceptions mechanism, which is precisely intended to avoid the transaction costs of obtaining a licence.

– In order to obtain any of the required licences, it is necessary to go through an application process that is mostly off-line and requires a decision making

---

[48] See Law 2121/1993: A. 18–28C, Copyright, Related Rights and Cultural Issues Government Gazette (FEK) A' 1993.

process per application by the Central Archaeological Council (ΚΑΣ) (Law 3028/2002: A. 46 & 50). This imposes high transaction costs that, while they make sense in the context of professional reproduction and distribution, make little sense in the case of private use of content.

Overall, the clash between the provision of the Archaeological Law and the technological, market and licensing reality of the sharing and commons-based economies is evocative of the huge dilemma the Ministry of Culture is faced with. On the one hand, it could technically still try to implement the Archaeological Law provisions, by forcefully requiring the obtaining of all types of licensing and issuing cease and desist notices. The lack of control in the use of images of antiquities, as well as the loss of revenue are evident. However, the question of how to mitigate such losses remains open. A strategy of enforcement of the current regime may be highly problematic. It would not only entail substantial costs and require resources that the Ministry is doubtful it could spend, but it is also questionable whether such tactics would support the primary objectives of Law 3028/2002, namely the promotion of Greek culture, the protection of antiquities and the promotion of the image of Greece as intertwined with the antiquities in a continuous spectrum ranging from the prehistory to today.

Owning the Law

A first response to the inability of Law 3028/2002 to keep up with the changes in the technologies of capturing and digitally distributing surrogates of protected antiquities would be to amend the law so as to reflect more accurately the technological and market landscape of our times. While this is a reasonable response, it would only patch the problem. It would address its symptoms rather than its actual causes and, hence, obfuscate rather than resolve the problem.

An underlying assumption behind the Archaeological Law, as indeed behind most of our laws, is that law maintains the hegemony within the regulatory ecosystem. As we know from a range of regulatory theorists, from Easterbrook (1996), and Lessig (1996; 1998) to Brownsword (2005; 2006; 2008) and Black (2000; 2001; 2002), regulation is increasingly dominated by other forms of regulation, mostly technologies and the markets they sustain. It is the immediacy of technology as a regulatory form and its enforcement, unmediated by social meaning that renders it a supreme regulatory force, more often than not dominating the regulatory environments where the state is dwarfed by the techno-economic power of the originators of the technology. In addition, it is the characteristics of netocratic technologies, mostly sharing economy platforms, that enable them to exercise an almost irresistible force over the regulated subject and hence turn law into a second order if not insignificant source of regulation.

Platforms have some key characteristics that both accelerate and intensify their regulatory features. For example, when a search is made through the Google search engine, it is drawing from the collective experience of all previous searches ever made on this keyword before. In other words, it draws from and contributes to a form of commons that operates temporally and cyberspatially: it is affected and affects all searches that have ever been made. At the same time, it is also affected by the history of searches, the location of the individual and the other uses of services they have made in the past, as well as by Google's own confidential algorithm. In a sense, it contributes to a public and to a personal commons, but at the same time the mechanics of these commons and its constituting governing mechanism remain by and large opaque. Most importantly the ranking of the search is monetized by Google and sold as a service to third parties. In this sense, there is a degree of extraction that draws from the commons and nullifies them at the same time: it is commons-based, since it requires the collective interactions in order to draw the data that constitute the blood in the veins of the Google ecosystem; and it is extractive as it keeps sucking data produced by and large by all types of human activity, both individual and collective, it can lay its digital hands on. The more humans use Google's apps and services, the more the algorithm is fed with their data and provide services that are better and hence may attract more users.

This symbiotic relationship, which makes Google a counter-rival good, i.e. a good whose value increases with its use, is at the heart of its regulatory force. It is not merely the immediacy of the technology that only allows the user to follow its predetermined path, but it is the gradual incapacitation of the user to opt for another service, because of the network economics that makes Google a much more powerful regulator compared to the law: Google is a textbook example of the 'There Is No Alternative' dictum.

To make things even worse, the law and particularly the Archaeological Law has to face other forms of inevitabilities as well: the dominance of Google as a search engine and as a gateway to access the web makes any other distribution system subservient to it. The regulation of a digital publisher is relevant only after it is spotted by the user and Google controls its findability.

The case of most of social media platforms is pretty much the same, though the control they exercise over the search and display of results is much greater than that of Google's: it is not only the search and display algorithm they control, but the entirety of the environment. The extraction here is much more unhindered and the devices of control much more obscure. In fact, both in the case of Instagram and Facebook, the revelation of the mechanisms of searching and displaying, i.e. the basic operation of the algorithm, is only revealed to the extent it is necessary to fulfil the respective corporate programme of action.

It is necessary here to ponder a bit more on this aspect of controlled revelation.

The items that remain in the commons on these platforms are mostly third party content or more specifically hyperlinks to the URIs of third party content, plus a minor contribution by the end user in the form of either a search (as is the case of Google Search) or a comment/ post (as is the case in social media). It is the collective and individual choices of content over time that are shared but, as we have seen, in a rather filtered way: the result of these contributions, the digital information commons that is created from these choices and actions is not shared with everyone or with the same terms. It is the information asymmetry that characterizes netocracies, which is expressed in a three tier pyramid: at the top there are the owners of the platform who extract the entirety of the information and use it as they wish; at the middle layer there are the commercial users who buy aggregate information, usually packaged as a service, as well as the way in which information is displayed to the end user; at the bottom of the pyramid are all the users whose activity, including even biodata, is continuously harvested in order to produce value for all three layers of the pyramid. The flows of data and value are inverse: the users provide all the data and get a minimum of value, the professional users are buying data and attention and provide some data and the netocrats obtain both data and monetary value and they offer as a service the platform that produces value for them.

The revelation of the workings of the algorithm has a regulatory quality: as the professional users are instructed as to the operation of the algorithm, they alter their behaviour in order to correspond to its function and maximise the value produced for them, mostly to maximise the exposure of their products and services and achieve specific results (e.g. tickets, purchases, views, interactions etc.). The user is also instructed as to how the algorithm operates through the use of the service and adjusts their behaviour accordingly, e.g. by altering the nature of the posts in order to achieve the impressions or the following they desire.

Such is the totality of these platforms that there is very little space left for the law to operate. This is apparent in the ways in which search results that rank and are depicted on Google or hashtags operate in the context of social networks. How can the State achieve control of the collective imaginary through the control of the dissemination of image(s) of antiquity, when the distribution network is totally outside its control? How is it possible for the law to retain its regulatory supremacy when the state from which it derives its power is in the best-case scenario positioned only at the middle layer of the netocrats information/value pyramid? How can the state be seen as the hegemonic source of regulation, when it struggles to increase its ranking in Google search results or appear in hashtags the production and value of which it does not control?

Rhizomes of Regulation

Appreciating that the regulation of the making and distribution of images of antiquities is positioned within a polycentric rather than a state-driven environment is perhaps the first and most important realisation required for the development of a consistent cultural heritage policy. This is not just a question of how to regulate a set of technologies, but rather how to interact with another source of regulation that is, if not of more, then at least of equal power.

The particular regulatory features that platforms have make them a particularly strong regulatory source, with their own programme of action and enforcement tools. This is not something that has evaded the attention of policy makers and legislators. While platforms in their original form have been exempted from liability, especially in the context of Intellectual Property Rights, through the World Intellectual Property Organisation (WIPO) treaties (Adams 1997) and the e-commerce Directive (European Parliament and The Council 2001), there is increasing discussion as to whether we need to reconsider such legislation in order to exercise a greater form of control over them. This is an interesting trend, since it marks a transition from a generation of legal instruments that saw Internet Service Providers as private sources of enforcement and encouraged them to create their own mini-regulatory regimes in order to handle primarily IPR infringements in return for their lack of liability to a new generation of laws that sought to increase their level of liability and position them within the regulatory regime of the law.

The recent draft Copyright Directive (European Commission 2016) is an example of such an approach: it imposes upon platforms the obligation to clear any content before it is uploaded on their servers, especially when it is then shared by its users. This kind of legislation explicitly acknowledges, first that the value created for platform owners stems from the sharing and interactions of their users and that these, in turn, are facilitated by the content they share. Hence, the draft copyright directive argues, there must be some sort of revenue sharing of the platforms with the original owners of the material. This approach reflects the value structure of the European economy, which is much stronger in content creation compared to platform ownership, is also a clear appreciation of the regulatory strength of platforms as well as an effort to combine the State's regulatory programme of action with that of the platforms: if the latter wish to lawfully extract value from users, then, first, they need to share revenue with the content owners and second, submit to the regulatory force of the state regulators by increasing their liability.

This is not an isolated regulatory intervention. We have seen similar types of regulatory responses in cases such as Uber, where it is obliged to conform to labour and transport regulations, AirBnB in terms of paying city taxes and collaborating with the tax and planning authorities and all social media platforms in relation to their compliance with the GDPR. What is common in all of these cases is the tacit appreciation of the regulatory force that these platforms have, the concerted effort to make them comply with the rule of law and the aim to protect the relevant industries and markets that are threatened by the rise of the techno-markets that platforms constitute. What is also common in all these efforts is that they are most successful when they occur at a mass scale level that goes either beyond the nation state (e.g. the EU) or involves mega-national jurisdictions, such as the US or China. In all of these cases scale matters in order to be able to meaningfully negotiate with platforms that have hundreds of millions of users and budgets that surpass those of an average nation-state. Size, here, matters precisely because of the market that brings with it and the regulatory capacity that they themselves carry.

However, this type of approach means that a country the size of Greece can only operate in terms of its cultural policy response within the framework of the regulatory tools and policy framework of the EU. Any intervention that is solely local and does not in one way or another bootstrap on the EU level is destined to fail or have the exact opposite effect. For instance, a regulatory response banning pictures of the Acropolis from Google or Instagram, is not really possible in terms of enforcement costs. In this case, the individual users would have been targeted and it would be almost impossible to defend it legally in all the jurisdictions solely by means of Greek legislation.

This is, of course, not a source of major surprise. Even in the case of the regulation of classical antiquities, while the content of it remains in the competency of the Greek state, it is hugely influenced by other policies, mostly financing, infrastructure and environmental policies. The way in which funding is channeled for most restoration works is through the Greek Regional Authorities and the Ministry of Development, following the regulatory framework and priorities of the Greek Partnership Agreement (Partnership Agreement 2016) as approved by the EU. In a practical sense this means that the funding, which operates a form of signaling and hence regulation for the state agencies and services, again does not stem directly from the Archaeological Service, nor is it possible to be seen as a purely sectoral or isolated Greek policy.

Similarly, a new cultural heritage policy for global mega platforms can only be seen and implemented in the framework of the broader EU platform policies (Goudin & European Added Value Unit 2016). This 'Cost of Non-Europe' study examines the current economic, social and legal state of play regarding the sharing economy in the European Union, and identifies the cost of the lack of further European action in this field. The assessment of existing EU and national legislation confirms that there are still significant implementation gaps and areas of poor economic performance. The subsequent examination of areas where it was believed that an economic potential exists highlighted that substantial barriers remain, hindering the achievement of the goals set out in the existing legislation. Moreover, some issues are not or are insufficiently addressed (e.g. status of workers employed by sharing economy service providers and in the same way that it acted in relation to Copyright law almost two decades ago, it needs to do the same now understanding this as a horizontal rather than sectoral policy. It needs to focus on developing strategies of regulation and negotiation with mega platforms emphasizing liability, licensing of operation, reporting and flow of value to the Archaeological Service.

Another policy trend which is of equal value and importance is the dual practice of supporting and encouraging the free flow of data while regulating it in order to conform to the policy objectives of state or super-state regulators. Such policies appreciate the need to increase the flow of data with the minimum transaction costs, while ensuring that the state regulatory programmes are respected and advanced. The EU Digital Single Market (DSM) policies (European Commission 2017) are an exemplary case of this trend, particularly the initiatives related to the building of European Data Economy, such as the PSI Directive, the Regulations for the Free Flow of Personal and non-Personal Data, the European Open Science Cloud and the Communication "Towards a common European data space". All of these policies and regulatory measures have as an underlying assumption the need to increase low transaction cost flows of data within the European Union, while ensuring that the services offered by non-EU providers conform to the policies set out by the regulators with respect to IPR ownership, confidentiality, personal data protection, competition law rules and other sectoral legislation.

While such regulations that increase the flow of data are necessary for the development of most of the services provided by the mega platforms and in that sense eradicate the regulatory power of the state, at the same time they are essential for the existence and growth of the commons. It is in this growth of the Commons, as expressed in Wikipedia and Wikimedia Commons, Free and Open Source Software (FOSS) or open scientific content that the state will be able to produce or cultivate its narrative: by providing access to the monuments for which it is the custodian and allowing for their reproduction with conditions of proper referencing as well as of further sharing of the surrogate on the same terms and conditions as the original surrogate.

These conditions allow for the maximum circulation of the work, which reinforces the narrative of the producer of the picture while ensuring referencing to the locus of the creation of the collective imaginary, that is the state. Even in the case of extractive platforms that own the regulatory habitat within which their users interact and produce value, there is still a communication and interaction commons that the platform uses in order to extract value from the users, whereas the state could use it in order to support the types of meaning and symbolic value it wishes to promote.

This requires a set of regulatory devices and techniques that are substantially different from the ones now at hand: it is essential to focus on maximizing access to digital surrogates with proper referencing at a close to zero transaction cost rather than broad prohibitions of access with limited interest on how referencing is effected; to seek moderation and instigation in the production of meaning through working with communities rather than approving and controlling access to space and content; to negotiate at all possible levels with netocrats, while always attempting to deploy the EU policy toolkits and frameworks; to appreciate and accept the regulatory power of mega-platforms and hold them liable for the actions which are monitored and are taking place over their platforms; to appreciate the role of the materiality of the monument and the interplay of the monument with local communities, the civil society and the markets in order to increase the leverage against the netocrats.

The existence of a polycentric regulatory landscape (Bell 1991/1992; 1998) signifies the transition of the function of regulation from a means of state policy implementation to a domain of conflicting or colluding regulatory regimes and modalities. While the regulatory positioning of platform technologies, is clearly privileged in a techno-market driven context, the nation-state, supranational formations like the EU or mega-jurisdictions such as the US or China are likely to reassert their regulatory role through the concentrated targeting of the netocrats at all possible levels. This reaction, which we have seen forcefully and under different strategic models in the US, China and the EU, is likely to become more consolidated in the future. As the regulatory wars saga unravels, the positioning of small/medium states, such as Greece, that still wish to form a national rhetoric can only be sustained within the broader regulatory formations that envelope their action. Whether their control of images as a form of control of the collective imaginary of the nation community will persevere remains an open question. The only certainty is that the battle for regulatory dominance has just begun; and the state is not the only game in town.

Bibliography

Adams, J. N. (1997). WIPO: Intellectual property. *European Intellectual Property Review, 19*(4), 113–116.

Anderson, B. (2006). *Imagined communities: Reflections on the origin and spread of nationalism.* London, United Kingdom: Verso.

Baldwin, R., Cave, M. & Lodge, M. (2012). *Understanding regulation: Theory, strategy, and practice.* New York, NY: Oxford University Press.

Bard, A. & Söderqvist, J. (2002). *Netocracy: The new power elite and life after capitalism.* London, United Kingdom: Reuters/Pearsall.

Bell, T. (1991/1992). Polycentric law. *Humane Studies Review, 7*(1). Retrieved November 20, 2019, from https://theihs.org/w91issues/.

Bell, T. (1998). Polycentric law in the new millennium. Retrieved November 20, 2019, from http://www.tomwbell.com/writings/FAH.html.

Benkler, Y. (2002). Coase's Penguin, or Linux and the nature of the firm. The *Yale Law Journal, 112,* 369–446.

Benkler, Y. (2006). *The wealth of networks: How social production transforms markets and freedom.* New Haven, CT: Yale University Press.

Black, J. (2000). Proceduralising regulation: Part I. *Oxford Journal of Legal Studies, 20*(4), 597–614.

Black, J. (2001). Proceduralising regulation: Part II. *Oxford Journal of Legal Studies, 21,* 33–58.

Black, J. (2002). Regulatory conversations. *Journal of Law and Society, 29*(1), 163–196. DOI: https://doi.org/10.1111/1467-6478.00215.

Brownsword, R. (2005). Code, control, and choice: Why East is East and West is West. *Legal Studies, 25*(1), 1–21.

Brownsword, R. (2006). Neither East nor West, is mid-West best? *Script-Ed, 3*(1), 15–33. DOI: https://doi.org/10.2966/scrip.030106.15.

Brownsword, R. (2008). *Rights, regulation, and the technological revolution.* Oxford, United Kingdom: Oxford University Press.

Derrida, J. (2010). *Athens, still remains: The photographs of Jean-François Bonhomme.* New York, NY: Fordham University Press.

Easterbrook, F. H. (1996). Cyberspace and the Law of the Horse. *University of Chicago Legal Forum, 207–216.*

European Commission. (2016). *Proposal for a directive of the European Parliament and of the Council on copyright in the digital single market, Pub. L. No. COM(2016)593.* Retrieved September 7, 2018, from https://ec.europa.eu/digital-single-market/en/news/proposal-directive-european-parliament-and-council-copyright-digital-single-market.

European Commission. (2017). *Digital single market.* Retrieved September 7, 2018, from https://ec.europa.eu/commission/priorities/digital-single-market_en.

European Parliament and The Council. (2001). Directive 2000/31/EC of the European parliament and of the Council of 8 June 2000 on certain legal aspects of information society services, in particular electronic commerce, in the Internal Market ('Directive on electronic commerce'), *Official Journal of the European Communities, L. 178,* 1–16.

Gawer, A. (Ed.). (2009). *Platforms, markets and innovation.* Cheltenham, United Kingdom: Edward Elgar. DOI: https://doi.org/10.4337/9781849803311.

Goudin, P. & European Added Value Unit. (2016). *The cost of non-Europe in the sharing economy: economic, social and legal challenges and opportunities.* Brussels, Belgium: European Union. Retrieved September 7, 2018, from http://bookshop.europa.eu/uri?target=EUB:NOTICE:QA0116059:EN:HTML.

Hamilakis, Y. (2007). *The nation and its ruins: Antiquity, archaeology, and national imagination in Greece.* Oxford, United Kingdom: Oxford University Press.

Hamilakis, Y. (2013). *Archaeology and the senses: Human experience, memory, and affect.* Cambridge, United Kingdom: Cambridge University Press.

Harman, G. (2018). *Object-oriented ontology: A new theory of everything.* London, United Kingdom: Pelican.

Latour, B. (1996). *Aramis, or the love of technology.* Cambridge, MA: Harvard University Press.

Law 3028/2002. *On the protection of antiquities and cultural heritage in general.* Retrieved November 20, 2019, from https://www.bsa.ac.uk/wp-content/uploads/2018/11/Archaeological-Law-3028-2002.pdf.

Lessig, L. (1996). The zones of cyberspace. *Stanford Law Review*, 48(May), 1403–1411.

Lessig, L. (1998). The new Chicago school. *The Journal of Legal Studies*, 27(S2), 661–691.

Lessig, L. (1999). *Code and other laws of cyberspace*. New York, NY: Basic Books.

Manovich, L. (2001). *The language of new media*. Cambridge, MA: MIT Press.

McLuhan, M. (1994). *Understanding media: The extensions of man*. Cambridge, MA: MIT Press.

Morando, F. & Tsiavos, P. (2011). *Diritti sui beni culturali e licenze libere (ovvero, di come un decreto ministeriale può far sparire il pubblico dominio in un paese)*. Retrieved September 7, 2018, from https://www.researchgate.net /publication/256034821_Diritti_sui_beni_culturali_e_licenze_libere _ovvero_di_come_un_decreto_ministeriale_puo_far_sparire_il_pubblico _dominio_in_un_paese_Cultural_Heritage_Rights_and_Open_Licenses _ie_How_a_Ministerial_Decre.

Orlikowski, W. J. & Scott, S. V. (2008). Sociomateriality: Challenging the separation of technology, work and organization. *The Academy of Management Annals*, 2(1), 433–474. DOI: https://doi.org/10.5465/19416520802211644.

Partnership Agreement. (2016, February 22). *Partnership Agreement (PA) 2014–2020*. Retrieved September 7, 2018, from https://www.espa.gr/en /Pages/staticPartnershipAgreement.aspx.

Schmidgen, H. (2014). *Bruno Latour in pieces: An intellectual biography*. New York, NY: Fordham University Press.

Scott, S. V. & Orlikowski, W. J. (2013). Sociomateriality — taking the wrong turning?: A response to Mutch. *Information and Organization*, 23(2), 77–80. DOI: https://doi.org/10.1016/j.infoandorg.2013.02.003.

Surowiecki, J. (2005). *The wisdom of crowds*. Washington, DC: Anchor.

Szegedy-Maszak, A. (2001). Felix Bonfils and the traveller's trail through Athens. *History of Photography*, 25(1), 13–43. DOI: https://doi.org/10.1080 /03087298.2001.10443433.

Winner, L. (1993). Upon opening the black box and finding it empty: Social constructivism and the philosophy of technology. *Science, Technology, & Human Values*, 18(3), 362–378.

CHAPTER 6

"Capture and Release of the Chthonic Beasts": Archaeological Heritage as Digital Commons in Contemporary Art Practice. Various Thoughts on the Occasion of the Artwork 'Future Bestiary'

Marina Markellou and Petros Moris

This chapter is a formal attempt at an unstructured informal exchange of opinions and thoughts between Marina and Petros on the occasion of Petros' art show titled 'Future Bestiary'. Through this specific case study, the aesthetic, artistic and ethical impact of contemporary artistic practices that transgress the traditional notions of originality and authenticity were explored, while questions about how digital creations are controlled through Copyright Law and the Archaeological Law and how Intellectual Property is managed were also raised. The rise of contemporary art practices such as that of Petros', clearly inspired by archaeological heritage, produces unprecedented and unusual digital reconstructions through prompts to reconsider the fundamental structure of traditional legal systems and move towards an alternative legal framework that enables creativity in a collaborative fashion.

How to cite this book chapter:
Markellou, M. and Moris, P. 2020. "Capture and Release of the Chthonic Beasts":
Archaeological Heritage as Digital Commons in Contemporary Art Practice.
Various Thoughts on the Occasion of the Artwork 'Future Bestiary'. In Lekakis, S.
(ed.) *Cultural Heritage in the Realm of the Commons: Conversations on the Case of
Greece*. Pp. 127–140. London: Ubiquity Press. DOI: https://doi.org/10.5334/bcj.h.
License: CC-BY

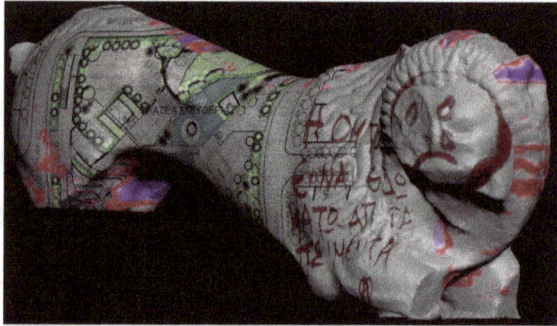

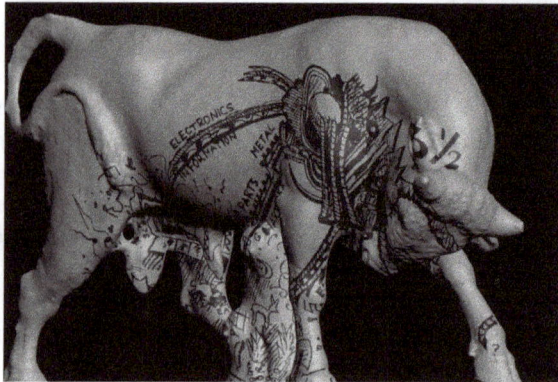

Figures 1, 2, 3: Petros Moris, Future Bestiary, 2019, HD video projection (5:00) (Source: PM).

Future Bestiary

The work 'Future Bestiary' is a video-projection that could be perceived as a type of fragmented, open-ended visual essay. The primary material that makes up this digitally animated narrative was gathered by Petros during an autumn afternoon around the idyllic archaeological site of Kerameikos ancient cemetery, and its adjacent elegant museum in the centre of Athens.

The primary material of 'Future Bestiary' is a series of photogrammetric documentations, rendered within the video as three-dimensional digital forms. The original subjects of these forms come from the funerary sculptures of Kerameikos. More specifically, they focus on the mythical and naturalistic animal sculptures that once adorned the ancient cemetery, inducing depictions of a molossian hound, sphinxes, lions and a mighty bull. This system of sculptural forms is understood here as a type of chthonic bestiary, which is lined up sequentially throughout the video in the form of rotating three-dimensional depictions. In the video, these perpetually rotating digital surfaces, which emerged by means of the photogrammetric process, become the 'canvas' for the inclusion of visual elements recovered online. These elements find their way onto the 3D reconstructions via an 'intrusive' style, simulating immaterial graffiti, tattoos, talismans or other graphic typologies.

In this way, the digital reconstructions of the ancient forms become a system of mnemonic ethereal bodies, onto which the fantasies and mythologies that concern realities of the present and speculations of the future are inscribed. More specifically, these are prospects, fears and desires that concern the future of the city of Athens, a future which is evoked here through references to urban development projects, technological innovations, algorithmic economic systems, social upheavals and cultural metamorphoses. Beyond providing an informational and narrative layer that orchestrates the conceptual premise and aesthetic character of the work, this series of visual projections functions inevitably as an 'iconoclastic' gesture, a simulated 'defacement'. As is the case with the non-destructive technique of documentation and reproduction involved in photogrammetry, this equally immaterial, non-destructive gesture further hybridises the perplexed status of these digital clones of archaeological remains, of this 'captured' and 'released' cultural material. It also triggers a further exploration of the essence and affordances of cultural heritage in the Greek context.

The photogrammetric technique and its affordances

If we set aside this additional layer of artistic conceptual and formal remix for a moment, we can see that, for a significant part, the complications that can be found in the way 'Future Bestiary' deals with material cultural heritage lie in the nature of the photogrammetric technique itself. Photogrammetry is a non-destructive technology used to derive accurate 3D metric and descriptive object information from photographs. It is a well-established technique for archaeological documentation and cultural heritage conservation, as it provides a precise method of acquiring three-dimensional information relating to sculptures, cultural monuments and historical sites (Al-Ruzouq 2012). In recent years, photogrammetric processing has been used as a basis for further analysis and interpretation of cultural goods from an artistic perspective.

There is a telling semiology in the alternative terminology for the technique of photogrammetry, known as Structure-from-Motion. As its most common applications would suggest, one can imagine a bodily and active practice, a process of corporeal motion around objects, involving a series of repetitive photographic shots from different angles. This fundamentally 'analogue' element of human motion, bound always to physical and cultural aspects, introduces us to an overall set of particular, non-quantifiable attributes, a series of complexities of the photogrammetric practice.

Indeed, in contrast to other hi-precision, non-destructive documentation tools, such as laser scanning, there is a significant degree of estimation that takes place in photogrammetry; a logic that suggests a special kind of 'interpretative' quality. This has to do, in the first place, with the relative inconsistency of the primary photographic material that is used in the digital reconstruction process. Photography is highly sensitive to the shifting environmental light conditions that are to be found in open-air and non-studio spaces, while it is also subject to a variety of photographic glitches that usually originate from reflective, transparent or complex surfaces. The algorithmic architecture of photogrammetric software, based on the fundamental rules of trigonometry and stereoscopy, tackles these inconsistencies with an estimative approach, attempting to reconstruct the original object by closing gaps, bridging inconsistencies and filling up whatever information has been accidentally left out during the photographic documentation. This has the result of creating a number of divergences from the actual three-dimensional topology of the original object. Often these divergences take the form of structural distortions, or even empty holes on the digital surfaces that make up the resulting 3D file. One could easily suggest that the reconstructed digital objects gain a 'ghostly' character from this algorithmic process, inherently imperfect, inevitably incomplete.

It is true that many of these faults can be prevented through the careful and experienced planning and execution of the documentative part of the process. This is often the case for scientific applications of the technique, although – as already explained – the limits of the photographic apparatus and the contingencies created by an uncontrolled environment will inevitably introduce inaccuracies.

The deficiencies of photogrammetry would not concern us further, were it to be solely dealt with within a professional scientific context. However, photogrammetry is a digital technique that has recently become increasingly popularized to the general public through a number of proprietary and open source software platforms and even more so through the launch of several mobile apps. In many cases, these apps or desktop software platforms simplify the overall process through accessible interfaces and playful instructions while, most importantly, outsourcing the demanding computational work that photogrammetric reconstruction requires to the digital Cloud. It is important to note here that this momentum of democratization in photogrammetry has been closely related to another field of the (post) digital market (Campbell et al. 2011). This is none other than the expanding industry of inexpensive desktop 3D printers and the variants of plastic-based filament materials that these machines use as consumables. Marketed to a broad public of non-professionals as a hobby aligned to the general character of the 'makers culture', cheap desktop computer-aided-manufacturing has been increasingly entering classrooms, workshops and households alike over the last decade. As this target group of customers is not necessarily familiar or experienced with 3D design, the printable content comes, more often than not, from online repositories that provide open source, free, or payable 3D models, or simple template-based apps that let their users customize already existing designs.

Given these limited options, it is obvious how simplified photogrammetry applications have strategically infiltrated this maker-culture industry as a tool that allows for a more intimate and interactive audience engagement with digital crafting and desktop manufacturing: the ease of reconstructing a familiar physical object in digital form through the common practice of taking photographs with a smartphone adds greatly to a personalised creative and productive experience, stirring the cultural fantasy of a 'cloning' type of mechanical reproduction. What is important to note here is that the popularisation of similar maker-culture tools and practices provides a novel context to think about the current state of technological appropriation and reproduction, which calls for an overall updating of our theoretical, cultural and legal understandings. Needless to say, it was also inevitable that such techniques would diffuse into contemporary art practices, not only because of their growing cultural relevance, but also as they are tools that make accessible and sustainable production techniques that were until recently only offered as expensive services by specialised rapid-prototyping studios or through acquiring unapproachable unattainable industry-grade equipment.

However, one must ask what is the nature of usage of such digital production techniques by the general public? Experienced users and amateurs of digital technological trends have been using such accessible 3D reconstruction applications for various purposes and for a plethora of subjects. A typical search on 3D model online-sharing repositories (e.g. Scan The World, Sketchfab and many more) reveals a focus on themes such as small-scale design objects or knickknacks, human portraits, sleeping pets, as well as museum exhibits or public sculptures. It is true that, apart from the engaging process of constructing such digital objects, the actual cases of (re)usage of such 3D files in further creative projects remains a study that has still to be pursued in a critical way. However, in most cases it is easy to obtain some information on the files' popularity by, for example, consulting download-count statistics or comment-posts showcasing derivative projects. As mentioned above, downloading such files for 3D-printing is a possible type of usage, speculating that mixing these 3D files in visual compositions, gifs or other type of digital animations is another possible application. However, the technical expertise needed to manipulate such formats, especially in contrast to common bitmap images or sound files, renders debatable the degree of utility or relevance of such digital 'offerings'. It would appear that, for the moment, the capturing, sharing and collection processes of casual photogrammetric files remains an end in itself for the casual user, driven by the enthusiasm and relative ease, attributed to the non-professional usage of the technique. When it comes to artistic production, on the other hand, the subjects and applications of the photogrammetric technique can be considered more broad and ambitious in relation to their subjects and scope. In recent years, artists have been increasingly using photogrammetry as an alternative to custom-made or ready-made 3D models, usually welcoming the technological limitations (or working around them) in order to either use its products as intermediate stages for analogue sculptural production (as mere references or 3D-printed artefacts), or as elements for the composition of digital videos and interactive or virtual narratives.[49]

If the general or specialized audiences consider the current (or better inherent) technical limitations of photogrammetry as a small price to pay for getting one step closer to the productive emancipation promised by the imaginary of the desktop-industrial-revolution, 'Future Bestiary' embraces them wholeheartedly. For the work, the three-dimensional faults and structural distortions are employed in a contemplative and critical manner, towards the introduction of a fluid, impartial and transformative aesthetic that rewires movements and hierarchies between the material and the digital. In other words, the technical slippage becomes part of an aesthetic style and a conceptual inquiry into the relationships between original and copy. And it does so by embracing the composite nature of this interpretative technical process: a synergy between bodily subjectivity, material complexity, technological limitations and algorithmic automation.

Heritage implications

This interpretative logic, inherent in the way we have been producing and experiencing representational images and reproductions since early modernity, is not novel or without historical precedent. However, its technical specificities call for a more multifaceted and entangled inquiry into the scientific, academic and legal discourse concerning the documentation and use of cultural heritage. For once we have to consider the implications of a general understanding of

---

[49] Examples of artists and filmographers utilizing photogrammetry include Morehshin Allahyari, Timur Si-Qin, Hito Steyerl, Clement Valla and Liam Young among many others.

machine vision; the approach of algorithmic automation towards a novel kind of gaze (Steyerl 2016). This debate goes beyond any technical or physical limitations of our devices, since it is in fact a domain of computer engineering that implies design decisions of practical, but also ideological nature.

The special question that arises in the context of this article's premise, is what is the nature, status and implications of the production and distribution of these digital 3D objects created by photogrammetry (and by extension, through other 3D scanning techniques), when their subject is an object of cultural heritage? If it were possible to somehow filter the total amount of existent digital content that derives from three-dimensional documentation of cultural heritage, it would be possible to observe three basic categories: a) 3D models that are produced by institutional and scientific initiatives related to archaeology, preservation or museology, b) 3D models that were created by ordinary users (cultural heritage enthusiasts, museum-goers, tech enthusiasts and anyone that might experiment with such technologies as an alternative to taking normal photos or videos of historic artifacts) and c) artists and other cultural producers working within the creative industries (from 3D animators to cinematographers, graphic designers and so on).

To some degree, it is easy to distinguish the intentions behind each category, as well as to imagine the respective applications and even assume the level of quality and precision attributed to the outcomes produced in the different cases of researchers, the general public and art professionals. However, quality and precision aside, all of this digital material comprises an overall ecology of documentative representations that, as we suggest, maintains an unprecedented potentiality of current and future applications that can generate further reproductions not limited in the digital realm. Even if we keep the conversation about the implications of digital documentation, editing and distribution of cultural heritage within the limited and privileged discourse of artistic production, the cartography of such an ecology is still important, since it reveals an overall techno-cultural tendency of an ongoing, massive and complex project of digitisation of cultural heritage. This process is at the same time both 'accidental' and systematic, bringing together the activity of the general public, of institutional endeavours and corporate forces. Some illustrative projects within this trend, showcasing theoretically contrasting ideologies and attitudes towards their subject, are the totalitarian efforts of the Google Arts & Culture project (spanning from digitisation to 3D reconstruction of cultural artefacts, the production of virtual versions museum spaces, mass archiving and online content curation) and the Perpetuity | Palmyra project, which attempted to reconstruct a 3D model of the Arch of Triumph of Palmyra destroyed by ISIS in 2015, by using a photogrammetry field with photographs taken by tourists before the event.[50]

---

[50] See https://the-arckives.org. Last accessed July 2019.

How can one evaluate such a technical process in relation to what we already know about media distribution and reproduction? It would seem that it becomes even more complex on a technical level. It is revealing to just take note of one practical aspect of the photogrammetric technique: once a digital photogrammetric reconstruction is obtained in the form of a 3D file, the collection of digital photographs that were used as primary material can be (and usually are) discarded. This leaves us with a three-dimensional reproduction with no familiar documentation source, as it would be the case with photography for example, which has already been debated broadly in relation to the question of its potential to mechanically reproduce cultural material.[51] What we obtain here is a 'unique object', with no familiar traceable past, a generated mathematical abstraction brought into existence only by a visual reference to an original counterpart, a reference that does not exist anymore. In contrast, this dynamic format of the 3D file provides us the possibility for a new series of reproductive activities, such as the translation to new material objects through computer-aided-manufacturing discussed above.

Perhaps, this idiosyncratic character of the photogrammetric technique, its inability to provide us with a) exact technical representations b) familiar media formats that have already been debated in relation to their reproductive status and c) its fluent ability to generate new reproductive potentials, could be a crucial opportunity for a discussion beyond the technical and institutional characteristics that the issue of usage of cultural heritage has been officially built upon. If our technical apparatuses can bring us with such ease in front of extremely hybrid and transformative examples of the original-copy scheme, then questions of technical resolution and quality, of professional and profit-oriented usage and of cultural heritage could start being replaced with more broad and fundamental ones. What are the novel cultural potentials of our digital reproductions? To whom do they belong intellectually and legally as cultural material? What does the possibility for their further accessibility and dissemination mean in a practical sense?

Legal implications

Petros Moris' artwork 'Future Bestiary' perfectly reflects this artistic practice of using the image of pre-existing culturally significant works of art and re-contextualizing them. For Petros, the exploration of the Structure-from-Motion photogrammetric technique and its incorporation into his creative process transgresses the boundaries between materiality and immateriality,

---

[51] See for example the seminal essay by Walter Benjamin, 'The Work of Art in the Age of Mechanical Reproduction'.

challenging the notions of reproduction and authenticity as traditionally perceived by legal scholars.

Within this framework, some interesting questions regarding the interpretation of heritage accessibility from a legal standpoint may arise. What are the
implications of the emergence of these contemporary artistic practices for cultural heritage appropriation? How does the Greek legislation on antiquities
and cultural heritage deal with this issue in general?[52] In other words, could a
hypothesis for increased cultural heritage preservation along with that of cultural heritage accessibility for artistic purposes be envisaged?

Greek Archaeological Law 3028/2002 "on the protection of antiquities and
cultural heritage in general" broadens the scope of cultural heritage protection
as it provides an extensive definition of cultural objects as "testimonies of the
existence and the individual and collective creativity of human kind" (A.2) and
it covers manifestations of both tangible and intangible cultural heritage.

Article 46 of the Greek legislation regulates the accessibility and use of
"monuments"[53] and sites. According to the paragraphs 4 and 5 of article 46
of the Archaeological Law 3028/2002, a previous permission granted by the
Ministry of Culture is required for the production, reproduction and dissemination to the public of impressions, copies or depictions of monuments
belonging to the Public Sector, or immovable monuments that are located
within archaeological sites and historical places or are isolated, or movable
monuments that are kept in museums or public collections, in any way and by
any means whatsoever, including ICT. Such permission is granted to natural or
legal persons for a fee paid to the Fund of Archaeological Proceeds (TAP) upon
decision of the Minister of Culture, while the decision also specifies the temporal validity of the permission, the terms on which the permission is granted and
the fee that must be paid. The production, reproduction and use of the aforementioned goods for other purposes, such as artistic, educational or scientific

---

[52] Archaeological Law 3028/2002 on the protection of antiquities and cultural heritage in general, Government Gazette, (hereinafter FEK) A' 153.
For an official translation of this law into English see: http://www.unesco
.org/ulture/natlaws/media/pdf/greece/grelaw_3028_engtof.pdf. Last access
April 2019.

[53] The Greek legislator used the term "monuments," a term referring to
memory, to describe ancient and other protected tangible cultural objects.
According to Article 2, sub para. (b), by "monuments" are meant cultural
objects which constitute material evidence and belong to the country's cultural heritage, whose special protection is called for. Monuments are divided
into ancient and modern (or "recent" in the official translation) (i.e., those
later than 1830), and also divided into "immovable" and "movable".

purposes, is again allowed for a fee paid to TAP, however, the fee can be waived upon decision of the Minister of Culture[54] (See also Tsiavos this volume).

When reading the relevant regulatory framework, two main considerations arise with respect to the creative use and reuse of cultural heritage content for Greek monuments and other cultural goods. Firstly, it is obvious that there is a state-centric character for heritage protection resulting from historical reasons related to the centralized cultural policy tradition of the country. This conservative approach exclusively establishes antiquities and other protected cultural goods as a privileged symbolic foundation for national identity (Voudouri 2010). Under this framework, the mediation of ICT tools and methods can be interpreted as being in line with this state-centric vision for cultural heritage only if it is used for preservation, protection, educational and research purposes. The creative and artistic aspect of re-purposing and re-using digital cultural heritage content is clearly underestimated – if not excluded – from the scope of the national legislator. Even where the legislator acknowledged the primacy of heritage's social function,[55] the limitations of experiencing heritage by individuals and communities is still a challenging issue, affecting the essence of heritage as a public good to be fully accessed and enjoyed by everyone.[56]

Secondly, the existing rules on the use of digital technologies for the reproduction, use and preservation of cultural heritage content is obviously out-

---

[54] Common Ministerial Decree no 81397/2199/21-09-2005 provides a number of dispositions regulating the permission procedure for using cultural heritage content digitally. The Public Sector and the TAP are excepted from paying fees for any kind of use, however the relevant permission by the Ministry of Culture should be granted in any case.

[55] Within the Archaeological Law 3028/2002, it is evident that the preservation is not understood as an end in itself. See mainly A.3 on the content of the protection, A.45 on museums and A.46 on access to end use of monuments and sites.

[56] With regards to the re-use of Public Sector Information (PSI), despite the fact that Directive 2013/37/EU, amending PSI Directive 2003/98/EC, is or at least was meant to be a determinant pillar of the European Union's open data strategy, the amended PSI Directive permitted the contractual restriction on the commercial reuse of public domain works which have been digitised under a Public Private Partnership (PPP). The contractual restrictions are in principle restricted to ten years but may run longer as long as they are subject to review. See Pekel, Fallon & Kamenov, Public Sector Information in Cultural Heritage Institutions, June 2014, https://www.europeandataportal.eu/sites/default/files/library/201406_public_sector_information_in_cultural_heritage_institutions.pdf. Last access July 2019.

dated. Since the beginning of the 20th century, the development of services supporting the implementation of digital technology in the cultural heritage sector has significantly contributed to bridge the gap between ICT research and cultural heritage. Beginning with the introduction of digital technology into the infrastructure of cultural institutions and the digitisation of cultural heritage content, this process eventually led to considerations for updating the regulatory framework regarding the digital content use. These considerations should not only be limited to educational or research purposes; the artistic factor should also be taken into account. A most interesting possibility raised by the digitisation of cultural heritage content is transmitting the value of original sources and finding sophisticated ways to reintroduce the past into everyday life. Not only serving students, scholars, and educators, but also inspiring new artists and fostering future interest in cultural heritage collections is critical to the longevity and relevance of cultural heritage itself.

Moving forward

It is necessary to move away from the official approaches to heritage that exclusively view monuments as a privileged symbolic foundation for national identity and it is essential to strongly support an open, accessible cultural heritage that will serve as an inspirational pole for contemporary artistic practices. It is urgent that we explore new ways of collectively rethinking our approach to reproduction, storage and sharing of artworks and cultural heritage in the 21st century.[57] New technologies provide great opportunities so that cultural heritage be more accessible, and cultural experience be more meaningful. It is urgent that the dialogue opens up globally by offering opportunities for creative collaboration and coexistence between the ancient and the contemporary, between the past and the future, the original and the copy, by constructing realistic legal licencing systems that promote accessibility, reuse, and thus creativity.

---

[57] The ReACH project (Reproduction of Art and Cultural Heritage) was a valuable initiative coordinated by the Victoria and Albert Museum in partnership with the Peri Foundation, the Louvre Museum, the Smithsonian Institute and other key research partners, which resulted in the production of a Declaration embracing digital technologies and offering new ways to produce, store and share museum and heritage assets, see https://www.vam.ac.uk/research/projects/reach-reproduction-of-art-and-cultural-heritage. Last access June 2019.

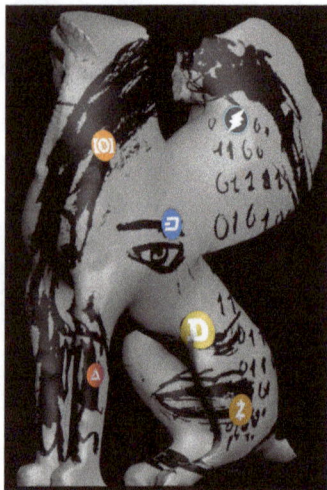

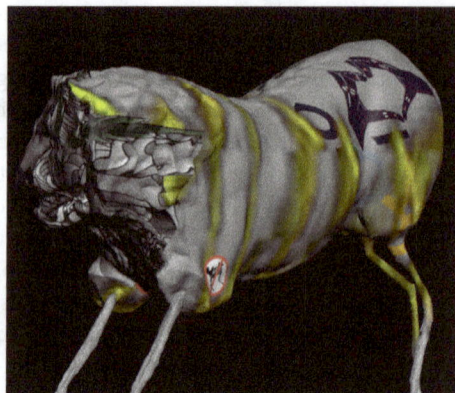

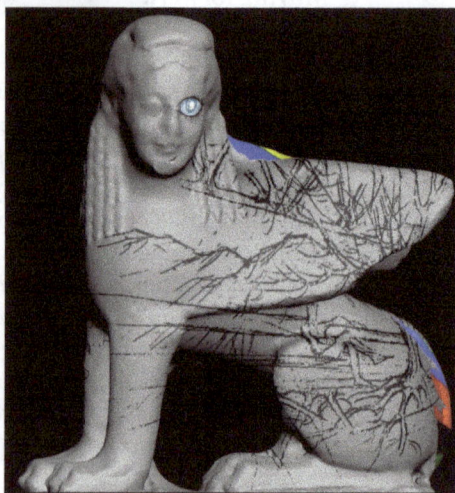

Figures 4, 5, 6: Petros Moris, Future Bestiary, 2019, HD video projection (5:00)
(Source: PM).

Bibliography

Al-Ruzouq, R. (2012). Photogrammetry for archaeological documentation and cultural heritage conservation. In Da Silva, D. C. (Ed.), *Special applications of photogrammetry* (pp. 97–110). Retrieved April 7, 2019 from www.intechopen.com.

Campbell, T., Williams, C., Ivanova, O. & Garrett, B. (2011). Could 3D printing change the world?: Technologies, potential and implications of additive manufacturing. *Strategic Foresight Report, October.* Retrieved April 7, 2019, from https://www.atlanticcouncil.org/wp-content/uploads/2011/10/101711_ACUS_3DPrinting.PDF.

De Clippele, M.-S. & Lambrecht, L. (2015). Art law and balances: Increased protection of cultural heritage law vs. private ownership: Towards clash or balance? *International Journal of Cultural Property, 22,* 259–278. DOI: https://doi.org/10.1017/S0940739115000119.

Eschenfelder, K. R. & Caswell, M. (2010). Digital cultural collections in an age of reuse and remixes, *First Monday, 15*(11). Retrieved April 7, 2019, from https://firstmonday.org/article/view/3060/2640.

Hamilton, G. & Saunderson, F. (2017). *Open licensing for cultural heritage.* London, United Kingdom: Facet Publishing.

Ioannides, M., Chatzigrigoriou, P., Bokolas, V., Nikolakopoulou, V., Athanasiou, V., Papageorgiou, E., ... & Sovis, C. (2017). Educational creative use and reuse of digital cultural heritage data for Cypriot UNESCO monuments. In: M. Ioannides M., E. Fink, A. Moropoulou, M. Hagedorn-Saupe, A. Fresa, G. Liestøl ... & P. Grussenmeyer (Eds.), *Digital heritage: Progress in cultural heritage: Documentation, preservation, and protection.* 6th International Conference, EuroMed 2016, Nicosia, Cyprus, October 31 – November 5, 2016, Proceedings, Part I. Lecture Notes in Computer Science, vol. 10058 (pp. 891–901). Cham, Switzerland: Springer.

Kuan, C. (2014). 7 Lessons learned for digital culture. In H. Din & S. Wu (Eds.), *Digital heritage and culture: Strategy and implementation* (pp. 41–52). Singapore, Singapore: World Scientific. DOI: https://doi.org/10.1142/9789814522984_0004.

Law 3028/2002. *On the protection of antiquities and cultural heritage in general.* Retrieved November 20, 2019, from https://www.bsa.ac.uk/wp-content/uploads/2018/11/Archaeological-Law-3028-2002.pdf.

Newell, J., Lythberg, B. & Salmond, A. (2012). Old objects, new media: Historical collections, digitization and affect. *Journal of Material Culture, 17*(3), 287–306.

Panezi, A. (2018). Europe's new renaissance: New policies and rules for digital preservation and access to European cultural heritage. *Columbia Journal of European Law, 24*(3), 596–611.

Pary, R. (2007). *Recoding the museum: digital heritage and the technologies of change*. London, United Kingdom: Routledge.

Ruthven, I. & Chowdhury, G. G. (Eds.). (2015). *Cultural heritage information: Access and management*. London, United Kingdom: Facet Publishing.

Steyerl, H. (2016). A sea of data: Apophenia and pattern (mis-)recognition. *E-Flux Journal, 72*. Retrieved April 7, 2019 from https://www.e-flux.com/journal/72/60480/a-sea-of-data-apophenia-and-pattern-mis-recognition/.

Voudouri, D. (2010). Law and the politics of the past: Legal protection of cultural heritage in Greece. *International Journal of Cultural Property, 17*, 547–568.

Wachowiak, M. J. & Karas, B. V. (2009). 3D scanning and replication for museum and cultural heritage applications. *Journal of the American Institute for Conservation, 48*(2), 141–158.

Younan, S. (2015). Poaching museum collections using digital 3D technologies. *Journal of Science and Technology of the Arts, 7*(2), 25–32.

CHAPTER 7

Seeds as Common Cultural Heritage

Vasso Kanellopoulou

The seeds of cultivated plants are nourishing, charming and creative. They belong to the past and to the future. They have an amazing memory, which becomes activated when conditions are favourable. This memory is continuously modified as the plants respond to selection and management by humans while adapting to new geographic and climatic data.

Traditional seeds,[58] as plant reproductive material of the cultivated species that we have collectively inherited, belong to the Common Pool Resources. Initially a gift of nature, they are consecutively the result of continuous interaction between nature and humanity, as expressed in the evolutionary modification of the memory of the seeds. This natural and at the same time cultural heritage is expressed by a huge number of edible plant varieties created by farmer-breeders, through the domestication of wild plants over the past 10,000 years of agriculture. The relevant knowledge relating to seed saving is also included in this common heritage.

Other terms for traditional and locally adapted agricultural plants include landraces, heirloom, heritage, local, unimproved, conservation varieties, populations and ancient or old varieties (although they can also be new). In addition, the term heterogeneous genetic material, implying lack of strict genetic

---

[58] This article refers mainly to seeds, however, the majority of the information also applies to other plant reproductive material such as tubers, cuttings, grafts etc.

How to cite this book chapter:
Kanellopoulou, V. 2020. Seeds as Common Cultural Heritage. In Lekakis, S. (ed.)
Cultural Heritage in the Realm of the Commons: Conversations on the Case of Greece.
Pp. 141–158. London: Ubiquity Press. DOI: https://doi.org/10.5334/bcj.i. License:
CC-BY

uniformity, has been recently adopted in European legislation as a description of the reproductive material (seeds etc.) of the traditional types of agricultural plants (EU 2018). These plants have a large genetic base and are not characterized by uniformity.

The seeds of traditional varieties, bred by farmers, are at the time of writing rarely found on the European market. They are more frequently exchanged among passionate breeders and cultivators. The global and European market is currently dominated by industrial/commercial seeds belonging to new varieties bred by scientists and covered by the Plant Variety Protection (PVP), i.e. Intellectual Property Rights (IPRs) or patents. These are predominantly owned by large multinational companies, which also focus on the production of chemicals for agriculture and/or pharmaceuticals.[59]

Genetic erosion, loss of biodiversity

Unfortunately, the majority of traditional plants and their seeds are being lost to humanity. This phenomenon is known as "genetic erosion" or loss of agricultural biodiversity. According to the UN's Food and Agriculture Organization (FAO) this represents a vanishing heritage for agriculture and it poses a serious threat. The FAO estimates that in the previous century about 75% of the genetic diversity of agricultural crops was lost.

> "We are becoming increasingly dependent on fewer and fewer crop varieties and, as a result, a rapidly diminishing gene pool. The primary reason is that commercial, uniform varieties are replacing traditional ones, even and most threateningly, in the centres of diversity" (Food and Agriculture Organization of the United Nations n.d.).

The Mediterranean region is regarded as one of these biodiversity centres, where principal crops such as wheat originated (Food and Agriculture Organization of the United Nations 2019; Vishnyakova et al. 2017). Greece is known to be particularly rich in natural and cultivated biodiversity (Stavropoulos et al. 2000). However, even here the local loss of biodiversity appears to be dramatic. In 1994 it was estimated that cultivation of local 'unimproved' wheat varieties amounted only to 2% of cultivated wheat in the country (Samaras & Matthaiou 1994).

---

[59] Industrial-Commercial seeds are available today in the global seed market either in their conventional form or in a genetically engineered (GE) form. In the European market only one GE corn variety is allowed for cultivation. In Greece, its cultivation is not allowed. Imports of GE grains to be used as food for the animals but not for cultivation, are allowed all over Europe including Greece.

Cultivated plant varieties as common goods

Initially all plant seeds were common goods. Nowadays only traditional seeds belong to the realm of the commons. However, their commercial circulation in Europe and accordingly in Greece, is very restricted. The generally accepted principle of the free movement of goods does not apply in this case.

The development of this amazing biological and cultural wealth by man was based on three cultural pillars that apply for common goods:

a. The freedom of the farmer to save seeds from his crop in order to plant them the following year (farmers' right to use farm-saved seed)[60]
b. The free exchange of seeds between cultivators
c. The freedom to use the seed to create a new variety (breeders' right)
d. The free movement of the seed to other regions

Existing European regulations, also adopted in Greece, restrict these freedoms in various ways, depending on the seed category. For example, once the plant is officially registered in the catalogue, which is a prerequisite for any seed entering the market, commercial seeds are free to travel and be sold without any restrictions. In contrast, registration of traditional seeds is extremely difficult, in many cases almost impossible. In addition, once some traditional plants are finally registered, their seeds are restricted both quantitatively and geographically. They are restricted to their region of adaptation, known as the 'region of origin'.[61] This is in spite of the fact that the wealth we have inherited – i.e. the wealth we are losing – resulted to a large extent from the free travel of seeds.

The tomato in Greece

The history of the tomato in Greece highlights the importance of free movement of seeds. The tomato was unknown in Greece until 1814. In that year the first tomato seeds were planted in the courtyard of the monastery of the French Capuchin monks in the centre of Athens (Plaka) (Marangou 2018). In other regions of Greece tomato seeds came from elsewhere: for example, tomato seeds came to the Aegean island of Amorgos with the boat of captain Nicolas Platis from the eastern Aegean town of Izmir (Marangou 2018). Consequently, the farm-saved tomato seed was freely distributed and thus travelled

---

[60] 'Farm-saved seed' is not always identical to 'farmer's seed'. The latter is potentially one of the denominations for a traditional variety although it is ambiguous as a term because sometimes it is used to indicate 'farm-saved' seeds.

[61] The region of adaptation is named by European legislation as 'Region of origin' (Commission Directive 2009).

to the various regions of Greece. It gradually adapted to the local climatic and cultural conditions and has offered us important 'local Greek' varieties of tomatoes. This was made possible by the free circulation of the seed, and resulted in the traditional Greek salad – with onions and feta cheese – which is commonly regarded to be Greece's most popular national dish.

If the current approach and the consequent restrictive legislation had prevailed 200 years ago, we would not be enjoying local Greek tomatoes today. The same case could be made for local Greek apples, which initially arrived as gifts from farmers in other continents. Indeed, the apple originated in Kazakhstan, but it has adapted locally in many other areas all over the planet, offering a tremendous wealth of 'local' traditional varieties. In Greece the well-known 'Pilafa' variety became adapted in the area of Tripolis –southern Greece. The sale of its seed is restricted to this region of 'origin' (i.e. one of the apple's numerous regions of adaptation).

Traditional Seeds: Profile of an enclosed common good

As a common good, not covered by Intellectual Property Rights (IPRs) or patents, traditional seeds can be freely reproduced both legally and technically. Practically this means that the farmer can save his seeds for the following year. Thus, the potential seed-market size is much smaller than in the case of commercial seeds, where new seeds have to be bought every year (for annual plants). In addition, traditional seeds are resilient and do not require heavy inputs of fertilizers and pesticides, thus protecting the environment and limiting cash dependencies for the farmer. Nevertheless, from the point of view of agribusiness companies, they also limit the size of the agricultural input market.

There are traditional varieties with substantial yields. There are others with much lower yields than industry seeds. They are all suited to the multifunctional farming model of the small and medium-scale farmer, for non-intensive, low-input agriculture and the related agro-ecological practices. Agro-ecology is a link between nature and science. Like ecology, it is mainly a cultural issue. According to FAO, agro-ecology is a scientific discipline, a set of practices and a social movement. "One of the main features of agro-ecology is that it looks for local solutions and linkages with the local economy and local markets and keeps farmers in the field with improved livelihoods and a better quality of life" (Food and Agriculture Organization of the United Nations 2019).[62]

Unlike many commercial varieties, traditional varieties have a large genetic base, so they are diverse and have a greater evolutionary capacity. They are optimally suited for climate-change adaptation, because their vast range of genes offers them the ability to evolve and adapt to new conditions, while also contributing to the preservation of valuable rural biodiversity. The fact that they

---

[62] For more on agroecology see Moss & Bittman 2018.

require lower inputs makes it possible to save energy and to keep other important environmental resources – again common goods such as soil and the water table – relatively clean.

Diversity versus homogeneity

The large genetic base of traditional seeds is penalized by the current legislation in Europe. The large base means less uniformity than with commercial seeds. While traditional seeds remain a common good, their commercial circulation is treated as an exception by the current legislation, which focuses on the characteristics of industrial/commercial seeds.

As already mentioned, the registration of a variety in an official catalogue in Europe is a prerequisite for the seed to enter the market. The basic criteria for this registration are distinctiveness, uniformity and stability (DUS criteria), which correspond exactly to the characteristics of the commercial varieties but do not cover those of traditional varieties. Lighter DUS criteria have been accepted for the registration of traditional varieties, although the process is problematic as a very large degree of uniformity is still required and traditional varieties are basically not uniform. What makes matters worse is that once the traditional variety is registered, quantitative and geographical restrictions apply to the marketing of the seed (Magarinos-Rey 2015). As a result, the sale of traditional seeds is restricted while commercial seeds can travel freely to be sold and cultivated once the plant is registered.

What is more, the sale of traditional seeds is restricted under the pretext of preserving purity, to the so-called region of origin of the variety or more precisely the region of adaptation during its evolutionary history. For example, if a variety has been locally adapted on the island of Crete, its registered seed cannot be sold in any other regions of Greece. This local variety is thus officially not allowed to adapt to other areas and create 'new local varieties'. The purity of a locally adapted variety is precious indeed. However, it could be protected through the well-known tool of geographic indications,[63] while allowing for the free travel of the seed to bring about new adaptations.

In this way, it is obvious that the further evolution of the variety and its adaptation in other regions is hindered. The catalogue criteria and the additional restrictions have contributed greatly to the genetic erosion of the common pool of traditional varieties and pose a great obstacle to their regeneration. Seed laws were a critical factor in many countries. By making seed certification mandatory

---

[63] Geographical Indications could be used to ensure the variety's local name and purity. Even if the seed could be freely traded in other areas, only the variety's region of origin (adaptation) should have the right to use the initial variety's name. Protected designation of origin is one of the frequently used geographical indications for agricultural products.

and trade in uncertified seeds illegal, governments supported commercial seeds against traditional seed-exchange systems (GRAIN 2007). For example, in Greece by 2018, only one traditional variety among hundreds has been registered in the official catalogue so that its seed can be sold, and this is limited to the narrow region of origin and only in restricted quantities. All the seeds of the other Greek traditional varieties are actually out of the market, except for just a few vegetable varieties that have been genetically stabilized and registered by a public institution in a way that their seeds are considered commercial.

The restrictions on the sale of traditional seeds offers a monopoly to commercial seeds within the seed market. This phenomenon has been reinforced by the schemes for agricultural insurance and subsidies, which in recent decades many European governments, including Greece, have applied (GRAIN 2007). The genetic material of traditional seeds is currently propagated only by passionate professional or amateur cultivators. One can find their seeds in seed exchanges which take place in many parts of the country. The exchange of seeds is tolerated by the state, though considered to be on the margins of the law. Restrictions apply only to the plant reproductive material, whereas the fruit of these 'illegal' seeds can be legally marketed anywhere once the farmer can find the seed in order to plant it!

According to the International Federation of Organic Agriculture Movements, IFOAM-Organics International:

> "This seed is not 'legally' available to farmers because it is characterized by a high level of genetic and phenotypic diversity. This diversity is very good for organic farming – as opposed to the general seed law that requires high level of homogeneity of seed" (IFOAM 2018).

Diversity offers resilience and that is what organic farming needs.

In May 2018, there was a historic change in European law on seeds in organic agriculture, effective from January 2021. It will be finally possible, at least for organic farmers, to access, produce and sell traditional varieties, referred to as 'heterogeneous material' according to the text of the new Organic Regulation (Commission Regulation 2018). Secondary legislation by the Commission, referring to the practicalities of implementation, is expected by the middle of 2020. We hope that the expected delegated and implementing acts will not reduce or cancel the new opportunity for small and medium scale organic farmers to become once again seed producers and/or breeders.

The seeds of many endangered traditional varieties are stored in gene banks. In the majority of these banks, stored seeds have to be reproduced at regular intervals, since over time the germination capacity decreases depending on the storage conditions. Each reproduction weakens the initial purity of the variety, since it takes place away from the region of origin (actual region of adaptation) but it is important because it keeps the plant genetic resources alive. Gene banks are very valuable and must be supported. Nevertheless, they must not be used as a pretext for biodiversity to be kept only in a museum. Biodiverse seeds must also be cultivated and allowed to evolve in the fields and adapt to climate change, soil conditions and management by humans. Let us not forget that gene banks are more vulnerable than decentralized cultivation, due to a range of circumstances such as conflict situations as in Syria (Mesquida 2018), privatization, political control, inadequate infrastructure or climate change. Even the famous Svalbard global seed vault, located on a remote Norwegian island near the North Pole, unexpectedly flooded in 2017 due to melting permafrost – luckily no seed collections were damaged (Carrington 2017).

Gene banks keep accessions of seeds characterized by genetic erosion, and the seed industry relies partly on them to find traditional and/or wild plant material for breeding innovation and disease prevention. In accordance with international treaties, gene banks give samples to scientists for research and frequently in practice it is a multinational chemical or pharmaceutical company that obtains the legal right for the outcome of the scientists' research on the seed.

On the other hand, many gene banks, including the one in Greece, do not often provide samples to farmers for experimentation and new plant breeding in the field. Gene banks usually do not encourage dissemination of biodiversity in the fields. The prevailing mentality around traditional varieties is to be of no commercial interest; their basic role is thought to be that of forming the basis for the creation of new commercial varieties by scientists. The breeding role of the scientist is fostered, and the breeding role of the farmer denigrated. Nevertheless, the new movement for Participatory Plant Breeding –a collaboration between scientists and farmers – attempts to overcome these established conditions. It has already produced interesting results with well-adapted new varieties (Ceccarelli 2016). Unfortunately, this is not at all the prevailing practice, although it has the possibility to offer new important varieties, covered with open source breeding licenses.

The social movements that protect traditional seeds are supportive of the gene banks, but they also believe that the best guarantee for our future food security is the free decentralised cultivation and exchange or sale of traditional seeds, in parallel with the current system of cultivation and sale of commercial industrial seeds, so that:

1. Control of the seed is decentralised – this being a prerequisite for democracy – and open source breeding licenses are supported.
2. The plant breeding criteria are extended to include criteria such as health, taste, resilience in low input situations etc. so that creation of new varieties is not only restricted to the current commercial criteria with which modern varieties are bred, such as high yield with heavy chemical inputs, shelf-life, transport durability, etc.
3. The purity of locally adapted traditional varieties is kept in its region of adaptation (origin) while the seed is free to travel (under the standard sanitary requirements) to other areas for its genes to continue to evolve and adapt to other regions.

Figure 1: Peliti seed exchange in Greece (Source: Aris Pavlos).

Seed guardians

The Greek non-governmental organization called 'Alternative Community Peliti' organises seed exchange festivals at both a local and national level. Peliti was the first traditional seed regeneration organization in Greece, founded in 1995 by Panagiotis Sainatoudis.[64] 'Aegilops' is another important Greek seed regeneration organization founded by the organic breeder Kostas Koutis.[65] Over the last decade the citizens' movement has been growing in Greece. According to Peliti estimates, there are approximately 40 ad hoc independent traditional seed protection groups (Sainatoudis 2018).

Industrial or commercial seed: In practice, a privatized commodity

Industrial and/or commercial seeds belong either to a variety or to a hybrid plant (type F1). Unlike traditional seeds, which are not legally protected, the seeds of the private seed industry have become – in practice – private property, as they are covered by IPRs or patents and regulated by restrictive bureaucracy once the legal protection expires. This gradual privatisation has advanced

---

[64] www.peliti.gr/. Last access 20 November 2019.
[65] www.aegilops.gr. Last access 20 November 2019.

almost 'behind closed doors' and most citizens are not aware of this expanding private control over the food system.

Industrial plant varieties protected by PVP cannot be legally reproduced by the farmer without paying royalty fees to the breeder (with few exceptions). In addition, in the event that the plant is a F1 hybrid, (as is the case for most vegetables), the obstacles for seed saving are also technical. F1 Hybrids are productive in the first generation but in the following generations the offspring are unstable, they do not produce true to themselves. Therefore, either for legal and/or technical reasons, farmers do not save their seeds for the next year for annual crops. Instead they must buy the seed every year from the companies that own their legal right (IPR or patent).

In theory, the privatisation of industrial/commercial seed should be a temporary issue, because IPRs expire after 2–3 decades, however, in practice it is possible for the IPR owner to withdraw the plant variety from the market by deregistration when the legal protection period is about to expire. For example, according to the Environmental Justice Atlas, when the IPR of a popular commercial variety of potato named 'Linda' expired in 2004 it was deregistered from the German catalogue by the IPR owner. As a result, anyone who farmed it commercially would be acting illegally. It was to be replaced by new varieties for which profitable licensing fees could be charged once again (Environmental Justice Atlas 2015). German farmers organized the 'save the Linda potato' campaign and it was settled in the courts that 'Linda' could remain on the market for two more years. Thereafter it would not be available for cultivation. Yet it is today again available to farmers all over Europe because it was accepted for registration in another European country, this time in England.

> "The 'Linda' potato is seen as a success story against the industry. But the incident also made farmers acutely aware of how much they depend on the market and on the whims of the companies" (Environmental Justice Atlas 2015).

We conclude and propose that once a plant IPR expires – when the variety is ready to become a common good –EU authorities or national governments of EU member states should automatically register it in the official catalogue and a public institution should also automatically take care of the conservation of its purity. Unfortunately, this is not currently the rule, contributing to the loss of agricultural goods that have just returned to the realm of the commons. This proposal only applies to non-genetically engineered commercial plants.

Industrial/Commercial Seeds: Profile

According to scientific research the nutritional value of commercial seeds is lower than that of the traditional local varieties. For example, in the case of vegetables, the components of their nutritional value in commercial varieties are reduced or lost in relation to local varieties, as confirmed in bibliography, for various vegetables (Koutsika-Sotiriou et al. 2011).

Industrial/commercial seeds have high yields but at the same time they require significant inputs of fertilizers and pesticides during their cultivation. Therefore, industrial seeds intensify the farmer's dependence on inputs and on the purchase of new seeds every year. These seeds (either varieties or hybrids F1) are suitable for intensive agriculture. They are based on an initial plant improvement of traditional and/or wild seeds but recently it has been observed that the new varieties or hybrids entering the market are very closely related to the ones already registered for marketing. This raised a number of concerns as to the role of plant breeding science in the reduction and uniformisation of crop genetic diversity; it seems possible that the continuous selection efforts and crosses between genetically related cultivars could have led to a narrowing of the genetic base of cultivated crops (Batur 2014).

In addition, commercial hybrids type F1, have a narrow genetic base themselves. As a result, there is a reduced contribution of commercial seeds to the wealth of plant genetic resources, and they also have a reduced capacity for climatic adaptation, when compared to the corresponding capacity of the traditional ones. Thus, the new biodiversity created by commercial seeds has a narrow genetic base and it does not compensate for the loss of older biodiversity as claimed by the formal seed industry (European Seed Association n.d.).

A short history of the Plant Variety Protection

In 1961, the International Convention on the Legal Protection of Plant Varieties developed by the Union for the (legal) Protection of New Varieties of Plants (UPOV) defined the Intellectual Property Rights (IPRs) of plant breeders.[66] According to this, the owner of the variety had the monopoly of commercial sales of the seed, but farmers could freely reproduce and use their farm-saved seeds as many times as they wanted. Breeders could also freely use the protected varieties to develop new ones. Following pressures from the seed industry, the UPOV convention was revised in 1991. As a result, replanting of farm-saved seed belonging to a variety under legal protection was prohibited to farmers. The government could lift this prohibition in specific circumstances and even then, the seed company could demand payment of a royalty. Today in the so-called developed countries our diet is mostly based on industrial/commercial seeds and most farmers are almost exclusively dependent on the seed industry. Regulations do not allow many choices as farmers have to adhere to the formal commercial seed sector. Privatized seeds are gradually entering the developing world as well, however, in developing countries a considerable number of

---

[66] www.UPOV.int. Last access 20 November 2019.

farmers continue to save their seeds. These are estimated at 1.5 billion people, representing thus a huge potential market for companies: as a result, there are enormous political and commercial pressures to phase out traditional seeds from the market so that the farmers would rely almost exclusively on industrial seeds. The International Convention on the Legal Protection of Plant Varieties, which many developing countries are forced to sign, has much of the responsibility for this (ETC 1999). It is obvious that in these countries, the informal seed sector of seed saving and seed exchanging is still alive.

While according to UN sponsored reports (IAASTD 2009), small-scale farmers should be supported in order to end the current agricultural crisis (pollution and hunger), international conventions promote measures that destroy the small farmer who has no capital to buy costly agricultural inputs (seeds, fertilizers, pesticides etc.) and may prefer to use farm-saved seed. This age-old farmers' right is gradually being removed, with serious implications for our food security. The seed industry has modified the initial traditional plant-breeding criteria. Instead of taste, aroma, health and resilience, we now have commercial criteria such as productivity related to agro-chemical dependence, plant uniformity and stability, extension of duration of shelf-life, transport capacity. Thus, the farmer buying these seeds tends to follow the model of intensive chemical farming because these seeds work well only within this model. This model is suitable for the global movement of agricultural goods whereas the model for traditional seeds is suitable for local markets.

Strengthening privatization: Intellectual Property Rights are gradually replaced by patents on cultivated plants

Initially patents on agricultural plants covered only Genetically Engineered plants (GE). More recently patents have unfortunately also been extended to conventionally bred plants, i.e. the plants mostly cultivated in Europe where GE cultivation is mostly avoided.[67] For example, the European Patent Office has already granted 200 patents on conventionally breeding (No Patents on Seeds n.d.). Living organisms should not be patented.

Patents offer the breeder control over the genetic content of the variety, in contrast to IPRs. This means that patents not only restrict seed saving by the farmer (farmers' right), they also prohibit scientists or farmers from using this seed to create new varieties (breeders' right). Patents, therefore, lead to an even stricter enclosure of plant genetic resources, which are a biological and cultural

---

[67] Less than one percent of Europe's agricultural land is cultivated with GE plants (one GE corn type is allowed) taking place in only in 2–3 member states. In contrast a large amount of GE grain is imported for animal food. Thus indirectly, through the animals and their products, GE has entered the European food chain, including in Greece.

common good. In the case of digital commons, for example, the Creative Commons legal protection allows for further research, innovation and creation of new products whereas in the case of patents on plant varieties or plant traits, none of these is allowed.

The gradual change in plant breeding criteria towards the support of a large market for agrochemical products has led to the entry of genetically modified organisms into our diet. GE plants are the result of the invasion of agrochemistry into agriculture and also of the gradual privatization of seed through strengthening legal protection. Most GE plants currently on the global market are associated with the herbicide of the company that sells the seed, so the farmer must buy the whole package and follow the model of intensive chemical farming. In addition, let us not forget that a considerable body of scientific research indicates the alarming effects of GE plants on our health and the environment (Velot 2009; Seralini 2014; Fagan et al. 2014).

The commercialization of GE plants is being carried out by the same companies that also sell non-GE seeds and agrochemicals. This is particularly important as the seed breeding agricultural input industry has already acquired considerable commercial and political power and is able, to a large extent, to control the future of our agriculture and set it irreversibly on a path that we have not chosen (Corporate Europe Observatory 2018). For society to have a free choice for a different future of agriculture, we should fully support the return of bio-diverse traditional seeds –pool of common goods – to the fields, in parallel with cultivation of non-GE commercial seeds.

Vulnerability in our Food System: Market consolidation in the commercial seed sector

In recent decades, international seed industry consolidation has been increasing. Small and medium sized seed breeding companies are being bought by large agrochemical companies. By 2013, Monsanto, DuPont and Syngenta – producers of both agrochemicals and seeds – controlled over half of the global seed market. This is a dramatic shift since 1996, when the top three corporations controlled 22% of the industry.

This consolidating process is presented in the graphics by Dr Phil Howard that depicts changes in ownership involving major seed companies and their subsidiaries, primarily occurring from 1996 to 2018 (Cornucopia Institute 2018).

According to the ETC group, the oligopoly paradigm has moved to the entire food system, which becomes increasingly vulnerable: Six multinationals control 75% of all private sector plant breeding research, 60% of the commercial seed market and 76% of global agrochemical sales. The six companies are Monsanto, DuPont, Syngenta, Bayer, Dow, and BASF (ETC 2013). This consolidation intensified in 2018, when Monsanto was acquired by Bayer.

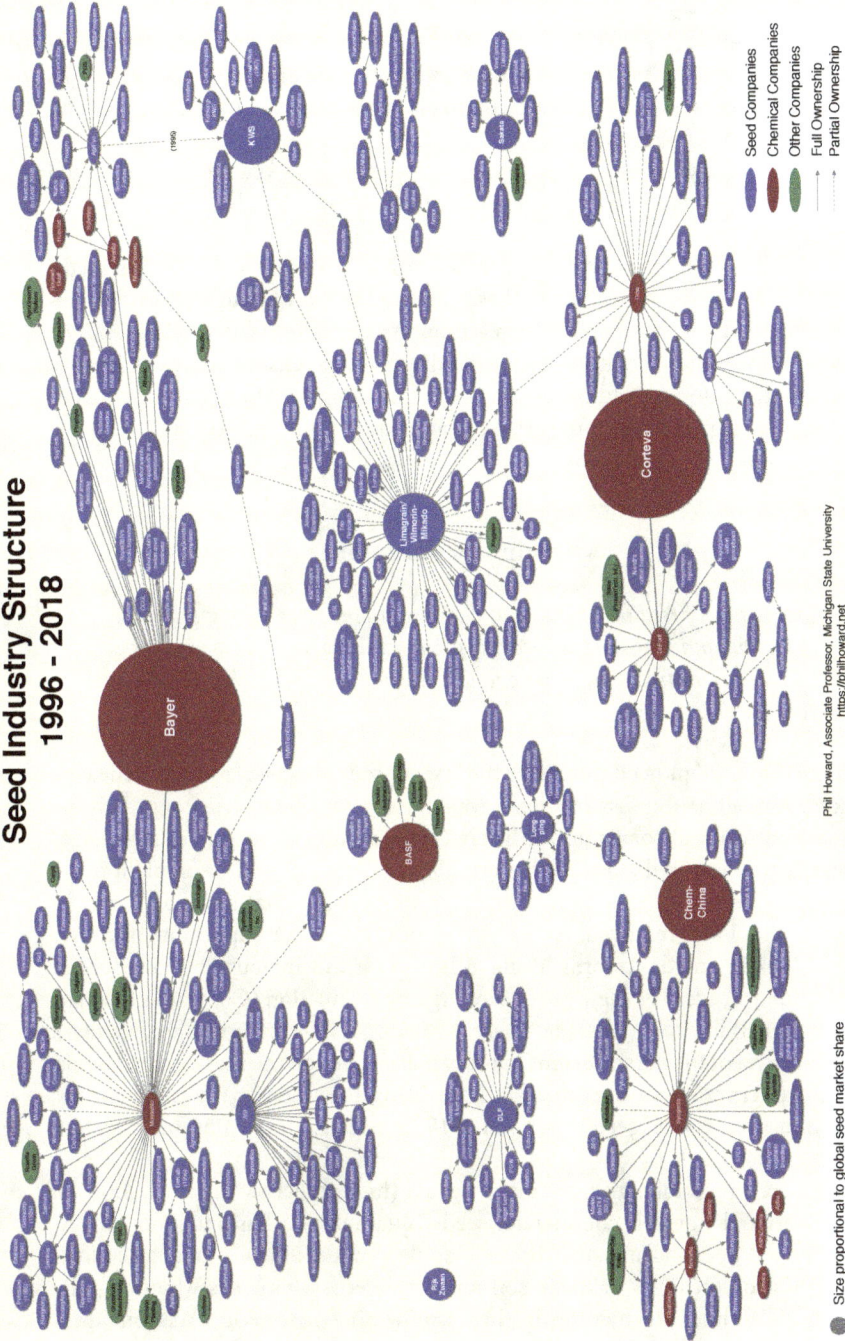

Figure 2: Seed industry structure 1996–2013. The largest firms are represented as circles, with size proportional to global commercial seed market share (Source: Cornucopia Institute 2017).

Seeds and Mediterranean diet

The Mediterranean diet is a vibrant part of our cultural heritage full of memories, colours, aromas and flavours, with sociability and sharing as its cornerstone. Greece's Mediterranean diet is included in the Intangible Cultural Heritage List (UNESCO 2018).

Unfortunately, when discussing the Mediterranean diet in public, much more attention has been paid to the table than to the field. Thus, it has not been made clear that the system of this valuable Mediterranean diet is deeply rooted in respect for biodiversity, the best expression of which is the traditional seeds, due to their broad genetic base. These common goods offer us the lost flavours that the Mediterranean diet enthusiasts are trying to maintain. This diet has its roots in the regional cultures and in biodiversity and ensures the maintenance and continuation of traditional farming and fishing activities and practices in the Mediterranean communities. It is accordingly inextricably linked to the universe of traditional seeds.

Seeding for our future

"Seed is the first link in the food chain and embodies a long sequence of evolution and thousands of years of plant breeding. In addition it expresses the culture of free seed production, conservation and exchange" (Buiatti et al. 2013).

There is an urgent need to reverse the loss of traditional varieties ('genetic erosion') as well as the loss of the relevant seed-saving knowledge and cultural traditions of local communities. There is also an urgent need to change European legislation so that no patents are allowed on plants and/or on plant traits. Restrictions on the commercial circulation of traditional seeds as common goods should be removed. As already mentioned, some important efforts are already being made towards lifting at least a part of the current enclosure of traditional seeds: The New European Organic Regulation (Commission Regulation 2018) is a good example, as are the national interpretations by Denmark and Austria of the harsh current European directives on the marketing of seeds. These interpretations are aimed at liberalising the trade in traditional seeds, for non-professional seed buyers. In 2018 France also moved in this direction (Artemisia 2018).

The regeneration of traditional seeds (in parallel with cultivation of conventional non-GE commercial seeds) guarantees a basis for food sovereignty and offers farmers the choice to apply a model of low-input agriculture, which also conserves valuable soil and water ecosystems. As Mpofu rightly claims: "Without our own seeds, there can be no agro-ecology. Without agro-ecology, we cannot build food sovereignty" (Mpofu 2014: 14).

Figure 3: From generation to generation (Source: Aris Pavlos).

Agricultural diversity must be accessible to all of us. Participatory breeding and open source licenses in breeding should be supported. The two parallel markets of non-GE commercial seed and of traditional seed can coexist. The latter is a small market, one that is not very important according to financial criteria, but which is absolutely essential for the preservation of very important common goods that are the basis of our food security: seeds and their biodiversity, decentralized seed saving knowledge, clean healthy soil with beneficial microorganisms and clean water. Food security is also strongly linked to a wide gene pool, or in other terms, to rich biodiversity. Let us not forget that evolutionary capacity is the basis for the continuation of life. The seed is based on the cumulative memory of a continuum of human and biological interactions. Whoever controls the seed also controls our diet and obtains the power to impose political and cultural choices on our future. That is why the seed must remain a decentralized common good, just like culture.

Bibliography

Artemisia. (2018, October 2). *Le projet de loi "Egalim" a été adopté: Encore une avancée pour les semences!* Retrieved October 15, 2018, from https://www.artemisia-lawyers.com/fran%C3%A7ais/publications-et-interventions/egalim-fr/.

Batur, F. (2014). *Agrobiodiversity conservation and plant improvement: Adjustments in intellectual property rights reclaiming the public domain towards sustainability and equity* (Unpublished PhD Thesis). Université Catholique de Louvain, Ottignies-Louvain-la-Neuve. Retrieved November 5, 2018, from http://www.apbrebes.org/files/seeds/files/2014-09-08%20BATUR%20 Fulya%20THESE%20final.pdf.

Buiatti, M., Ceccarelli, S., Dolder, F., Esquinas, J., Mammuccini, M. G., Magarinos -Rey, B., ... & Shiva, V. (2013). *The law of the seed*. Retrieved November 5, 2018, from https://seedfreedom.info/the-law-of-the-seed/.

Carrington, D. (2017, May 19), *Arctic stronghold of world's seeds flooded after permafrost melts.* Retrieved November 5, 2018, from https://www.theguardian .com/environment/2017/may/19/arctic-stronghold-of-worlds-seeds -flooded-after-permafrost-melts.

Ceccarelli, S. (2016, February 29). The centrality of seed: Building agricul- tural resilience through plant breeding. *Independent Science News for Food and Agriculture*. Retrieved November 5, 2018, from https://www.indepen dentsciencenews.org/un-sustainable-farming/the-centrality-of-seed -building-agricultural-resilience-through-plant-breeding/.

Commission Directive 2009/145/EC, on providing for certain derogations, for acceptance of vegetable landraces and varieties which have been traditionally grown in particular localities and regions and are threatened by genetic erosion and of vegetable varieties with no intrinsic value for commercial crop production but developed for growing under particular conditions and for marketing of seed of those landraces and varieties (article 8, on region of origin)(2009), *Official Journal* L312, 48.

Commission Regulation 2018/848 of the European Parliament and the Council of 30 May 2018, on organic production and labelling of organic products and repealing Council Regulation (EC) No 834/2007 (2018), *Official Journal* L150, 1–92.

Cornucopia Institute. (2018). *Seed industry structure*. Retrieved November 5, 2018, from https://www.cornucopia.org/seed-industry-structure-dr-phil -howard.

Corporate Europe Observatory. (2018, June 29). *Biosafety in danger: How industry researchers and negotiators collaborate to undermine the UN Biodiversity Convention*. Retrieved November 5, 2018 from https://corporate europe.org/food-and-agriculture/2018/06/biosafety-danger.

Environmental Justice Atlas. (2015, February 24). *Media campaigns to save the "Linda Potato", Germany*. Retrieved October 15, 2018, from https://ejatlas .org/conflict/media-campaigns-to-save-the-linda-potato-germany.

European Seed Association. (n.d.). *Biodiversity is our business: How plant breeders protect and promote biodiversity*. Retrieved November 5, 2018, from https://legacy.euroseeds.eu/voluntary-benefit-sharing-activities-european -seed-industry.

ETC Group. (1999, February 2). *UPOV '91 threatens Francophone Africa*. Retrieved November 5, 2018, from https://www.etcgroup.org/content /upov-91-threatens-francophone-africa.

ETC Group. (2013). Putting the cartel before the horse ...and farm, seeds, soil, peasants, etc.: Who will control agricultural inputs, 2013? *Communiqué, 111.* Retrieved November 5, 2018, from http://www.etcgroup.org/sites /www.etcgroup.org/files/CartelBeforeHorse11Sep2013.pdf.

Fagan, J., Antoniou, M. & Robinson, C. (2014). *GMO myths and truths: An evidence-based examination of the claims made for the safety and efficacy of genetically modified crops and foods.* London, United Kingdom: Earth Open Source. Retrieved November 5, 2018, from https://earthopensource.org /wordpress/downloads/GMO-Myths-and-Truths-edition2.pdf.

Food and Agriculture Organization of the United Nations. (n.d.). *Harvesting nature's diversity.* Retrieved November 5, 2018 from http://www.fao.org/ docrep/004/v1430e/V1430E04.htm.

Food and Agriculture Organization of the United Nations. (2019). *Family Farming Knowledge Platform. Agroecology and Family Farming.* Retrieved November 5, 2018, from http://www.fao.org/family-farming/themes/agro ecology/en/.

GRAIN. (2007, February 16). *The end of farm-saved seed?: Industry's wish list for the next revision of UPOV.* Retrieved November 5, 2018, from https://www .grain.org/article/entries/58-the-end-of-farm-saved-seed-industry-s-wish -list-for-the-next-revision-of-upov.

IAASTD. (2009). *Agriculture at a Crossroads, International Assessment of Agricultural Knowledge Science Technology and Development,* summary: IAASTD Fact Sheet Feeding the World, Greening the Planet Retrieved November 5, 2018 from ///E:/IAASTD%20Fact%20Sheet.pdf, also see global report at: http://www.fao.org/fileadmin/templates/est/Investment /Agriculture_at_a_Crossroads_Global_Report_IAASTD.pdf.

IFOAM. (2018). *The new EU organic regulation: What will change?* Retrieved November 5, 2018, from https://www.ifoam-eu.org/en/organic-regulations /new-eu-organic-regulation-what-will-change.

Koutsika-Sotiriou, M., Tsivelikas, A. L. & Gogas, Ch. (2011). Αγροκομικές δυνατότητες τοπικών ποικιλιών. Retrieved November 5, 2018, from http:// wwww.minagric.gr/gpa/omilies/Koutsika.pdf.

Magarinos-Rey, B. (2015). *Semences hors-la-loi. La biodiversité confisquée.* Paris, France: Éditions Gallimard.

Marangou, L. (2002). Αμοργός 1-Η Μινώα: Η πόλις, ο λιμήν και η μείζων περιφέρεια. Athens, Greece: Greek Archaeological Society.

Mesquida, S. (Producer). (2018). *Seeds of war* [TV documentary]. France: ARTE TV and What's up productions.

Mpofu, E. (2014). *Declaration of the General Coordinator of La Via Campesina,* in Saatgutkampagne.org home page, retrieved on Nov. 5 2018 from http:// www.saatgutkampagne.org/.

Moss, D. & Bittman, M. (2018, June 27). *Bringing farming back to nature.* Retrieved November 5, 2018, from https://www.grain.org/bulletin_board /entries/5975-bringing-farming-backtonature.

No patents on seeds!. (n.d.). *Patent cases*. Retrieved on November 5, 2018, from https://www.no-patents-on-seeds.org/en/patent-cases.

Samaras, S. & Matthaiou, A. (1994). Greek Gene Bank. Retrieved November 5, 2018, from http://www.nagref.gr/journals/ethg/images/23/ethg23p24–26 .pdf.

Séralini, G.-E., Clair, E., Mesnage, R., Gress, S., Defarge, N., Malatesta, M., ... & Spiroux de Vendômois, J. (2014). Republished study: Long-term toxicity of a Roundup herbicide and a Roundup-tolerant genetically modified maize. *Environmental Sciences Europe, 26*. Retrieved November 5, 2018, from https://enveurope.springeropen.com/articles/10.1186/s12302-014-0014-5.

Stavropoulos, N., Samaras, S. & Matthaiou, A. (2000). *Προστασία και βελτίωση φυτικών γενετικών πόρων: Απολογισμός-προπτικές στην απαρχή του 21ου αι. Πρακτικά 8ου Πανελλήνιου Συνεδρίου Γενετικής Βελτίωσης Φυτών, 23–25 Οκτωβρίου 2000*. Arta: Elliniki Epistimoniki Etaireia Genetikis Veltiosis Fiton. Retrieved November 5, 2018, from http://www.plantbreeding.gr /assets/pdf/8o_PROCEEDINGS.pdf.

UNESCO. (2013). *Browse the lists of intangible cultural heritage and the register of good safeguarding practices*. Retrieved November 5, 2018, from https:// ich.unesco.org/en/lists#2013.

Vélot, C. (2009). *OGM: Touts' explique*. Athée, France: Goutte de Sable.

Vishnyakova, M., Thanopoulos, R., Bebeli, P. & Ozerskaya, T. (2017). *Συλλογή τοπικών ποικιλιών και αγρίων συγγενών καλλιεργειών από τον Ν. Vavilov στην Ελλάδα το 1926*. Retrieved November 5, 2018, from http://www .minagric.gr/images/events/4th-scientific-consortium/vishnyakova -thanop-mpempeli-4hepsin-1hsyn-new.pdf.

CHAPTER 8

From Cooking to Commoning: The Making of Intangible Cultural Heritage in OneLoveKitchen, Athens

Penny Travlou

This chapter is a critical discussion of intangible cultural heritage (ICH) and its conceptual predicates through the lens of a self-organised, collective, culinary project: *OneLoveKitchen,* an African collective kitchen in Athens, founded and sustained by a group of undocumented migrants and refugees from Africa along with local and international activists. It examines the emergence of a very distinctive kind of translocal cultural heritage through the sharing of cooking practices, skills and knowledge, and discusses how sharing was conflated with the crossing and contesting of borders. *OneLoveKitchen* demonstrates how cultural values can be co-created by agents of diverse national, socio-cultural, economic, political and religious backgrounds, who have embarked upon a common project motivated by a desire to care for each other in a safe, communal space shared and owned by all. The obvious challenge here is how to re-define ICH by taking into account transcultural, transnational and nomadic contexts of cultural production. What are the cultural values shared within a newly constituted community of former strangers with different personal histories, geographies and everyday experiences? How can these differences be negotiated to create – and enrich – a shared common space of care and active citizenship?

How to cite this book chapter:
Travlou, P. 2020. From Cooking to Commoning: The Making of Intangible Cultural Heritage in OneLoveKitchen, Athens. In Lekakis, S. (ed.) *Cultural Heritage in the Realm of the Commons: Conversations on the Case of Greece.* Pp. 159–182. London: Ubiquity Press. DOI: https://doi.org/10.5334/bcj.j. License: CC-BY

Culinary Practices as Intangible Cultural Heritage (ICH)

In recent years, the discussion on cultural heritage has moved beyond its earlier (and arguably limited) focus on tangible objects such as artefacts, monuments, architectural and archaeological sites of historical significance. The concept of cultural heritage has been broadened to encompass a greater diversity of cultural manifestations, including intangible cultural practices *such as:*

> *"customs and oral traditions, music, languages, poetry, dance, festivities, religious ceremonies [...] systems of healing, traditional knowledge systems and skills connected with the material aspects of culture, such as tools and the habitat"* (Bouchenaki 2003: 1).

International organisations such as UNESCO and ICOMOS, the International Council on Monuments and Sites, have acknowledged that tangible and intangible cultural heritage (ICH) are bound inextricably (ICOMOS 2002). However, it has taken a very long time – particularly for UNESCO – to recognise intangible cultural heritage as equally important to tangible artefacts, monuments and sites. This came after much criticism by indigenous groups against the hierarchical, colonial and "unconditionally" elitist approach to cultural heritage by UNESCO (Brulotte & Di Giovine 2016: 12). As a response to this rightful criticism, UNESCO set up the *Representative List of the Intangible Cultural Heritage of Humanity* which follows the same structure with the World Heritage List, "yet purports to be more democratizing and even less determinate in its standards of selection" (Brulotte & Di Giovine 2016: 12). In this Intangible Cultural Heritage List, there is recognition of equal importance of people's everyday cultural practices, knowledge and skills to that of artefacts and monuments.

Specifically, UNESCO has proposed a set of criteria that would render a cultural practice recognised as Intangible Cultural Heritage. According to these criteria, such a cultural practice must be, a) traditional, and 'living' at the same time; b) inclusive; c) representative; and, d) community-based (UNESCO 2011). For UNESCO, ICH can represent traditions of the past as much as of the present; ICH practices can be deployed in rural and/or urban areas, by diverse groups, including groups that have migrated from one place to another. ICH contributes "to social cohesion, encouraging a sense of identity and responsibility which helps individuals to feel part" of a community (UNESCO 2011). ICH is, therefore, a cultural good that is passed from generation to generation and is shared between members of a community as well as with other communities. Most importantly, however, ICH can only be recognised as such by the communities wherein it is produced, maintained and transmitted. Along these lines, traditional culinary practices have recently been recognised as ICH, since these practices encompass voices, values, traditions, skills, knowledge, craftmanship, technologies, tools, storytelling and oral history (see ICH: ICH-UNESCO 2017).

In the introduction of their book "Edible Identities: Food as Cultural Heritage", Michael Di Giovine and Ronda Brulotte share their observation that:

> "[A]most immediately after the ratification of the Intangible Heritage Convention, nation-states in Latin America and Western Europe, for whom food already factore into heritage claims and touristic imaginaries, began drawing up inventories cataloguing, and thereby constructing, a systematic narrative about their cuisines" (Brulotte & Di Giovine 2016: 13).

In the 12th session of the *Intergovernmental Committee for the Safeguarding of the ICH* (Republic of Korea, December 2017), a culinary practice, the making of the Neapolitan pizza, was recognised as ICH for the first time; as such it became included in the *Representative List of the ICH of Humanity*. The Committee described the art of the Neapolitan *'pizzaiuolo'* (pizza maker) as,

> "a culinary practice comprising four different phases relating to the preparation of the dough and its baking in a wood-fired oven, involving a rotatory movement by the baker. The element originates in Naples, the capital of the Campania Region, where about 3,000 Pizzaiuoli now live and perform. Pizzaiuoli are a living link for the communities concerned. [...] The element fosters social gatherings and intergenerational exchange, and assumes a character of the spectacular, with the Pizzaiuolo at the centre of their 'bottega' sharing their art. However, knowledge and skills are primarily transmitted in the 'bottega', where young apprentices observe masters at work, learning all the key phases and elements of the craft" (ICH-UNESCO, 2017).

Notable in this description is the emphasis on the contribution of the *pizzaiuolo's* art on sociability, knowledge exchange and the maintenance of community links. Evidently, these criteria weighted heavily in the recognition of the pizzaiuolo's art as ICH. It is, thus, the potential of this culinary practice to bring people together and to enable them to share the knowledge of pizza recipes that is considered to hold cultural value. The official recognition of the Neapolitan pizzaiuolo's art as ICH exemplifies this understanding of cultural value and invites an enquiry on 'food' as a social practice that holds cultural value. Beyond this, it looks at the way food and culinary practices bond people together and build new and/or strengthen existing communities through sharing cooking practices, skills and traditional knowledge. The art of the Neapolitan pizzaiuolo has also crossed borders creating a strong transglobal network of pizza makers whose skills and knowledge have bonded together the Italian diaspora and connected with other local and translocal communities to redefine ICH in a mobile transcultural context.

Being Collaborative – Being Ethnographic

Building upon previous ethnographic work on collaborative and peer learn-ing practices within emerging networks of digital art practitioners (Travlou 2013), while on sabbatical in Athens in 2015, I embarked on a project look-ing at the influx of newcomers to the city– mainly artists and activists from the Global North and immigrants and refugees from Africa and the Middle East. The arrival of refugees in Greece peaked in the summer of that year, with hundreds of people arriving daily after a perilous Aegean crossing. I was inter-ested in exploring the solidarity networks emerging within Athens to support migrants and refugees. At the same time, I became involved with several initia-tives within this solidarity network as an active participant. *OneLoveKitchen*, the African collective kitchen that forms the focus of this chapter, was one such initiative in which I participated from the outset. A brief comment on my multi-fold role as a researcher, activist and member of the kitchen is warranted here; this can also serve as a short testimony on the collaborative methodology I used in the course of the project.

Reflecting the current shift of ethnographic research towards the investigation of nomadic and multi-sited communities (Marcus 1998), this ethnography of *OneLoveKitchen* looked at a mobile group. Local and international activists and migrants/refugees had been in constant movement across international bor-ders and the urban space(s) of Athens; many refuges/migrants hoped to con-tinue their journey further, to Germany or other countries in Northern Europe. The ethnographic methodology was shaped by – and mirrored – the networks, spaces, practices of co-creation and the collaborative ethos of this 'subject' community, which, for my sojourn in Athens also became my community.

This was a collaborative ethnography (Lassiter 2005). Collaboration was employed as a tool to contest knowledge hierarchies: it enabled horizontal prac-tices of doing fieldwork *together*, with everyone else involved in the kitchen. Kitchen members were active participants in the fieldwork process, while I par-ticipated in all the tasks and practices that sustained the kitchen.

Creativity is understood as emerging from the synergy of spaces, practices and artefacts, interlinked so that they constitute an assemblage (Deleuze & Guattari 1987). Spaces are inhabited by bodies; practices are performed by bodies; arte-facts are made by (and in some sense are themselves) bodies. The underpin-ning commonality here is, therefore, a network of interacting bodies linked by actions, biographies, stories. In *OneLoveKitchen*, collective making and sharing takes place at the intersection, and through the weaving together, of multiple storylines. This topology of distributed agency and interconnection resembles that of a mesh network: a rhizome. Ethnographic fieldwork in *OneLoveKitchen* thus became a quest for interactions between places, people and things. My attempt to follow the storylines embodied in the making of the kitchen led me to a "rhizomic ethnography" (Leach 2003; Travlou 2013). This rhizomic topology also permitted me to explore various entry points to *OneLoveKitchen*, both during fieldwork and while writing the ethnographic text. To do justice to the rhizomic, multivocal and horizontal nature of the kitchen (and fieldwork), this chapter eschews a linear narrative structure.

Nomadic subjectivities, active citizenship and intangible culture

OneLoveKitchen was founded in 2015, in what was, for Athens (and Greece as a whole), a socio-political turning point: a moment of accelerated economic, social and demographic change, often referred to, in both the media and everyday conversation, as '*I Krisi*', the *Crisis* (see Mitsopoulos & Pelagidis 2011; Douzinas 2013; Pleios 2013; Mylonas 2014; Tsilimpounidi 2016). This crisis is usually portrayed as an impeding, even accomplished catastrophe. Yet, amidst the very real pressures generated by massive state debt, neoliberal austerity, extensive impoverishment and large numbers of newcomers in need (refugees, other migrants), there are also processes and agents that make possible the emergence of innovative models of living, sharing of resources, surviving and resisting oppressive state policies. Departing from current mainstream representations of the '*crisis*' ('financial'/'debt crisis'; 'refugee crisis') as (only) a catastrophe, I wanted to explore opportunities for socio-political change and novel forms of participatory citizenship that could emerge from the collaboration, friendship, care, trust – in one word, comradeship – between people that this 'crisis' brought together. *OneLoveKitchen* offered me an appropriate – and very welcoming – place in which to attempt this exploration.

I also wanted to move beyond the stereotypical representation of migrants/refugees as outlined in Giorgio Agamben's *Homo Sacer* (Agamben 1998) – people with fewer rights than the citizens of nation-states – and explore their nomadic experiences and practices of active political engagement as possible catalysts of social and cultural change in the host-society. This theoretical shift challenges the tendency to view refugees/migrants as (merely) economic, rather than socio-political actors – a tendency that often obscures the numerous ways in which refugees/migrants exercise political agency. Many practices of refugees and migrants are, indeed, political acts, even though they often differ from the forms of mobilisation and protest readily recognised as 'political' in the host society.

Rosi Braidotti's (2011) notion of "nomadic subjectivity" helps us to realise how refugees/migrants – newcomers and 'strangers' who inhabit space in a non-sedentary manner, challenge the bounded territory of the nation-state. For Deleuze and Guattari (1987), nomadism designates a way of occupying space while subscribing to a kind of rule, a custom, outside that of social respect or engagement. Nomadic citizenship can be seen as a new paradigm of citizenship that, while contributing to the making of shared cultural values in the city, at the same time challenges and contests these values. This paradigm of citizenship is predicated upon the sense of belonging to a transnational network detached from the bounded territory of the nation-state and, therefore, potentially oppositional to the myriad exclusions and the proclivity to violence that state citizenship entails (Holland 2012). As Arjun Appadurai concludes in an essay on the future of patriotism, citizenship "become[s] plural, serial, contextual and mobile" (Appadurai 1993: 428). In this respect, nomadic citizenship entails voluntary membership of self-organising groups of various kinds and scales. Borrowing Papadopoulos and Tsianos' words, what constructs mobile citizenship is *the sharing of knowledge and infrastructures of connectivity, affective cooperation, mutual support and care among people on the move*" (2013: 178). Nomadic citizenship thus tends to break the state's monopoly on controlling citizenship: it re-distributes social belonging among other groups and across other, non-state sanctioned forms of group organisation (Holland 2012). *OneLoveKitchen*, founded and sustained by nomads, people on the move, is a case in point.

How does nomadic citizenship relate to the intangible cultural heritage? The vital question here is one of *practices* and *conditions* of cultural production: *who* produces ICH in the transient, contested spaces shared and shaped by newcomers and locals alike? *Where*, by what *means*, and through what *practices* does this production take place?

As already mentioned, one of UNESCO's four identifying criteria of ICH is its community-based character. This criterion may be taken to imply that ICH can only be (re-)produced within a settled, localised community. This implication is further supported by the claim (often made by symbolic anthropologists) that a community is the result of 'boundary construction through identity and shared systems of meaning' (Cohen 1985 qtd. in Guimarães 2005: 146). The nomadic constituents of *OneLoveKitchen* clearly fall short of this criterion. Is this then to imply that the mingling of ingredients, recipes, food, stories and bodies in *OneLoveKitchen* does not qualify as intangible culture?

This impasse brings into focus the limitations of the concept of community as an identifying criterion for ICH. Community is predicated upon a disposition of boundaries – be they boundaries in space or/and boundaries in membership. As such, a community often excludes newcomers, especially those who do not share its common (foundational) histories and values. The nomadic citizenship practiced in *OneLoveKitchen* challenges this limiting and exclusionary understanding of the concept of community.

It seems that a more appropriate organisational concept – permissive, open, and fluid enough to accommodate nomadic lives on the move – is that of a network, a *meshwork* (Ingold 2010). Unlike the conception of community, based on (fixed) identity and the construction of boundaries, a meshwork is an emergent phenomenon in constant flux. It is constituted from "interwoven lines of growth and movement" (Ingold 2010: 4); trajectories of bodily movement across continents, oceans and time, stories of lives in motion that render multivocality explicit within an ever-changing structure of entanglement. Understood in this way, a meshwork cannot be static: it is always in-the-making, as new actors arrive and continuously reshape it. Neither can it be closed and firmly fixed in space: the ever-changing storylines that constitute it are formidably extendable.

An ever-growing number of people – migrants, refugees, 'cosmopolitans' and others – are constantly on the move. They meet and constitute meshworks of co-existence and solidarity, where they enact nomadic citizenship and, in the course of this, produce intangible culture. Our understanding of what counts as ICH, therefore, needs to take these practices, social contexts and distributed topologies and cultural production into account.

Sharing is caring: Food and politics in *OneLoveKitchen*

Compared with other European capital cities, Athens is not regarded as a hub of 'ethnic' cuisines. This may be due to the dominance of the Greek culinary tradition: there may be less of a local interest in experimenting with different tastes. However, Greek cuisine itself manifests the country's geopolitical situation on the crossroad between East and West in its eclectic merging of flavours and recipes from Turkey, the Balkans, Italy and France. A number of emblematic Greek dishes (e.g. *tzatziki, moussakas, imam, soutzoukakia, baklavas*) come straight from the culinary tradition of the Ottoman Empire/Turkey – particularly from that of Istanbul and the urban centres of the Aegean coast where many Greeks lived before the 1923 Greece-Turkey population exchange. Dishes of these earlier Greek refugees brought new flavours to the local palette: cumin, aniseed, cloves etc. Since the 1990s, with the arrival of economic migrants of different nationalities in Athens, there has been an expansion in restaurants dedicated to 'ethnic' cuisines. Migrants from China, Pakistan, India, Ethiopia, Kurdistan and Iraq have established restaurants in and around the city centre, mostly catering for a migrant clientele. These restaurants are usually in neighbourhoods with populous migrant communities. A smaller number of more 'upmarket' 'ethnic' restaurants cater for a mixed clientele of Greeks, migrants and tourists.

As African cooks informed me, alongside these licensed restaurants there is also a network of homemade food catering businesses that serve migrant communities. These businesses are part of an informal economy where non-monetary exchanges of services are often permissible (e.g. someone can provide home-cooked lunches in exchange of a haircut or child minding). Our Eritrean cook in *OneLoveKithen*, for instance, would often bake bread in her basement flat in exchange for haircuts. This informal economy can be viewed as a form of collaborative economy where "assets or services are shared between private individuals, either for free or for a fee" (Gañigueral 2015).

As mentioned earlier, the African collective kitchen consisted of undocumented (*sans papiers*) African migrants and refugees along with local and international Greek activists. We were from Senegal, Gambia, Nigeria, Ethiopia, Eritrea, UK, Hungary, Italy, the USA and Greece, of different age, gender, sexuality, race, religion, education, employment and economic status. Languages within the group varied too: we spoke English, Greek, French, Wolof and Amharic. When necessary, we would interpret between these languages. Some of us were professional chefs; others had just started learning how to cook; a few others were responsible for organising and promoting our events. Each member of the collective had one or more distinct roles, according to individual skills and interests (Social Innovation Europe 2016).

Our aim was to create a safe, shared, social space where we would care for each other, cook together, share food and organise pop-up events across the city where people could come together to taste well cooked and novel dishes and to meet one another. We hoped that this interaction could facilitate cultural exchange and social transformation. Equally important to us was our desire to challenge hegemonic notions of exchange value and the idea that value is produced only through "action that is considered labour" (see Wilson 2017: 132). We wanted to show that, independent of their potential to produce goods and services for exchange, actions of solidarity constitute value-in-themselves. We saw value as determined by the potential of people's actions to translate into, inform and enrich meaning; to be "meaningful [and, in our project, explicitly political] action" (Taylor 2017: 191 in Wilson 2017: 132).

We applied a model of solidarity economy, based on practices of participatory budgeting, heterarchy, horizontal decision-making, collective self-organisation and peer learning. Many of our African members brought their experiences of informal economy to the project. These experiences were cross-pollinated with experiences of collaborative economy that other members had practiced. Our principles and operational practices were explored, discussed and reinforced in regular (weekly) assemblies.

For five months, *OneLoveKitchen* organised regular pop-up events in various locations across Athens: from the rooftop of *Nosotros*, a free social space in Exarchia, at the very centre of Athens (Figure 1), to an anti-racist festival in the occupied space of Votanicos Park, a former botanic garden, and academic conferences in two squatted art spaces: EMBROS theatre and café-bar Green Park (Figure 2). The collective kitchen was self-funded through fees charged for catering services and individual donations. Due to the self-organised and non-legal status of the kitchen, we were not able to invoice for our catering services. We kept our prices low to make our food accessible to people who, in the midst of the financial crisis would have found it difficult to spend much on eating out (Figure 3). We never managed to make much profit, but what we

Figure 1: Pop-up event in Nosotros (Source: author).

earned from each event was shared equally among all of us regardless of our individual financial situation. We thought that unequal distribution of earnings would have disempowered some members by placing them in the position of recipients of charity. Those of us who were in less precarious financial position and had a steady income, however, used our share of the earnings to purchase cooking equipment and to cover other expenses incurred from our catering events (e.g. hire and repair of a van). We also followed a participatory budgeting framework to collectively decide how and where to spend our budget. In this, we were inspired by citizen and neighbourhood assemblies in Latin American cities, which use participatory budgeting as a tool for economic democracy, to involve those (e.g. low-income residents, non-citizens, the youth) left out by conventional methods of public engagement (Participatory Budgeting Project 2012). In our case, this was particularly relevant for migrant and refugee

Figure 2: Senegambian cooks in occupied Votanikos Park (Source: author).

members (*sans papiers*) who, by lacking a residence and work permit, had no legally sanctioned access to employment.

Our decision-making practices aimed explicitly at challenging power structures. All decisions pertaining to the functioning of *OneLoveKitchen* were made collectively in weekly assemblies (Travlou 2017; see Figure 4). Some members already had considerable experience of participating in assemblies; others did not. Speaking in front of the whole group was not easy for some, particularly at the beginning, when most of us were just beginning to get to know each other. To enable communication and allow all members to find a voice, one of us facilitated the assembly, using the *Art of Hosting*, "a suite of powerful conversation processes to invite people to step in and take charge of the challenges facing them" (Art of Hosting n.d.). Our assemblies started in a circle: the 'host' addressed a generic question to the group and each member responded in their turn. On one such occasion, in the early days of the project, the host asked us: "*are you in love today?*" To our surprise, all of us responded, and by the end of the assembly that morning some remarked that they felt a stronger bond with the rest of the group. This is how we came up with a name for our project: *OneLoveKitchen*.

The assembly was not only a platform for discussion of operational matters, but also for the exchange and sharing of personal stories, struggles and reflections on everyday life in Athens. In the assemblies, particularly in those facilitated through the *Art of Hosting*, it became evident that we cared for

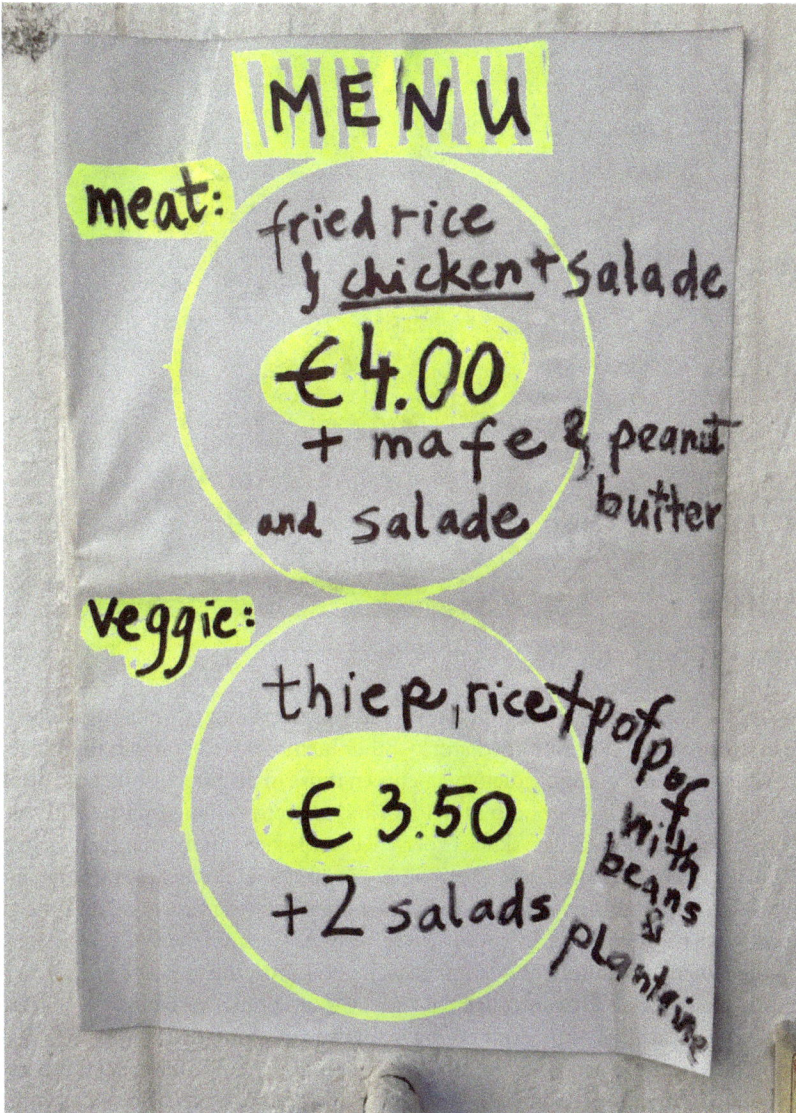

Figure 3: OneLoveKitchen Senegalese Menu (Source: author).

each other and that we were all determined to ensure that each of us was healthy and content.

A further, equally crucial function of the weekly assemblies was the building and maintenance of trust between members. This was not always easy: conflict was unavoidable on several occasions, and this became apparent in the assemblies. In a group of people as diverse as ours, from so many different cultures, political ideologies and religious beliefs, conflict was expected – even valued, as it helped

Figure 4: OneLoveKitchen Assembly (Source: author).

us to better understand our differences and positionalities. Conflict was dealt with in the assemblies, with mediators – other members – stepping in to resolve issues through encouraging dialogue between those in dispute. Conflict can also be regarded as a driver for both individual and collective change, particularly as it challenges the knowledge, skills, experiences and expectations that each member brings into the community. Overcoming conflict was about, firstly, recognising difference, and then allowing individual members to unlearn; to shift their knowledge paradigm and accept to learn afresh. As Carmen Elena Cirnu argues "[T]he concept of unlearning is intrinsically bound to the concept of change" (2015: 131). In our African collective kitchen, our conflict resolution practices involved unlearning. This is something we arrived at spontaneously. Some of us learned to be more accepting of racial, gender and religious differences; others learned to share more openly our stories; while others learned to do things with others and to value collective interest more than individual gain.

What enabled us to sustain our project through these episodes of conflict was our trust on our common values of equality and sharing. These common values were constantly reinforced in the assemblies. It became evident that, beyond our differences, we all desired to care for each other, share knowledge and skills and act in solidarity whenever the need arose. By solidarity, here, I mean both the principle that can inspire and guide action in support of one another (Arendt 1990: 88–89) and the relationships built upon this principle (Vasiljevic 2016: 381).

Cooking is often regarded as a gendered, feminine activity, a characteristic of the domestic, a private sphere related to social reproduction.

"[F]ood work has typically been relegated to women or otherwise marginalized peoples and excluded from the purportedly more sophisticated, abstract activities of knowledge production" (Brady 2011: 322).

This confinement in the domain of 'home economics' – women's unpaid labour, as part of their house chores – disassociates cooking from political action. Yet, it is its very nature as an act of *care* for the other members of the household/collective that makes cooking a political praxis (see Arendt 1958). Care encompasses:

"being mindful, looking after, attending the needs, and being considerate, [...] both awareness of dependency, possession of needs, and relatedness as basic elements of the human constitution and also concrete caring activities in a broad sense. It involves "caring for the world", not only by means of nursing and social-work activities or housework in the narrow sense, but also by dedication to a cultural transformation" (Knecht et al. 2012: 37).

In *OneLoveKitchen*, care played a central role in bringing us together and transforming our lives in various ways. Some of us lived precarious, 'bare lives' (to use Agamben's term), without legal status, housing and steady employment, and confronted with harsh and challenging daily experiences. The kitchen was a caring and safe shared space sustained through its members' actions of solidarity. When our Eritrean cook was threatened by her landlord with eviction, another member from Sierra Leone reassured her: "you are not alone, we are together. And together, we are power". Members of *OneLoveKitchen*, came together to organize legal support. Her eviction was overturned and she managed to remain in her rented flat.

Care work – the material and affective labour of seeing to another person's needs – was also a paid professional activity for many *OneLoveKitchen* members. Most of the African women participating in the kitchen also worked, for very low wages, as home carers and cleaners in residential care homes for the elderly, hospitals, bars and restaurants. The intersectional oppression that these women experienced as racialised, gendered and underclass subjects in Greece has motivated them to self-organise and set up the *United African Women Organisation* which lobbies for equal rights for migrant women and their children in Greece. Their first-hand experiences of exploitation and marginalisation, where their affective labour, although monetised as 'paid labour', remained underpaid and devalued, led them to deploy 'care' as political action. In this way, they became political subjects demanding visibility and justice. This "politics of care" encouraged African migrant women care-workers to develop a political consciousness in which caring is invoked as the power to build new

Figure 5: OneLoveKitchen event poster (Source: Nosotros & author).

kinds of active citizenship and solidarity (see also Hill Collins 2000; Bassel & Emejulu 2018).

These African migrant women brought their distinctive political subjectivity and their know-how of grassroots activism and politics of care to *OneLoveKitchen*. Most importantly, they decolonised political action and made their means and methods of struggle relevant and instructive to local and foreign activists in our group. We should note that sharing and caring are concepts deeply rooted in African traditions of political struggle: '*Ubuntu*', originally a Zulu concept, is widely used across Africa to describe a universal bond of sharing that connects all humanity: the notion that "a person is a person through other persons" (Shutte 1993: 46). The concept of '*Ujamaa*', a Kiswahili term translated as 'familyhood' or 'brotherhood' (Cornelli 2012), central to Julius Nyerere's formulation of African Socialism (Nyerere 1968), is another case in point. For Nyerere, Ujamaa is "an attitude of mind [...] needed to ensure that the people care for each other's welfare"; this is a precondition for a just society (1977: 1).

Caring was thus valued as an empowering political act from the very beginning of *OneLoveKitchen*. Since our cooking took place not in a domestic or commercial setting but out in the public sphere (the *polis*), we saw the opportunity to develop the kitchen as a political space for empowerment and emancipation rather than (just) a space to perfect recipes and experiment with ingredients. Our common belief that "sharing is caring", our intention to act as recipients and providers of care and solidarity and to contest the multiple facets of the crisis that Athens experienced, formed the very core of our kitchen politics. The poster publicising our very first pop-up event, on the rooftop of *Nosotros* in Exarchia, declared that "*freedom is our basic ingredient*" (see Figure 5). From the outset, we wanted to make it explicit that *OneLoveKitchen* was a platform for active citizenship, a political praxis.

Breaking bread together:
Com panis –> Companion –> Comrade

As OneLoveKitchen members and political actors, we became companions and comrades. A companion (from Latin 'com panis') is a person you share bread with, you "break bread together". The Greek cognate is 'σύντροφος' (syntrofos): one you share food ('τροφή') with. With a comrade (from Latin 'camera': chamber) you share intimate living space. As all these cognates demonstrate, relationships of political solidarity are reinforced by acts of sharing and intimacy.

Food making and sharing is a social act of hospitality ('*filoxenia*' in Greek; '*teranga*' in Wolof – both meaning the gift of unconditional generosity to a stranger) and connection: a means for celebrating and constantly reinforcing relationships of reciprocity. By bringing people together, a shared meal facilitates "the togetherness of the social actors" (Adapon 2008: 37). In Georg Simmel's terms, a meal mediates socialisation (1994: 350). This companionship through the sharing of food can even be achieved with very little resort to conversation. In this sense, we can think of food as an object of exchange, a gift (in Marcel Mauss' terms) that can be shared and exchanged (Mauss 1990). In her ethnographic monograph, "*Culinary Art and Anthropology*", Joy Adapon (2008) suggests that,

"Food sharing is dynamic and self-extending whereas eating is socially static and self-collapsing. So, cooking is an inherently social act, and so, conversely, eating what one cooks oneself is antisocial, unless one is sharing the food" (2008: 41).

In *OneLoveKitchen*, we ate together regularly, in a conscious act of group bonding. This fitted in well with the culinary practices many of us had grown up with. In both Senegambian and Eritrean/Ethiopian traditions, you commonly eat with others, sharing food from the same plate. In Senegal, 'thieboudienne', a rice and fish dish, is served in a large round tray from which everyone partakes. Likewise, in Eritrea and Ethiopia, people share food served on *injera*, a type of flatbread. In the Greek tradition, 'mezedes' are served in small plates to be shared among all those sitting around the table.

Eating together was of great importance to us all, as we had previously been strangers, with different personal histories, geographies and points of departure. In his eponymous text, Georg Simmel defines the stranger as "somebody who comes today and stays tomorrow" (unlike the wanderer, "who comes today and goes tomorrow", Wolff 1950: 402). The stranger is,

"[a] fundamentally mobile person; [s/he] comes in contact, at one time or another, with every individual, but is not organically connected, through established ties of kinship, locality, and occupation, with any single one" (Wolff 1950: 403).

By this definition, we were all strangers: the kitchen was where we all came together, to work on a project that we collectively owned. It was our cooking and eating together that shaped our project as a common shared space of care and solidarity wherein we could enact our citizenship.

Cooking as intangible cultural heritage – Cooking as commoning

Arguably, acts of commoning were implicit to the kitchen's ethos and practice. To speak about commoning rather than commons follows a current shift in the relevant theory, where authors such as Bollier and Helfrich (2012; 2015) advocate the importance of recognising the processes of creating and nurturing community. This recognition is also a critique of the limited view of the commons as only a pool of resources (see Ostrom 2015). As Linebaugh puts it:

"To speak of the commons as if it were a natural resource is misleading at best and dangerous at worst. The commons is an activity and, if anything, it expresses relationships in society that are inseparable from relations to

nature. It might be better to keep the word as a verb, an activity, rather than as a noun, a substantive" (Linebaugh 2008: 279).

Julie Ristau (2011), co-director of *On the Commons*, suggests:

> "*The act of commoning draws on a network of relationships made under the expectation that we will each take care of one another and with a shared understanding that some things belong to all of us—which is the essence of the commons itself. The practice of commoning demonstrates a shift in thinking from the prevailing ethic of "you're on your own" to "we're in this together"* (*On the Commons* 2011).

Many of the practices, relationships and ethical considerations outlined in this quotation were indeed manifested in *OneLoveKitchen*. Nonetheless, when it comes to the spatial configuration of the *OneLoveKitchen*, we still need to refer to common space (which is definitely not just a pool of resources). Our kitchen was a common space: shared, porous, constantly in the making, redefined and never complete, collectively owned and relatively free from interference by external power structures (Stavrides 2016a).

> "*In common space, differences meet but are not allowed to fight for a potential predominance in the process of defining, giving identity to space. If common space is shared space, then its users-producers have to learn to give, not only take. Common space can thus essentially be described as "offered" space. Space offered and taken the way a present is. True, the offering and acceptance of a present can mediate power relations. But the commoning of space presupposes sharing as a condition of reciprocity"* (An Architektur 2010: 23).

Further to this, in his recent monograph on 'common space' (2016b), Stavros Stavrides points out that:

> "*common space may be shaped through the practices of an emerging and not necessarily homogeneous community that does not simply try to secure its reproduction but also attempts to enrich its exchanges with other communities as well as those between its members. Common space may take the form of a meeting ground, an area in which 'expansive circuits of encounter' intersect"* (Stavrides 2016b: 11).

OneLoveKitchen was precisely such an intersection in our 'expansive circuits of encounter', where we, (previously) strangers, took the opportunity to share a "common world-in-the-making". To realise forms of cooperation through sharing, commoning has to overspill any fixed community boundaries by always being open to 'newcomers', strangers (Rancière 2006: 42). As argued earlier, the topology most conducive to this act of commoning is that of a meshwork, rather than that that of the (bounded) community. Huron also makes this point quite explicitly:

> "In order to change the balance of power in the contested urban environ-ment, what is precisely needed is to create networks with people who were once strangers but could become allies, or even friends. This is the specific challenge of urban commons: to weave new networks of trust and care amid the alienating pressures of the capitalist cityscape" (Huron 2015: 14–15).

The strangers that make and sustain porous common spaces within the capitalist cityscape are (also) people on the move, nomad citizens: activists from Global North; migrants and refugees from Global South. Common spaces are often reclaimed and/or reconstituted at a point of crisis, when deep human bonds of caring and mutual aid (bonds that are often imperiled by, for instance, forced displacement, migration, precarious labour, class exploitation, gender and race discrimination) are (re-)forged between people who were up to that point strangers. So, through commoning, these otherwise strangers come together to negotiate co-governance and affective practices of caregiving and taking (see Kurtz 2001). Here, the commons are revalued as an economy of care, love and mutual aid (after Hardt 2007; Hardt and Negri 2009 Hardt, see also Kropotkin 1902).

As noted, commoning is never complete. It is perpetually in the making; its horizon is tenuous, ever-retreating. In this emerging commons, strangers look into the mist and strive to locate others, an unrealised potential for non-territorially bound, porous and inclusive networks of comradeship built on the sharing and co-shaping of common values.

In *OneLoveKitchen*, our act of commoning extended beyond our kitchen and our cooking and eating together, to embrace and, by doing so reshape, a wider network of other spaces in Athens. Since we did not have a fixed venue to serve our food, we moved across the city like nomads, making use of spaces made available to us within Athens' wider solidarity network. In our peregrina-tion, we weaved lines that linked together various spaces across the city into a mobile commons, or, rather, a nomadic, rhizomic commons in the making. It is important to clarify here that nomadic commons as a term is not a synonym to a frivolous, ephemeral space of flows (see Castells 2009). Nomadic space is still predicated upon relationships and trust. Along with the members of the *OneLoveKitchen*, there was an infrastructural network of helpers who worked with us during our pop-up events: from those who lent us kitchen equipment, a van to transport the food to the event venues, the catering/serving staff and the kitchen porters to the food suppliers, venue occupants and clients. The infrastructure of the *OneLoveKitchen* was based on relations and collective work: friends and comrades made our events happen by offering their skills and facilities, but most importantly their solidarity. Together with a network of spaces, we created an over-expanding community who was present, relevant and empowering.

The configuration of the rhizomic topology of our network of solidarity was ever-changing, contingent upon the emergence and disappearance of transient entry points i.e. new occupied spaces, members arriving and departing (see Deleuze & Guattari 1987). The rhizomic topology and relational infrastructures of our African collective kitchen may offer another layer into the definition of ICH where the 'intangible' is connected to the affective and immaterial assets rather than what is produced within. Here, the relational is in sync to 'affective infrastructures' as defined by Lauren Berlant (2016) accommodating multiplicity and difference as much as allowing movement while recognizing collective affect inprinted on patterns, habits, norms within the common shared spaces. Speaking of movement and action (i.e. following Berlant's (2016: 399) argument that "the commons is an action concept that acknowledges a broken world"), affective infrastructures are discovered by looking at the making of cultural heritage by aterritorial communities. The latter implies those who are either displaced as refugees and/or intentionally (trans)located as for example activists and artists from the Global North. The cultural values produced within a collective project such as the *OneLoveKitchen* are relational and affective *par excellence*. Since there was no past history connecting its members and spaces (as most of us were newcomers in Athens, and knew each other for a short time), our sharing practices and common values of solidarity and care gave shape to our community in the here-and-now and strengthened relations between us and those we collaborated with throughout the five months of our kitchen's existence. It is, therefore, pertinent to redefine ICH in the context of displacement and mobile citizenship, to challenge notions of the 'cultural' as predicated (only) on borders, nation-states and localities. The *OneLoveKitchen* demonstrates how cultural value can be created and shared through an ever evolving and emerging heritage of commoning practices.

Concluding remarks

The nomadic, networked nature of *OneLoveKitchen*, an African collective kitchen in Athens, compels us to question the limitations of current understandings of cooking as intangible culture (and, I argue, intangible culture more generally). In times of increasing population mobility, migration and global nomadism, the concept of intangible cultural heritage needs to open up to include cultures produced by people on the move. Culinary culture, especially, cannot be seen as situated only at long-established, clearly demarcated communities at fixed geographical locations. By crossing and contesting borders, both geographical and cultural, and through enacting their nomad citizenship in networks of interaction, sharing, care and solidarity, migrants and refugees cross-pollinate culinary and political practices in their host countries. *OneLoveKitchen,* a common shared space co-created by migrants, refugees and other nomad citizens, exemplifies the practices of interchange whereby 'strangers' and 'newcomers' subvert current understandings of intangible cultural heritage as a prerogative of demarcated, spatially fixed communities. *OneLoveKitchen,* has enriched Athenian culinary culture with recipes and ingredients from Africa, and, also, with the practices of sharing, caring, solidarity and hospitality that emerged within it. These practices, shaped through the political actions of care and commoning, arguably constitute a distinctive kind of intangible cultural heritage: not fixed, but in perpetual flux; always in the making; socially and politically transformative.

Acknowledgements

Special thanks to the *OneLoveKitchen* members: Addis, Cheikh, Christos, David, Elisa, Esther, Jeff, Katlin, Lauren, Lauretta, Luisa, Mageb, Omar, Senait, Susan, Thanassis, Vicki.

Bibliography

Adapon, J. (2008). *Culinary art and anthropology.* Oxford, United Kingdom: Berg.

Agamben, G. (1998). *Homo Sacer: Sovereign power and bare life.* Redwood City, CA: Stanford University Press.

An Architektur. (2010). On the commons: A public interview with Massimo De Angelis and Stavros Stavrides. *e-flux – Journal, 17* (June–August). Retrieved November 20, 2019, from https://www.e-flux.com/journal/17/67351/on-the-commons-a-public-interview-with-massimo-de-angelis-and-stavros-stavrides/.

Appadurai, A. (1993). Patriotism and its futures. *Public Culture, 5*(3), 411–429.

Arendt, H. (1958). *The human condition.* Chicago, IL: The University of Chicago Press.

Arendt, H. (1990). *On revolution.* London, United Kingdom: Penguin Books.

Art of Hosting. (n.d.). *What is the art of hosting conversations that matter?* Retrieved November 20, 2019, from http://www.artofhosting.org/what-is-aoh/.

Bassel, L. & Emejulu, A. (2018). *Minority women and austerity: Survival and resistance in France and Britain.* Bristol, United Kingdom: Policy Press.

Berlant, L. (2016). The Commons: Infrastructures for Troubling Times*. *Environment and Planning D: Society and Space, 34*(3), 393–419. DOI: https://doi.org/10.1177/0263775816645989.

Bollier, D. & Helfrich, S. (Eds.). (2012). *The wealth of the commons: A world beyond market and state*. Amherst, MA: Levellers Press.

Bollier, D. and Helfrich, S. (Eds.). (2015). *Patterns of commoning*. Amherst, MA: The Commons Strategy Group & Off the Commons Books.

Bouchenaki, M. (2003). The interdependency of the tangible and intangible cultural heritage. In *14th ICOMOS General Assembly and International Symposium: Place, memory, meaning: preserving intangible values in monuments and sites, 27–31 October 2003, Victoria Falls, Zimbabwe*. Retrieved November 20, 2019, from http://openarchive.icomos.org/468/.

Brady, J. (2011). Cooking as inquiry: A method to stir up prevailing ways of knowing food, body, and identity. *International Journal of Qualitative Methods, 10*(4), 321–34. DOI: https://doi.org/10.1177/160940691101000402.

Braidotti, R. (2011). Nomadic subjects: *Embodiment and sexual difference in contemporary feminist theory*. New York, NY: Columbia University Press.

Brulotte, R. L. and Di Giovine, M. A. (Eds.). (2016). *Edible Identities: Food as Cultural Heritage*. London: Routledge.

Castells, M. (2009). *The rise of the network society, Vol. 1* (2nd ed.). Malden, MA: Wiley-Blackwell.

Cirnu, C. E. (2015). The shifting paradigm: Learning to unlearn. *Internet Learning, 4*(1), 126–133.

Cohen, A. P. (1985). *Symbolic construction of community*. London, United Kingdom: Routledge.

Cornelli, E. M. (2012). *A critical analysis of Nyerere's Ujamaa: An investigation of its foundations and values* (Unpublished PhD Thesis). University of Birmingham, Birmingham.

Deleuze, G. & Guattari, F. (1987). *A thousand plateaus: Capitalism and schizophrenia*. Minneapolis, MN: University of Minnesota Press.

Derrida, J. & Dufourmantelle, A. (2000). *Of hospitality*. Stanford, CA: Stanford University Press.

Douzinas, C. (2013). *Philosophy and resistance in the crisis: Greece and the future of Europe*. Cambridge, United Kingdom: Polity.

Gañigueral, A. (2015). Can digital sharing economy platforms pull Latin America's informal sector into the mainstream? Yes. *Americas Quarterly, Summer 2015 Issue: Trade is Back!* Retrieved November 20, 2019, from https://www.americasquarterly.org/content/can-digital-sharing-economy -platforms-pull-latin-america%E2%80%99s-informal-sector-mainstream -yes.

Guimarães Jr., M. J. L. (2005). Doing anthropology in cyberspace: Fieldwork boundaries and social environments. In C. Hine (Ed.), *Virtual methods: Issues in social research on the internet* (pp. 141–156). Oxford, United Kingdom: Berg.

Hardt, M. (2007). About love. *European Graduate School*. Retrieved November 20, 2019, from: www.youtube.com/watch?v=ioopkoppabI.

Hardt, M. & Negri, A. (2009). *Commonwealth*. Cambridge, MA: Harvard University Press.

Hill Collins, P. (2000). Gender, black feminism, and black political economy. *The Annals of the American Academy of Political and Social Science, 568*(1), 41–53.

Holland, E. W. (2012). Global cosmopolitanism and nomad citizenship. In R. Braidotti, P. Hanafin & B. Blaagaard (Eds.), *After cosmopolitanism* (pp. 149–165). Oxon, United Kingdom: Routledge.

Huron, A. (2015). Working with strangers in saturated space: Reclaiming and maintaining the urban commons. *Antipode, 47*(4), p. 963–979.

ICH-UNESCO. (2017). *Art of Neapolitan 'Pizzaiuolo'*. Retrieved November 20, 2019, from https://ich.unesco.org/en/RL/art-of-neapolitan-pizzaiuolo -00722.

ICH-UNESCO. (n.d.). *What is intangible cultural heritage?* Retrieved November 20, 2019, from https://ich.unesco.org/en/what-is-intangible -heritage-00003.

ICOMOS. (2002). *International Cultural Tourism Charter: Managing tourism at places of cultural and heritage significance*. Retrieved November 20, 2019, from https://www.icomos.org/charters/tourism_e.pdf.

Ingold, T. (2010). Bringing things to life: Creative entanglements in a world of materials. *Realities Working Paper, 15*. Manchester, United Kingdom: University of Manchester. Retrieved November 20, 2019, from http://hummedia.manchester.ac.uk/schools/soss/morgancentre/research/wps/15-2010-07-realities-bringing-things-to-life.pdf.

Knecht, U., Krueger, C., Markert, D., Moser, M., Mulder, A.-Cl., Praetorius, I., ... & Trenkwalder-Egger, A. (2012). *ABC des guten Lebens*. Russelsheim am Main, Germany: Christel Goettert Verlag.

Kropotkin, P. (1902). *Mutual Aid: A Factor of Evolution*. New York: McClure Phillips & Co.

Kurtz, H. (2001). Differentiating Multiple Meanings of Garden and Community. *Urban Geography* 22(7): 656–670. DOI: https://doi.org/10.2747/0272 -3638.22.7.656.

Lassiter, L. E. (2005). *The Chicago guide to collaborative ethnography*. Chicago, IL: The University of Chicago Press.

Leach, J. (2003). *Creative land: Place and procreation of the Rai Coast of Papua New Guinea*. New York, NY: Berghahn Books.

Linebaugh, P. (2008). *The Magna Carta Manifesto: Liberties and commons for all*. Berkeley, CA: University of California Press.

Marcus, G. E. (1998). *Ethnography through thick & thin*. Princeton, NJ: Princeton University Press.

Mauss, M. (1990). *The gift: The form and reason for exchange in archaic societies* (2nd ed.). *London, United Kingdom*: Routledge.

Mitsopoulos, M. & Pelagidis, T. (2011). *Understanding the crisis in Greece: From boom to bust*. London, United Kingdom: Palgrave Macmillan.

Mylonas, Y. (2014). Crisis, austerity and opposition in mainstream media discourses of Greece. *Critical Discourse Studies, 11*(3), 305–321.

Nyerere, J. K. (1968). *Ujamaa: Essays on socialism*. Dar-es-salaam, Tanzania: Oxford University Press.

Papadopoulos, D. & Tsianos, V. S. (2013). After citizenship: Autonomy of migration, organisational ontology and mobile commons. *Citizenship Studies, 17*(2), 178–196.

Participatory Budgeting Project. (2012). *Mission*. Retrieved November 20, 2019, from https://www.participatorybudgeting.org/mission/.

Pleios, G. (2013). Τα ΜΜΕ απέναντι στην κρίση: Έντονη υιοθέτηση της λογικής των ελίτ. In G. Pleios (Ed.), *Η κρίση και τα ΜΜΕ* (pp. 87–134). Athens, Greece: Papazisis.

Rancière, R. (2006). *The politics of aesthetics*. London, United Kingdom: Continuum.

Ristau, J. (2011, March 3). What is commoning, anyway?: Activating the power of social cooperation to get things done – and bring us together. *On the Commons*. Retrieved November 20, 2019, from http://www.onthecommons .org/work/what-commoning-anyway#sthash.6oYDUwk8.dpbs.

Shutte, A. (1993). *Philosophy for Africa*. Rondebosch, South Africa: University of Cape Town Press.

Social Innovation Europe. (2016, January 26). Options Foodlab: How food making and sharing is supporting migrant integration in Greece. Retrieved November 20, 2019, from https://socialinnovationexchange.org/insights /options-foodlab-how-food-making-and-sharing-supporting-migrant -integration-greece.

Stavrides, S. (2016a). *Common space: The city as commons*. London, United Kingdom: Zed Books.

Stavrides, S. (2016b) Common space as threshold space: Urban commoning in struggles to re-appropriate public space. In *Public-open spaces as common goods: A park for all at Hellinikon: File: Public event*. Biennale Architectura 2016, 25 September 2016 (pp. 9–20). Retrieved November 20, 2019, from https://www.academia.edu/30344547/Public-open_spaces_as_common _goods._A_park_for_all_at_Hellinikon._File_of_public_event_2016_.

Symons, M. (1994). Simmel's gastronomic sociology: An overlooked essay. *Food and Foodways, 5*(4), 333–351. DOI: https://doi.org/10.1080/07409710 .1994.9962016.

Taylor, T. (2007). The commodification of music at the dawn of the era of 'Mechanical Music'. *Ethnomusicology, 51*(2), 281–305.

Travlou, P. (2013). Rhizomic ethnographies: Rhizomes, lines and nomads: Doing fieldwork with creative networked communities. In S. Biggs (Ed.),

Remediating the social (pp. 65–69). Bergen, Norway: University of Bergen, ELMCIP.

Travlou, P. (2017). The making of *OneLoveKitchen:* Commoning the assembly. In J. Marketou & S. Bailey (Eds.), *Organizing from Below/HOW Assemblies Matter?* (pp. 6–7). New York: Naked Punch Publications.

Tsilimpounidi, M. (2016). *Sociology of crisis: Visualising urban austerity.* London, United Kingdom: Routledge.

Vasiljević, J. (2016). The possibilities and constraints of engaging solidarity in citizenship. *Filozofija I Društvo, 27*(2), 373–386.

Wilson, D. (2017). Commoning in sonic ethnography (or, the sound of ethnography to come). *Commoning Ethnography, 1*(1), 125–136.

Wolff, K. H. (1950). *The sociology of Georg Simmel.* New York, NY: The Free Press.

CHAPTER 9

Urban Experiments in Times of Crisis: From Cultural Production to Neighbourhood Commoning

Giorgos Chatzinakos

'Everything will be as it is now, just a little different'
Giorgio Agamben (1993:53)

Introducing the Context

This chapter describes the development of the *Alexandrou Svolou Neigbour-hood Initiative*[68] (ASNI), a bottom-up and self-organised activist group that was founded in 2013 in Thessaloniki. Broadly speaking, the projects organised by ASNI aim to connect people to place by fostering an imaginative and intersectional framework, namely the 'Neighbourhood'. The latter is seen as a common representation of place that can address and promote the role of locality and peoples' ability to engage with urban commons. The research is influenced by the 'new politics of place' (Amin 2004), the revaluation of the role of culture in urban regeneration (Oakley 2015) and the right to the city (Harvey 2012). By interrogating contemporary theoretical debates around human geography,

---

[68] Official Facebook page: https://www.facebook.com/geitonia.svolou/. Last access 20 November 2019.

How to cite this book chapter:
Chatzinakos, G. 2020. Urban Experiments in Times of Crisis: From Cultural Production to Neighbourhood Commoning. In Lekakis, S. (ed.) *Cultural Heritage in the Realm of the Commons: Conversations on the Case of Greece.* Pp. 183–212. London: Ubiquity Press. DOI: https://doi.org/10.5334/bcj.k. License: CC-BY

sociology, cultural analysis and event management, the broad scope of this project is driven by the emerging roles of cities at a global level in a continuous, globalised and interconnected 'world of cities'. Likewise, the research considers the various socio-cultural representations of the city as fundamental to understanding urban life. It has been argued that "cities have always constituted typical spaces of exchange, where conflicting and confusing perceptions and representations crisscrossed continually, spaces where memories have been negotiated and processed" (Spiridon 2013: 206). The metropolis itself can be seen as "the site of biopolitical production, because it is the space of the common, of people living together, sharing resources, communicating, exchanging goods and ideas" (Hardt & Negri 2009: 250). In this light, urban space can be subjected to a broad range of geographies of experimentation (Kullman 2013).

The overall relevance of urban experimentation lies in the fact that in recent decades cities have been undergoing globally radical transformations. According to the United Nations' report on global urbanisation prospects (2014), 54% of the world's population now resides in urban areas. This proportion is expected to increase to 66% by 2050. As the world's population is increasingly concentrated in urban settlements, new conditions and challenges emerge in a fast-changing context. A reasonable macro-sociological question that arises is how will this 'world of cities' would look in 30 years' time? In this direction, Barber (2013) believes that cities, and the administrations that run them, offer the best possible new patterns of global governance and can be viewed as a formidable alternative to the conventional nation-state paradigm. In this sense, cities and urban networks can play a key role in engaging with global challenges that manifest locally. On the contrary, some argue that often those responsible for strategising management scenarios for cities forget that they are constituted by real people with real needs, desires and motivations (Miles 2017), producing hegemonic exclusion policies, incapable of creating impactful solutions to overcome actual problems through applicable interventions and practices.

With this in mind, this research focusses on Thessaloniki, at the same time both an ordinary and an extraordinary city (Mazower 2004; Robinson 2006). Thessaloniki would seem to embody an ongoing struggle to redefine its image and rewrite its urban myth, by integrating culture within its broader strategic development and planning initiatives. On the local level, there is an ongoing discussion around the role of residents in the midst of a 'more-than-financial' crisis (Athanassiou et al. 2018), coupled with an outlook aimed at developing Thessaloniki into the 'Metropolitan city of the Balkans' (Labrianidis 2011; Frangopoulos et al. 2009). However, evidence suggests that there is a "particular dynamic of interests established by specific elite categories that are capable of intervening and claiming public funding for their benefit" (Thoidou & Foutakis 2006: 40). Along similar lines as Miles (2017), Christodoulou (2015) emphasises that there is a significant and stable deviation between the projected aims/priorities and the implemented interventions made by the municipal authorities compared to the needs and desires of the local community itself. Those symptoms of colonisation by a dominant economic, cultural and political hegemony, highlight the fact that the city is constructed around the needs of a privileged audience that, in turn, tend to relentlessly reproduce idealised and commodified images of the city, until they become more real than the reality itself (see Goodwin 1997). In addition, in terms of urban management it appears that the city's administration is not able to take into consideration the socio-cultural plurality and place-based particularities of its urban neighbourhoods, contributing to a particularly problematic governance of the city and its broader metropolitan area (Chatzinakos 2016: 167). Within the context of the chapter, findings highlight some limitations experienced in practice when it comes to the broader management of the urban fabric of a Greek city.

In this respect, this research tries to go beyond traditional definitions of participation and governance, attempting to design a tentatively transformative approach, through which we can learn from different experiences and representations, directly derived from urban communities. According to Providência (2015: 218) such an approach "privileges personal readings of an urban site and conceives of the "townscape" in terms of the public perception of urban space. This, in turn, fosters a planning attitude that privileges the particular, the lived space and the sidewalk, and that fights any abstract general planning that does not focus on improving quality of life". This approach (1) focuses on an overarching view of individual needs and collective desires, (2) offers a new dimension of thinking and opportunities for experiential learning, through various practices of everyday appropriation and commoning, (3) promotes the design of more inclusive neighbourhoods, (4) addresses and/or prevents social problems, (5) contributes to a broader understanding regarding the impact of crisis on the quality of life of a city, (6) allows for a new perspective on the complexity of urban life and (7) opens up new political imaginaries, essential for the transformation of urban life. This experience so far has introduced new elements on the discussion around the role of bottom-up initiatives in the midst of a 'more-than-financial' crisis.

A Brief Historical Overview

The crisis has initiated major transformations, which have brought with them new socio-cultural realities and forms of living, political imaginaries and spatial configurations. It is argued that the legacy of the crisis has not only impacted on local economies, but by now has become an embodied subjectivity, a material and sensory experience in everyday encounters in public space. As a response to this gradual yet inter-temporal stagnation, a highly diverse group of locals, comprised of residents, shopkeepers, researchers, activists, artists, students and one journalist, who lived in close proximity, formed the Alexandrou Svolou

Neigbourhood Initiative in December 2013. The initial aim of the Initiative could be summed up in the phrase 'let's become a neighbourhood again'. In that sense, the revival of the notion of the 'Neighbourhood' is seen as a response to the economic crisis, which creates constant insecurity and fear, followed by the alienating effects of contemporary neo-liberal politics.

ASNI was first conceived on Facebook and then moved gradually from cyberspace to urban space. This informal social structure gradually began to acquire permanent standards and a social dimension. From the very beginning the main challenge was to develop a diverse network of people that would engage in common activities; creating a nodal space for communication and knowledge exchange. Upon creation, in order to set an organisational and ethical framework that would allow the creation and co-formulation of shared meanings, ASNI published a founding declaration and thereafter disseminated it to various individuals and community groups. This declaration is comprised of 10 social values.

These are:

1. We reinforce social ties by promoting self-action.
2. We highlight the value of collegiality and we actively contribute to the creation of an everyday urban 'warmth'.
3. We rejuvenate local creativity and inventiveness.
4. We exercise our right to the city, through exemplary actions. We critically highlight, document, and refer to the appropriate public institutions, the problems and the needs of our Neighbourhood.
5. We preserve the collective memory of our Neighbourhood and we learn its history.
6. We show that important things can be done without funding.
7. We facilitate the development of solidarity through horizontal, self-organised social structures.
8. We undertake things we had expected the institutions would provide.
9. We develop mutual relationships; cultivating trust and intimacy between residents and shopkeepers.
10. We improve the quality of life of our City and Neighbourhood…our common life.

Over the last six years, ASNI has organised a variety of cultural activities, such as concerts in public and private spaces, a street parade with various new urban movements and activist groups, place-making activities and workshops in local schools and public spaces (e.g. urban gardening), cultural mapping workshops, artistic and tactical urbanism interventions (e.g. street zebra), memory nights, thematic walking tours, a movie festival on urban commons, a reading group entitled 'Cities and Literature', a revival of a local carnival, a picnic for the "global Degrowth day", solidarity actions (e.g. 'save the water' campaign, refugee support), and place-identity fundraising (e.g. neighbourhood annual sticker). The most successful activity so far been has been the organisation of a collective dinner: it has not only promoted the transfer of a cultural practice from Spain to Greece, but it has also allowed the creation of a gregarious community network of residents, shopkeepers and local institutions. Currently, ASNI is creating a DIY Pocket Park, through participatory methodologies and is also initiating a Memory Bank. These projects presuppose the existence of informal and loose networks that operate as experimental laboratories for the articulation of identities and the production of culture (Melucci 2009).

ASNI's narration draws on Charles Baudelaire's poetic flâneries and "celebrates the city as an 'allegorical' place where the phantasmagoria of mass culture mixes with the melancholia of everyday life" (Benjamin 1997 as cited in Lowry et al. 2015: 319). Respectively, the Initiative approaches the neighbourhood's space as an urban laboratory. This empirical approach to urban space claims to engage and learn about a city's everyday life, including its neighbourhoods and focuses on the different meanings of public space, which is directly affected by the crisis in every aspect (social, cultural, political, economic) of everyday life. Accordingly, ASNI tries to recreate a local public sphere, not only at neighbourhood but also at the city-wide level, and attempts to produce different uses, perspectives and significances of the urban landscape. For this reason, it evaluates the capacity of Common Pool Resources, such as neighbourhood-based organisations and networks, highlights and fosters potential synergies in the micro-environment of the neighbourhood with combined actions in public space (Chatzinakos 2016). Gradually, this approach enabled the Initiative to capitalise on place-based dynamics by mapping and constantly reinventing an inclusive, yet highly diverse network of assets, within a peculiar neighbourhood-scale symbolic economy. According to Zukin (1988; 2010) the scope of the symbolic economy can be used in order to explore how people develop a sense of place and value their neighbourhoods. In this project, this value emanates from the social constructs of place, the cultural understandings of the particular place and the conscious choices people make regarding its use.

Methodology: Linking Theory to Action

The overall methodological approach of the project is informed by action research and activist ethnography (Plows 2008; Sutherland 2013). The starting point of this longitudinal research was inspired by Svolou TV,[69] a journalistic audio-visual street project that was already conducting research on a local level in 2013; publishing several short films on YouTube. In the period examined a distinct mode of inductive knowledge co-production was generated through interviews, focus groups, participant observations, cultural mapping, surveys,

---

[69] ASNI official Facebook page: https://www.facebook.com/geitonia.svolou/. Last access 20 November 2019.

questionnaires and audio-visual projects.[70] This gradually enabled the development of a more credible argumentation through a scientific, evidence-based ontology and created a broader space for discussion across a range of disciplines including urban geography, anthropology, sociology, cultural studies, community economics, environmental studies, history, early childhood education, urban planning and so on.

At this point, it should be noted that the data presented here is auto-ethnographic (see Dashper 2016) in its intention and thus reflects upon the author's own engagement with ASNI. In this respect, the data presented is done so in a manner which bears in mind the blurring of boundaries between the researcher and the researched, not least given the fact that the researcher is also an activist who grew up in the particular locality. In terms of reflexivity then, Maguire's (1988: 190) advice that the 'sociologist-as-participant must be able to stand back and become sociologist-as-observer-and-interpreter', has been particularly helpful. In other words, the data reflects Beck's (1995: 15) model of reflexive modernity, and seeks to reconcile "the science of data and the science of experience through real world experiments".

In order to avoid "the sharp separation between the academic world and the world of practice" (Whyte 1989: 382), the overall research approach is built around the concepts of people, power and praxis (Finn 1994). It thus incorporates research design, analysis, reflection and action (Finkel & Sang 2016) including various methods which can be employed. Participatory research often involves multiple instruments and techniques and is often utilised in conjunction with mixed methods, such as interviews, focus groups, and/or surveys. One of the key elements of participatory research is the equitable partnership approaches to planning and conducting the research in conjunction with community members and/or community-based organisations. The basic assumption of the research is to take social science closer to society and provide an intersection between practice and theory; enabling in such a way an iterative process that reflects and is shaped by the context of the lived experience. One of its key elements is the equitable partnership in planning, as well as conducting the research in conjunction with participants who "effectively mix, sequence and integrate appropriate tools to support genuine dialogue and the exercise of reason in real settings, including complex situations marked by uncertainty and the unknown" (Chevalier & Buckles 2013: 7). For this reason, it focuses on individual participants who are involved actively in the production of knowledge and emphasises their full involvement at every stage of the research process. In this sense, this research is being conducted and developed together *with* participants, who combine different skills interdisciplinary, constructively and complementarily in a process of mutual dialectical understanding.

---

[70] ASNI Youtube channel: https://www.youtube.com/channel/UC6Yn4bZN iZ00AN7JvG_kQiw. Last access 20 November 2019.

Alexandrou Svolou: An Ordinary Neighbourhood?

The neighbourhood of Alexandrou Svolou is located within the administrative boundaries of the 1st Municipal District, which is comprised of five sub-neighbourhoods that include the historical (landmark monuments), administrative (City Hall), cultural (museums) and commercial centre of Thessaloniki (Figure 1). However, those sub-neighbourhoods (Σ1, Σ2, Σ3, Σ4, Σ6, M1, Figure 2), are not officially recognised as separate units by the city's administration. For this reason, ASNI demarcated an area of broader interest and named it after Alexandrou Svolou Street, a central mild-traffic axis that lies between the two major streets of the city that horizontally divide its historical centre (Figure 2 & 3). The urban fabric can be characterised as continuous, interrupted only by several vertical streets and pathways. The area is characterised by high density housing that follow the model of vertical social segregation, a typical characteristic of the Greek city (Maloutas & Karadimitriou 2001) (Figure 4). Although it is a relatively residential neighbourhood that mainly houses middle class families, the elderly and students, it is full of cultural life and spaces of consumption. Analysing the position of the neighbourhood and its relationship

Figure 1: The administrative boundaries of the 1st Municipal District (Source: Municipality of Thessaloniki).

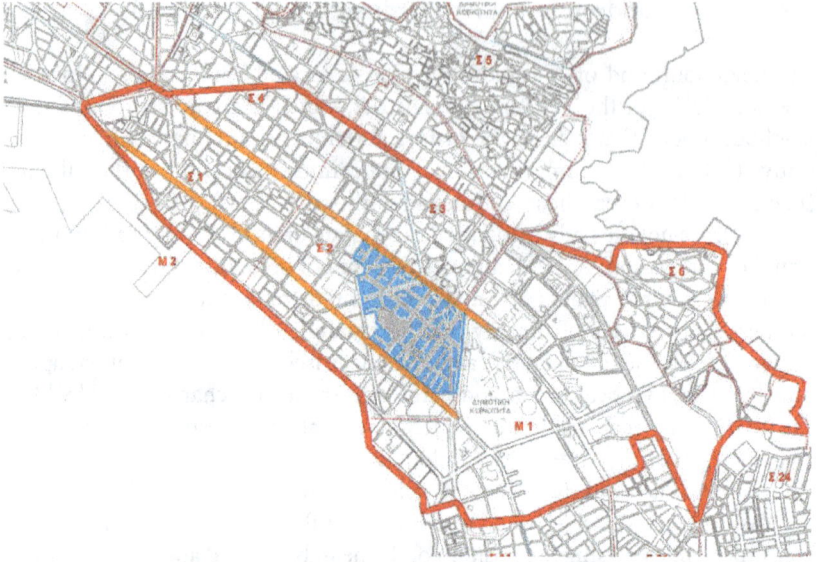

Figure 2: With red: the boundaries of the 1st Municipal District. With orange: the two main streets of the city (Tsimiski & Egnatia str.) that divide the historical centre. With blue: the sub-neighbourhood of Alexandrou Svolou (Source: Municipal Department of Urban Planning & Architecture, edited by the author).

Figure 3: Alexandrou Svolou's Neighbourhood, according to ASNI (Source: GIS Thessaloniki, edited by Periklis Chatzinakos).

to the broader city, one must take into account its proximity to the Aristotle University, the Municipal Central Library, the International Helexpo, the History Centre of Thessaloniki, the church of Hagia Sofia, the Arch of Galerius

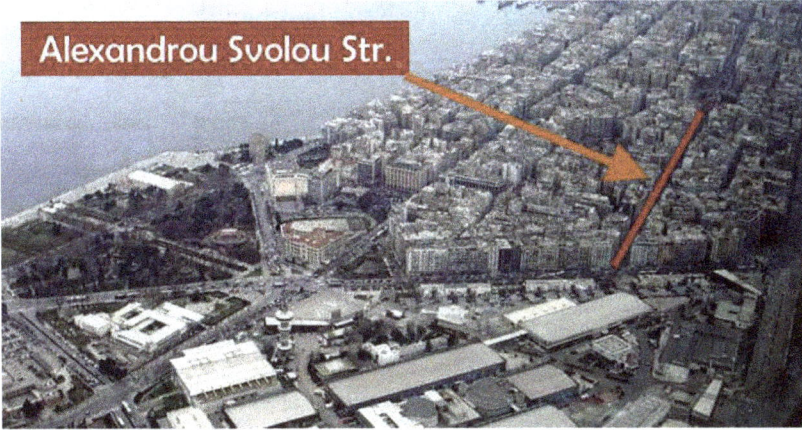

Figure 4: An aspect of the historical centre of Thessaloniki (Source: Airphotos. gr, edited by Lazaros Chatzinakos).

and Navarinou Square.[71] Apart from this square, of city-wide importance and consisting of a public space that has traditionally been shared by a mosaic of different sub-cultures and urban tribes, there is a significant lack of open and green spaces. In order to provide an in depth understanding of the geographical specificities of the particular neighbourhood, the most ideal approach would be a detailed, demographic analysis of specific administrative boundaries. However, quantitative data is not available for the sub-area under consideration. The only census data available is the total population of the 1st Municipal District,[72] which is considered too large an area for the focus of this study. It must be noted that in Greece it is not common for researchers and/or residents to be afforded access to demographic data through open-source neighbourhood monitoring systems, as is the case in many other cities around the world (e.g. Brussels,[73] Manchester,[74] Vienna[75] etc.). For this reason, the empirical understanding of the social landscape of the neighbourhood is shaped through the qualitative elements of the research, such as interviews, observations and secondary sources.

---

[71] Navarinou square is emphatically characterised by a local musician as the "centre of the entire world". https://www.youtube.com/watch?v=3zEaLO 60Bik. Last access 20 November 2019.

[72] The population of the district is 44.434 people (FEK 718/B'/21.05.2014).

[73] Website: https://monitoringdesquartiers.brussels/. Last access 20 November 2019.

[74] Website: https://dashboards.instantatlas.com/viewer/report?appid=962615 537fc24dda8a0a29dc86bd4e37. Last access 20 November 2019.

[75] Website: https://www.wien.gv.at/statistik/bevoelkerung/bevoelkerungsstand/. Last access 20 November 2019.

Searching for the Neighbourhood

A neighbourhood can be seen as a contested archipelago of objectivity (streets, squares, buildings etc.) and subjectivity (peoples' perception, sense of place, place identity, local heritage etc.). Nonetheless, a single and straightforward definition of what actually constitutes a neighbourhood is difficult to capture in simple terms. Such a broad use of the concept "has a transcendent nature and cannot simply be equated with particular groups or a place. Nor can it be reduced to an idea, since they do not simply exist outside social relations, socially-structured discourses or a historical milieu". Even if there is a lack of a broad consensus, a neighbourhood can be associated with the sense of reciprocity and collective action within a delimited space and is based on an underlying expectation that an urban community might exist in the arena of residential life (Martin 2017: 79). Subsequently, a neighbourhood captures the idea of social interaction, since as a term it highlights propinquity as the primary dimension of urban social relations.

However, even if the notion intuitively involves spatiality and it is widely acknowledged that it affects locals in a special way, precise measurement of this spatial dimension is often treated as problematic (Spilsbury et al. 2009). Moreover, when identified, neighbourhood impacts are often small in magnitude, leading to controversy about whether such effects actually exist (Dietz 2002; Sampson et al. 2002; Sellström & Bremberg 2006). Still, a neighbourhood can be defined also as an experience, not limited to specific geographical constraints. Relatedly, in order to invoke the notion of neighbourhood as a commoning practice, one has to recognise that it is real and material as well as an ideal. It is both an experience and an interpretation (Wagner 2008). In this sense, a neighbourhood can be approached not just as a practice constructed by mental or even physical boundaries, but as having a symbolic character, which to a certain extent creates links between different social sub-groups (Turner 1969; Cohen 1985). In such a way, it can be seen as a symbolic unity composed by practices, shared symbols and values that allows its members to form a collective consciousness.

In summarising this short overview of different concepts about the neighbourhood, one could agree that the different uses of the term are inevitable. The main reason this project embraces the concept of the neighbourhood is that community-building at a local, decentralised level can be seen as a response to the crisis, engendering solidarity and belonging, notions that have been 'exacerbated' and at the same time induced by globalisation (Delanty 2009). Subsequently, even if the particular neighbourhood does indeed have some geographical limits, the overall research approach has mostly focused on the relational and symbolic aspects of the definition; involving relationships that do not depend solely on physical proximity. In other words, this project considers an Aristotelian perspective that views the 'neighbourhood' as a civic society of mutual interdependence and reciprocity, a kind of social co-existence comprised by diverse individuals that live, share and use common resources and public space. According to this conceptualisation the neighbourhood is approached as a micro-sociological context within a particular locale, in which a broader crisis – entailing long-lasting insecurity, despair and alienation – is played out. This pertains to both processes of space production and forms of social reproduction (Lefebvre 1991); allowing for the creation of "a space designed for interactions between an urban context and a research process to test, develop and/or apply social practices" (Voytenko et al. 2016: 3). In this light, the *locality* (a neighbourhood) becomes not only the setting but also the means for collective experimentation with possible alternative forms of social organisation.

Challenging Conventional Strategies through Urban Experiments

"Nobody knows the answers to city living in the future, and, when answers are unknown, experiment is essential" (Spilhaus 1967: 1141).

Urban experimentation is an emerging field of practice, and one that has come rapidly to prominence across a broad spectrum of practice and thought. The term has been used broadly to reshape practices of knowledge production in urban debates, across different regions and cities. An urban experiment can be defined as a flexible set of practices that centre on processes of social change, and on the emergence of new practices and concepts that constitute belonging (Karvonen & van Heur 2014: 380). Every experiment can be analysed according to "the degree to which it is inclusive, systematic, practice-based, challenge-led, a site of social learning and adaptive in the face of uncertainty and ambiguity" (Sengers et al. 2016: 26). The latter, are seen as places for representing, encountering, incorporating and researching aspects of cultural difference. Essentially, the symbolic significance of an experiment can attempt to modify the concepts of perception and appreciation of the social world; making "visible the ways local stories, practices, relationships, memories, and rituals constitute places as meaningful locations" (Duxbury et al. 2015: 19).

Furthermore, there is a growing effort to situate urban experimentation as a mode of governance within a broader understanding of the material and political production and reproduction of cities and parts of cities (Evans et al. 2016). Previous research demonstrates that such interventions, either organised in a top-down or bottom-up fashion, managed to increase participation in neighbourhood-based activity, changing the spatial and social environment of various cities (Zenk et al. 2009; Kinney et al. 2012; Brindley et al. 2014; Dulin Keitaa et al. 2016). In this sense, place-based experimentation can offer novel modes of engagement, governance and politics that both challenge and complement conventional strategies.

Nevertheless, as urban experimentation has become an important way of understanding and governing the city and of trying to steer processes of urban change in specific directions, "the social inclusiveness and disruptive potential of the 'improvements' sought through experimentation begs more critical scrutiny" (Evans 2016: 430). Even if researchers have been studying this phenomenon for quite a long time, only recently have urban geographers brought a range of new terms and ways of thinking about urban experiments to contemporary cities (Evans & Karvonen 2011; Bulkeley & Castán Broto 2012). According to May & Perry (2016: 33) whilst urban scholars have examined the 'sustainable' city, less emphasis is placed on the relationships between knowledge production, the city and experimentation from a social epistemological point of view. In other words, there is little research done on how knowledge is implicated within urban strategies and how experimentation is attributed with social value in the context of neoliberal politics. Bearing this in mind, ASNI's approach to experimentation promotes experimental cultural productions that challenge established norms and highlight various networks of opposition to the dominant culture, proposing their own cognitive and evaluative structures (Bourdieu 1984; Melucci 1996; see Souzas 2015: 267). Likewise, experimentation on a neighbourhood level has enabled knowledge acquaintance from real-world interventions and procedures of collective reflection and analysis. Specifically, ASNI has organised three grassroots urban experiments, namely Spring Dinner, Pocket Park and Memory Bank. The rest of the chapter will reflect on the most significant theoretical and empirical outputs these experiments have produced.

Spring Dinner: From One Southern Mediterranean City to Another

Inspired by a picture of an urban dinner that took place during the Fiestas de Gràcia in Barcelona (Sanclemente 1990; Sobrequé 1996; Lafarga, 1999; Mercado 2004; Crespi-Vallbona & Richards 2007; Richards 2010) ASNI initiated the Spring Dinner in 2014. In terms of cultural geography, the organisation of the dinner examined whether it was possible to transfer a rooted cultural practice from another southern European city to Thessaloniki in an organic fashion. In other words, the key to this experiment was to adapt this cultural practice to the local identity without diluting it. It is important to note that these cultural practices can be traced in a variety of regions and cities around the world and are considered important cultural practices, with long-established associations with urban culture. In fact, they can be found under different names in cities all across the word (Fiestas del barrio, Nachbarschaftsfest, Fête des voisins, Grätzelfest, Neighbours' day, Dzień sąsiada etc.). Although they might differ from city to city in terms of organisation, social characteristics, cultural practices undertaken and legal status ('eventful framework', see Richards & Palmer 2010), they share some common attributes: urban space, people, identity negotiation, practice as well as evoking cultural heritage. In contrast to this, urban dining was until recently something that was almost unknown in the contemporary urban landscape of Greece and as a result there is a lack of legal frameworks that allow for the appropriation of public space for communal use and culture.

The concept behind an urban dinner is to get the neighbours together to share their food, thus symbolically reclaiming public space. By confronting people with the unfamiliar, this sort of liminality aims to provoke free thinking, self-questioning, self-discovery and reflexivity (see van Heerden 2011). The concern in this experiment is with the potential that a gathering of this kind has to, temporarily, disrupt the everyday order. In earlier societies liminal rituals, such as the medieval carnival, provided a sanctioned forum for the unleashing of societal tensions, a place where peasants were able to enjoy and consume the surplus produced by the intense labour of harvest (Bakhtin 1984; Turner and Rojek 2001). In this regard, the Spring Dinner aims to transform the neighbourhood from a space of daily routine and monotony into a place of sharing and entertainment. It can be considered a way to discuss the possibility of *communitas*, which frees residents from the constraints of 'everyday' life and provides both the opportunity and a space for reflection on basic cultural values and norms (see Turner 1982). By following Jepson & Clarke's (2013: 3) definition of community festivals, the Spring Dinner is a *"themed and inclusive community event or series of events which have been created as the result of an inclusive community planning process to celebrate the particular way of life of people and groups in the local community with emphasis on particular space and time"*. It can be framed by five essential characteristics: (1) the performance of cultural symbols, (2) sharing and entertainment, (3) it is undertaken in a public place, (4) it reclaims urban space for community use and (5) it constitutes a social strategy to combat the growing alienation and insecurity felt in public space (see Hughes 1999).

The first Spring Dinner was not holistically embraced by the neighbourhood. However, it did produce some social links between different individuals, groups and institutions, which in the past did not have any form of synergy. Essentially, locals, shopkeepers and community groups who previously did not know each other, gradually, established a new sense of confidence and conviviality; encouraging a stronger interaction between existing community organisations and activist networks. This was achieved not only through their participation but also through active involvement in the organisation of the dinner (a period of approximately 5 months). In this regard, cultural production and consumption can produce a sort of profound social interaction, with identifiable social consequences and impacts, providing people with an opportunity to get to know each other better and develop an interactive relationship with

Figure 5: The 1st Spring Dinner in 2014 (Source: Eleni Vraka).

public space. With the passage of time, ASNI established a flexible event management plan by experimenting with different research approaches and methodologies, mixing various 'good practices', and effectively integrating the local creative capital and its socio-cultural attributes. Subsequently five consecutive Spring Dinners, variations on the above model, have taken place on an annual basis. Since 2016 each dinner has attracted around 5,000 people, including local musicians and artists. It would seem that this pilot urban experiment created a more fertile ground for carrying out further activities and, indeed, is nowadays considered to be a benchmark in the city.[76]

Nevertheless, it should be noted that the Spring Dinner is a standalone one-day event. Essentially, each year ASNI builds an urban stage, a theatrical scenery that for a few hours converts the neighbourhood into a highly diverse street ballet set (Jacobs 1961). Despite the socio-cultural mixing and the appropriation of public space, there is the danger that this could create a feeling of managed or "staged culture" (MacCannell 1973). Such a feeling might remind one of a theatricalised and aestheticised city, not one that has been built up organically (Williams 2004). However, ASNI considers these urban dinners not an end in themselves but as a means to create a different/temporary atmos-

---

[76] In 21.06.2016 the Mayor Yiannis Boutaris invited the citizens of Thessaloniki to take more initiatives in order to improve their everyday life, through a rhetoric of 'citizenship', using as an example Spring Dinner.

Figure 6: The 3rd Spring Dinner in 2016 (Source: Argiris Karagiorgas).

phere in a stagnant and crumbling reality. In this sense, although the dinner constitutes a heterotopic performance that creates a short-term community, its focus is on the 'next day' and the potential changes in social attitudes and perceptions. The concern here is how far the Spring Dinner has managed to provide the foundations for more diverse networks (extrovert or introvert) that might add to an evolving but gradual process of neighbourhood-building, connecting people to their locality over a period of time far beyond the confines of the event itself.

Pocket Park: From Participatory Planning to Participatory Action

The reflective evaluation that followed the 3rd dinner in 2016 raised the questions as to whether its impact was sustainable throughout the rest of the year and whether such a non-permanent and culturally produced intervention is enough to contribute towards a deeper experiential appropriation of the neighbourhood. Bearing this reasonable limitation in mind, ASNI discussed ways of achieving a more permanent presence and further visibility in the neighbourhood. Undeniably, the creation of a self-managed space would serve as a meeting place for collective action. To this end, the Initiative decided to engage with student groups (Iliopoulos & Kaligas 2017) by focusing on and appropriating an urban 'void' located in the neighbourhood.

Figure 7: The urban 'void' from above (in the centre) (Source Vaggelis Ameranis, The White Dot).

What is particularly significant about this urban 'void' (431,65 m²) is its ownership regime. It consisted of a vacant piece of public land that had been left to become derelict. 70% (337,05 m²) of its total area belongs to the School Buildings Organisation SA, a state-owned public limited company based in Athens, with the other 30% (94,60 m²) belonging to the Municipality of Thessaloniki. A reasonable question that arises from this situation is why an urban 'void' should belong to two public institutions? Why would the Municipality of Thessaloniki purchase a piece of wasteland from another public institution, especially when this space does not have any other apparent use other than landfill? Comparative research on other cities revealed the remarkable fact that, for example, in Helsinki (Finland) all the public land belongs to the city itself, whilst the revenue from public services (see Helen Electricity Network Ltd) is mostly reinvested back into the urban fabric. In contrast, Greek cities seem to be unwilling or incapable of managing their urban fabric. Therefore, the creation of this space is highly relevant in relation to urban planning and the production of alternative spaces, while also holding the potential to encourage more inclusive and democratic forms of planning.

Essentially, this experiment consists of a collective effort to convert an urban 'void' into a pocket-sized neighbourhood park through a social process of commoning. In order to kick-start this activity, ASNI organised a participatory planning workshop in its premises in the 1st Municipal District of Thessaloniki. This workshop offered 'average residents' an effective outlet for collective and creative expression. Subsequently, in order to engage with the broader neighbourhood, the Initiative organised a number of campaigns, placing

Figure 8: (left): How the space looked at the time of the participatory planning workshop in 22.04.2017 (Source: Maria Stefanouri), (right): How the Park looks now, about a year and a half later (Source: Anthi Antoniadi).

information points in various spots in the locality and collaborating with the local primary school. Passing from participatory planning to participatory action, the Initiative has so far organised 9 consecutive 'construction acts' (cleaning, embankment fill, urban garden, plantings, cob workshop, self-made urban infrastructure/benches, gym, entrance, feeders for stray animals) and a variety of cultural events (fundraising concerts, a summer cinema, collective dinners, workshops, artistic performances etc.) demonstrating a particular appetite for community engagement along the way. Despite profound bureaucratic limitations,[77] ASNI is still developing this project, without any external sources of funding. The methodology that was used is considered groundbreaking for the city, as there have been no other cases effective bottom-up participation in urban planning.

Thus far, the main challenge that has emerged through this experiment is finding ways to build trust with the surrounding urban micro-environment, breaking the negative impacts of vertical and horizontal social segregation. Arguably, this approach will assist socio-spatial appropriation on a regular basis whilst avoiding exclusionary or elitist practices.

Memory Bank: Towards a more Conscious Local History

In 2018, ASNI initiated a Memory Bank in an attempt to highlight the role of memory on an individual and neighbourhood level. The aim of this project is to identify and crystallise elements that can shape a more conscious and intimate historical and experiential knowledge, involving locals in "the creation of their own history" (Grele 1985: xvi). Together with the Greek Oral History

---

[77] The Kallikratis reform (Law 3852/2010), for instance, does not illuminate in detail how citizens can actually participate in decision making and urban planning. For further scrutiny see Katsoulis 2011: 4).

Figure 9: The gradual transformation of an urban 'void' (Source: Periklis Chatzinakos).

Association,[78] ASNI organised an introductory seminar that took place in the Municipal Central Library. The seminar aimed to familiarise participants with the theoretical, methodological and ethical aspects of oral history. Oral history is closely linked to local cultural heritage, since it is

> "built around people… It brings history into, and out of, the community. It helps the less privileged, and especially the old, towards dignity and self-confidence. It makes for contact – and thence understanding – between social classes, and between generations … It can give a sense of belonging

---

[78] Official website: http://www.epi.uth.gr/index.php?page=aboutus. Last access 20 November 2019.

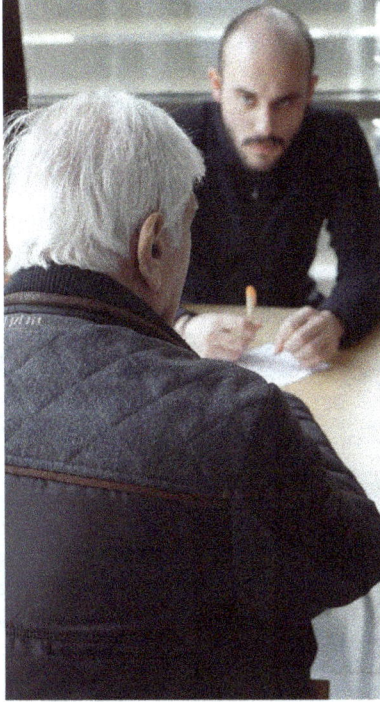

Figure 10: A two days seminar on oral history in the Municipal Central Library
(Source: author).

*to a place or in time ... It provides a means for a radical transformation of
the social meaning of history"* (Thompson 1978: 18).

The main influence behind this urban experiment lies in Burnage, a working-
class suburb of Manchester, where local groups and individuals try to collect,
share and celebrate the stories of their place of residence. In a similar fashion, ASNI's Memory Bank has started to collect personal narrations, stories,
local myths and archival material (bibliography, photographs, postal cards,
newspapers, personal letters, etc.) and the intention is to deposit them in an
open-source platform (see Burnage Memory Bank[79]). The aim is to "include
within the historical record the experiences and perspectives of groups of people who might otherwise have been hidden from history" (Perks & Thomson
2006: ix). Such an approach can develop intercultural story-telling, memory

---

[79] Official website: http://www.burnageactivityhub.org.uk/wp/?page_id=1306.
Last access 20 November 2019.

Figure 11: 30 years from the Earthquake of 1978: A Night of Memory in the History Centre of Thessaloniki (Source: Periklis Chatzinakos).

visualisation and aestheticisation, making it possible to reclaim the neighbourhood as a "collective work of art" (Lefebvre 1996: 174).

Discussion: From Cultural Production to Neighbourhood Commoning

In a world where notions of culture are becoming increasingly fragmented, such experiments and cultural practices have gained an important position when it comes to the consumption of the city (Ritzer 1999). However, the mass standardisation of cultural production and consumption that lie at the very heart of the contemporary city (Miles 2017), has led to phenomena that have been characterised variously as the "serial reproduction of culture" (Harvey 1989), "placelessness" (Relph 1976), "non-places" (Augé 1995) and so forth. Within a continuously globalised environment, places start to look the same and the ability to create the sense of "uniqueness" within a city diminishes (Richards & Wilson 2006). As Zukin (2011) points out, the more contemporary cities have sought to distinguish themselves from one another, the more they have in fact ended up looking and feeling the same. Within this emerging geography of connectivity there is a growing tension between culture as something grounded in place and culture as a pattern of non-place globalised events and experiences (Scott 2000).

Although the experiments presented here are very similar to corresponding practices that take place across the world (e.g. urban dinners, DIY parks, memory banks etc.), it can be said that they are trying to adapt to the existing social resources and local dynamics. Even though they consist of a pluralistic mosaic of different cultural practices, their main feature is that they constitute a significant aspect of the socio-economic and cultural landscape of everyday life. Key to their transfer is the extent to which such cultural events previously held in other cities can be replicated in such a way as to not dilute the unique nature of the local identity (Richards & Wilson 2006). Arguably, if a community maintains its proactivity, creativity and inclusive character, it can retain its identity without being alienated by the global massification, since "people are the ones making a cultural practice unique and not the practice itself" (Chatzinakos 2015: 50). This approach can bypass the limitations derived from the codified definitions of culture and engage in practice with different experiences and representations, derived directly from the neighbourhood's "collective imaginary" (Castoriadis 1987).

Thus, in a variety of ways these urban experiments build-up expertise and a capacity for urban commoning practices, while serving as a process for collective reflection on communal issues and problems and providing an open platform for locals to meet and share their thoughts. ASNI has developed a model of direct democracy where social relations are organised around place, urban identity, peer to peer knowledge exchange and intersectionality, without any hierarchical regulation imposed by a legal framework. In this sense, this paradigm of neighbourhood organisation can be considered to be an informal social structure that aims to integrate objective and subjective considerations of reality. This can assist, to a certain extent, in the creation of a relational and interactive collective identity (Melucci 2009), which is embedded in a shifting social-cultural and political context. The latter is not proposed as a consolidated, rigid, homogeneous and integrated reality, but rather as a changing context characterised by emotion, diversity and flexibility, a subject of continuous construction and re-construction. It constitutes both a dynamic space of relationships that crystallises the effects of collective action and a springboard for action (see Souzas 2015: 268). Therefore, it only truly exists in a state of permanent and dialectic re-invention.

Overall, the research presents elements that can potentially enhance the skills and the resources of a community, dismantle barriers and isolation through active engagement; promoting community self-governance and knowledge exchange. This process allows participants to understand the importance of initiative and taking action. Essentially, this longitudinal activist project aims to create an *identity effect* that will enable locals to become more aware, re-evaluate, regain, and/or strengthen their sense of place through an empowering process. Chiesi & Costa (2015) argue that this identity effect can be intangible but very significant. It is related to a process that allows for the emergence of a shared view regarding strategies to promote local culture, a detailed definition of local needs related to social and cultural necessities, a raised awareness of the importance of local cultural heritage and deeper spatial and place-based understandings. This process might enable a growing synergy among locals in public space, acquiring an in-practice understanding of the importance of cooperative practices in solving common social issues, enriching cultural and spatial imaginaries. However, every neighbourhood and place is different, with unique characteristics and particular dynamics. Therefore, even if the experiments presented can be transferred and replicated further, the findings cannot be generalised.

Additionally, from this perspective there is a danger of seeing the topic either in a personal and even biased light or in an institutionalised fashion that might dilute community dynamics and spontaneity. This experimental approach should take place on an ontological level, far from normative. As Caprotti & Cowley (2017: 1445) critically note, in some cases an urban experiment might lend itself to a potentially normative epistemological approach to the city: presenting the city as a set of variables, a messy set, but still a collection of parameters that can be tinkered with and controlled. In this direction, the experiments presented are being developed in parallel with all the surrounding material conditions, which include the creation of shared cultural meanings, social interaction, and community engagement. Neighbourhood-building depends on a variety of processes and critical factors, while social transformation is an ongoing process that can not solely solve structural inequalities. Arguably, the quest of belonging is the inevitable process of meaningful re-production. Therefore, future research should pay attention to the motivations and meanings participants develop i.e. devotion, perseverance, dialectics, language, power relations, conflict-resolution, critical evaluation, reflection and realisation of the overall set aims and objectives.

Conclusions

This chapter highlights the role that key neighbourhoods can play in urban management and local governance. It can be argued that cities taking advantage of the liminal attributes provided by urban experiments can develop a municipal strategy based upon the promotion and expansion of urban commons and social solidarity. In such a way, cities can actually use urban experimentation in their favour, overcoming specific challenges they might be facing on a community level, and generating novel, bottom-up solutions that respond effectively to the local socio-cultural contexts, engendering a sort of neighbourhood culture. If respective neighbourhood initiatives flourish then they can create a domino effect, leading the history of a city into a new era of participation and solidarity, challenging social conventions, strengthening social ties and creating a new relationship with public space. Nevertheless, when faced with everyday lives that are heavily personalised, the reproduction of this social structure cannot alone provide a practical approach to neighbourhood organisation. This can only happen when respective commoning practices start to flourish, becoming important pre-figurations of an emancipated society. Urban commoning must remain a collective struggle to re-appropriate and transform 'at the same time' a society's common wealth (Hardt & Negri 2009: 251–253), extending this structure beyond its own limits. This entails an approach that is consultative, informed, and democratic, and which considers both the whole population (past, present, future) and culture in all of its diverse and collective manifestations (Evans 2015). Such an approach may provide the basis for the development of further approaches to resident empowerment and participation, by encompassing a variety of sustainable, locally based, place-making projects that promote neighbourhood-building and more inclusive urban futures.

This project makes the case for more effective and decentralised governance capacity. Accordingly, the long-term outcome of the project discusses a common reflection that concerns the future of the Greek city, given the fact that during financial crises, cities are not only the epicentre, but also the context that shapes residents' daily routine and their relationship with the urban fabric (Harvey 2012). In terms of urban management, activism and local level research reveals the main limitations, trends, hegemonic norms, and issues experienced in practice. These include the lack of an open-source neighbourhood monitoring system and the absence of a framework that supports locally organised collective action in urban planning and culture. As a result, in Greece, citizens do not have the opportunity to participate in local governance and collectively address the problems of their place of residence. Therefore, they cannot (re-)produce applicable actions in a bottom-up fashion that may provide practical solutions and physical improvements to shared spaces.

Nonetheless, the potential of such bottom-up neighbourhood initiatives may foster a more locally-based participatory and activist culture that can be associated with the creation of a different urban identity: one that is built around urban commons and is created by the people, instead of being imposed upon them. Long's (2013) argument on the sense of place, drawing on Massey (1994), tells us to pay close attention to the cultural specificity of places; the myths, narratives and memories that surround them, and the cultural production that is shaped by them. In this regard, this project highlights the fact that if a city is considered to be a common (Pusey & Chatterton 2017), it can be governed by and for its residents to maximise internal democracy and well-being (see De Angelis 2007; Linebaugh 2008). The priority then is to create a systematic approach for effective and efficient group collaboration on neighbourhood level, thereby ensuring improved decision-making in urban-scale politics. To this end, it is peoples' ability to work together that this longitudinal research seeks to understand by setting the foundations for common urban futures in the 'real' world.

Acknowledgements

I would like to express my warmest thanks to all the magnificent people from the Alexandrou Svolou Neighbourhood Initiative. This long-lasting journey would not have been possible without you. My deepest appreciation goes to Giorgos Synefakis, Aikaterina Georgiadou and Periklis Chatzinakos whose companionship, solidarity and invaluable contribution played a decisive role in the development of the project. I am grateful to the guidance and mentoring given by Professor Steven Miles (Manchester Metropolitan University). Through all these years, not only has he been a second father to me, but also a tireless and critical observer of this project. I would also like to sincerely express my gratitude to Eleftheria Deltsou, Stelios Lekakis, Konstantinos Theodoridis and Natalia Natsika for providing me with valuable feedback and constructive comments. This chapter is dedicated to the memory of Lazaros Chatzinakos, a Journalist who believed in a modern society that could maintain the innocence of earlier times. May you travel in tamed seas and rest in power, father.

Bibliography

Agamben, G. (1993). *The coming community*. Minneapolis, MN: University of Minnesota Press.

Amin, A. (2004). *Regions unbound: Towards a new politics of place*. Geografiska Annaler: Series B, Human Geography, 86(1), 33–44.

Athanassiou, E., Christodoulou, C., Kapsali, M. & Karagianni, M. (2018). Hybridising 'ownership' of public space: Framings of urban emancipation in crisis-ridden Thessaloniki. In S. Knierbein & T. Viderman (Eds.), *Public space unbound: Urban emancipation and the post-political condition* (pp. 251–265). New York, NY: Routledge.

Augé, M. (1995). *Non-Places: Introduction to an anthropology of supermodernity*. London, United Kingdom: Verso.

Bakhtin, M. (1984). *Rabelais and his world*. Bloomington, IN: Indiana University Press.

Barber, B. R. (2013). *If mayors ruled the world: Dysfunctional nations, rising cities*. New Haven, CT: Yale University Press.

Beck, U. (1995). *Ecological enlightenment: Essays on the politics of the risk society*. Atlantic Highlands, NJ: Humanities Press.

Benjamin, W. (1997). *Charles Baudelaire: A lyric poet in the era of high capitalism*. New York, NY: Verso Books.

Bourdieu, P. (1984). *Distinction: A social critique of the judgement of taste*. New York, NY: President & Fellows of Harvard College, Routledge & Kegan Paul.

Brindley, P., Goulding, J. & Wilson, M. L. (2014). Mapping urban neighbour hoods from internet derived data. In *22nd GIS Research UK Conference*.

Glasgow, UK, 16–18 April 2014 (pp. 355–364). Retrieved November 20, 2019, from https://www.gla.ac.uk/media/Media_401753_smxx.pdf.

Bulkeley, H. & Castán Broto, V. (2012). Government by experiment?: Global cities and the governing of climate change. *Transactions of the Institute of British Geographers, 38*(3), 361–375.

Caprotti, F. & Cowley, R. (2017). Interrogating urban experiments. *Urban Geography, 38*(9), 1441–1450.

Castoriadis, C. (1987). *The imaginary institution of society.* Cambridge, United Kingdom: Polity Press.

Chatzinakos, G. (2015). *Community festivals and events in the post-industrial European city: The impact of liminal practices on community-building.* Saarbrücken, Germany: Lap Lambert Academic Publishing.

Chatzinakos, G. (2016). Mapping the neighbourhood: Problems, suggestions and approaches to urban futures: A methodological approach to the management of bottom-up community synergies and cultural initiatives. In Rocco, R. (Ed.), *Jane Jacobs is still here: Jane Jacobs 100: Her legacy and relevance in the 21st century, 24–25 May 2016, Faculty of Architecture and the Built Environment, TU Delft, The Netherlands* (pp. 166–173). Delft, The Netherlands: TU Delft, BK Bouwkunde. Retrieved November 20, 2019, from https://issuu.com/robertorocco/docs/jane_jacobs_report.

Chevalier, J. M. & Buckles, D. J. (2013). *Participatory action research: Theory and methods for engaged inquiry.* London, United Kingdom: Routledge.

Chiesi, L. & Costa, P. (2015). One strategy, many purposes: A classification for cultural mapping projects. In N. Duxbury, W. F. Garrett-Petts & D. Mac Lennan (Eds.), *Cultural mapping as cultural inquiry* (pp. 69–85). New York, NY: Routledge.

Christodoulou, C. (2015). *Τοπία αστικής διάχυσης: Αστικοποίηση και πολεο δομικός σχεδιασμός: Η περιφέρεια της Θεσσαλονίκης.* Thessaloniki: University Studio Press.

Cohen, A. P. (1985). *The symbolic construction of community.* London, United Kingdom: Tavistock Publications.

Crespi-Vallbona, M. & Richards, G. (2007). The meaning of cultural festivals: Stakeholder perspectives in Catalunya. *International Journal of Cultural Policy, 13*(1), 103–122.

Dashper, K. (2016). Researching from the inside: Autoethnography and critical event studies. In R. Lamond & L. Platt (Eds.), *Critical event studies: Approaches to research* (pp. 213–229). London, United Kingdom: Palgrave Macmillan.

De Angelis, M. (2007). *The beginning of history: Value struggles and global capital.* London, United Kingdom: Pluto.

Delanty, G. (2009). *Community* (2nd ed.). London, United Kingdom: Routledge.

Dietz, R. D. (2002). The estimation of neighborhood effects in the social sciences: An interdisciplinary approach. *Social Science Research, 31*(4), 539–575.

Dulin-Keita, A., Hannon, L., Buys, D., Casazza, K. & Clay, O. (2016). Surrounding community residents' expectations of HOPE VI for their community, health and physical activity. *Journal of Community Practice, 84*(1), 18–37.

Duxbury, N., Garrett-Petts, W. F. & MacLennan, D. (Eds.). (2015). *Cultural mapping as cultural inquiry.* New York, NY: Routledge.

Evans, G. (2015). Cultural mapping and planning for sustainable communities. In N. Duxbury, W. F. Garrett-Petts & D. MacLennan (Eds.), *Cultural mapping as cultural inquiry* (pp. 45–68). New York, NY: Routledge.

Evans, J. (2016). Trials and tribulations: Conceptualizing the city through/as urban experimentation, *Geography Compass, 10*(10), 429–443.

Evans, J. & Karvonen, A. (2011). Living laboratories for sustainability: Exploring the politics and epistemology of urban transition. In H. Bulkeley, V. Castán Broto, M. Hodson & S. Marvin (Eds.), *Cities and low carbon transitions* (pp. 126–141). London, United Kindom: Routledge.

Evans, J., Karvonen, A. & Raven, R. (2016). *The experimental city.* Abingdon, United Kingdom: Routledge.

Finkel, R. & Sang, K. (2016). Participatory research: Case study of a community event. In R. I. Lamond, & L., Platt (Eds.), *Critical event studies: Approaches to research* (pp. 195–211). London, United Kingdom: Palgrave Macmillan.

Finn MSW, J. L. (1994). The promise of participatory research. *Journal of Progressive Human Services, 5*(2), 25–42. DOI: https://doi.org/10.1300/J059v05n02_03.

Frangopoulos, I., Dalakis, N. & Kourkouridis, D. (2009). Urban structure and mobility in the context of sustainable development: Citizens' opinion about the Thessaloniki submerged tunnel. *International Journal of Sustainable Development and Planning, 4*(4), 333–344.

Goodwin, M. (1993). The city as commodity: The contested spaces of urban development. In Kearns, G. & Philo, C. (Eds.), *Selling places: The city as cultural capital, past and present* (pp. 145–162). Oxford: Pergamon Press.

Grele, R. J. (1985). *Envelopes of sound: The art of oral history* (2nd ed.). Chicago, IL: Precedent Publishing.

Hardt, M. & Negri, A. (2009). *Commonwealth.* Cambridge, MA: Belknap Press.

Harvey, D. (1989). *The condition of postmodernity: An enquiry into the origins of cultural change.* Cambridge, MA: Blackwell.

Harvey, D. (2012). *Rebel cities: From the right to the city to the urban revolution.* London, United Kingdom: Verso.

Hughes, G. (1999). Urban revitalization: The use of festive time strategies. *Leisure Studies, 18*(2), 119–135.

Iliopoulos, S. M. & Kalligas, N. G. (2017). Σχεδιάζοντας συμμετοχικά τα Πάρκα Τσέπης ως εργαλείο αναζωογόνησης κεντρικών αστικών περιοχών: Η περίπτωση του ιστορικού κέντρου της Θεσσαλονίκης (Unpuplished Bachelor Thesis). Aristotle University of Thessaloniki, Thessaloniki.

Jacobs, J. (1961). *The death and life of great American cities.* New York, NY: Random House.

Jepson, A. & Clarke, A. (2013). Events and community development. In R. Finkel, D. McGillivray, G. McPherson & P. Robinson (Eds.), *Research themes for events* (pp. 6–17). Wallingford, United Kingdom: CABI.

Karvonen, A. & van Heur, B. (2014). Urban laboratories: Experiments in reworking cities. *International Journal of Urban and Regional Research*, 38(2), 379–392.

Katsoulis, D. (2011). *Καλλικράτης: Ενδοδημοτική αποκέντρωση*. Athens, Greece: Elliniki Etaireia Topikis Anaptyxis kai Aftodioikisis. Retrieved November 20, 2019, from https://www.eetaa.gr/ekdoseis/pdf/139.pdf.

Kinney, A. M., Hutton, L., Carlson, B., Perlick, L. M., Minkler, K. K. & Kimber, C. (2012). Isanti County active living: Measuring change in perception and behavior. *American Journal of Preventive Medicine*, 43(5), S392–S394.

Kullman, K. (2013). Geographies of experiment/Experimental geographies: A rough guide. *Geography Compass*, 7(12), 879–894.

Labrianidis, L. (2011). Thessaloniki's arrested development: Missed opportunities. *Antipode*, 43(5), 1801–1827.

Lafarga, J. (1999). *Gràcia: de rural a urbana: Territori i nomenclator*. Barcelona, Spain: Taller d'Història de Gràcia.

Lefebvre, H. (1991). *The production of space*. Oxford, United Kingdom: Blackwell.

Lefebvre, H. (1996). *Writing on cities*. Oxford, United Kingdom: Blackwell.

Linebaugh, P. (2008). *The Magna Carta Manifesto: Liberties and commons for all*. Berkley, CA: University of California Press.

Long, J. (2013). Sense of place and place-based activism in the neoliberal city: The case of 'weird' resistance. *City*, 17(1), 25–67.

Lowry, G., M. S. Levin, M. & Tsang, H. (Maraya). (2015). Maraya as visual research: Mapping urban displacement and narrating artistic inquiry. In N. Duxbury, W. F. Garrett-Petts & D. MacLennan (Eds.), *Cultural mapping as cultural inquiry* (pp. 319–337). New York, NY: Routledge.

MacCannell, D. (1973). Staged authenticity: Arrangements of social space in tourist settings. *American journal of Sociology*, 79(3), 589–603.

Maguire, J. (1988). Doing figurational sociology: Some preliminary observations on methodological issues and sensitizing concepts. *Leisure Studies*, 7(2), 187–193.

Maloutas, T. & Karadimitriou, N. (2001). Vertical social differentiation in Athens: Alternative or complement to community segregation? *International Journal of Urban and Regional Research*, 25(4), 699–716.

Martin, D, G. (2017). Community. In M. Jayne & K. Ward (Eds.), *Urban theory: New critical perspectives* (pp. 74–83). Abingdon, United Kingdom: Routledge.

Massey, D. (1994). *Space, place and gender*. Cambridge, United Kingdom: Polity Press.

May, T. & Perry, B. (2016). Cities, experiments and the logics of the knowledge economy. In J. Evans, A. Karvonen & R. Raven (Eds.), *The experimental city* (pp. 32–46). Abingdon, United Kingdom: Routledge.

Mazower, M. (2004). *Salonica, city of ghosts: Christians, Muslims and Jews, 1430–1950*. London, United Kingdom: Harper Perrenial.

Melucci, A. (1996). *Challenging codes: Collective action in the information age*. Cambridge, United Kingdom: Cambridge University Press.

Melucci, A. (2009). *The playing self: Person and meaning in the planetary society*. Cambridge, United Kingdom: Cambridge University Press.

Mercado, B. G. Fl. (2004). *"La festa de Gracia sóc jo i jo sóc la festa". La construcción psicocultural de la participación ciudadana en una fiesta popular*. Unpublished PhD Thesis. Universitat de Barcelona, Barcelona.

Miles, S. (2017). Consumption. In M. Jayne & K. Ward (Eds.), *Urban theory: New critical perspectives* (pp. 99–108). Abingdon, United Kingdom: Routledge.

Oakley, K. (2015). *Creating space: A re-evaluation of the role of culture in regenaration. Research* Report. University of Leeds. Retrieved November 20, 2019, from http://eprints.whiterose.ac.uk/88559/3/AHRC_Cultural_Value_KO%20Final.pdf.

Perks, R. & Thomson, A. (Eds.). (2006). *The oral history reader*. New York, NY: Routledge.

Plows, A. (2008). *Social movements and ethnographic methodologies: An analysis using case study examples. Sociology Compass, 2*(5), 1523–1538.

Providência, P. (2015). City readings and urban mappings: The city as didactic instrument. In N. Duxbury, W. F. Garrett-Petts & D. MacLennan (Eds.), *Cultural mapping as cultural inquiry* (pp. 217–230). New York, NY: Routledge.

Pusey, A. & Chatterton, P. (2017). Commons. In M. Jayne & K. Ward (Eds.), *Urban theory: New critical perspectives* (pp. 63–73). Abingdon, United Kingdom: Routledge.

Relph, E. (1976). *Place and placelessness*. London, United Kingdom: Pion.

Richards, G. (2010). Tourism development trajectories: From culture to creativity? *Revista Encontros Científicos – Tourism & Management Studies, 6*, 9–15.

Richards, G. & Palmer, R. (2010). *Eventful cities: Cultural management and urban revitalisation*. Oxford, United Kingdom: Butterworth-Heinemann.

Richards, G. & Wilson, J. (2006). Developing creativity in tourist experiences: A solution to the serial reproduction of culture? *Tourism Management, 27*(6), 1209–1223.

Ritzer, G. (1999). *Enchanting a disenchanted world: Revolutionizing the means of consumption*. Thousand Oaks, CA: Pine Forge Press.

Robinson, J. (2006). *Ordinary cities: Between modernity and development*. London, United Kingdom: Routledge.

Sampson, R. J., Morenoff, J. D. & Gannon-Rowley, T. (2002). Assessing "neighborhood effects": Social processes and new directions in research. *Annual Review of Sociology, 28*, 443–478.

Sanclemente, V. (1990). *Gràcia: Història de la festa major més gran del pla*. Barcelona, Spain: Carrer Gran.

Scott, A. J. (2000). *The cultural economy of cities: Essays on the geography of image-producing industries*. London, United Kingdom: SAGE Publications.

Sellström, E. & Bremberg, S. (2006). Review article: The significance of neighbourhood context to child and adolescent health and well-being: A systematic review of multilevel studies. *Scandinavian Journal of Public Health, 34*(5), 544–554.

Sengers, F., Berkhout, F., Wieczorek, A. J. & Raven, R. (2016). Experimenting in the city: Unpacking notions of experimentation for sustainability. In J. Evans, A. Karvonen & R. Raven (Eds.), *The Experimental City* (pp. 15–31). Abingdon, United Kingdom: Routledge.

Sharpley, R. & Stone, P. R. (2012). Socio-cultural impacts of events: Meanings, authorized transgression and social capital. In S. J. Page & J. Connell (Eds.), *The Routledge handbook of events* (pp. 347–361). Abingdon, United Kingdom: Routledge.

Sobrequés, J. (1996). *La difícil construcció d'un poble*. Barcelona, Spain: Lunwerg.

Souzas, N. (2015). Ο ρόλος των πολιτισμικών πρακτικών στη συγκρότηση των κοινωνικών κινημάτων. In K. Athanasiou, E. Vasdeki, E. Kapetanaki, M. Karagianni, M. Kapsali, V. Makrygianni, ... & C. Tsavdaroglou (Eds.), *Urban conflicts* (pp. 266–277). Thessaloniki: Ergastirio synantiseis kai sygkrouseis stin poli. Retrieved November 20, 2019, from https://www.academia.edu/12776105/Urban_Conflicts.

Spilhaus, A. (1967). The experimental city. *Daedalus, 96*(4), 1129–1141.

Spilsbury, J. C., Korbin, J. E. & Coulton, C. J. (2009). Mapping children's neighborhood perceptions: Implications for child indicators. *Child Indicators Research, 2*, 111–131.

Spiridon, M. (2013). "The wasteland quest": Cityscapes of memory in postmodern fiction. *Philologica Jassyensia, An IX, 1*(17), 201–207.

Sutherland, N. (2013). Book review: Social movements and activist ethnography. *Organization, 20*(4), 627–635. DOI: https://doi.org/10.1177/1350 508412450219.

Thoidou, E. & Foutakis, D. (2006). Μητροπολιτική Θεσσαλονίκη και αστική ανταγωνιστικότητα: Προγραμματισμός, μετασχηματισμός και υλοποίηση ενός 'οράματος' για την πόλη. ΓΕΩΓΡΑΦΙΕΣ, *12*, 25–46.

Thompson, P. (1978). *The voice of the past: Oral history*. Oxford, United Kingdom: Oxford University Press.

Turner, B. S. & Rojek, C. (2001). *Society and culture: Principles of scarcity and solidarity*. London: SAGE Publications.

Turner, V. (1969). *The ritual process: Structure and anti-structure*. New York, NY: Aldine de Gruyter.

Turner, V. (Ed.). (1982). *Celebration, studies in festivity and ritual*. Washington, DC: Smithsonian Institution Press.

UN (2014) *World Urbanization Prospects: The 2014 Revision (Highlights)*. Department of Economic and Social Affairs, Population Division. New York: United Nations Available at: https://esa.un.org/unpd/wup/publications /files/wup2014-highlights.pdf.

Van Heerden, E. (2011). The social and spatial construction of two South African arts festivals as liminal events. *South African Theatre Journal, 25*(1), 54–71.

Voytenko, Y., McCormick, K., Evans, J. & Schliwa, G. (2016). Urban living labs for sustainability and low carbon cities in Europe: Towards a research agenda. *Journal of Cleaner Production, 123*(Special Issue "Strategies for Sustainable Solutions: An Interdisciplinary and Collaborative Research Agenda"), 45–54. DOI: https://doi.org/10.1016/j.jclepro.2015.08.053.

Wagner, P. (2008). *Modernity as experience and interpretation: A new sociology of modernity*. Cambridge, United Kingdom: Polity Press.

Whyte, W. F. (1989). Advancing scientific knowledge through participatory action research. *Sociological Forum, 4*(3), 367–385.

Williams, R. J. (2004). *The anxious city: British urbanism in the late twentieth century*. Abingdon, United Kingdom: Routledge.

Zenk, S. N., Wilbur, J., Wang, E., McDevitt, J., Oh, A., Block, R., … & Savar, N. (2009). Neighborhood environment and adherence to a walking intervention in African American women. *Health Education and Behavior, 36*(1), 167–181. DOI: https://doi.org/10.1177/1090198108321249.

Zukin, S. (1988). *Loft living: Culture and capital in urban change*. London, United Kingdom: Radius.

Zukin, S. (1998). Urban lifestyles: Diversity and standardisation in spaces of consumption. *Urban Studies, 35*(5–6), 825–839. DOI: https://doi.org /10.1080/0042098984574.

Zukin, S. (2011). *Naked city: The death and life of authentic urban places*. Oxford, United Kingdom: Oxford University Press.

CHAPTER 10

Commoning Over a Cup of Coffee: The Case of Kafeneio, a Co-op Cafe at Plato's Academy

Chrysostomos Galanos

The story of Kafeneio

Kafeneio, a co-op cafe at Plato's Academy in Athens, was founded on the 1st of May 2010. The opening day was combined with an open, self-organised gathering that emphasised the need to reclaim open public spaces for the people. It is important to note that every turning point in the life of Kafeneio was somehow linked to a large gathering. Indeed, the very start of the initiative, in September 2009, took the form of an alternative festival which we named 'Point Defect'.

In order to understand the choice of 'Point Defect' as the name for the launch party, one need only look at the press release we made at the time:

'When we have a perfect crystal, all atoms are positioned exactly at the points they should be, for the crystal to be intact; in the molecular structure of this crystal everything seems aligned. It can be, however, that one of the atoms is not at place or missing, or another type of atom is at its place. In that case we say that the crystal has a 'point defect', a point where its structure is not perfect, a point from which the crystal could start collapsing'.

How to cite this book chapter:
Galanos, C. 2020. Commoning Over a Cup of Coffee: The Case of Kafeneio, a Co-op Cafe at Plato's Academy. In Lekakis, S. (ed.) *Cultural Heritage in the Realm of the Commons: Conversations on the Case of Greece.* Pp. 213–226. London: Ubiquity Press. DOI: https://doi.org/10.5334/bcj.l. License: CC-BY

There is an obvious analogy in this statement between a crystal and social structures. The vision of our gathering was to create a small crack[80] that would enable the new imagined realities to surface. Realities of equality, self-organization, creativity and mutual respect. It could be argued that in the vision of September 2009 launch party, one can find the soul of the Kafeneio, the co-op cafe at Plato's Academy.

From vision to realisation

In order, however, to properly convey the atmosphere of the Kafeneio and its evolution over time, maybe the story should start a little earlier. To begin with, it is important to clarify how we found ourselves in the area of Athens called 'Plato's Academy', especially given the fact that almost none of the members of the founding team lived there. In fact, some of us had never heard of the area that took its name from the adjacent archaeological park, on either side of the Cratylus street in the area of Kolonos, bearing the remains of the school (387 – 86 BC) founded by the legendary philosopher.

Towards the end of May 2007, Kerameikos Metro station, 2.5 kilometres from Plato's Academy, opened its gates to the public. One direct effect of this was the rapid increase in business development in the wider area, especially in the domain of entertainment, food and music. As most of us lived in the affected areas, we experienced the consequences of this development and observed the distortion inflicted upon the coherence and the character of the neighbourhood. The continuous incorporation of more and more public spaces into the commercial zone was one of the main issues. Formerly abandoned corners were now cafés and restaurants and sidewalks where people used to gather and talk were now covered with tables and chairs.

Seeking to somehow act against this trend, we were lucky to find support from a very active residents' group in the neighbourhood of Plato's Academy.[81] The 'Residents' Committee for Plato's Academy' created a few years earlier as a result of collective activist attempts, already had noteworthy success in blocking the construction of a multi-storey building at the edge of the park, as well as a building for the Prefecture of Athens that would have had a significant impact on the life of the neighbourhood. Our collaboration started from the 'Point Defect party' and their solidary assistance was crucial for the creation of the Kafeneio.

Although our inauguration party took place in September 2009, it was only in May 2010 that Kafeneio opened to the public. The first few months were necessary to deal with several practical issues, such as forming the founding team,

---

[80] It is perhaps interesting that at that point we completely ignored the work of John Holloway and his book *Crack Capitalism* (Holloway 2010).

[81] https://akadimia-platonos.com/. Last access 20 November 2019.

Figure 1: Panoramic view of Athens' city centre (Source: Google Earth).

deciding the goals of the initiative, choosing the right legal form, sorting out financial issues, dealing with interpersonal problems and much more.

From the beginning, we aimed to network with other initiatives in the field of the Social and Solidarity Economy that either already existed or were also starting at the time. Back in 2010 we were pioneers, as the only known initiative to exist before us was 'Sporos'[82] in Exarcheia, while about a month after the founding of Kafeneio, a workers' collective named 'Pagkaki' was founded in the area of Koukaki in Athens. It is interesting to note that within a few months dozens of formal or informal groups had come to life, trying to respond to the obvious contradictions and malfunctions of the dominant economic model and to experiment with new types of social organisation.

A defining factor for the extension and growth of similar ideas and initiatives was without doubt the 'Aganaktisménoi' (Indignants) movement and the square protests that spread throughout Greece in May 2011. The most important of these were the demonstrations at Syntagma square in Athens (Papapavlou 2015). One might think that including these facts in the narrative here might be irrelevant to the story of Kafeneio, however, these historic moments helped us define and update our role and our relationship to the prevalent social issues of the day. This period was very important, since it was the first time that relatively newly appearing notions and practices, such as common goods, eco-communities, time banks, alternative currencies and Social & Solidarity Economy (SSE), were experientially introduced into the everyday vocabulary of the people participating in collective processes. In my view, these terms helped people obtain a common vocabulary for things they were already doing but were uncertain of how to express or communicate them.

---

[82] Seized operation in Autumn 2012.

This transformational language of the commons helped us to escape the bipolar view between the market and the state and the hidden pitfalls in the ways in which we defined problems and located solutions (Bollier & Helfrich 2012). From the moment, a third dimension, this of the commons, was introduced to the system dominated from the market and the state and a new horizon opened up regarding action and thought towards the co-creation of a different world.

This was a period in which we also discovered the vocabulary to articulate the fact that the main drive that propelled us to take action next to the archaeological park was the need to protect the park itself and highlight its value as a common good.

A further, very important event for the development of relations between the emerging alternative initiatives, as well as for the adoption of a commons vocabulary was the Alternative Festival of Solidarity and Cooperative Economy (fest4sce), which took place for the first time in the Ellinikon Cultural Center in October 2012. The festival aimed to become a central event in facilitating local and international initiatives to introduce themselves to each other and to network. The event was subsequently repeated annually for four years, with the last two, in 2015 and 2016, taking place in Plato's Academy. The high levels of interaction and osmosis among the actors of the emerging world of the commons and the success of the events were applauded. As a result, in October 2017 the festival was incorporated into the Festival of the Commons[83] in Athens. Kafeneio, both as a project and through its members, was present from the first moment in these five years, participating in the Festival's organising committee. It is also worth mentioning that the first ever presentation made in the Festival was about Kafeneio in Plato's Academy.

Thus, since 2012 an active community of social, cooperative and solidarity economy and of the commons has emerged, with a clear vision of a social transformation rather than merely dealing with the neoliberal financial crisis. As a part of this community, our goal was to make Kafeneio a welcoming space, where groups and individuals could meet, exchange opinions and present their ideas; a hub of collaborative energy, information and knowledge in the developing horizontal ecosystem of an emerging new world.

Issues within the team and how we dealt with them

Every initiative has its difficulties, even more so when many individuals, business activity, financial problems and unprecedented bureaucratic issues are involved. In fact, the combination of all the above created an unstable situation for the management of the initiative. In our case, we had to go through various difficult paths and many times we almost abandoned the project. However, in

---

[83] https://commons.gr/festival/. Last access 20 November 2019.

spite of all of this, we are still there, offering Zapatista coffee to anybody who wants to enjoy it.

A major difficulty that we had to deal with, from the very beginning, was to choose the right legal form. We were very conscious about what we wanted to do as an informal group, but when it came to be settling into a specific legal form, there was a gap in the law. We wanted to create an initiative that would function as a part of the social, cooperative, non-profit economy. Back in 2010 there was no specific law for SSEs, such as exists today (L.4019/2011 amended by L.4430/2016), that provided directions to the local authorities on how to deal with projects like ours. In our case, we came to the conclusion that the legal form closest to our aspirations was the non-profit civil company. After long discussions and clarifications with the local authorities that almost made us give up the project before it even started, we eventually managed to be granted an operating license as 'European Village', a pre-existing, civil, non-profit company, aligning in vision and objectives with the idea of the Coop Café.

Even more central and harder to deal with are the interpersonal issues that arise among the members of a team and are related to topics such as the decision making processes, the conscious or unconscious power games, conflict management, the definitions of goals and the balance between financial viability, efficiency and self-management. This is a long list of crucial issues about which we learned nothing in school or university, since the dominant system does not teach us how to collaborate but how to function as individuals within a hierarchy. Soon we realised that good intentions are usually not enough, because the way we are brought up has created automatic reactions that prevail against well-meaning ideals.

Tools that helped us

It is very important to know that it is not necessary to reinvent the wheel over and over again and it is relieving to find out that your unpleasant experiences have most likely already been dealt with by others. There are people out there who have already carried out many experiments and are in a position to suggest solutions[84] for anybody who wants to take them and adapt them to their needs. If this sounds like commons-based peer production of solutions for collective issues, it really works like this!

An issue that required a long time to understand was the fact that an assembly is not just a gathering where each participant shares their opinion, especially when there is an agreement for the decisions to be taken with consensus. Any tool can become a disadvantage when used improperly, thus the assembly, the soul of any cooperative initiative, can easily become a synonym for time wasting. One thing that helped us a lot was the creation of supporting roles for

---

[84] For example, http://www.circleway.org/. Last access 20 November 2019.

the assembly. A facilitator and a rapporteur are the minimum required set of roles. Indeed, specific roles such as that of the facilitator's are admittedly quite demanding and for this reason it was necessary for quite a few members to get the relevant training.

The circle is also a very important part of the process, since it facilitates the equal participation and creation of a safe environment. In practice, we realised that even if we focused overly on specific decision-making processes, there were often emotional blockages that prevented us from reaching solutions. In order to avoid this, we decided to include a monthly meeting in our shared practices, which we named 'assembly of emotions', aimed at dealing exclusively with personal issues. While we only followed this practice for a short while, it produced clear results and we would argue that it has significant potential. Although also in this case it must be said that the presence of at least one experienced facilitator is crucial.

Another important practice that helped us crucially is the tool of Nonviolent Communication (NVC). NVC is a process that helped us realise, locate and deal with the violence we receive and give to others and ourselves every day (Nonviolent Communication 2018). We were lucky enough to host some of the first NVC workshops in Greece, which of course had an influence on the members of our group. In fact, the first NVC certified trainer in Greece is a member of our group.

Mediation is also a practice that gave us positive results whenever we used it. A mediator is a trained person who holds a neutral position and their job is to help two conflicting parties to understand each other's needs and thus find new, mutually acceptable solutions (Mediation 2018). Some of our members were also trained to be able to play the role of mediator.

However, there were moments when we realised that we had to ask for external help, since the team by itself did not have the knowhow or the emotional strength to deal with certain issues. In one of those cases we asked for the help of 'Metaplasis', a non-profit informal group which organised structured dialogue and communication processes (Metaplasis 2018). The process lasted for almost three months. It started with one on one interviews with all of the members carried out by the representatives of 'Metaplasis' and proceeded to meetings with the whole team. It really helped us to deal with the communication crisis we were undergoing, and it also stressed the importance of facing up to issues instead of trying to hide them.

What is more, on two occasions we organised Strategic Planning gatherings: in April 2015 and November 2017. The members of our organisation met and spent 3 days discussing our issues, thoughts, feelings and desires. This was followed by a stage in which we redefined our vision and goals. Living together for a few days outside Athens under the same roof helped us substantially to get over certain situations and move on. These meetings combined communal living with a specific set of activities and practices. Some of the tools we used were Open Space Technology, Mind Maps, Collective Story Harvesting, S.W.O.T analysis, graphic facilitation and many more. In our 2015 gathering, we had support from external facilitators,[85] while in the 2017 event we used our acquired skills and knowledge to manage the processes ourselves.

Finally, since 'European Village' takes part in European Mobility Programs, its members and affiliated participants have often had the opportunity to travel throughout Europe, to acquire new experiences in non-typical, experiential education and to become familiar with initiatives outside Greece. One of the most notable cases was our participation in the program 'Hétérotopies',[86] which was inspired by the ideas of the philosopher Michel Foucault and aims to discover alternative existent worlds where things are different from the mainstream. It is through becoming aware of the existence of all of these different spaces that we have kept on working for social transformation and for the transformation of our everyday life.

Developing urban commons

As mentioned previously, many of the activities that were carried out in the first period were the result of the needs that existed among the members of the group, who did not always have the vocabulary to express them and communicate them properly. For example, it has been stated that it was necessary to ensure our presence next to the archaeological park as a point of resistance to possible future commercialisation efforts in the area with the consequence of altering the character of the neighbourhood. It also felt important to preserve a point in the city that allows citizens to have contact with the natural environment.

Over time, we realised that what we were promoting through our activities, in relation to the park, was the development of the urban commons. Our first contact with the area was through a celebration that was primarily aimed at socialising, reclaiming the public space and the self-management of our entertainment. These key features have remained central to the events we have held or helped to take place in the area since. In the words of one inhabitant of the area "you broke the neighbourhood taboo of organising activities in the park" (Resident 2010, pers com.), a sentiment that gave us great strength in continuing our activities.

The root of our actions is always linked to the following question: '*If a neighbourhood is not accustomed to using its space, then who is going to claim it, if private interests attempt to appropriate it?*'

Indicative examples of the conscious development of the idea for Plato's Academy as an urban commons are the following activities:

---

[85] http://www.aoh-athens.gr/. Last access 20 November 2019.

[86] http://www.viabrachy.org/h%C3%A9t%C3%A9rotopies/le-projet. Last access 20 November 2019.

- a discussion organized, on the initiative of Kafeneio members, at the 3rd Alternative Festival of Solidarity and Cooperative Economy, titled: 'Plato's Academy collectives: Transforming public space to common space while building human relationships. The case of the Plato's Academy's archaeological park'.
- a discussion at Commons Fest 2015 in Athens by 'Koino Athens' team, titled 'Urban Commons Practices', where one of the three examples discussed was the case of the Plato's Academy Park (Theodorou 2015).
- an open discussion / participatory design workshop, titled 'Common Goods – Common Objectives: The Plato's Academy Park as a Common Good and the struggle against the construction of the Mall' that took place at Kafeneio at 21st November 2017 in co-organization with the team Urban Transcripts Unit 4 (European Village 2018a).
- in the framework of the 4th meeting 'Dialogues in Archaeology' held in Athens, May – June 2018, Plato's Academy hosted many activities in the neighbourhood (https://www.archaiologia.gr/blog/2018/05/11/αρχαιολογικοί -διάλογοι-2018-πόλεις-ασ/). Associated with our objectives were the following two:
  - A 'Silent Walk at Plato's Academy', co-organised by the Plato's Academy participatory design team. The Silent Walk was completed with an open discussion with residents of the area, debating on the significance of the Park as a cultural heritage asset and a common good for the city.
  - 'The Museum as a common good' workshop by SOMA team (Scattered Open Museum of Attica), aimed at contributing to the wider effort of the residents to 'see' the park of the Plato's Academy as common good. In the workshop, appropriate museological practices were discussed, highlighting the cultural identity of the Park and the dynamics of the area as its central and symbolic core (Nonplan 2018).

Events with a similar aim are the many self-organized, community festivals that have taken place at Plato's Academy in recent years.[87] It is important to put an emphasis on some of the events that took place in the park of Plato's Academy, which were of particular importance. The first was the two-day event organized by collectives of the neighbourhood on March 30–31, 2013. The central slogan of the event was 'We defend the Commons, we are creating communities of active solidarity' (European Village 2018b). The other two were the 4th and the 5th 'Alternative festivals of Solidarity and Cooperative Economy' that took place on October 16th–18th 2015 and June 3rd–5th 2016, with the central slogan 'Come to our Autonomous village'.

There are two reasons to focus specifically on these two events: Firstly, because they were large-scale events, with thousands of visitors; secondly because they

---

[87] For a very good example check: https://www.youtube.com/watch?time _continue=108&v=8pKy3PZCAUQ. Last access 20 November 2019.

Figure 2: 5th fest4sce at Plato's Academy: "Come to our Autonomous Village" (Source: author).

were powerful events that allowed the space to acquire the character of an urban commons. These events were created through assemblies of collectives that, if only for a few days, took over total responsibility for the space. By creating these Temporary Autonomous Zones, we succeeded in projecting ourselves into non-hierarchical systems of social relations (Temporary Autonomous Zone 2018).

Who really manages cultural heritage?

The great difference between this park and other green areas is its significant cultural heritage. We must not forget that we are dealing with an archaeological site of global importance. One need only point to the fact that Plato's 'Republic' is the most widely cited in Universities curricula (Ingraham 2016) whereas the word 'Academy' derives its origin from this place.

A central question is 'who is the most competent body to manage this cultural heritage'? Or to put the question differently 'who are the stakeholders whose opinion should be taken into account?'. In many cases the Greek state has shown that the citizens and their opinion do not have any validity in its plans. A prominent example of this was the construction of a small museum at the edge of the park. Most residents expressed a positive opinion about the construction of the museum, but were opposed to the choice of the site, putting forward reasonable arguments. They went as far as to propose an alternative spot in the immediate vicinity with many comparative advantages. However, in the end, the museum was erected in an area that everyone knows is inappropriate, and the neighbourhood lost valuable green space as a result.[88] Thus, a situation that could easily be mutually beneficial, ultimately becomes problematic simply because it does not take into account the suggestions of those who are most involved; the residents of the area.

---

[88] http://www.plato-academy.gr/museum. Last access 20 November 2019.

Figure 3: Defending the park (Source: author).

The question is, how much democracy is involved in a state mechanism that constantly treats citizens as immature agents and displays a paternalistic manner of dealing with problems? Furthermore, when local communities are excluded, can a heritage resource remain alive and an asset for future genera-tions or does it become void of meaning? Our experience tells us that ordinary people spontaneously and rapidly demonstrate most of the necessary skills for collaboration, problem solving and shared responsibility. Provided that appro-priate tools for identifying and recording collective intelligence exist, there can be a lot of positive surprises.

From our experience in the perimeter of the Park, a number of relevant successful examples can be discussed, ranging from symbolic human chains to defend the Park against any kind of private interests but also activist and free Park tours for visitors and public engagement events for the wider public; the fire jumping event on St. John's 'Klidonas' name day, admittedly remains the most successful engagement scheme.

The looming threat has a name: Academy Gardens Mall

As Harvey (2013: 78) insightfully discusses, there is a palpable threat for those who create a stimulating everyday neighbourhood life, as they can easily loose it to the predatory practices of the "real estate entrepreneurs, the financiers and

Figure 4: Plato's Academy is not for sale: Open, public, free park (Source: author).

upper-class consumers bereft of any urban social imagination". And this threat of appropriation by private profit-maximizing interests is more imminent the better the common qualities a social group creates.

The most difficult battle the local actors and citizens of Plato's Academy have been taking part in over the last few years is against the plans of the omnipotent multinational BlackRock, which – through its subsidiary Artume – aims to construct a massive, 55.000 square meter mall in the area. This effort to appropriate the huge cultural heritage of the area is shamelessly highlighted by its very name, 'Academy Gardens Mall'.[89]

Despite the fact that before coming to power the previous governing political party (SYRIZA) passionately opposed the construction of the mall, the previous Environment Minister gave the green light to the project by signing the required licenses (GTP editing team 2018), reiterating the promise of development and job creation; this is an empty narrative fabricated to lure people, living in job uncertainty or socially precarious conditions.

The residents and the actors of the area know very well that the only thing they can use against the ways of the private capital and the state is agility and solidarity. The 'Open Co-ordination Committee Against the Mall' has already taken action to highlight the looming threats; There is no doubt that the construction of the Mall will have serious and non-reversible impact on the natural environment of the area. A recent economic study, concluded that the Mall will also result in the loss of 6.000 jobs in the local markets, thus dealing a fatal blow to the local economy. What is more, side to imminent issues rising as the traffic pressure for the wider area, more detriment effects as those on the social

---

[89] More info and an international petition against the mall here: http://academy gardens.org/. Last access 20 November 2019.

fabric of the area are still unaccounted for. Lastly, but most disturbingly, is the fact that a multinational company is trying to appropriate a place of universal cultural value to make private profits (Plato's Academy blog 2018).

The citizens have submitted a series of concerns and proposals to the authorities without receiving an adequate answer. What they are focussing on is a mindful development strategy based on the local and regional needs, respecting the culture, the resources and the residents of the area (Plato's Academy blog 2018). This could be the overarching goal leading the upgrade of the neighbourhood and the enhancement of the archaeological site, open and accessible as a common good; extending the 'Unification of the Archaeological Sites of Athens' project to include the area in question and the development of a 'Museum of the City of Athens' could be important milestones in the process (Garidi 2018).

Within all this, where do we stand?

Kafeneio is still open to the public at the corner of the Park. We still view our initiative as an urban experiment of social transformation. With our stance, with the sharing of our space, with the tools we have developed and in any other way we can, we are trying to support actions that lead us away from the monoculture of the dual logic 'Market or State'. There are many alternatives, there are various heterotopies. We can create temporary autonomous zones and breathe clean air. Our motto 'building human relationships' says it all: Our

Figure 5: "Building human relationships", outside of the co-op Café (Source: author).

hope is that we are doing our part in the process of commoning and in the protection of the Park as a common good.

Acknowledgements

The author wishes to thank the "family" of Kafeneio for co-creating this amazing journey and especially Katerina Troullaki and Giorgos Tsitsirigkos for their support in the translation of the text.

Bibliography

Bollier, D. & Helfrich, S. (Eds.). (2012). The wealth of the commons: A world beyond market and state. Amherst, MA: Levellers Press.

European Village. (2018a). Τρίτη 21/11, το πάρκο στην Ακαδημία Πλάτωνος ως κοινό αγαθό – Ενάντια στο Mall. Retrieved July 18, 2018, from http://www.european-village.org/eventsview.asp?id_newsdata=3466&ekdosi=eve nts&katigoria=dromena_sto_kafeneio.

European Village. (2018b). Διήμερο δραστηριοτήτων για ένα ανοιχτό-ελεύθερο-δημόσιο αρχαιολογικό πάρκο πολιτισμού. Retrieved July 17, 2018, from http://www.european-village.org/eventsview.asp?id_newsdata =195&ekdosi=events&katigoria=sinvainoun_kai_mas_aresou.

Garidi, E. (2018, February 1). Ακαδημία Πλάτωνα: Να μπλοκάρουμε τα σχέδια για Mall. Retrieved July 18, 2018, from https://dea.org.gr/ακαδημία-πλάτωνα-να-μπλοκάρουμε-τα-σχέδια-για-mall.

GTP editing team. (2018, January 11). Athens' Academy Gardens Mall gets green light. Gtp-Greek Travel Pages Headlines. Retrieved July 17, 2018, from http://news.gtp.gr/2018/01/11/athens-academy-gardens-mall-gets-green -light/.

Harvey, D. (2012). Rebel cities: From the right to the city to the urban revolution. London, United Kingdom: Verso.

Holloway, J. (2010). Crack Capitalism. London, United Kingdom: Pluto Press.

Ingraham, C. (2016, February 3). What Ivy League students are reading that you aren't. The Washington Post. Retrieved July 17, 2018, from https://www.washingtonpost.com/news/wonk/wp/2016/02/03/what-ivy-league -students-are-reading-that-you-arent/.

Mediation. (2018). Retrieved July 17, 2018, from Wikipedia: https://en .wikipedia.org/w/index.php?title=Mediation&oldid=845420140.

Metaplasi. (2018). Metaplasi. Retrieved July 17, 2018, from http://metaplasis .org.

Nonplan. (2018, June 10). Museum as Commons @ Academy of Plato (II). Retrieved October 12, 2018, from http://soma.nonplan.gr/2018/06 /museum-as-commonsacademy-of-plato-ii/.

Nonviolent Communication. (2018). Retrieved July 17, 2018, from Wikipedia: https://en.wikipedia.org/w/index.php?title=Nonviolent_Communication &oldid=848528006.

Platos' Academy blog. (2018, January 26). Κάλεσμα του Συντονιστικού για Κυριακή 28 Γενάρη. Retrieved July 18, 2018, from https://akadimia-latonos. com/2018/01/26/κάλεσμα-του-συντονιστικού-για-κυριακ/.

Temporary Autonomous Zone. (2018). Retrieved July 17, 2018, from Wikipedia: https://en.wikipedia.org/w/index.php?title=Temporary_Autonomous _Zone&oldid=849740148.

Theodorou, K. (2015). «Πρακτικές των αστικών κοινών» – Σάββατο 16 Μάη: Παρουσίαση & εργαστήριο στο Commons Fest από το Koino Athina. Retrieved July 17, 2018, from https://koinoathina.wordpress. com/2015/05/09/πρακτικές-των-αστικών-κοινών-σάββατ/.

PART 3

CHAPTER 11

The Alternative of the Commons, New Politics and Cities

Alexandros Kioupkiolis

In the years between 2011 and 2012 history appeared to be "born again" (Badiou 2012) through the Arab Spring, the15-M movement in Spain, the 'squares movement' in Greece and the global Occupy movement. Seven years later, a bleak picture dominates in Europe and across the world as a whole. The global hegemony of neoliberalism remains firmly in place, while reactionary, xenophobic, right-wing politics is on the rise. The scenes of democratic uprisings, mass mobilization, collective empowerment, glimpses of real, egalitarian democracy, and popular aspirations to progressive political change in countries such as Spain and Greece seem to have been consigned to the distant past.[90]

At the time of writing, the financial crises are no longer as acute as they were back in 2011, and a normalization of crisis has taken hold in many countries, with Spain and Greece being the most prominent examples. But the looming ecological catastrophe, the popular disaffection with elitist politics, the devastating consequences of neoliberalism in terms of social justice, equality and meaningful democracy remain our historical horizon. More than ever, it is time

---

[90] This chapter is part of a project that has received funding from the European Research Council (ERC) under the Horizon 2020 research and innovation programme (grant agreement 724692).

How to cite this book chapter:
Kioupkiolis, A. 2020. The Alternative of the Commons, New Politics and Cities. In Lekakis, S. (ed.) *Cultural Heritage in the Realm of the Commons: Conversations on the Case of Greece*. Pp. 229–252. London: Ubiquity Press. DOI: https://doi .org/10.5334/bcj.m. License: CC-BY

to act. But it is also time to take a step back, to re-think and refigure our strategies of egalitarian social change.

In tune with many activists and champions of the commons across the world, the present argument holds that contemporary theories and practices of the commons outline a horizon of historical change which is already in motion, in fits and starts. At the dawn of the new millennium, from the Bolivian Andes (the water wars in Cochabamba, 1999–2000) to the U.S. (e.g. the Creative Commons licences established in 2001) to Southern Europe (e.g. the Italian city regulations for urban participation and self-management) the commons have arisen as a socio-political, economic and cultural paradigm that provides an alternative to both neoliberal capitalism and defunct socialism, social democracy and revolutionary communism.

The commons are not only about co-producing, co-managing and sharing collective resources within a certain community. Numerous social movements, city governments, advocates and political thinkers have made the case in recent years that this is an emergent new historical paradigm, a new mode of production, a new culture, a deeply democratic and ecological politics which can offer a guide, a material foundation and a rallying point for historical change beyond capitalist hegemony and statist socialism or communism. Crucially, in the contemporary European context, a commons-based politics could counter the rise of the nationalist populist right by advancing a progressive way of dealing with social dislocation and alienation, thus restoring solidarity, social trust, collective ties and common welfare. At the same time, alternative commons harbour a radical egalitarian and emancipatory ideal, a visionary pragmatism and an emphasis on massive, bottom-up participation which hold the promise –but only the promise – of overcoming the political frailty, the hierarchical centralism around personal leaders, and the impoverished programmatic imagination of leftist populist parties and governments in Europe, from Podemos to Syriza and Mélanchon.

The following discussion will outline the new paradigm and will introduce certain political propositions on the commons as a counter-hegemonic project. It will then indicate how they lack an adequate political strategy of transition, broad-based mobilization and counter-hegemonic struggle, which could effectively further social transformation in contemporary Europe and the world, transcending the limitations of left-leaning populist parties and governments. In an attempt to start plotting such a strategy, we will draw on the 2011 cycle of democratic mobilizations in Southern Europe and the latest pro-commons politics in Spanish and, mainly, Italian cities. The aim is to explore how powerful counter-hegemonic praxis could be pursued in ways which renew Gramsci's (and Laclau's) hegemonic politics in the direction of alternative commons –horizontal self-government, equality, sustainability, plurality, openness and sharing – and can reshuffle the decks of power.

In the study of commons-oriented politics in the Italian context, we will dwell on the artistic and political community of 'l'Asilo' in Naples, which followed in the footsteps of the famous occupation of Teatro Valle in Rome, in 2011, the first of its kind in recent years which explicitly identified itself with the new commons. Among others, the two cases initiated novel, commons-based, practices of governing cultural heritage 'resources'. In effect, they have both striven to act as an alternative to both private and public modes of governance in this field, valuing, revitalizing and 'commoning' cultural heritage. They broke with the conception of cultural heritage as a 'resource' managed bureaucratically or run by private corporations for private benefit.

Both the conceptualization of the commons and, mainly, the fieldwork underpinning theory took place within the context of an ERC-funded project, 'Heteropolitics' (2017–2020);[91] This project set out to re-think contemporary democratic change from the bottom through the lenses of contemporary commons and radical political theory, from Laclau & Mouffe to Hardt & Negri, among others. The present chapter condenses some of the main themes and preliminary conclusions of this research into actual alternative politics which gestures towards an emancipatory and egalitarian direction. The research agenda fostered a close interaction between political theory and reflection, on the one hand, and engagement with praxis on the ground, through ethnographic fieldwork conducted by three post-doctoral researchers in Greece, Spain and Italy (Dr Antonio Vesco was in charge of the fieldwork in Italy).

The guiding intuition behind this composite methodology was that in order to re-think historical transformation in our times, contemporary political theory, attending to the lessons of the 20th century, should engage closely with present-day collective thought so as to learn from ongoing experiments, social creativity, innovation and actual processes of social change on the ground. If the commons are collective goods and processes which are managed autonomously by communities according to egalitarian principles of self-government for the common benefit, commons-oriented thought should likewise unfold as a common endeavour in which all participants are equal co-producers. Crucially, reflection tending to the commons should proceed as a critical interaction with and elucidation of actual initiatives and communities which build the commons of our times. The principles of collective self-direction and emancipation on a footing of equality cannot be dictated from outside and above, otherwise they would suffer the pains of self-contradiction.

From a standpoint situated in present-day Greece, an immersion in the new urban commons in the Italian context assumes particular significance. The two countries share a socio-economic and political crisis, considerable cultural heritage and a huge stock of abandoned historic buildings which are listed for preservation but are barely maintained by state authorities or private capital. The Italian case charts new paths in civic politics and the governance of cultural heritage and social infrastructure more broadly, which could inspire similar initiatives in other places, including Greece.

---

[91] See heteropolitics.net. Last access 20 November 2019.

The commons as an alternative world

The 'commons' or 'common-pool resources' (Ostrom 1990: 30, 90) or 'commons-based peer production' (Benkler & Nissenbaum 2006: 395) comprise goods and resources that are collectively used and produced. Access to them is provided on equal terms, which may range from totally open access to universal exclusion from consumption, with many possibilities in-between. The common good is collectively administered in egalitarian and participatory ways by the communities that manufacture or own it. *Sharing* is a fundamental process which lies at the heart of the commons (Walljasper 2010: xix).

There are many different classes of common goods, from natural common-pool resources (fishing grounds, irrigation canals etc.; Ostrom 1990: 30) to common productive assets, such as workers' co-operatives, and digital goods, such as open source software and Wikipedia (Benkler & Nissenbaum 2006; Dyer-Witheford 2010). Their common baseline, however, is that they involve shared resources which are managed, produced and distributed through collective participation in ways which contest the logic of both private-corporate and state-public property (Ostrom 1990: 1-30, 90; Benkler & Nissenbaum 2006: 394-396; Dyer-Witheford 2010; Hardt & Negri 2012: 6, 69-80, 95). Equally important is the fact that existing 'commons' are all threatened by the predatory, privatizing greed of corporate forces and the top-down, monopolistic authority of state powers (Walljasper 2010: xix; Caffentzis 2013; Bollier 2008).

Furthermore, it is now widely held that all commons in their diversity tend to display a tripartite structure. Most definitions render commons as an artifice which consists of three main parts: (a) *common* resources/goods, (b) institutions (i.e. *commoning* practices) and (c) the communities (called *commoners*) who are implicated in the production and reproduction of commons (Dellenbaugh et al. 2015: 13; see also Bollier & Helfrich 2015: 3).

Finally, it is currently a *topos* of critical thought on the commons that the commons are not primarily resources or goods, but practices of *commoning*, that is, of actively forging and reproducing communities of collaboration and action around different dimensions of social life and the environment. Commoners improvise and amend these rules on an ongoing basis, in ways that respond to particular socio-ecological situations and historical contexts. As a result, there is "an incredible range of commoning across time, geography, resource domains and cultural tradition" (Bollier & Helfrich 2015: 7), which defies any simple formulas and predetermined taxonomies.

But how could dispersed practices and communities around a heteroclite diversity of commons add up to a world-changing process and force? Some enthusiastic champions of the digital commons have asserted that this is already happening. Other, more politically minded thinkers, such as Hardt and Negri, and Dardot and Laval, have laid out political conceptions of the commons which could foster a global shift. In all these cases, however, the shallowness of strategic political thought is glaring.

To begin with, since the dawn of the new millennium, with the spread of new digital technologies and the Internet, a large body of thought and action has veered attention away from the 'commons of nature' to the 'immaterial' commons of culture, information and digital networks (Benkler 2006; Bollier 2008, 2016; Bauwens 2005, 2009, 2011). Technological change has given rise to new modes of production and collaboration, which enact novel patterns of association and self-governance. These new modes not only reinvent and expand the commons as a culture of co-creation and social sharing outside their traditional bounds of fisheries, forests and grazing grounds, they also represent new schemes of community and collective self-governance beyond the closely knit, stable and homogeneous communities of face-to-face interaction (Benkler 2006: 117–120; Bollier 2008: 2–4; Bauwens 2005). Spanning diverse fields, from software development to online encyclopaedias (Wikipedia) and social media platforms, the new digital environment enables the proliferation of decentralized communities. These combine individual freedom with autonomous social collaboration, holding the promise of more democratic participation, openness, freedom, diversity, creativity and co-production without the hierarchies of the state and the market (Benkler 2006: 2; Bollier 2008: 1–20, 117; Bauwens 2005).

'Digital commoners' argue, in effect, that the networked information commons immensely expand the commons model beyond its traditional, small-scale natural location in forests, land, irrigation channels and fishing grounds. Digital commons remake in their image a wild diversity of social fields, from music to business, law, education and science, refashioning them after the logic of the open, plural, creative and participatory commons (Benkler 2006: 2–3; Benkler & Nissenbaum 2006; Bollier 2008: 14–18; Bauwens 2005) and disseminating the values and the practices of the commons: sharing, free collaboration for mutual benefit, egalitarian self-organization, openness (Bauwens 2005). According to Bollier (2008: 190), this amounts to a 'Great Value Shift' which has brought about a crucial transformation in subjectivity by propagating, among other ideas and values, a deeply different conception of wealth as commons. As far back as 2005, Bauwens envisioned a new form of society, 'based on the centrality of the commons, and within a reformed state and market' (Bauwens 2005).

Prominent advocates of the digital commons, such as Bollier (2008). Benkler (2006) and Bauwens (2005, 2014) concur in a techno-legal and economic fix when they anticipate transitions in the direction of the commons. Despite allusions to 'Common-ist' movements, we are left in the dark as to how these will gather a critical mass, how they will overhaul the 'neoliberal dominance' and how they will reform the state and the market (Bauwens 2005; see also Bauwens 2014: 28). Technology, economic practices, and the law, including Creative Commons Licences, are the main entries. The guiding idea of this movement is to change society, not by fighting the system, but by designing a new model which makes the existing model obsolete (Bollier 2008: 294).

Historical transformation would be mostly incremental and immanent, arising from within actual social relations and productivity (Bollier 2008: 305–310). "Superior working models – running code and a healthy commons – will trump polemics and exhortation. Ideological activists and political professionals are likely to scoff at this scenario" (Bollier 2008: 305). Society will not be re-ordered, then, by taking political power but through a long process of technologically induced development which advances new social logics of production (Bauwens 2009).

In recent years, an awareness that the techno-economic and legal path runs up against overpowering obstacles has been significantly growing among the peer commons school (see e.g. Bauwens & Kostakis 2014). Hence, they place an increasing emphasis on the 'partner state', on social and political movements and on assembling commons counter-power by crafting parallel institutions, such as the 'Chambers of Commons'. Still, the techno-economic and legal steps are always accorded pride of place in both analysis and practice, and the political comes second (Bauwens et al. 2019). They acknowledge that this approach to social renewal "is based solely on the structural changes that take place within the political economy. An integrated strategy needs to also take particular notice on the relevant cultural and subjective changes that vary in every different context" (Bauwens et al. 2019: 55–70).

In effect, an 'integrated strategy' that takes on board political dynamics would need to deploy a full-fledged politics of *hegemony*, which precisely diffuses cultural and subjective transformations, but is also bent on organizing sociopolitical struggle and on welding together wide, transversal alliances. Work on the regulatory and institutional framework that could push forward the commons is not enough if we lack the agents and the political practices which could reconstruct state structures and economic policies in order to put in place such a framework in the face of bureaucratic resistances and elite opposition.

In the peer commons current, one can also currently discern a heightened consciousness of the fact that political power struggles would be required in order to turn the actual 'market state' into a 'partner state' that tends to common interests and is internally "commonified" (Bauwens et al. 2019: 52–53). Majoritarian social movements of a global reach and new, parallel institutions of the commons should be enlisted and bolstered in this enterprise. But how is it possible to overcome social fragmentation and widespread disaffection in order to band together such movements at a time when economic and political crises push the majority of citizens towards xenophobic and conservative politics across the world? Who could bring them around to a 'common' political perspective, construct a historic bloc for the commons and orchestrate a political transition towards a true 'partner state'? And how could this be achieved? It is this paramount political question that remains unaddressed and cries out for proper political reflection on the level of strategy, agency and organization.

Counter-hegemonic politics

Herein lies the political importance of a Gramscian argument for the commons in our times. The principle of the common could rearrange prevalent institutions and structures only if social renewal on the ground – new communities of the commons, new, open and collective technologies of production, and so on – is embedded in a larger political movement contesting hegemony: in a *historical bloc* (Hoare & Nowell Smith 1971: 137, 168, 366, 376–377). A fully-fledged hegemonic politics of revolutionary change à la Gramsci is anchored in a broad-based historical bloc which knits together a multiplicity of social resistances and political struggles; economic projects and productive activities that tend to social needs; and the making of a new collective identity, a common political program, values and critical ideas. All these elements are organized through the cohesive force of a committed political alliance.

To put together such a popular front, political actors need to weave organic bonds with large social sectors in their everyday lives, seeking popular outreach and conducting a sustained 'war of position' in civil society and the state, in a way which bridges micro – and macro-politics. Political activity dwells on the micro-level of everyday social activities and groups, engaging directly with social relations and subjectivities so that they transform into a new collective identity, culture and political orientation. At the same time, a common political platform connects the multiplicity of micro-political processes, draws up a coherent and comprehensive political plan adapted to an entire social formation, and wrestles with macro-structures and institutions of the state, the economy, culture and so on.

However, to harness a Gramscian strategy of hegemony for commons-oriented reform today, core elements of Gramsci's thought should be problematized, beginning with his centralizing *Party* and moving on to working class politics. Class inequalities have skyrocketed in our epoch of neoliberal hegemony. Global wealth is amassed world-wide in the hands of a super-rich minority. Middle classes are being increasingly impoverished in many western countries. And the global expelled population – the poor, workers, the unemployed, precarious people, dwellers of shanty towns – who live at or below subsistence level is in the billions. Nonetheless, the 'working class' does not constitute today a unified, massive category which can yield the basis for majoritiarian political identities and mobilization (see Crouch 2004; Dyer-Witherford 2015; Standing 2011). Social differentiation and fragmentation, the pervasiveness of (neo-) liberal individualist values, the decline of industrial labour in developed countries, the growth of precarious labour and the service sector are some of the factors which account for the actual failure of working people across the globe to become politically interpellated as 'working class,' to coalesce and to hit back as 'workers' in a single country or internationally. Moreover, the politics of democratic commons needs to devise new patterns of effective political organization which break with the centralized, hierarchical and homogenizing party, and are now in tune with the horizontalist, pluralist and egalitarian animus of the commons.

It is worth noting, also, that in a Gramscian strategy the state remains a central site of the struggle, but a protracted 'war of position' in civil society is the effective anchor of historical change against any state-centred politics that aspires to topple neoliberal hegemony and transform society from the top. One of the main challenges today is to work out political structures and agencies that conduct struggles and reconstruct society on all levels in an alliance that prevents top-down direction and the autonomization of parties and leaderships in the political system.

Laclau and Mouffe's relaunch of hegemonic politics in 1985 addresses key predicaments of transformative commons today: how to rally a popular will for antagonistic commons and how to catalyse an expansive convergence of social forces which will overturn the dominance of neoliberal capital and will extend equal freedom around the commons, under circumstances of social fragmentation and complexity, which do not cohere around any simple and given antagonism. Crucially, their reconstruction of hegemony is largely attuned to the spirit of alternative commons, rooted as it is in the "open, unsutured character of the social", "plurality and indeterminacy", the dispersion of power, the autonomy of social movements, the diversity of political spaces and antagonisms (Laclau & Mouffe 1985: 192, 152). They rid hegemony of Marxist determinism, the determining force of the economic base and class. Their accent on social contingency brings to the fore the always present possibility of historical change against TINA. In doing away with any historical assurances, e.g. technological innovation and networks as the trigger of social transformation, they force us to think politically and to seriously ponder how to organize political action, so as to attain the desired transformations.

Articulation, discourse, plurality and *antagonism* become the pillars of a post-Marxist idea of hegemony. *Hegemony* is primarily a process of articulation which operates in a contingent terrain and strives to piece together an organized system of relations out of disaggregated elements and differences by way of instituting nodal points (Laclau & Mouffe 1985: 134–135). Hegemony consists, then, in a particular type of political relation and activity whereby a social force moves outside itself to connect itself with other conflicts through "chains of equivalence" in order to aggregate a collective will. Social actors aspiring to hegemony go beyond their narrow identities and assume broader organizational functions in a community, building coalitions and imputing wider meanings to social practices or resistances (Laclau & Mouffe 1985: 134–135, 141).

Furthermore, beyond specific demands or negative protests, a winning hegemonic strategy installs nodal points from which a process of different, positive reconstruction of social structures can be set in motion. An effective alter-politics of social transformation thrives on the capacity of subordinated groups to positively direct and renovate a broad range of social spheres. A hegemonic strategy for the "construction of a new order" must also conjoin an understanding of existing structural limitations –on the level of the state, the economy etc. – with a utopian vision for another social order (Laclau & Mouffe 1985: 184, 189, 190).

However, Laclau and Mouffe's hegemonic politics could be reclaimed for a political strategy of alternative commons only if it were released from certain biases of their thought which clash head-on with the horizontalist, pluralist, open and autonomous logic of the commons. Laclau affirmed the vertical distribution of power within the hegemonic alliance, populist homogenization and the need for individual leadership in a counter-hegemonic (see Laclau 2000b: 303; Laclau 2005: 100). However, the distribution of power among the constituents of a radical democratic front can tend towards horizontality rather than towards vertical direction from one particular group at the helm. Unity could be pursued in ways that nurture diversity and pluralism both inside and outside itself. Decision-making and the construction of a collective will could be a participatory and collective process rather than an affair of individual representatives.

Another hegemony for the commons

Recent democratic activism, such as the 2011 square movements and the 'municipalist' politics from 2015 onwards, provide important insights which can help to re-imagine counter-hegemonic politics around a commons vision.

Unity, the formation of a collective identity, the concentration of force, and leadership make up the backbone of hegemonic politics (Hoare & Nowell Smith 1971: 152–3, 181–2, 418; Laclau 2000a: 207–212; Laclau 2000b: 301–303). In recent years, egalitarian movements have also made such hegemonic interventions in order to alter the balance of forces. The Occupy Wall Street and the Spanish 15-M movement (or 'Indignados') converged around common ends, practices and signifiers (such as 'the 99%' and 'the people'). They centralized the co-ordination of action in certain 'hubs' (such as Puerta del Sol in Madrid). They sought to reach out to broader sectors of the population affected by neoliberal governance, and they strove to initiate processes of deeper democratic transformation. They voiced aspirations to radical socio-political change (e.g. 'real democracy'), and they confronted dominant structures of power with vast collections of human bodies and networks.

These civic politics combined 'hegemony' with horizontalism. The 'square movements' of 2011 took aim at the institutionalized separation of political leaders from the people and the sovereign rule of representatives. They set out, instead, to open up the political representation and leadership to ordinary citizens. The very choice of public squares and streets to set up popular assemblies highlights the desire for publicity, transparency and free accessibility of political power to all (Nez 2013). Moreover, in order to preclude the monopolization of authority by any individual or group, the assemblies of 2011–2012 enforced binding mandates and alternation in the functions of spokespersons, moderators and special working-groups. Institutional devices such as lot, rotation, limited tenure, increased accountability and the casual alternation of participants in collective assemblies work against the consolidation of lasting divides between rulers and ruled, experts and lay people.

Moreover, *diversity* and *openness* became themselves the principle of unity in collective mobilizations such as Occupy Wall Street. *Open pluralism* has been persistently pursued through a multiplicity of norms, practices and organizational choices. The construction of *open spaces of convergence* for collective deliberation and coordination stands out among them (Nez 2013). Openness and plurality are further nurtured by a certain *political culture* which dismisses dogmatic ideologies and strict programmatic definitions in order to appeal to all citizens *in their diversity* (Harcourt 2011). This culture nurtures tolerance, inclusion, critical respect for differences, civility, generosity, a relaxed atmosphere of debate, and an affective politics of care and love among diverse people who struggle in common despite their differences (Dixon 2014).

The network form, which is widespread among democratic action today, is also crucial. Distributed networks enable a loose coordination among different groups and individuals which need not subordinate their distinct identities to an overarching collective identity or a hegemonic agent, yet they are nested in the same web of communication and act in concert. New organizations, such as the *Plataforma de Afectados por la Hipoteca* in Spain, illustrate how a more coherent organising core can tie up with a loose group of diverse agents who participate in different degrees, constituting an open 'network system' that allows for plurality and resists strong centralization and fixed hierarchies (Nunes 2014; Tormey 2015).

Finally, *pragmatism* facilitates modes of convergence and common identity which sustain diversity and openness. A heterogeneous assemblage of agents and practices can more easily cohere around practical objectives rather than around group identities and definite programs or ideologies. Collective action can thereby avoid the fragmentation of 'identity politics.' Acceptance of empirical 'messiness' and hybridity, a flexible approach oriented to concrete problem-solving, an open mind and a reluctance to take universal, dogmatic positions compose a pragmatic outlook which can depolarize strategic choices, supporting broad pluralist assemblages in the interests of the many.

Cities as incubators of counter-hegemonic change

Massive civic mobilizations, which sought to refigure counter-hegemonic politics along these lines in the years of crisis have failed, however, to reshuffle the decks of power and to rein in, at least, the neoliberal onslaught of austerity policies. Spain and Greece are just two dramatic examples. In both countries, large popular movements and insurrections from 2011 onwards strove to alter the fundamental co-ordinates of neoliberal governance and even to transform the main economic and political institutions. But governments and institutions remained largely impervious to the demands for 'real democracy', economic fairness and the protection of social rights.

In a broader perspective, any effective politics for the expansions of the commons would need to engage state and market forces in order not only to relax the daily constraints they exert on social majorities deeply embedded in their networks of power but also to defend and recover public goods for the commons, also halting environmental degradation and climate change. Strategies of exit and prefiguration, whereby civic initiatives construct their own alternative institutions of social reproduction and self-government in the interstices or 'outside' dominant systems, can only be one part of the larger equation. For the great bulk and a vast range of resources, from energy grids to internet, transport, water, health, cultural heritage and educational infrastructures or large-scale means of production, it is either infeasible or unreasonable and environmentally disastrous to create other, parallel structures. The vexing challenge remains, thus, to place major social resources and infrastructures under collective control for the common benefit of society and our planet, reclaiming them from state bureaucracies, neoliberal governments and predatory private interests. Culture and cultural heritage stand out among such resources and infrastructures, particularly in urban settings. It is no accident, therefore, that they have become hubs of commoning activity, particularly in the Italian case, as we will see below.

In Spain, from 2014 onwards, several citizens' initiatives and political platforms were put together in order to gain a grip on institutional power on the city level. They all opted for hybrid schemes of action and structure in order to both uphold grassroots mobilization and to pursue centralized co-ordination, electoral politics and institutional intervention. Civic platforms set out to propel commoning and participatory self-governance in the city by contesting municipal elections and gaining local power (see Barcelona en Comú 2016). This process introduced in effect a certain political strategy of 'municipalism' which purports to expand the logics and practices of the commons on the scale of cities and is instantiated in diverse locations across Spain, from Barcelona to Madrid, Zaragoza, Valencia.

Their objective in building a coalition to win local elections was to advance a new, participatory model of local government, a system of transparent and accountable governance that would be under citizens' control. They wanted to initiate fair, redistributive and sustainable policies starting from the grassroots. Crucially, the proximity of local government to the citizens enables collective platforms which act as mediators to take social change from the streets to state institutions. Although the autonomy of municipal authorities was curtailed in the years of the crisis in Spain, the institutions of city government remain the closest to citizens and their demands. At the same time, they maintain varying degrees of control over important common goods, from land to transport, housing, the health system, education, energy and water, which they have come under increasing pressure to privatize or further commodify or subject to austerity cuts (Observatorio Metropolitano 2014: 106–109, 135–137). The city is, therefore, a central site of the struggle around the common goods.

In Italy, civic politics around the commons has walked along different, albeit parallel, pathways, in which complex relations have been woven between grassroots movements, citizens' groups, municipal authorities and progressive jurists, such as Ugo Mattei and Francesco Gregorio Arena. The 2011 national referendum against the privatization of water was a milestone in these processes, followed by the occupation of Teatro Vale in Rome, which was explicitly informed by a commons discourse. Since then, 'bene comuni' has become a buzzword of feel-good and 'alternative' politics in Italy (Kioupkiolis 2018). Discourse and political practice around the commons are pervasive in present-day Italy, and they are perceived by several political actors as a constructive response to the economic, social and political crisis. Commons-related activity has often focussed around specific issues, such as water and culture, and is anchored at the level of the municipality.

The role of law and jurists is particularly prominent in commoning processes in the Italian context

The quasi 'empty signifier' of bene comuni refers to different realities in the country, but it signals a shared commitment to denounce the concentration of power, to attend to local inequalities, and to pursue other ways of possessing and producing, which would transcend the market order imposed by the neoliberal model (Kioupkiolis 2018). Through the common goods, a dialogue has opened up with the militant academy. Law has furnished a potent tool for articulating an incisive criticism of the existing structures. Movement practices and legal mediation have become two fundamental pivots for critical reflection on the legitimacy and the quality of public management and private property in the light of the most urgent social needs and contradictions, reviving the profound meaning of substantial equality and introducing a grammar of inclusion. This is based on the relational and shared dimension of the use of resources that should be conducted in ecological and qualitatively responsible ways, governed by the principle of equal access.

Lawyers and municipalities catalysed the expansion of the commons in the Italian context. Municipal authorities have introduced pro-commons regulations on the city level, drawing on provisions of the Italian constitution. In effect, in Italy there are currently three main approaches to the use of law for the purposes of urban commons: the 'Labsus model', the approach worked out by Ugo Mattei and his associates, and 'civic use' as articulated in Naples by social movements and jurists.

The 'Labsus model' is based on the Italian constitution and, crucially, on the principle of 'subsidiarity' which calls for citizen participation in the administration and collective works. This was introduced into the Italian constitution in 2001 (A.118), and stipulates that all state institutions, on all levels, must favour the autonomous initiatives of citizens, individuals or associations, in order to foster the general interest on the basis of subsidiarity. Citizens, as allies of the administration, in horizontal relations, should address together the various crises that face them – economic, climatic, of migration etc. Jurists directly drew on the constitution in producing a regulatory framework that bypasses national legislation by introducing municipal legislation on the basis of the constitution. The Labsus group was established in 2005 by professors of administrative law to further this project (Heteropolitics 2018a).

The ambiguous but dynamic process of pro-commons regulations was inaugurated in Bologna in 2014 and has attracted thousands of citizens who have submitted hundreds of projects for the collective management of urban goods and infrastructure. It was largely a top-down institutional initiative, advanced by lawyers (mainly the Labsus group) and taken up by left-leaning mayors who sought to fill in the gap left by the demise left wing party politics in Italy. However, it has subsequently been embraced by more than 150 cities in the country, including Turin and Parma. Through the regulations, the local administration intends to transform itself into a facilitator (enabler) rather than a supplier of goods and services. Under this scheme, the administration has the task of helping those who discern in a building, a run-down area, or a flowerbed, the potential for a collective project of care and recovery of the asset, simplifying and streamlining the procedures required in order to obtain the necessary authorizations to start the reuse (Heteropolitics 2018a).

The cornerstone of the Bologna regulatory framework is Article 5: the pacts of collaboration, i.e. the contracts made between groups of citizens and the municipality in order to serve bene comuni. The most diverse combinations of actors enter into these pacts, from scouts to citizens' associations to migrant groups (Heteropolitics 2018a). The political vision driving the Bologna regulations is a society of care, trust and sharing, which fills in the lack of ideas about the future. This lacuna has come about due to the demise of the grand ideologies of the past. The void generates fear, but this can be remedied through trust and sharing. The communities of the commons could become a new collective subject, appealing to 'normal people.'

Jurists have also contributed to the 'commoning' processes in various other ways. These include the so-called 'Commissione sui Beni Comuni' chaired by the jurist Stefano Rodotà, which initiated a process that culminated in the 2011 water referendum. In 2007, the committee was commissioned by the Ministry of Justice to draw up a law to amend the rules of the Italian civil code on public goods. The proposal presented by the Commissione at the end of their activity enriched the taxonomy of public and private goods with a new category; common goods. The common goods are described as resources with widespread ownership, which may belong to public bodies or private subjects. Therefore, beyond the proprietary title, common goods possess the concrete possibility of collective access, within the limits and according to the procedures established by law, and therefore their management must serve this possibility (Kioupkiolis 2018).

In 2011, members of the Rodotà Commission were among those that framed the referendum questions that were put to vote on the 12th and the 13th June that year. The great success of the consultation (in which the 'yes' prevailed by 57% of those entitled to vote) popularized and advanced the concept of common goods. This became the key signifier of many different disputes and transformed it into a political category, freeing it from the confines of the legal realm in which it originated. Movements for the defence of land against speculative use and for the preservation of historical and cultural heritage, trade unions and housing movements have included the common goods among their slogans, not only because it is politically fashionable to do so, but above all because the term highlighted the concentration of power and processes of exclusion. Moreover, through the common goods, a dialogue opened up with the militant academy, and law was considered a necessary tool for a rigorous critique of the existing structures. Movement practices and legal mediation became two fundamental components for questioning a crystallized proprietary equilibrium (Kioupkiolis 2018).

According to Ugo Mattei (Kioupkiolis 2018), common goods have thus had the strength of the empty signifier. They have offered, thanks to their flexible content, a negative unity to different struggles which have become equivalent in a post-ideological scheme, by way of participating in 'struggles' for the defence of the commons. Moreover, the commons have also implied the possibility of taking part in the management of different assets, or even the possibility of inventing new institutions or rethinking old mechanisms. So, in Naples, the administration of the public water company was set to include also users in the governance of the company, while the Teatro Valle in Rome planned to organize its management through a private law entity. However, the foundation charter was modified in order to increase shared decision-making, to spread power and to advance participation in the management of the foundation's assets (Kioupkiolis 2018).

The commons as an alternative model of co-governing and co-creating cultural goods and the example of L'Asilo in Naples

This civic and institutionally driven path to the expansion of the commons in Italy is risky and tortuous, as it may in effect devolve public financial and administrative responsibilities to citizens, substituting cheap and voluntary labour for public funding and administration. On the other hand, it outlines another model of preserving, reusing and revitalizing cultural heritage. Society is no longer confined to the role of the consumer of privately managed goods or the passive recipient of public management. Democratic communities re-appropriate cultural spaces and goods as active co-administrators and co-creators – from theatres and museums to abandoned historic buildings that host artistic activities – as active co-administrators and co-creators. They craft different figures of communal living and bonding, which are freer, more equal, participatory, self-governing, creative, open, diverse, solidary and caring. They make cultural goods and infrastructure a site of renewed collective life, participatory governance, cultural revitalization, new creation, and socio-political experimentation. Hence, they open up cultural goods and heritage to the common, turning them into common goods and an activity of a heterogeneous, inclusive community that involves ordinary people. The case of L'Asilo Filangieri will serve to illustrate these transformations.

As a key hub of urban commoning activity in Italy, Naples, has framed its own institutional scheme in favour of the commons. The municipality has promoted civic participation in the management of urban infrastructure, such as water, and the use ('uso civico') of public buildings by associations of artists; also in the emblematic ex-Asilo Filangieri, among others. This development was largely the outcome of a synergy between independent social movements and the singular populist persona of the mayor, Luigi de Magistris. The case of L'Asilo elucidates the different paths taken in Italy by social movements which seek to gain leverage on institutions in order to advance the commons and civic empowerment. In contrast to Spain, where social movements, activists and citizens came together in electoral municipal platforms with a view to becoming city administrators, in Italy they strive to make an impact on the formal political system through an intelligent, diverse and inventive use of the law. This charts a different avenue to gaining leverage on political institutions, which is worth considering and debating. Perhaps, it allows egalitarian social movements to uphold a higher degree of political independence and creative autonomy.

'L'Asilo', as it is called by participants, pursues further the process of commoning artistic activity, community and politics which was initiated by Teatro Valle in Rome in 2011, a landmark in the recent history of the commons in Italy. In a sense, l'Asilo takes up where Teatro Valle left off. L'Asilo was a convent located in the historic centre of Naples and established in the 16th century. In 2008 it was restored in order to host a Universal Cultural Forum. This event was organized by a private association which was funded with public money. L'Asilo started with a symbolic occupation staged by a group of artists and cultural workers ('Balena') in March 2012, who protested against the public sponsorship of such events at time when artistic work was under-funded and neglected. Gradually, the assembly brought together 300-400 people who decided to stay in the building (Heteropolitics 2018b).

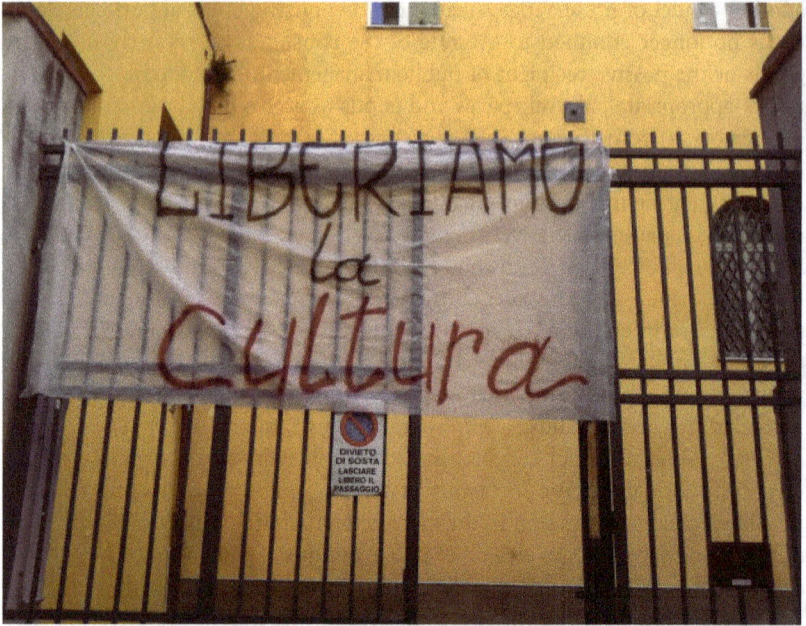

Figure 1: L'Asilo Filangieri: The first day of occupation (Source: Riccardo Siano).

This movement was part of a broader pro-commons political mobilization in Italy in 2011, which included the national campaign for the defence of water as a common good, the occupation of Teatro Valle in Rome and Macao in Milan. There was then a contagion of movements for the commons. In Naples, the city administration was already sponsoring the commons, having introduced the notion of culture as a common good in the City Statute (Heteropolitics 2018b).

The commons in 'L'Asilo' embodies a civic and cultural praxis which pivots around a) collaborative artistic creation and experimentation; b) egalitarian democratic self-management; c) self-legislation through the production of an internal regulation that was finally ratified by the municipality after a long struggle; d) the making of a different community and politics informed by openness, plurality, horizontality, non-violence and non-domination, consensus, collaboration, and experimentation; e) the negotiation of a different relationship with the municipality characterized by both collaboration, struggle, conditional municipal support and autonomous self-organization of the community in l'Asilo (see Heteropolitics 2018b).

More specifically, l'Asilo illustrates the 'uso civico' approach to the commoning processes of Italian cities, the relations of pro-commons social movements with municipalities and the attitude of city administrations towards the commons and civic groups. The lawyers who joined after the beginning of the occupation suggested a legal route, which would combine the legal provision of civic use, concerning originally natural resources and 'traditional' commons, with the Article 43 of the Constitution, which allowed for the takeover of a public service by the community of its workers in certain conditions. Finally, in December 2015, the municipality issued a new administrative act, co-authored by l' Asilo and based on a self-regulation statute wholly drawn up by l'Asilo. L'Asilo has subsequently extended these explorations and their collaborative work with the de Magistris administration to other seven spaces, totalling about 40.000 square meters of occupied real estate (Heteropolitics 2018b).

Through this regulation, the main idea of the community of l'Asilo was to 'hack' the law. They made a declaration of *urban and collective* civic use. The legal instrument worked out by l'Asilo can now also be used by others and it has been deployed for the recognition of eight more spaces, which are now drawing up their declarations of use. The idea of the recognition of a 'collective use' that has already started is powerful, and it is different from the 'constitution' of such a use only after the municipality decides. L'Asilo is thus an attempt to connect social movements with a juridical path. It involves an endeavour to hack the legal system in order to configure new institutions, using the law to change the system 'from within.' L'Asilo can offer an example, a precedent in legal terms, which introduces the idea of self-organization in new juridical institutions (Heteropolitics 2018b).

What is more, l'Asilo seeks to combine the 'civic use' of the commons with public property and support. It relies on public funding from the municipality for some of its functions (for the maintenance of the building and basic operational expenses, such as electricity; Micciarelli 2018). L'Asilo is not and does not desire to become, 'self-sustainable' on the market, in financial terms. This contrasts to some degree with other models of urban commons in Italy, whereby collectives and associations collaborate with municipalities and sign 'pacts' with the city administration on the condition that they become self-sustainable financially. The political predicament here is whether cultural activities should operate according to the logic of the private market or whether they should be sponsored by public funds and the redistribution of wealth. In a commons-based society, a part of the wealth produced in the narrower economic sphere of material production could, or should, be redistributed to other activities, from education to health and culture, which are likewise productive or creative in a broader sense. Such activities contribute to the 'economic basis' by sustaining social reproduction but also by fostering the growth of knowledge, creativity, culture and ideas, which again feed into material production for social needs in a narrower sense.

Regarding the alternative politics of the commons and the alternative model of governing cultural heritage which are performed in l'Asilo, these are focused on the public assembly which makes the key decisions in the space. In l'Asilo, there is no collective, only a public assembly and different worktables which were established as the self-governance system of a heterogeneous community. Different people are involved in l'Asilo, both in terms of their profession (artisans, actors, cultural workers, researchers, unemployed and students) and in terms of political identity (from anarchists to greens, communists to social democrats and even non-political people). All of them work together on the understanding that they are not driven by a monolithic ideology and they do not vie for internal hegemony, but they resist the dominant legal in order to invent a new institution (Heteropolitics 2018b). To develop this common process of collaboration, they mobilize the law (the regulation), humour, and psychology. It is the commoning (activity in common) that forges the bond. Thereby, a diverse and open community comes into being (Heteropolitics 2018b).

L'Asilo represents an attempt to invent new institutions for the communal self-management of public infrastructure and cultural heritage, through which people in a building can regulate in concert the ways in which they can enter public spaces, use means of production, decide and co-decide as a deliberating subject. This practice contrasts with the hegemonic political model, in which only one or few subjects decide. To realize this other practice, they also draw on a certain interpretation of the Italian Constitution and a theoretical idea of fundamental rights (including the radical right of the freedom to create new democratic institutions). They propose a practice of direct administration in which people perform public functions, coordinating themselves with the public administration, where necessary, in order to demand services, rights and duties that they cannot always provide themselves. Starting from the management of buildings and cultural heritage, this model could extend to public services and beyond. Three core elements make up this political ideal: 1) the collective use of the means of production; 2) direct administration through an assembly which is open to everyone, but follows certain rules and excludes racism, fascism and gender violence; 3) the right to different uses spread among different experiments (Heteropolitics 2018b).

More broadly, l'Asilo combines long-term political reflection with an everyday attention to social relations within itself. The community does not always engage in actual politics. L'Asilo is, rather, an ongoing and fluid experimentation, by an ever-shifting community that is not animated by a precise vision for the future but undertakes an experimentation about which it is very conscious. Hence, l'Asilo is now developing a broad reflection on the assembly itself and its functions of information-sharing and decision-making. A principal focus of the assembly is its opening to newcomers. They seek, thus, to be conscious and clear about the workings of the assembly through systematic internal reflection and external projection (Heteropolitics 2018b).

In short, l'Asilo is a gate for all, and a galvanizing place, bringing together people from all around the world. Every process comes from people who have different points of view. To work for the common good, they need and they try to be open-minded and to trust each other. Hence, l'Asilo is not a place to reach a final answer but a means of dreaming about a different way of living in the future. A core political idea of l'Asilo lies in practicing different relations. Participants do not want to use more power over others and to compete. Rather, they want to share their different knowledge, without seeking any advantage

Figure 2: L'Asilo Filangieri (Source: Sabrina Merolla).

from the exchange. They offer help to others for free. This knowledge exchange occurs not only between two individuals, but the community as a whole. A person may conceive the project of an installation, which s/he shares with others in order to produce a common project. The will to share and do things in common referred to as 'interdependence'. For participants in l'Asilo, the future lies in this kind of community, in which one's freedom is more open to the freedom of others. Moreover, people in l'Asilo try out ideas in practice and they use them when they work. But everything is always changing in an unexpected way, as a never-ending river, and a process, not an institution. The whole point of l'Asilo is 'to let a seed become a tree' (Heteropolitics 2018b).

The political creation of the commons

In a time of fascist deviations, imperial neoliberalism and apparent impasse, the common(s) have gained salience as the nodal point of an emergent political imaginary and a growing constellation of forces. The commons uphold and renew what is best in the egalitarian traditions of modernity, from communism to socialism and anarchism: social self-government, collective property, equal freedom, solidarity, inclusion, open creativity, care for the environment. At the same time, they can resonate beyond the historical left and they are free of the darkest pages in the modern history of radical politics.

Since the turn of the century, multiple forms of democratic agency and mobilization have also sketched the rudiments of another counter-hegemonic strategy, which can assemble forces, attain cohesion, exercise leadership and make a universal address without succumbing to the logics of fusion, top-down direction and 'realist' power games. Grounded in prefiguration and in grassroots control, counter-hegemonic politics could guide the whole process of transformation from below and could effectively expand the political logic of the commons: horizontal participation, sharing, diversity, openness, sustainability and care. Such strategies of 'another politics' mix horizontalism and verticalism with a clear emphasis on the former, combining heterogeneous spatialities and temporalities. They are anchored in the here and now; this world, its urgent needs and its ordinary people. Yet they are also oriented towards new worlds of freedom, plurality, openness and equality, which pertain to the long term and require arduous processes of reflection, struggle and invention.

In contrast to the central stage of national politics, cities are a privileged site in which these alternative strategies for the commons could take hold, unfold, engage with dominant institutions and reshuffle the balance of power. On account of their proximity, municipal institutions are more easily accessible to direct civic influence and participation. At the scale of the city and urban neighbourhoods, ordinary citizens can also exert effective control over their representatives, if they craft proper forms of political organization through public assemblies and digital or other networks, enforcing transparency and accountability. Recent experience from the new 'municipalist politics' suggests the need to sustain new schemes of 'dual power' or 'disjunctive conjunction.' To build autonomous bases of collective power that will gain leverage on ruling institutions and alter hegemonic formations in politics, economy and society, people should construct alternative institutions of the commons, wherever this is meaningful, they should self-organize at the grassroots and multiply civic initiatives of social reconstruction and empowerment over existing social structures. But without losing their primary focus on autonomous self-activity, participants in these processes should also take part in, or forge ties with political platforms which can exert influence on institutions of government or even strive to directly control them in order to open them up to people's power, to democratize the management of public goods and to divert resources to the commons.

The cities remain an apposite site in which extensive direct participation of lay citizens in political decision-making can take place, and institutions of government can become directly accountable to the people. At the same time, and despite the growing fiscal and political constraints inflicted on them by central governments, international institutions and global markets, cities are hubs of economic, social, cultural and political activity. And their governments maintain a degree of control over urban resources, infrastructures and flows of capital. City-based politics can scale up to address national and international structures of power by federating and networking municipalities and movements to put strong pressure on higher scales, while maintaining a solid anchorage in extensive participation and political direction at the bottom in each locality.

This is not simply an ideal projection. It is already occurring at an incipient stage, both in Europe and across the world. City-based politics along these lines promises to foster a progressive egalitarian populism for the common good(s) where traditional and new leftist parties have failed. Fundamental democratic change is, of course, premised on the active desire and engagement of large bodies of citizens. But in the presence of such a will and mobilization, city politics re-organized along the lines of disjunctive conjunctions between people and their representatives promises to aggregate, to channel and to amplify the power of the many against the entrenched rule of the few.

This alternative city politics can take place and flourish in a multiplicity of social spaces, practices and relations, combining distinctive activity and creativity with broader political processes and experiment. The case of l'Asilo in Naples illustrates these innovative potentials and the dynamic of the commons in the field of art, culture and cultural heritage. L'Asilo mixes art, culture and politics in ways which are open, pragmatic, critical, free, democratic, creative, experimental and caring. The commons in l'Asilo thus break with the logics of top-down, bureaucratic government, profit-seeking capitalist entrepreneurship and cultural elitist administration. In their words: "The Ex Asilo Filangieri, former seat of the Forum of Cultures, is since 2 March 2012 a public space dedicated to artistic and cultural production and flourishing. This space is self-governed by a heterogeneous, mutable, solidary and open community, through practices of shared and participatory management, which are akin to civic use. In l'Asilo, the organization of space and the planning of activities take place in a public and horizontal way, through the assembly and roundtables which promote encounters, sharing and experimentation".[92]

Those who inhabit l'Asilo recognize themselves:

- in the repudiation of every form of fascism, racism, homophobia and sexism through active policies of inclusion and the affirmation of singularities;
- in the liberation of artistic expression and culture from the logic of profit and the market, as a manifestation of creativity, freedom and human personality, and as a fundamental contribution to the qualitative growth of society;
- in interdisciplinarity and the sharing of arts, sciences and knowledge, with a view to liberating labour by fostering a vision of cooperative and non-competitive human relationships that follows the principle 'from each according to their own possibilities and capabilities, to each according to their needs and desires';

---

[92] Self-presentation of l'Asilo, available at https://www.facebook.com/lasilo/. Last access 21 July 2018; translated from Italian into English by Maria Deligiannidou.

- in the independence of cultural and artistic organization from interferences external to the practice of self-government;
- in interdependence, understood as the dependence of the community on the collaborative capacity of the individuals who recognize themselves in it;
- in the pursuit of consensus in decision-making, in order to build a common, 'co-divided' process of decision-making process through an inclusive and non-authoritarian method.

Bibliography

Badiou, A. (2012). *The rebirth of history: Times of riots and uprisings.* London, United Kingdom: Verso.

Barcelona En Comú. (2016). *How to win back the city En Comú: Guide to building a citizen municipal platform.* Retrieved May 3, 2017, from https://barcelon aencomu.cat/sites/default/files/win-the-city-guide.pdf.

Bauwens, M. (2005). The political economy of peer production. *CTheory, Issue 1000 Days of Theory.* Retrieved March 20, 2017, from http://www.ctheory .net/printer.aspx?id=499.

Bauwens, M. (2009). *Marx, cognitive capitalism and the transition to the commons.* Retrieved March 20, 2017, from http://dev.autonomedia.org /node/13285.

Bauwens, M. (2011). *Should we worry about capitalist commons?* Retrieved March 20, 2017, from https://blog.p2pfoundation.net/should-we-worry -about-capitalist-commons/2011/03/23.

Bauwens, M. & Kostakis, V. (2014). From the communism of capital to capital for the commons: Towards an open co-operativism. *tripleC, 12*(1), 356–361. DOI: https://doi.org/10.31269/triplec.v12i1.561.

Bauwens, M., Kostakis, V. & Pazaitis, A. (2019). *Peer to Peer: The commons manifesto.* London: Westminster University Press.

Benkler, Y. & Nissenbaum, H. (2006). Commons-based peer production and virtue. *The Journal of Political Philosophy, 14*(4), 394–419.

Bollier, D. (2008). *Viral spiral: How the commoners built a digital republic of their own.* New York, NY: New Press.

Benkler, Y. (2006). *The wealth of networks: How social production transforms markets and freedom.* New Haven, CT: Yale University Press.

Caffentzis, G. (2013). *In letters of blood and fire: Work, machines, and the crisis of capitalism.* Oakland CA: PM Press.

Crouch, C. (2004). *Post-Democracy.* Cambridge, United Kingdom: Polity.

Dellenbaugh, M., Kip, M., Bieniok, M., Müller, A. K & Schwegmann, M. (Eds.). (2015). *Urban commons: Moving beyond state and market.* Basel, Switzerland: Birkäuser Verlag GmbH.

Dixon, C. (2014). *Another politics: Talking across today's transformative movements.* Oakland, CA: University of California Press.

Dyer-Witheford, N. (2010). The circulation of the common. Retrieved August 20, 2015, from http://www.globalproject.info/it/in_movimento/nick-dyer -witheford-the-circulation-of-the-common/4797.

Dyer-Witheford, N. (2015). *Cyber-proletariat: Global labour in the digital vortex.* London, United Kingdom: Pluto Press.

Harcourt, B. E. (2011, October 13). Occupy Wall Street's 'political disobedience'. *The New York Times.* Retrieved June 20, 2012, from https://opinionator.blogs .nytimes.com/2011/10/13/occupy-wall-streets-political-disobedience/.

Hardt, M. & Negri, A. (2012). *Declaration.* Argo-Navis Author Services.

Heteropolitics. (2018a). *Report on the fieldwork in Bologna, Italy, as conducted by the PI: Alter-politics and commons in Bologna, 4–10 June 2018.* Retrieved June 21, 2019, from http://heteropolitics.net/index.php/ethnographic-mat erial/.

Heteropolitics. (2018b). *'To let a seed become a tree': Urban commons in Naples: Short report on the field visit by A. Kioupkiolis and interviews 30 November– 5 December 2018, with A. Vesco.* Retrieved June 21, 2019, from http://hetero politics.net/wp-content/uploads/2019/01/Short-report-on-commons-in -Naples.pdf.

Hoare, Q. & Nowell Smith, G. (Eds.). (1971). *Selections from the Prison Note-books of Antonio Gramsci.* London, United Kingdom: Lawrence and Wishart.

Kioupkiolis, A. (2018, July 17). Audio from the 2nd day of the Torino work-shop on law, the commons and politics in Italy, with Ugo Mattei, Ales-sandra Quarta and Rocco Albanese. Retrieved June 21, 2019, from http:// heteropolitics.net/index.php/2018/07/17/audio-from-the-2nd-day-of-the -torino-workshop-on-law-the-commons-and-politics-in-italy-with-ugo -mattei-alessandra-quarta-and-rocco-albanese/.

Laclau, E. (2000a). Structure, history and the political. In J. Butler, E. Laclau & S. Žižek (Eds.), *Contingency, hegemony, universality: Contemporary dia-logues on the Left* (pp. 182–212). London, United Kingdom: Verso.

Laclau, E. (2000b). Constructing universality. In J. Butler, E. Laclau & S. Žižek (Eds.), *Contingency, hegemony, universality: Contemporary dialogues on the Left* (pp. 281–307). London, United Kingdom: Verso.

Laclau, E. (2005). *On populist reason.* London, United Kingdom: Verso.

Laclau, E. & Mouffe, C. (1985). *Hegemony and socialist strategy: Towards a radi-cal democratic politics.* London, United Kingdom: Verso.

Nez, H. (2013). Among militants and deliberative laboratories: The Indig-nados. In B. Tejerina & I. Perugorria (Eds.), *From social to political: New forms of mobilization and democratization. Conference Proceedings.* 9–10 February 2012 (pp. 123–139). Retrieved November 20, 2019, from https://addi.ehu.es/bitstream/handle/10810/15294/UWLGSO5952.pdf? sequence=1&isAllowed=y.

Nunes, R. (2014). *Organisation of the organisationless: Collective action after networks.* Berlin, Germany: Post-Media Lab/Mute Books.

Observatorio Metropolitano. (2014). *La apuesta municipalista: La democracia empieza por lo cercano*. Madrid, Spain: Traficantes de Sueños.

Ostrom, E. (1990). *Governing the commons: The evolution of institutions for collective action*. Cambridge, United Kingdom: Cambridge University Press.

Standing, G. (2011). *The precariat: The new dangerous class*. London, United Kingdom: Bloomsbury Academic.

Tormey, S. (2015). *The end of representative politics*. Cambridge, United Kingdom: Polity Press.

Walljasper, J. (2010). *All that we share: A field guide to the commons*. New York, NY: The New Press.

CHAPTER 12

Making Politics Meaningful: The Pitfalls of the 'Commons' and the Importance of Anthropological Analysis

Dimitris Markopoulos

The political significance of the commons

In the past few years a lively discussion regarding the so called 'commons' has taken place within certain political circles and movements in Greece but also around the globe. Firstly – and for reasons of political consistency – we must admit that the subject of enquiry introduced here does not entail a new theoretical discovery or a new field of social activism. The so called 'commons' is a subject related to common goods and the institutions via which they are utilized and distributed within societies. In fact, it concerns the social relationships which are inherited, created, called into question, transformed, or even cease to exist depending on the moment of human history.

It is therefore probably wise to avoid the ostentatious use of the term 'commons' – seemingly as a neologism – as it is deceptive and runs the risk of becoming worthlessly sensationalist and inane. In this sense, a conversation dealing with the 'commons' becomes meaningful and interesting only if it revives the historical issue of social transformation of the public agenda, as it has been historically and politically set by the social movements of the last

---

How to cite this book chapter:
Markopoulos, D. 2020. Making Politics Meaningful: The Pitfalls of the 'Commons' and the Importance of Anthropological Analysis. In Lekakis, S. (ed.) *Cultural Heritage in the Realm of the Commons: Conversations on the Case of Greece.* Pp. 253–258. London: Ubiquity Press. DOI: https://doi.org/10.5334/bcj.n. License: CC-BY

centuries. This is exactly the political significance of the 'commons': the effort of people to reclaim their agency and self-regulate their lives as well as the public –'common'– space, by going against the existing heteronomous social structures.

Naturally, the matter of correlating the self-regulation of the commons with the existing political conditions arises at once. Hence, we must engage with the more general subject of politics and the meaning we assign to it. Everything included in the term 'common goods' –such as the use of natural and cultural resources, technology, law, the concept of property, and even the binary of public / private itself– is associated with our beliefs regarding the concept of the citizen as well as with our daily social activity. As a result, the elaboration of new theories concerning the 'commons' demands (and necessitates) the re-examination of the present societies' political context and of their potential to be radically transformed. Before proceeding to some comments on the subject (which will be unfortunately brief due to the size of the present enquiry), we will note some general political observations, which might prove useful in the current era of unprecedented general flux dominating both words and actions.

An anthropological overview of the crisis

It should be very clear to all who think about politics that politics is not defined as the professional occupation of certain executives, specialists, or experts on public matters. Nor is it limited, obviously, to representation and to the passive handover of power from the many to the few or the handling of current affairs through oligarchical institutions, such as, to name an example, political parties. On the contrary, it should always be emphasized that politics is precisely the disruption of such passivity. Politics is defined as the active and constant engagement with the commons and the direct participation in making and implementing decisions concerning public life. Such participation should occur in every domain of life: from our neighbourhood and workplace to a broader co-operative organization on a local or nationwide scale. Naturally this kind of organization cannot be realized within the existing institutional framework which maintains passive representation, but only within new democratic institutions which will promote agency and equality.

Yet what is the current situation in modern western societies? On the one hand we are experiencing a deep crisis, not merely financial but in essence socio-political and moral. This fact is now a generally accepted truth. On the other hand, however, we are in the middle of an unprecedented anthropological annihilation of the western societies (a phenomenon that has been gradually developing in the past few decades), which constitutes both a cause and at the same time a symptom of the present crisis. What we are referring to here is the especially problematic social organization of people, i.e. the general narcissism and common conformism that certain sociologists –such as

Christopher Lash, Richard Sennett and Zygmunt Bauman– have discussed and which perpetuates the phenomenon of political apathy. To be more specific, contemporary societies are in a state of complete disorientation, and incapable of finding a way out of their standstill: crisis of representation, rise of social inequalities, delegitimisation of authority, loss of meaning (Castoriadis 2010).

Under such conditions, the attempts that we can observe to shift towards even more oligarchic societies, which on certain occasions resemble the practices of the mafia (the example of Greece is in this case characteristic), is not a symptomatic or impermanent development. Nor is it simply the consequence of such and such a ruling political party's momentary choices. It is, nevertheless, fuelled by the decrease of political resistance and the lack of social sensitivity that characterises a fundamental part of the population.

The expression 'lack of social sensitivity' demands, of course, further clarification. At this point we should explore the real effect of the neoliberal policies adopted in recent years. A series of 'innovations' (e.g. those promoted by political personnel) such as technocratic governments, full incorporation of all kinds of 'specialists' into public affairs, an authoritarian manner of governing that circumvents the primary principles of the parliamentary system itself etc. seem to clearly ensure the remission of political pathologies that greatly defined past governments. The aforementioned shift towards oligarchic societies does not necessarily mean, however, that we are heading towards a radical institutional transformation, i.e. towards unparliamentary regimes or fascistic policies. This is the reason why the adoption of slogans referring to 'dictatorship', 'totalitarianism' or 'state of exemption' indicate a great degree of naivety, since in this way every political criterion and categorization is undermined for the sake of a rambling 'hyper-revolutionary' rhetoric. Besides, with a government of left origins, such as that of SYRIZA, it has become apparent that there can be a 'smoother' or social-democratic (and in no way fascistic or reactionary) way to apply authoritarian austerity policies.

But presently what seems to be the crucial issue is the possibility of people reconsidering the significance of each political system in relation to their own lives. In fact, our general perception concerning the commons and social solidarity is called into question. Thus, when we grow accustomed to every transgression and depreciation of a statute, we are inevitably eased into a collective nihilism that rejects more or less any collective action or common project and encourages opportunism, according to the logic of 'every man for himself'. The process of losing any sense of social sensitivity is thereby entrenched. The new political scenery fosters the existing (and ever emerging) general politicisation of the population. The previous attitude of indifference for the commons is gradually replaced by the logic of technocratising politics, i.e. limiting ourselves to finding the best person (whether trustworthy or socially 'prestigious') to save us from the political and financial predicaments with which we are faced. In other words, whereas the nouveau riche and the consumerist middle class of the past used to depend upon antagonism in order to claim the best positions in the system (whether through bribery or through personal relationships and political patronage), nowadays this antagonism tends to develop into social cannibalism in order to endure and stay unaffected by the crisis.

So, as the political problem we are facing is serious, we must face it with all our seriousness, as the response to the modern authoritarian political transformation must not be a mere defensive stance. A cry to defend the public interests against privatizations or the relinquishing of rights is destined to become fruitless rhetoric as long as it does not encourage an opposition to the technocritisation of the commons as described above. Consequently, any discussion regarding the commons should transcend the binary opposition of public/private, at least as a point of reference or as the horizon of our political direction. This is not because we do not favour the public in many aspects of social life, but because referring to it can be a very treacherous, political pitfall if the meaning of the term is not radically reinvented in the minds of the people.

We are confronted with similar problems when approaching the issues from the angle of self-organization and acting socially through horizontal structures. They are, of course, largely positive and politically tenable, both as practices and values, but the peril of applying them to a clearly instrumental framework is apparent. The adoption of horizontal structures and institutions of direct democracy should always develop together with a deep questioning of the existing social conditions. Herein lies the significance of anthropological analysis that we need to practice if we wish, naturally, to move towards a revolutionary direction, towards a truly different society that has progressed beyond capitalism. The goal, therefore, is not to intervene in the system 'morphologically', through methods of self-organization, but to criticize not only the hierarchical structures, but also the individual constituents of the institutions and of human activity in general. Let us consider briefly how revolutionary instances such as the direct democratic operation of the trade unions can be when they fight for better though uneven wages and better though lopsided (depending on the professional group) working conditions. Or how positive for the project of emancipation the self-organization of the modern capitalist technique and science is. We will proceed to present some characteristic examples which reveal the depth of the problem.

Modern technology and overcoming the limits

In order to render our analysis of the 'instrumentalism' of the commons comprehensible, let us examine an issue which is often presented as crucial: the use of technology and more specifically of the internet. No matter how long we discuss the legal context and property on the one hand or the distribution of knowledge and the democratic potential of the internet on the other, the respective analyses will always remain incomplete as long as we do not address the issues of the structure and content of the medium itself. Unfortunately, analyses often focus on the subject of a commodity's property, in this case the commodities of technology, without referring to the public's actual stance towards the medium.

Renowned sociologist Richard Sennett (1977), referring to radio and television, insightfully comments that mass media has greatly increased people's knowledge about social activities but significantly diminished their ability to turn this knowledge into political action. This valid argument is equally true regarding the case of the internet, as also in this case visualization, the playful nature, and the temptation to infinitely collect information eventually affect the technology user in a stupefying way. This seems to be the main effect on the average human. Let us consider this simple example: How much time would we gain to engage with the commons if we did not on a daily basis aimlessly waste so much useless time online or how many of our thoughts would be converted into political actions if we were not so numbed by our immoderate online commenting and narcissistic verbosity. Consequently, even if we are working using a 'free software' or if we are sharing the whole world's knowledge and data equally, the reality at the end remains ruthless: *information does not amount to freedom and knowledge is a necessary but certainly not sufficient prerequisite for the development of critique and for the emancipation of people*, since the qualitative element of the tyranny of the useless and the trivial surmounts the quantitative element of boundless information and directs people towards an abyss of utter inertia.

Similar problems are apparently caused by the unquestioning faith in new technologies and innovations that are conquering our world nowadays. Probably the most characteristic example is the recent trend of 3D printing. This invention is promoted and advertised as revolutionary based on the argument that the production of commodities can become, to a certain degree, personalized and move from a 'corporate' to a 'personal' level, thus becoming more 'familiar' and 'monitored'. But it is easy to understand that 3D printers only seem to democratize the production of commodities. In fact, this technological innovation does not alter in essence almost anything in the relationship between man and commodity. At least the relationship is not altered in a positive way. Indeed, it could be argued that it contributes to a kind of alienation in the following way: as it provides an almost magic sense of being the 'producer', the user is captivated by this productive power and his consumerist manias are reinforced. This is because discussions never entail questions as to what we wish to produce, why we need the product, how much is enough or how much is too much. Who ultimately sets the limits? Or rather, is it perhaps the case that such technological innovations offer us the opportunity to not think about the limits? Do they merely succeed in intensifying our already prevalent mass consumption hysteria? In this way, the 'power' to personally design a commodity soon turns into a playful, yet uncreative imitation of mechanical and calculating methods, an illusion of a limitless autonomy of producing and consuming. Therefore, the 'reform' of the technical procedures is also in this case insufficient and what is needed is a re-evaluation of the content of the technical system itself as well as of the consumerist constants and models it provides, a subject, which can be further discussed and greatly analysed.

Conclusion

Returning to the more general political framework, we would finally argue that nowadays our primary objective should be the conflict with the liberal approach to politics, i.e. with the approach that prioritizes individual welfare and allows only for the power of the few to define limits (financial, political, ecological etc.). To limit the power of others or even to set the rules in the management of any commodity by the few is completely different to being allowed to manage these commodities ourselves via institutions of our own. So the problem is the following: in politics (in making and implementing decisions) and in social life in general (work, the production and management of commodities, use of technology, culture etc.), we have not considered the fact that a truly public management of the commons demands a brand new institutional framework of public participation and a brand new content of human creativity. Naturally, these institutions would not only provide the possibility of equal participation but would impel (or even compel!) the public to claim control over the commons. These institutions will construct a new anthropological type, correspondingly democratic, who will in turn constantly claim this participation.

Certainly, there is no absolute gap between the modern liberal world and a democratic society with an active public participation. We do not suggest, nor is it the right time for Manichaeism and absolutism. Nevertheless, whatever the first step might be, we should not retreat or distance ourselves from the horizon of a more radical criticism in politics and herein ultimately lies the meaning of this enquiry.

Bibliography

Castoriadis, C. (2010). *A society adrift: Interviews and debates, 1974–1997.* New York, NY: Fordham University Press.
Sennett, R. (1977). *The fall of public man.* New York, NY: Knopf.

This is not a Manifesto: Precipitating a Paradigm Shift in Cultural Management

Stelios Lekakis

In this volume, we set out to approach heritage as a commons, in an exploratory and comparative way, inspired by the processes and trends already taking place in Greece, and contrasting this with the pressing neoliberal agendas that have become established over the last decade across Europe. We have attempted to avoid drawing up a manifesto, such as often found in the last pages of many heritage publications but instead provide an introduction to a political horizon for heritage management, already advocated by a number of writers in different fields. We tried to do so by gathering argument from neighbouring fields of public resources, looking for interdisciplinary lessons to be adapted in the present for the future.

Commons – not as another grand narrative but as a summative practice, a political modus operandi – engages with goods, management processes and values, and allows us to step away from dichotomic discussions in private and government instrumentalities and move towards a mixture of modes and methods of democratic and polycentric governance systems. However, commons is mostly about people, in a plural, inclusive and enticing way; a symbol of human ideals and values, it re-examines on the ground concepts of exclusive identities, challenges established ideas on ideals and values and provides the

How to cite this book chapter:
Lekakis, S. 2020. This is not a Manifesto: Precipitating a Paradigm Shift in Cultural Management. In Lekakis, S. (ed.) *Cultural Heritage in the Realm of the Commons: Conversations on the Case of Greece.* Pp. 259–262. London: Ubiquity Press. DOI: https://doi.org/10.5334/bcj.o. License: CC-BY

foundations of instituent praxis for the here and now, assembling new worlds in the shell of the old.

Heritage commons

In attempting to ideologically challenge and politically treat heritage management through the lenses of the commons, a re-interpretation based on the social characteristics of heritage and current participatory/inclusive management tools, we set in motion a more systematic framework of discussion, a prolegomenon aimed at more sustained research and analysis.

In the framework of this new paradigm, heritage is envisaged as a cohesive mix of material and immaterial goods, surrounding communities and processes of governance and production, whether we emphasise on knowledge or services. Through this, a number of collateral issues are opened: material-wise, we are reminded that an ontological and anti-essentialist discussion is needed, exploring the ways in which the past is enclosed to heritage and its affordances. Valuation/valorisation processes and resource-based approaches in practice are part of this reconsideration along with the ethics of growth and the yoke of economism. The role of stakeholders and their right to heritage, aside from the normative documents' general prescriptions, must also be re-examined, in terms of structures of power and priorities of assigned values. Their identity is also crucial; how do we define the participant communities, how much we open up the schema to avoid confrontation but also represent diversity and how ready we are to engage with those unsettled, constantly becoming communities? The methodologies of participation are abundant; however, it must be asked whether they are political (in terms of intentions, agency and organisation), they deal with issues on the ground (e.g. speaking in front of others, enabling marginalized people, resolving conflict, extending effects beyond the timetable of a project) and they deliberate anything else other than a passive engagement circuit, another tick box in a cultural heritage project.

Given the volatile paradigm that emerges from this process, calls for self-governing institutional arrangements and bottom-up decision-making can be considered a starting point, stemming from fundamental qualities of the human condition: collaboration and sharing. Governance is a central pillar in this schema, but commoning allows us to re-orient heritage production towards use-value creation and distribution and also consider physical products and sophisticated services in non-extractive enterprises; examples of this could include simple establishments as a community-managed museum and a co-operative café located at a heritage site or more complex organisations as a workers' co-operative for restoration and heritage management projects. In this case, collectively owned market agents use their surplus to further social and environmental causes in a cycle of open input, participatory process, and commons-oriented output that can allow for the accumulation of the commons instead of capital. On that front, a more coherent discussion of heritage commons' institutions is due.

Feeding back to the mainframe: Cultural Commons

Apart from the apparent contribution to the emerging field of heritage commons, this volume allows for some reflection on cultural commons that even though an incremental concept to the aspiring commons democracy, the surrounding narratives seem to suffer from broad, all-inclusive descriptions that overly resemble the economistic appropriation of culture in order to make it market-ready.

Thus, the case studies presented here point towards the need for a systematic discussion of cultural commons, through a number of vital steps which are necessary to take in the process. These are as follows:

Cultural centric discussion for cultural management: The terminology used in the discussion of cultural/heritage management has delved deep into the economic core that seemingly offers efficient and proof ready concepts. There is an apparent need for re-examination of the tools used and their functions in context. Even though managerial processes are not to be condemned, we should relate them to the resources/goods at hand and not apply them externally to the resources, revisiting important, basic, overlooked elements of their internal mechanics – i.e. their social features. A new cultural language for culture is needed, one that is both decisive, convincing and relevant to the qualities of the resources in question.

Locally based culture: There is a considerable advantage in discussing and experiencing culture in its context. Culture and especially heritage relate to the production of locality and bind communities to a place. They formulate identity and answer vital questions for the present and the future: who we are, who we are not and who we want to be in the future. Thus, we need to re-localise culture and explore the new roots in society, networked with the global processes that go further than identity and memory politics. This process is critical in the everyday commoning as explained in the cases of the Alexandrou Svolou Neigbourhood Initiative, OneLoveKitchen and Plato's Academy Kafeneio Initiatives, dealing with soft issues of *being and working together* commonly lost in theoretical appraisals or generic vaunted declarations for democracy and the future. This can be the tool for the re-enchanting of culture and heritage, appearing with new meanings and forms, tending to the main characteristic of cultural commons, as rising unexpectedly and with great potential. Currently, this emerges as a topical process for the diversification of the municipalist movements, infusing cultural content to the political agenda, providing solutions synchronised with the local conditions, spanning from bureaucratic activism

– as in the case of l'Asilo Filangieri – to claiming the municipal leadership as in Barcelona. It also presents a great opportunity for valid, meaningful and inspiring research in arts/heritage management.

Political praxis: However, apart from academic exercises on definitions or symbolic political gestures of occupation, heritage commons will be more viable if active involvement of all interested stakeholders is sought through meaningful and open participation schemata. And this needs a political background to make cultural commons as porous and volatile as they could be. Having priced the bare necessities and put people into debt to acquire them, neoliberal politics now push for the extraction of non-use values, commonly residing on cultural goods. There is a need to transform these goods into rights, acknowledging their social importance for the communities and avoiding hyper-revolutionary or over-ambitious narrative. And this can be done through collective action, focused to prefigure change in managing the public texture of culture and heritage.

As a result of this approach, commons can emerge as a possible and realistic strategy for culture and heritage, establishing connections with other goods and giving rise to commons ecologies, towards a multi-modal commons-centric transition, where participants are a polity in action tending to a new world already blossoming under our feet.

Bibliography

Bauwens, M., Kostakis, V. & Pazaitis, A. (2019). *Peer to peer: The commons manifesto*. London, United Kingdom: Westminster University Press.

Dardot, P. & Laval, C. (2019). *Common: On revolution in the 21ˢᵗ century*. London, United Kingdom: Bloomsbury Academic.

Biographical Notes

Nicholas Anastasopoulos is an architect, researcher, and assistant professor at the School of Architecture, National Technical University of Athens. He holds a Ph.D. from the same university in alternative communities and sustainability and a MArch from Yale. Has taught at Patras University, Parsons School of Design (NYC) and elsewhere. As post-doctoral Prometeo Researcher (IAEN, Ecuador2014) he contributed to the FLOK Society project and conducted research on aspects of Buen Vivir and sustainability. Has conducted extensive research and collaborated with architects, artists, and researchers in Ecuador, Europe, and South America. Initiated the MET workshop and the Ports in Transition Workshops (Europe and South America) for spatial policies. Other research interests concern the commons, communities, systems theory, ecology, and complexity. Currently academic representative and senior researcher in charge on behalf of NTUA for SoPHIA, a H2020 consortium research program aiming to create a Social Platform on Holistic Impact Assessment of European Cultural Heritage.

Despina Catapoti read History and Archaeology at the University of Athens, Greece (1995). She was awarded an MA in Archaeology and Prehistory (1997) and a PhD in Archaeology (2005) from the University of Sheffield. Since 2008, she teaches at the Department of Cultural Technology and Communication, University of the Aegean, Greece. Her research and teaching interests centre on cultural theory, history of science and epistemology, with particular focus on the history and philosophy of archaeology. Currently, she works at the inter section of digital technologies and the broader cultural heritage field, with the aim of assessing the impact and contribution of New Media on archaeological/ historical heritage outreach and engagement.

Giorgos Chatzinakos is an urban and cultural geographer from Thessaloniki. Since 2012, his life has developed into a peregrination across different European cities. He studied political science at the University of Athens and he holds an interdisciplinary master's degree in European urban cultures (Vrije Universiteit Brussel, Tilburg University, Manchester Metropolitan University, Estonian Academy of Arts). He received his MPhil/PhD in 2020 at Manchester Metropolitan University for his research on the everyday life of the suburbs. Currently, he is based in Barcelona where he is investigating the role of 'neighbourhood associations' in the broader management of the city. His long-term aim is to develop a municipal strategy based on the co-creation and promotion of urban commons. His research interests are focused on neighbourhood-building and the commons, place-theory, urban and cultural policies, festivals, and the commons. He is a visitor research fellow at the Policy Evaluation and Research Unit at Manchester Metropolitan University.

Mina Dragouni is a researcher at the Dep. of History & Archaeology, University of Patras in Greece and an adjunct lecturer at Open University of Cyprus. Before receiving her doctorate by UCL Bartlett Institute for Sustainable Heritage, Mina had studied cultural management at the University of Ioannina and cultural studies at the University of Nottingham. Her main research interests revolve around heritage economics, community involvement in heritage management and grassroots-led cultural synergies. She has been involved in research, teaching and public engagement activities at various academic institutions and cultural organisations, including UCL, the University of Portsmouth, Bournemouth University, Panteion University of Social and Political Sciences, MONUMENTA and the Greek Association of Heritage Management Consultants. In the past few years, Mina publishes her work systematically in international peer-reviewed journals. She also serves as editor of the *Critical Studies in Cultural Heritage* journal.

Graham Fairclough studied archaeology and history at Nottingham University (UK) in the 1970s and worked in the UK government agency 'English Heritage' until 2012; he is presently a research member of the McCord Centre for Landscape at Newcastle University (UK). His main interests and work have been in heritage and landscape, particularly landscape characterisation, including work with the Council of Europe on its European Landscape Convention and Faro Convention initiatives. He coordinated the EU CHeriScape network (2012–20) and is currently a member of the EU HERILAND project (2018–2022). He has published widely on the relationship between landscape, heritage and sustainability, and since 2011 has co-edited the journal *Landscapes*.

Chrysostomos Galanos studied Business Administration in the University of Patras and acquired a MSc in Geoinformation for Environmental Management from CIHEAM. At the moment he is concluding a MSc in Social and Solidarity Economy (SSE) at the Hellenic Open University. In 2006, he founded the NGO 'European Village' which in 2010 gave birth to the Cooperative Cafe at Plato's Academy. After almost a decade of intensive activity for the SSE field in Athens, he decided to "escape" from the big city and move to Chania (Crete), where he is currently a member and a worker of the social cooperative 'Terra Verde'. His main area of work concerns the local development of SSE in Chania.

Georgia Gkoumopoulou: Architect Eng. (NTUA, 2001), MSc holder in Urban-Regional Planning (NTUA, 2006), PhD candidate and research fellow (NTUA). Her academic research concerns the recognition of "urban voids" as special open spaces with unique dynamics and potential as action fields of sociocultural relations and natural processes. She participates in projects, conferences, workshops and architectural competitions; a freelancer professional, she collaborates with architectural offices, local authorities, scientific, civic groups and NGO's (member of MONUMENTA).

Vasso Kanellopoulou is an environmental journalist, writer, documentary producer, born in Athens Greece. She graduated from Columbia University, New York, with a B.A. in social sciences. She worked with ERT, Greek public Radio TV in 1977 as a writer for radio broadcasts and later as a TV documentary producer and writer, specializing in culture and the environment. In 2001 she left ERT to become a freelance environmental journalist producing documentaries and working as chief editor and writer for a monthly environmental magazine for ten years. Following participation in the European social movement against genetically engineered food, she authored a book on this subject published in 2006. Since 2007, she has been working for PELITI a prominent seed regeneration association in Greece, representing it to the relevant European and international networks and raising public awareness in Greece on the issue of seeds as an enclosed common good. Recently she joined a network of other Seed Initiatives in Greece to work on the preparation of a database of seed guardians' interviews.

Alexandros Kioupkiolis is Assistant Professor of Contemporary Political Theory at Aristotle University, Thessaloniki, Greece. His research interests are focussed on radical democracy, the commons, social movements, and the philosophy of freedom. He is directing an ERC COG project on these topics (Heteropolitics, 2017–2020) and has published numerous relevant books and papers, including the monograph Freedom after the critique of foundations (Palgrave Macmillan 2012), and the collective volume Radical democracy and collective movements today (Ashgate 2014). His last monograph is entitled The Common and Counter-hegemonic Politics (Edinburgh University Press, 2019).

Stelios Lekakis studied classical archaeology and heritage management at the University of Athens and the University College London. He is currently a researcher at Newcastle University (landscape archaeology, characterization, perception and management) and teaches cultural management at the Open University of Cyprus and political economy at the Hellenic Open University. He works with NGOs (a founding member of MONUMENTA) and university departments – in Greece and abroad – as a cultural heritage consultant, focusing on participatory management and cultural informatics projects. He has published extensively in various academic journals and edited volumes. He is also the creative director of the LTD company: Mazomos Landscape and Heritage Consultants BVBA.

Marina Markellou is a Law Attorney and Adj. Lecturer at the Panteion University of Greece. Her primary research interests concern intellectual property, law and art, protection of cultural heritage. Member of the Ethics and Deontology Committee of NCSR DEMOKRITOS, of the Greek ALAI group and of the French Association Open Law, she often participates as an Independent Ethics Expert in many HORIZON 2020 Projects and as legal expert in many European programs. She speaks English, French and Spanish.

Dimitris Markopoulos studied physics at the Universities of Patras and Athens. For some years he was a member of the political group 'Autonomy or Barbarism'. While working in the publishing house 'Gutenberg', he was active in the book workers trade union in Attica. He now has his own publishing house, 'Magma', together with Nikos Malliaris, and they also publish the political journal 'Protagma'.

Petros Moris is an artist and PhD Candidate at the University of Thessaly. He studied art at the Athens School of Fine Arts and the Goldsmiths University of London. He has presented his work in international institutions including the New Museum in New York, EMST, the Cycladic Art Museum and the Singapore National Gallery. He is an Onassis Scholar and an SNF ARTWORKS fellow.

Ioulia Skounaki is a PhD candidate at the Department of Cultural Technology and Communication, University of the Aegean. She holds a degree in History and Archaeology (University of Athens) and Masters' in Classical Archaeology (University of Crete) and in Heritage and Museums (University of Cambridge). Her research and professional work focus on the areas of public archaeology, cultural management and museology.

Penny Travlou is a Lecturer in Cultural Geography and Theory (Edinburgh School of Architecture & Landscape Architecture, University of Edinburgh). Her research focuses on social justice, the commons, collaborative practices, cultural landscapes and ethnography. She has been involved in international research projects funded by the EU and UK Research Councils. Since 2011, she has been doing ethnographic research on collaborative practices in emerging networks (e.g. digital art practitioners, collaborative economy initiatives, translocal migrants); her most recent research is on cultural commons in Colombia. Alongside her academic work, Penny is an activist on social justice and the commons. She has been actively involved in a number of grassroots and self-organised initiatives on housing and refugees' rights. She is Co-Director of the Feminist Autonomous Centre for Research in Athens, a non-profit independent research organisation that focuses on feminist and queer studies, participatory education and activism.

Prodromos Tsiavos is the Head of Digital Development at the Onassis Cultural Centre and a Senior Research Fellow at The Media Institute at University College London (UCL)/ BBC. Prodromos has worked for the National Hellenic Research Foundation, the European Commission, Oxford and Oslo Universities, the Athens University of Economics and Business and the London School of Economics and Political Science (LSE). He read law and Information Systems in Athens and London and holds a PhD in Law and Information Systems from the LSE. Prodromos has worked as an adviser for the Greek Ministry of Infrastructure, Transport and Networks, the Special Secretary for Digital Convergence and a number of public sector bodies as well as companies in the cultural and creative industries. He has over 120 publications and talks on legal and business aspects of open data, Free/ Open Source Software, open hardware and open innovation/ fabrication. Prodromos is currently chairing the administrative council of the Greek Industrial Property Organisation.

Index

A

Alexandrou Svolou Neigbourhood Initiative   183, 186, 261

Athens   5, 8, 26, 28, 36, 37, 38, 40, 41, 42, 43, 44, 67, 71, 73, 74, 75, 76, 77, 81, 82, 83, 84, 86, 89, 90, 92, 93, 104, 106, 116, 125, 126, 128, 129, 143, 157, 159, 162, 163, 165, 166, 168, 176, 177, 181, 198, 209, 214, 215, 216, 218, 220, 224, 225, 263

austerity   2, 7, 24, 42, 43, 44, 49, 93, 163, 178, 181, 182, 238, 240, 255

B

biodiversity   5, 103, 142, 144, 146, 147, 150, 155, 156

bottom-up   3, 42, 54, 58, 68, 75, 85, 88, 183, 185, 193, 199, 204, 205, 207, 230, 260

C

capitalism   vi, 2, 5, 10, 59, 70, 72, 87, 91, 92, 93, 100, 105, 107, 124, 206, 230, 250, 256

Central Archaeological Council   110, 118

citizenship   7, 58, 159, 163, 164, 165, 172, 173, 174, 177, 178, 180, 181, 182, 196

collective action   xi, 10, 47, 52, 53, 55, 56, 64, 65, 92, 192, 197, 203, 205, 252, 255, 262

Common Pool Resources   3, 8, 30, 141, 187

commoners   vi, ix, 30, 36, 37, 51, 52, 72, 104, 232, 233, 250

commoning   ix, x, 5, 6, 8, 9, 10, 30, 31, 34, 37, 72, 73, 84, 85, 88, 98, 99, 100, 102, 105, 174, 175, 176, 177, 178, 179, 181, 185, 192, 198, 203, 205, 225, 231, 232, 239, 240, 241, 243, 244, 246, 260, 261

commons-based   2, 5, 30, 31, 34, 35,
    36, 40, 53, 112, 116, 117, 118,
    119, 217, 230, 231, 232, 245
copyright   98, 114, 117, 121, 125
CPR.
    See Common Pool Resources
Creative Commons   11, 117, 152,
    230, 233
crisis   vii, x, 7, 8, 11, 24, 35, 36, 38,
    40, 42, 44, 48, 49, 54, 63, 64,
    70, 86, 88, 89, 94, 100, 102,
    151, 163, 166, 173, 176, 179,
    181, 182, 184, 185, 187, 192,
    206, 216, 218, 229, 231, 238,
    239, 240, 250, 254, 256
crowdfunding   98
crowdsourcing   112
cultural policy   18, 38, 64, 109, 112,
    122, 136

D

decision-making   33, 45, 47, 52, 53,
    54, 55, 56, 57, 60, 75, 166,
    168, 205, 218, 242, 246, 248,
    250, 260
digital commons   5, 33, 97, 98, 100,
    101, 152, 232, 233

E

ecosystem   60, 103, 114, 118,
    119, 216
Ecuador   103, 104, 106
enclosure   vi, 1, 2, 3, 5, 6, 17, 21, 23,
    24, 25, 26, 29, 46, 50, 51, 59,
    67, 69, 72, 75, 82, 83, 99, 105,
    151, 154
enframing   67
EU Digital Single Market   123
European Commons Assembly   102

F

filoxenia   173
FOSS.
    See Free and Open Source Software

Free and Open Source Software   123
free ride   47
Fund of Archaeological Proceeds   135

G

Google Arts & Culture project   133
governance   x, 2, 5, 6, 7, 10, 11, 13,
    17, 21, 22, 30, 31, 33, 34, 35,
    36, 37, 38, 40, 47, 50, 52, 53,
    54, 57, 58, 59, 60, 61, 62, 71,
    72, 83, 84, 85, 88, 93, 176,
    184, 185, 193, 203, 204, 205,
    231, 233, 237, 239, 242, 243,
    245, 259, 260
growth   vi, vii, 19, 49, 59, 60, 64, 123,
    165, 215, 235, 245, 249, 260

H

Homo Economicus   3, 60
Human Genome Project   100

I

ICH.
    See Intangible Cultural Heritage
intangible cultural heritage   135,
    158, 159, 160, 164, 174, 177,
    179, 180
Intellectual Property Rights   117,
    121, 142, 144, 150, 151
IPR.
    See Intellectual Property Rights

K

Kerameikos   75, 78, 128, 129, 214

L

l'Asilo   230, 243, 244, 245, 246,
    249, 262
Labsus model   240, 241
landscape   v, vii, ix, x, xi, 2, 20, 34,
    38, 42, 48, 50, 73, 77, 79, 81,
    82, 86, 99, 107, 111, 115, 118,
    124, 187, 191, 195, 203, 264

Law 3028/2002   12, 23, 40, 68, 91, 110, 115, 118, 125, 135, 136, 139

M

maker   131, 161
Ministry of Culture   26, 29, 42, 68, 79, 115, 116, 117, 118, 135, 136
municipalist politics   248

N

neoclassical economics   60
neoliberal   2, 5, 7, 10, 19, 24, 25, 28, 39, 46, 48, 50, 64, 70, 87, 93, 99, 103, 104, 105, 163, 194, 209, 216, 230, 233, 235, 236, 237, 238, 239, 240, 255, 259, 262
netocrats   9, 111, 120, 123, 124
new commons   6, 99, 231
New Public Management   19, 21
non-excludability   45, 46, 51
non-use values   20, 22, 51, 262
Nonviolent Communication   218, 226

O

Occupy movement   5, 229
OneLoveKitchen   vii, 9, 159, 162, 163, 164, 165, 166, 168, 169, 170, 171, 172, 173, 174, 175, 176, 177, 178, 182, 261
openness   8, 58, 69, 70, 71, 73, 83, 84, 86, 87, 88, 97, 230, 233, 238, 244, 248
open-source   3, 6, 30, 98, 99, 191, 201, 205
Ostrom   vi, xi, 3, 4, 22, 30, 33, 39, 45, 46, 47, 50, 51, 52, 53, 54, 55, 58, 60, 65, 71, 72, 85, 92, 174, 232, 252
ownership   vi, ix, x, 6, 18, 20, 21, 23, 32, 33, 59, 60, 68, 70, 72, 83, 89, 112, 121, 123, 139, 152, 198, 206, 242

P

P2P.
  See peer to peer
peer to peer   99, 100, 203
Philopappos Hill   8, 67, 73, 79, 81, 82, 83, 84, 85, 86, 87
photogrammetry   129, 130, 131, 132, 133, 139
Plato's Academy   9, 67, 73, 75, 76, 77, 78, 79, 83, 85, 86, 87, 104, 213, 214, 216, 219, 220, 223, 224, 261
private good   20
property   vi, ix, x, 5, 9, 17, 18, 19, 20, 21, 22, 23, 24, 31, 37, 40, 44, 59, 68, 70, 89, 91, 117, 124, 148, 155, 232, 240, 245, 247, 254, 256
public engagement   48, 167, 222
public good   18, 20, 54, 79, 136
public participation   258
public / private   ix, 3, 6, 8, 50, 254
public resources   x, 2, 22, 25, 259
public space   71, 181, 185, 187, 191, 193, 195, 196, 204, 205, 206, 219, 249

R

refugees   7, 28, 159, 162, 163, 165, 166, 176, 177, 178
rhizomic ethnography   162
rivalry   20, 45, 51

S

seeds   2, 9, 141, 142, 143, 144, 145, 146, 147, 148, 149, 150, 151, 152, 154, 155, 156, 157, 158
self-organised   159, 166, 183, 186, 213
social dilemmas   45
Social Economy   4, 35
social media   5, 28, 69, 87, 99, 113, 116, 119, 120, 121, 233

Solidarity   4, 5, 8, 35, 64, 215,
      216, 220
Solidarity Economy   5, 8, 35,
      64, 215
Sumak Kawsay   103
sustainability   vi, 6, 7, 19, 37, 43,
      59, 85, 156, 208, 211, 212,
      230, 248

T

Temporary Autonomous Zones   221
teranga   173
The FLOK Society   103
top-down   vii, 18, 52, 54, 55, 57,
      58, 75, 88, 193, 232, 236, 241,
      248, 249
tourism   6, 7, 19, 21, 23, 24, 26, 31,
      32, 36, 37, 44, 46, 49, 50, 51,
      56, 58, 62, 63, 64, 65, 69, 88,
      89, 94, 180
tragedy   v, vi, vii, xi, 3, 50, 51, 52, 55

U

Ubuntu   173
Ugo Mattei   240, 242, 251
Ujamaa   173, 179, 181
UNESCO   viii, ix, x, xi, 11, 18, 19,
      21, 37, 44, 98, 139, 158, 160,
      161, 164, 180
urban commons   9, 71, 73, 90,
      91, 101, 176, 180, 183, 186,
      204, 205, 219, 221, 231,
      240, 245
uso civico   243, 244

W

welfare state   2, 7, 35, 48, 50
well-being   ix, 49, 65, 205, 211
Wikimedia   113, 114, 117, 123
Wikipedia   5, 98, 100, 110, 112,
      114, 117, 123, 225, 226,
      232, 233